Notes on Some

Figures Behind
T. S. Eliot

Notes on Some

Figures Behind
T. S. Eliot

Herbert Howarth

1964
Houghton Mifflin Company Boston
The Riverside Press Cambridge

For permission to use selections from copyrighted material the author is indebted to the following publishers and copyright proprietors:

Janice Biala: poems by Ford Madox Ford first published in *Chapbook*. Reprinted by permission of the copyright holder, Janice Biala.

Jonathan Cape, Ltd.: "Transitional Poem" and "From Feathers to Iron" by Cecil Day Lewis.

Editions Gallimard: *Correspondence* (*1905–1914*) by Alain-Fournier and Jacques Rivière; copyright Editions Gallimard 1926–1928. *La Cantate à Troix Voix* by Paul Claudel; copyright Editions Gallimard 1931. *Eloges* by Saint John Perse; copyright Editions Gallimard 1911. *Créances 1905–1910* by André Salmon; copyright Editions Gallimard 1926.

The Estate of Percy MacKaye: *Saint Louis, A Civic Masque* by Percy MacKaye, published by Doubleday and Company, Inc., and poems published in the *Harvard Monthly*.

Farrar, Straus & Company, Inc., and Faber & Faber, Ltd.: *Elder Statesman* by T. S. Eliot. Copyright © 1959 by Thomas Stearns Eliot.

Fischer Verlag: "Elektra" by Hugo von Hofmannsthal.

Harcourt, Brace & World, Inc., and Faber & Faber, ltd.: *The Complete Poems and Plays of T. S. Eliot:* "Ash Wednesday," "The Boston Evening Transcript," "Coriolan," "Whispers of Immortality," "The Waste Land," "Dry Salvages," "Little Gidding," "Mélange Adultère de Tout," "Preludes," "Rhapsody on a

*For
my mother
and in memory of
my father*

Acknowledgments

Some years ago, on the fringes of the British publishing world, I tried to persuade Edward L. Mayo to write a book about T. S. Eliot, but he chose, as perhaps a poet should, to concentrate on the carving of poems. In place of the work we imagined, which he would have written expertly, I only offer these tentative notes and sketches.

They were begun at the University of Pittsburgh, and I think with affection of W. George Crouch, Lawrence Lee, Donald Tritschler, Robert Gale, Richard Tobias, Raymond Cristina, Helene-Jean Moore, and that grand scholar, Hayward Keniston; and were continued at the University of Manitoba, where Lloyd Wheeler took me under his protective care, and the President and the Dean of Graduate Studies made a grant-in-aid from the President's Special Research Fund. The Modern Language Association's Committee on Research Activities generously enabled me to travel to distant libraries.

For their hospitality I thank the Directors and staffs of: the Widener Library; the Houghton Library; the Harvard University Archives; the Library of Washington University, St. Louis; the Missouri Historical Association, St. Louis; and the Mercantile Library, St. Louis. Information was kindly communicated by the Registrar of Harvard College; the Director of the Peabody Museum, Salem; the Reference Librarian of the American Naval Academy, Annapolis; the Reference Librarian

of the Enoch Pratt Free Library, Baltimore; the Registrar of
Antioch College; the Registrar of Framingham State Teachers'
College; the Superintendent in Charge of Personnel of the
Board of Education, St. Louis; the Director of the Massachusetts
Historical Society, Boston; and the Librarian of the American
Unitarian Association, Boston. In London Faber and Faber
Ltd. permitted me to consult their file of catalogues of the
thirties. Mr. and Mrs. John Cahill hospitably welcomed me at
their home, Eastern Point — the house which Henry Ware
Eliot Sr. built sixty-five years ago.

I record with gratitude my obligations to the following peri-
odicals: *Comparative Literature* and its editor Chandler B.
Beall; the *American Quarterly* and its editor Hennig Cohen; the
Georgia Review and its editor William Davidson; the *South
Atlantic Quarterly* and its editor W. B. Hamilton; and the *University of Toronto Quarterly* and its editor Millar MacLure.
Some of the material in Chapter I concerning Mrs. Eliot appears
in *Notable American Women 1607-1950*, the biographical dictionary sponsored by Radcliffe College and published by the
Belknap Press of Harvard University, and I am grateful for
permission to use it here to the editor, Edward T. James.

I have special debts to Theodore Hornberger of the University of Pennsylvania, Philadelphia; Lawrence Clark Powell
of the University of California, Los Angeles; Warner G. Rice
of the University of Michigan, Ann Arbor; Louis B. Wright of
the Folger Shakespeare Library, Washington, D. C., and the
late Charles Abbott of the University of Buffalo.

For advice or encouragement it is a pleasure to thank E. P.
Bollier; Michael Collie; Tom Crooks; Leona Davis; Alan Denson; Marilyn Denton; Edmund Freeman; Rudolf Germer; William Chase Greene; Mary Hottinger; Stanley Edgar Hyman;
Jeremy Ingalls; W. P. Kinne; Harry Levin; John F. McDermott,
who is assembling material for a life of William Greenleaf Eliot;
Louis L. Martz; Theodore Morrison; J. Mitchell Morse; Norman

Holmes Pearson; H. W. H. Powel Jr.; Justin Replogle; Myron Simon; C. F. Terrel. William Nixon Dehon devoted two terms to reading the *Criterion* with me at Montana State University. Mrs. Wylie Sypher so delighted me, during a Bread Loaf breakfast, with the story of her father at Harvard that, though the name of Eliot was not mentioned, I went back to the cottage with the plan for the Harvard pages taking shape. In making these acknowledgments there is perhaps more than the usual need to add that the conjectures and the mistakes in the book are my own.

The editor of the *New York Times Book Review* courteously printed an appeal for information about the Harvard teachers of "the Golden Era." I am glad to acknowledge the replies of: Robert H. Allen, Muncie, Indiana; J. Donald Adams of the *New York Times Book Review*; Walter C. Ames, Bronxville; Miss Elizabeth Booth, Boston; Grant Code of Talent Exchange, New York; Ronald M. Ferry, Concord, Mass.; Norman Foerster, Santa Barbara; Clarence E. Hale, New York; Courtenay Hemenway of the Choate School; Richard B. Hovey, Westminster, Maryland; Henry Levine, New York; Arthur J. Linenthal, Boston (who lent me his father's notebooks); Harold F. Smith, Kalispell, Montana; John Ives Sewall, Bristol, Maine (who lent me his notebook of Chase's course); T. N. Stensland, Warren, Virginia; Charles M. Storey, Boston; Jackson E. Towne, East Lansing, Michigan; Mrs. C. H. Wright, Boston. If in this—or another—paragraph I have inadvertently omitted names of those who have gone out of their way to give assistance, I ask pardon.

Like everybody who has written on the work of Eliot in the last few years I have continually fortified myself from Grover Cleveland Smith's book. Three unpublished works have been of help: Derek Colville's doctoral thesis (Washington University, St. Louis, 1953) on James Freeman Clarke, which surveys American Unitarian thought in the nineteenth century;

Anne C. Bolgan's doctoral thesis (Toronto, 1960) on Mr. Eliot's philosophy; H. W. H. Powel Jr.'s magistral dissertation (Brown, 1954), "Notes on the Early Life of T. S. Eliot," packed with significant material and acute in interpretation.

Jean Frampton in England has typed drafts and redrafts with unfailing skill and judgment, undismayed by impossible deadlines: —the warmest thanks to her.

HERBERT HOWARTH

Contents

Notes on Some

Figures Behind
T. S. Eliot

1. Family Figures

WHEN T. S. Eliot was growing up at 2635 Locust Street, St. Louis, his mother was writing a book, a biography of his grandfather, William Greenleaf Eliot. It was published in 1904. The dedication page says "Written for my children 'Lest they forget.'" Half a century later, when the poet revisited his native city and lectured at Washington University, he opened with memories of his early years, and said that, though he never knew his grandfather, who died a year before his birth, that figure seemed still to preside over the family, and his rules of conduct were the tables of the Law.

Barrett Wendell has written that the Unitarian leaders who, at the end of the eighteenth century, arose to convert New England from its grim Calvinism prevailed by their "astonishing personal purity and moral beauty." William Greenleaf Eliot represented their tradition in all its excellence. He led a life of pure, unfaltering, unflagging endeavor. "There is a sweet plain-speaking about him which is marvelously helpful . . . He never offends, because he is calm, quiet, kindly and sincere in his reproofs. His eye is single, and his whole body is full of light." So his friend, James Freeman Clarke, wrote in his journal in 1839. He added, "One feels rebuked in his presence . . . How can one be familiar with the Day of Judgment, which seems to attend him wherever he goes? Yet he is playful, fond of fun, and there is a sweet smile just ap-

pearing on the corners of his mouth. But there is no *abandon;*
he does not let himself quite go . . . in fact, I do not think he
ever quite gets away from his sense of responsibility."

William Greenleaf Eliot was born in New Bedford, Massachusetts, in 1811, and brought up in Baltimore, at the Friends'
Academy in New Bedford, and in Washington, D.C. He decided to enter the ministry and was trained at the Harvard Divinity School, from which he graduated in 1834. It was not
difficult for a young minister to find opportunities to go west;
pastorless congregations were asking for men; but few would
leave the security of the East. James Freeman Clarke, his senior
in the Divinity School, had gone out to Louisville in 1833, and
he was ready to follow the example and choose the frontier.
He accepted an invitation to go to St. Louis on a winter's engagement as preacher to the Unitarians, who had as yet no
minister or church. Featherweight, poor in health, looking almost like a girl, but quick, keen, and decisive, he arrived in St.
Louis in the late fall.

He might have seemed the last man to settle in a city which,
for all its fur-trade wealth and the elegance lent by its French
founders, was primitive: water in the cellars, no sewers, chills
and fever and someone bedridden in every poor family. But he
was one of those who, slight of frame, develop an indomitable
will. Within two months of his arrival he had founded the
First Congregational Society of St. Louis and opened a fund
for the erection of a church, and within two years his church
was ready and dedicated. Recognizing that the man who
would build up influence for the realization of his ideals must
stay in one place, he stayed in St. Louis. "The whole city was
his parish and every soul needing him a parishioner," reads the
tribute on his monument there.

Several times, lecturing on William Greenleaf Eliot, I have
felt obliged to mention that I am not a Unitarian, lest I might
appear to be pleading a special cause. He moves me regardless

of denomination. He loved his work: "The love of my profession, the ministry of Jesus Christ, is so ingrained that no other calling has any attraction for me. It has grown with my growth, and strengthened with my strength, and become stronger as the strength fails . . ." That is beautiful, and, spoken at his retirement, poignant; but it is the more beautiful, and above mere poignancy, because he translated it into action. He was the nineteenth-century descendant of Chaucer's parson:

> . . . Cristes lore, and his apostles twelve,
> He taughte, and first he folwed it himselve.

If some parishioner called at his house in his absence and left a message begging help, his wife and children knew that on return he would, however tired, act at once on it so long as they scribbled, when they laid it on his desk, the word "Pauper." He visited the poor, the sick, the prison, the asylum. He worked with the energy of a man of double his strength, gave with the bounty of a man of double his wealth. His small Church of the Messiah raised $50,000 annually for charity, his own name at the head of every subscription list. To give money, he once said, is easy, and sometimes it is only a means to exemption from the real giving of personal involvement. He involved himself without stint.

The year 1849 was a calamitous one in St. Louis. Cholera raged for six months and killed one in ten. While the epidemic was at its height, the levee and steamboats went up in flames and the business district was virtually destroyed. Soon after the fire, the Mississippi overflowed, the floods were swollen by unusual rains, and parts of the city became uninhabitable. The physicians, and the clergy of every faith, worked through six months of protracted crisis. Dr. Eliot's day was made up of visits to the sick, vigils by the dying, three hours' sleep, another call to the sick. When parents under his watch died, Dr. Eliot took care of their children. He had accepted responsibility for twenty-six by August, when the cholera began to slacken. Twenty-six besides five of his own! After the hardships of that year the muscles of his right arm were paralyzed. He taught himself to write with the left hand.

Amid so much work he still read constantly, especially the German philosophers. In public addresses he urged the West to cultivate an intellectual life. He founded an Academy of Science in St. Louis. Appointed a member of the city's School Board in 1848 he applied himself to the opportunity with zeal. In the early summer, with the thermometer at 95° in the shade, he walked to the First School Ward and instituted a searching inspection. He began to comb out defects in the system; to import teachers from New England; to claim land reserved for the schools under an Act of Congress of 1812 but currently withheld by obstructive officials; to purchase, with that shrewdness he always showed when investing in the public advantage, property for a new school. Within six months he was president of the School Board, and his reforms laid the foundations which enabled W. T. Harris gradually to make the St. Louis schools the best in the Union for their time. In the early fifties the state legislature passed, at the instance of his friends but without his prior knowledge, a charter for a center of higher learning, to be called the Eliot Seminary. He doubted whether the time was really ripe for a university of the West, but, examining the charter, found it so advantageous to the community that he could not let it lapse, and threw his energy into the enterprise. Not that he tolerated the proposed name. He requested that that be changed. He became the first president of the Board of Directors of the "Washington Institute." Washington University was inaugurated in 1857. He was installed as its third chancellor in 1872.

Missouri was a slave state. Dr. Eliot had arrived disposed by nature and training against the system. He regarded it as harmful to all parties concerned: to the whites, whose decencies it jeopardized and whose will to work and improve it sapped, as well as to the people it exploited. When he saw it in operation he realized like others that where it was benevolent it had more compensations than he had thought possible; but he also saw that wherever it was abused, it was worse than he had guessed. Early in his residence he looked out of his study window: a mulatto girl was hanging from a joist by her thumbs, and a man flogging her. He opened the casement and stopped him by a protest; then "I shut my book and went straight before the grand jury, then in session, and entered a complaint." The jury would not condemn, because "the penalty, affixed by law, was thought to be too severe" and the flogger was a person of respectability. "Attempt was also made to invalidate my testimony as that of a sentimental young preacher who knew nothing about slavery. That was a strong point to make."

Through two decades, during which the problem increasingly agitated the country, he considered whether it was his business as a minister to take a public stand against slavery. In private conversation he spoke freely as an opponent of it; but had he a right to speak openly from his pulpit, involving his congregation in controversy and almost certainly losing his church? Friends in the eastern cities would come quickly to his rescue if he were driven from St. Louis; they would, he wrote, have covered him with the honors of a martyr without the martyr's losses and have settled him in some flourishing church among them. Let us not be mistaken: he was tempted to the martyr's role, and to its suffering as well as its honors. He constantly and passionately thought how "It is to the holy throng of apostles and martyrs, God's saints on earth, that all progress in wisdom and goodness, and all triumphs over evil, are due." He would have liked to be the equal of Elijah P. Lovejoy, who protested against slavery and was driven out of St. Louis, and, continuing his protest, was murdered in Alton,

Illinois, in 1837. At the end of his life Dr. Eliot commemorated Lovejoy:

> The blood of the martyr is the seed not only of the Church, but of truth and liberty. Hundreds of those who half-approved of the outrages as they took place, were led by sober second thought not only to condemn them, but to hate the cause for which they had been committed.

It was with a deliberate patience, almost in the nature of a deeper martyrdom, that he controlled the impulse to the public protests which would have resulted in his expulsion from St. Louis. He was convinced that it was his duty to accumulate influence. He told himself in 1848:

> I have waited, "in patience possessing my soul"; perhaps I must wait a little longer — not much. The influence I have now acquired is real; by proper and fearless exertions it will become deeper and wider.

"A little longer" meant as long again. When he at length applied his influence, risking all the hazards, on a crucial issue, it was not less the problem of slavery than the peril of the Union that prompted him.

The families from which he sprang, the Eliots, the Greenleafs, the Daweses, were rooted in America. Some of them had played conspicuous parts in the American Revolution. Colonel Thomas Dawes had been so active a Whig that the British troops had thought it worthwhile to sack his house as they left Boston. William Greenleaf, as sheriff of Boston in 1776, had read the Declaration of Independence from the balcony of the State House, or begun reading it, till a cry went up from the crowd, "Read louder! louder!" and he passed the paper to an aide with a more resonant voice. William Greenleaf Eliot's ear-

liest memory was of "the booming cannon and shouts of rejoic-
ing in the city of Baltimore [in 1814], when the British armies
abandoned their attack on Fort McHenry, and the sweetest
cradle song, familiar to my childhood, was that glorious national anthem, then first written." The memory came back
vividly to him when the Republic was in danger in 1860. He
could not endure the possibility that the nation for which his
fathers had fought might fall into fragments and lose its power
to change the world.

So at the outbreak of the Civil War he terminated the years
of silence and made his position clear, or as clear as anything
could be in the intersecting tangles of that time: on the slavery
issue he stood for gradual emancipation, on the political issue
for unconditional union. A fourth of the congregation left his
church, the others remained.

Throughout the war William Greenleaf Eliot worked with
the energy that he had shown in the local crises of 1848. It had
seemed in the initial struggle that Missouri must go with the
South. Her background was southern, her settlers in the era
after the Louisiana Purchase had come mainly from Kentucky,
Tennessee, Virginia, North Carolina. Her governor was for secession. But her New Englanders, though very few, were active; and more active were her 80,000 Germans, convinced lib-
erals and opponents of slavery. When the governor moved his
state militia to the boundary of St. Louis, two congenital hazard seekers, the aggressive Francis Preston Blair Jr. and Nathaniel Lyon, overran his camp and disarmed the troops. That
was decisive (though Dr. Eliot was to tell a Phi Beta Kappa
meeting that the decision had really been effected twenty-
three years earlier when St. Louis voted to tax itself for the
public schools and so educated her young in time for them to
bring their influence to bear in 1860). The Confederates
would skirmish in southern Missouri and threaten the city, but
St. Louis remained in the Union and was anchor post of the

Northern operations against the lower Mississippi and the western flank of the Confederacy. Dr. Eliot was in constant touch with the military authorities, constantly addressing memoranda to Washington. When St. Louis was threatened, all his ardor was directed to the defense of the Union. He became chaplain of the volunteer Guard, men over the age for active duty, who mobilized to oppose the Confederate thrusts, and he exhorted them in sermons more patriotic than judicial, more animated than sage. But, these moments of sudden emergency excepted, he kept before his mind that the struggle was between kindred, and worked with that uncommon common sense of his alike to hasten the Union victory and to prevent the infliction of injustice by the Union authorities on southern prisoners and wounded or on southern sympathizers. His principal work, conducted with an extraordinary administrative capacity and success, was the organization of the Western Sanitary Commission to provide hospital services for the wounded of both sides and relief for refugees. He took a personal part in its work, from negotiating with the military commanders to raising funds and stringing parcels. There is a glimpse of him in Mrs. Eliot's biography finishing his parceling after midnight and walking, lantern in hand, to his home on the outskirts of the city. He still continued the regular work of his parish, and undertook additional work as unpaid Professor of Metaphysics at Washington University.

And though the slaves had apparently been allowed to recede to a somewhat remote second place in his mind, he had not forgotten them. In the course of the war there fell to him, and he accepted it, as a providential responsibility, his personal fight for the freedom of Archer Alexander. Alexander was a slave on a Missouri estate. He saved a Unionist company from ambush by walking five miles through the night to warn its officer. He then returned faithfully home; but the Confederates suspected him, and to save his life he took flight, and, after capture and a fresh escape, reached St. Louis. There he met Mrs. Eliot and asked her for work. She took him to her house; and, says Dr. Eliot, with a phrase which illustrates the courtesy and the warmth of his marriage, "She spoke to him once or twice on the way, and he gradually got courage as he looked at her, as well as he might." Eliot found him duties in the grounds — they were living at the time in a house set among four acres of garden, orchard, forest trees and outbuildings — and studied the implications of his action. It was generally his persuasion that the law, no matter if sometimes it falls short of justice, must be obeyed; and the law made it an offense to assist fugitive slaves. But he came to the conclusion that here was the exceptional case where a man must defy the law. He resolved to keep Alexander under his protection. But he also took the nearest means of bringing himself back within the law, by sending Alexander's master an offer to pay the fair purchase price for the runaway. He would buy Alexander so that he could give him liberty. But the master swore angrily that he wouldn't let "that little abolition preacher" beat him, and hired two men to go to St. Louis and fetch Alexander back by force.

On a sunny March morning in 1863 Eliot went out to Washington University with Hamilton's *Metaphysics* under his arm "and my mind intent upon the 'law of the conditioned' and 'excluded middle,' — how to explain it to a dozen not too eager youths, especially when I only half understood it myself." At one o'clock he came home from his classes and found the household in disorder. Alexander had been kidnaped. And now Dr. Eliot tells us something that shows that though he revered principles and dedicated all his action to them, action was his element. "Without taking off my hat, or waiting for dinner, I started with quick step for the provost-marshal's office; no more abstractions in my mind, nor 'law of the conditioned,' but a plain duty to rescue the captive." Which, enlisting the help of the authorities (whom he had learned to manipulate with the skill of a T. E. Lawrence), he did by the end of the day. He held on to Alexander till he was able to purchase him, then he freed him, and he looked after him with employment and assistance as long as he lived.

When he was on vacation in Italy in the post-bellum years, Eliot saw Thomas Ball's design for an "Emancipation" statue to Lincoln, and with his customary speed arranged for the execution of the project, subject to one proviso: that Alexander be the model for the slave. So today Archer Alexander kneels in Washington, D.C., breaking his chain in Lincoln's shadow.

The persistent efficiency which carried Eliot to his objective at every stage of the Alexander story is typical. A business enterpriser once said that if W.G.E. had been his partner, "we should have made most of the money west of the Alleghanies." But he lent his strength wholly to ideal enthusiasms. He used it for education. He used it to drive the Western Sanitary Commission. He fought for prohibition. He fought for women's franchise and education. He fought against the legalizing of prostitution; St. Louis regularized the traffic while Eliot was abroad; on return he went into action against it, for "from his knowledge of the working of the system in Paris, Berlin, and all the leading cities of Europe, he knew that it did not prevent the consequences of wrong-doing, while it increased the extent of the evil"; and after four years he had the ordinance expunged from the city books, and went campaigning for the purification of New York and Cleveland.

He had resigned from the active leadership of the Church of Messiah in 1870, to leave it to younger hands and to take up his work as Chancellor of Washington University. For seventeen more years he exerted his influence as a civic leader and reformer. In the summer of 1886, on his seventy-sixth birthday, he wrote a poem, "Nunc Dimittis," petitioning for release from the effort of life:

> Fain would I breathe that gracious word,
> Now lettest thou thy servant, Lord,
>   Depart in peace.
> When may I humbly claim that kind award,
>   And cares and labors cease?
>
> With anxious heart I watch at heaven's gate —
>   Answer to hear;
> With failing strength I feel the increasing weight
>   Of every passing year.
> Hath not the time yet fully come, dear Lord,
>   Thy servant to release?

In December he was ill, and his family, afraid that he could not tolerate the hard winter of the midwest, decided to move him in the New Year down to Pass Christian. That sounds like the geography of Bunyan and right for a devoted pastor; actually it is a resort to which the rich of New Orleans escaped from the swamp fevers. It is named after a French explorer of the Gulf coast, and Christian is pronounced with the accent on the last syllable and a southern *cantando*. The villas stand in lush gardens, each with its long wooden Regency-raked jetty running above the beach to the water, and a warm, salt wind blows in. William Greenleaf Eliot was in love with the sea, and here he might have revived. But the thirty hours' journey by rail shook the tired frame and he died in Pass Christian on January 23, 1887. His body was carried back to St. Louis where, though he had requested a simple funeral, the Church of the Messiah was full to overflowing on January 28.

He was one of those men in whose presence no one wishes to be at fault.

Within a liberal church he was a strongly conservative force. One reviewer of Mrs. Eliot's biography complained that she had not sufficiently revealed how conservative he was. As a young man it may have been a source of strength to him to feel that he was the evangelist of an outcast doctrine — "our

Church vilified and ourselves excluded from the Christian communion." But he came to emphasize what his Church shared with the Christian churches. He cherished "all that was sacred and memorable in the past, as a priceless legacy, a repository of truth, even though commingled with error." He loved the institutions of Christianity, baptism and the Lord's supper; "he considered the communion table the centre of the religious life of a church."

Like all Unitarians he was a believer in perfectibility; but he was most cautious in his estimate of man's capacity to arrive at perfection, cautious in his acceptance of the national assumption that everybody's opinion should weigh equally in the management of affairs. The objective of the wider and better education for which he pressed was to prepare all men to form and apply opinions; but he did not foresee any rapid general advance, and in the long meantime would have preferred to restrict the franchise by an educational qualification.

He sometimes promised himself to put time aside for writing, but the claims of his ministry, and of all the affairs of life for which he accepted responsibility, were always too pressing. Even so, he wrote, if no solid work, such as he would have liked, an extraordinary quantity of fugitive pieces: articles for newspapers; sermons and addresses. Several of his sermons were published by the American Unitarian Association and kept in print by successive impressions; and at least one group of them, *The Discipline of Sorrow*, studies in consolation after the death of his daughter, Mary, became well known. Just as businessmen envied him his energy and organizing ability, writers envied him "the literary finish" of everything he composed. He wrote without adjectives. He avoided flights that might encourage the "western grandiloquence" of his neighbors. His great-grandfather, Thomas Dawes, had introduced "the Greek simplicity" into New England architecture; there is a Greek simplicity in William Greenleaf Eliot's writing. But one work, while essentially depending on the same plainness and clarity, has other qualities, too. Towards the end of his life, when he had at last a little leisure, his family persuaded Dr. Eliot to set down *The Story of Archer Alexander*. Between the arts of the pulpit and the stage comparisons have often been drawn: preachers have to be actors, if they are to keep their listeners awake. Evidently Dr. Eliot had in reserve all the professional skills of the performer and entertainer, including the mimic. *The Story of Archer Alexander* is alive with regional voices. "I can tell you how we can fix it, short metre," says the Virginian Colonel Jones, squeezing a slave out of his miserable debtor, Parson Delaney:

> You just give me a bill of sale for that nigger Aleck out there, and it's done. He's a sassy boy and will get you into a big scrape some day; and you'd better get shet of him, anyway, for your own good and for the good of the country. There now, parson, the way I look at it, your religion and your pocket are on the same side. What do you say? But one thing's sure: money or its equiv-a-lent I'm a-going to have, down on the nail. There ain't no two ways about that.

There are passages of satirical understatement, which recall Swift and show how closely William Greenleaf Eliot was in touch with classical prose. A slave tried to escape with his wife and child. They were caught and brought back. "But they had suffered so much from exposure and in the struggle with their captors, *who had an unmanageable dog with them*, that they were never of much account afterwards." And there are one or two simple and penetrating sentences in the tradition of benevolence, which is a staple of the English essay and the English novel. William Greenleaf Eliot hardly allowed his literary and artistic sensibility to grow, holding it in check lest it prove too excitable, and always subordinating it to the claims of work. But it was alive in him and would not be extinguished. He handed it down to his children, who also kept it in a state of gentle submission. But it was then handed down to the next generation.

A Minister in Oregon

Dr. Eliot taught that a father should consciously require of his children the obedience that God requires of man: "It is an easy transition from filial respect to religious awe. Children who have been early taught the lesson of obedience to their parents, can easily learn the higher lesson of obedience to God. It is, in both cases, the respectful and reverential submission to authority, under the sense of duty . . ." And the father ruling an obedient family could best conceive God's tenderness for the world: "for as a father pitieth his children, so doth the Lord pity those who fear him." The relationship was his image of the eternal order.

His eldest son (not the poet's father, who was the second son) inherited and adopted almost without modification his doctrines and code of life. Thomas Lamb Eliot went west to the Pacific coast. He established a Unitarian church in Portland, Oregon, and called it the Church of Our Father.

In Portland he did everything Dr. Eliot had done in St. Louis. He indefatigably visited prisons, hospitals, the asylum and the sickbed. He struggled for social reform in the city and state. He acquired, as he stayed at his post, a local reputation and influence like his father's. A Massachusetts Unitarian sent to scout the Portland area in 1871 reported that people in the saloons and hotel rooms said, "Oh, that little Eliot and his set, they are different; if all were like him, religion would mean something."

Like his father, he thought constantly of the martyrs. During a European holiday in 1882 he went to Geneva, and tramped the streets to find the Place Champel where Calvin had burned

Servetus, who "gave his life in martyrdom to the distinctive principle of Unitarian theology." He found the square, but no plaque to commemorate the stake. He imagined a statue he would raise there if he could, "so costly, so significant, so prophetic, that not a traveller but shall visit it . . . I would put there a lofty figure of the Genius of Toleration, quenching the torch of persecution with her foot, and on the pedestal the dying words of the martyr: 'To whom should I call, except to God?'" But in the same article in which he recorded his search and his thoughts, he warned his readers that we are, all of us, so inured to habit that we cannot recognize the truth of the evangelist when he comes . . . "the chances are a hundred to one that, had you been in Palestine, you would have helped stone Stephen; that, had you lived in Rome, your shouts would be joined with the multitudes that doomed the hapless martyrs; that, had you been in Constance, you would have sincerely hated John Huss; and, had you lived in Geneva, you would have held up the hands that built the greenwood fire for a crazy Spanish heretic . . ."

It may be that an active minister in the Portland of the seventies met frequent calls on his courage. But there is no indication of it in the biography which his son-in-law, Earl Morse Wilbur, wrote. There is proof of a constant effort to keep abreast of current ideas and to support liberal movements. Eliot became a member of the local Woman's Suffrage Association in 1869, and his sermon on "Women's Political Enfranchisement" in 1883 was praised by his father as "the finest on the subject he had ever seen." Like his father, he was interested in comparative religion; going further than his father, he would make a whole sermon a lesson in religious history — would guide his congregation through the origins and evolution of the Christian Easter, for example. But the qualities of adventure, enterprise, energy, though not lacking in his story, are not the predominant quality. What most impresses in the biography is

the record of a Christian domestic fulfilment. It is as if Thomas
Lamb Eliot paid for his complete filial piety by a life deprived
of what he might have valued most, the martyr's experience,
and was rewarded for it by the perfection of his household life.

Wilbur describes the day and its regular rites in the Portland
home. He tells, for example, of the morning prayers:

> When breakfast was finished, chairs would be drawn back
> from the table and Bibles passed around. A selected book of the
> New Testament would be read in course, or one of the Psalms,
> each member reading a verse twice round the circle. Then one
> of the number would be asked to choose a hymn, and a stanza
> or two would be sung. After this the family would kneel while
> Dr. Eliot offered a brief prayer . . . But few fragments of these
> prayers have been preserved, jotted down by some one of the
> children from memory afterwards as far as they could be re-
> called; but could they have been taken down as spontaneously
> uttered, they would form a remarkable manual of domestic
> worship . . .
>   . . . these few minutes of daily worship had a profound ef-
> fect upon the members of the family, and were so greatly valued
> that not one was willingly missed. Grace at meals was rever-
> ently said, at supper always silently in the Quaker way . . .

The daily round and the round of the Christian year were kept
with pleasure. "As Christmas approached," Wilbur says later —

> there would be a trip into the woods to cut a Christmas tree;
> and on Christmas day all would gather at ten o'clock in the
> dining-room, where the shades would be drawn and the candles
> on the tree lit. Then after singing "Holy Night" and several
> other traditional Christmas songs the gifts would be taken from
> the tree by each in turn, beginning with the youngest, and
> handed to the person for whom they were intended. The tip of
> the tree was carefully saved to light the fire at the next Christ-
> mas, and thus one year was linked to another.

For the last twenty years, since Eliot published "Little Gidding," all his readers have been aware of an English seventeenth-century household dedicated to the round of religious
observance. There is something to be learned from the Portland household of the nineteenth century. The Ferrars observed, not the better to go out into daily life, but for the sake
of observance; their round of devotion was a choice of eternal
life in place of daily life. To the Eliots the round of observance
was, if satisfying in itself, the more satisfying because it gave
strength for work and was the most powerful agent of well-
doing. To help others was the purpose of life. A prayer Thomas
Lamb Eliot taught one of his daughters was "Dear God, help
me to be thoughtful, and helpful, and unselfish."

There is a supplementary record of his home. He married
Henrietta Robins Mack, who was interested in the education
of the young, especially in the Froebel method which Susan
Blow was introducing in St. Louis. As her children grew up,
she pleased herself by writing a storybook or two for them.
Laura's Holidays is a minuscule book of festivals: twelve chapters for the festive day of each month of the year. New Year's
Day — Laura's sled ride with her father. St. Valentine's Day —
visiting a sick boy in hospital. St. Patrick's Day — arranging a
holiday for their Irish serving girl. All Fools' Day — the Eliots
deplore fooling that hurts, and invent a useful kind, where the
surprise is a gift. May Day — May baskets, like Herrick's, hung
on the doorknobs of friends' houses. Midsummer Day — school
speech day. July 4 — Laura falls sick from the summer heat,
and her father puts her to bed and stays with her, and they see
the fireworks from the window while he tells her the story of
America:

how, a long time ago, grandpapa lived across the ocean, in a
country where the people would not let him pray and go to
church the way that he thought was right, and how he and some

other men and women that liked the same kind of church that he did came sailing across the ocean to this country, to live where they could do what they thought right; and how this country was all woods then, and how they built houses and schools and churches . . .

till by the time he had finished there were hardly any more rockets, and Laura was ready to go to sleep.

But I think, so long as she lives, she will never see rockets shooting upward in a still summer evening without feeling as if she were again a little girl with her dear father's hand holding hers.

Then August — Beach Day. September — Laura's birthday — and on each birthday her mother gives her a duty to do every day through the year ("and somehow she had come to care more about that, in one way, than the other presents, because she knew it helped her to grow up into a useful woman"). October — Halloween. November — Thanksgiving Day. December — Christmas — and making presents instead of buying them, since "we give presents to show our love."

The simple book has a beauty to which it never pretended: it reveals the life and hopes of the reticent people who constituted the finest stratum of American society in the late nineteenth century. We can construct from it, and from Wilbur, glimpses of the St. Louis home on which the Portland home was modeled, and glimpses of the corresponding daily and yearly round in which T. S. Eliot grew up.

A Businessman in St. Louis

Dr. Eliot had expected that all his sons would, like Thomas Lamb Eliot, emulate him, and enter the ministry. He never said it, because it was so perfectly plain to him. On graduation from Washington University Henry Ware Eliot told him that he wanted to go into some active business. "Then your education is wasted," said his father, in sudden anger. But he pulled himself up, paused, and added "except that it has made a man of you."

The ministry was the last thing Henry Ware Eliot wanted; he had had enough of church and Sunday school obligations in twenty years of a preacher's home. "Too much pudding choked the dog," he remarked. To learn something about business, he went into the St. Louis wholesale grocery store of Partridge and Company, later called Reed & Green. He was bill clerk, shipping clerk, purchaser of small items, receiving clerk, errand boy and assistant porter. He developed accuracy in preparing documents and efficiency in overseeing, and was proud of his acceleration of the movement of goods. He was a glutton for work. In the seven years he spent with Partridge he had two vacations and six weeks as a convalescent — after breaking a shin in the company's behalf rushing down an unlit wharf.

On his regular trips to the levee he took in, as he hurried by, the names of the steamboats; knew their names, *Grey Eagle, Bald Eagle, Great Republic, Sultana, Jewess.* But if he had a passion for far-away, it was subdued to the pleasure of sticking to a job and doing that well.

In 1870 Reed & Green were running down owing to managerial troubles. Eliot spent a year looking for other work. An acquaintance induced him to go into partnership to manufacture acetic acid for the St. Louis white lead companies. The enterprise was ill-starred; the factory was flooded twice by the Mississippi, burned once; and Eliot had to buy out his intemperate partner. He looked for support to men who had advised him to risk the undertaking, and found none, and that imbued him with a distrust of his fellows which it took many years to overcome. He closed down.

In the year of difficulties and unemployment that followed he found two sources of support. His wife supported him and their infant children by teaching. His father provided money to absolve the company's debts.

There were choice clays in the vicinity of St. Louis, in particular a superior red clay for building bricks and a valuable fire clay for firebricks, furnaces, retorts, tiles and sewer pipes. By the end of the century the St. Louis brickyards would employ four million dollars of capital and nearly three thousand hands and bring two and a half million dollars to the city annually. Searching for a fresh opportunity, Henry Ware Eliot became, in 1874, secretary of the Hydraulic-Press Brick Company. His drive was now rewarded quickly. He paid back to his father ten times the loan that had covered the chemical company debts. He remained in the work, as Secretary and Treasurer, then as President and Treasurer, then as chairman, to the end of his days.

He succeeded amply and gave amply: gifts to Washington University, and to other institutions in St. Louis that attracted his interest, such as the Academy of Science and the Missouri Botanical Garden, and to many charities. Even in his earliest Partridge days he and four other young men, three of them with equally small salaries and equally scanty spare time, had started a Newsboys' Home, paying for it themselves and conducting the evening classes themselves (in other words, like Dr. Eliot, they gave not only money but personal involvement). He kept the family pattern of giving.

He is to be seen in several of the family photographs now at the Houghton Library, Harvard. A penciled annotation by Henry Ware Eliot Jr. dates the earliest around 1885. This shows him with soft light hair, a soft beard, salient ears, a high Victorian collar and a bow tie, big hands, a straight if gentle look. The next, dated c. 1892, shows him posed in profile; he is wearing a fine morning suit; his strong hands are folded; the features seem a little delicate, though the ears are gnarled. The date of the next picture is uncertain, a year or two before the end of the century, but the place is Gloucester, and he is in holiday clothes — soft hat, soft collar and a tie instead of the formal bow tie, though he still has the gold watch chain hanging at his waistcoat as at home; his face is wizened, sharp, healthy, his head is thrown back, and he looks almost an old sea captain; he is on a seat with one of his sons, about ten years old, T. S. Eliot, and his left arm is thrown round him. In 1908 Henry Ware Eliot Jr. photographed him at home in St. Louis, playing chess, now bespectacled and his face lined; and later still the same devoted photographer, to whose care the collection is due, took a picture of the dining table in St. Louis: the old businessman in his high collar, spectacles, and a hearing aid strapped over his silky white hair; Mrs. Eliot in a woollen jacket, a long necklace.

Together with his brother, Edward Cranch Eliot, who had also turned aside from the ministry and chosen the profession of law and successfully practiced it in St. Louis, he wholly attached himself to the family tradition after his one act of nonconformism. His interests, as he aged, bent on the history of the family and set him collecting information about the descendants of the revolutionary William Greenleaf. In a similar way Edward Cranch Eliot collected information about William Greenleaf Eliot's children and grandchildren, published it, and left a fund for the publication of later editions to keep the record up to date.

Henry Ware Eliot died on January 8, 1919. He had not seen his youngest child, T. S. Eliot, since the summer of 1915 when that earnest migrant returned home for a brief visit. The First World War had impaired communications between the two continents. I fancy he felt rather bewilderedly separated from a child whose genius seemed to be wandering from the Eliot and the American folkways and seeking odd and scrappy ends — by that early month of 1919 very few of the great results of the errancy were yet to be seen in America. Henry Ware Eliot, like all the children of William Greenleaf and Abby Adams (Cranch) Eliot, was responsive to the arts: he had been in his younger days a member of the Philharmonic and Choral Societies; had some talent for painting; filled his home with pictures. But his taste was conservative. In politics he was staunchly Republican, in all matters conservative. It was hard for him to conceive of a life devoted to *experimenting* with words.

Charlotte C. Eliot

But Mrs. Eliot sympathized with her son's undertaking, and his progress as a writer was her happiness.

Before marriage, Mrs. Eliot was Charlotte Champe Stearns. Her ancestors included Charles Chauncy, the second president of Harvard, and Samuel Chapin, a founder of Springfield. Her father, Thomas Stearns Jr. of Lunenburg, Massachusetts, married the daughter of the Hon. Thomas Blood of Sterling, Massachusetts, in 1840. As a young man he appears to have been exploratory and restless, moving from town to town along the seaboard plain from his home to Maryland. In the early forties he was in Baltimore: the city directory of 1842 calls him a commission shoe merchant, that of 1845 a commission merchant. Charlotte, his second child and second daughter, was born in Baltimore in 1843. He settled down at last in Boston as a partner of the trading firm Stearns and Bailey, and took a home in North Lexington where Charlotte grew up — and there in due course her children made visits to their "Grandma Faraway."

She was educated at private schools in Boston and Sandwich, then at the State Normal School at Framingham. She did well, pleasing her teachers and herself. But all to no purpose, she thought later, because she had been unable, in the lack of opportunity for women to go to the university, to develop her aptitudes further. She used to look with nostalgia and bitterness at the testimonial given to her when she graduated at Framingham from the "advanced" class of 1862. "A young lady of unusual brilliancy as a scholar," it said. But what use, she thought, had her courses in trigonometry and astronomy served when she had gone, before she was twenty, into the teaching of young children? She did not take kindly to the stoppage of her growth, did not see it as compensated by what she could give her classes, saw herself as a failure as a teacher and a failure in her ambitions. Just as her father had been a restless mover in his early years, she moved restlessly: she taught in a private school in West Chester, Pennsylvania; in another in Milwaukee; for two years with a Quaker family; for a year at Antioch College; for a year at Framingham Normal School; and for the academic year 1867 to 1868 at St. Louis Normal School. In St. Louis she met Henry Ware Eliot. They married from her family's Lexington home in the summer of 1868.

Her seven children were born at 2635 Locust Street, in a large bed between walls covered with dozens of photographs, mirrors, engravings — engravings of a Mother and Child, of Theodosius and St. Ambrose, of a Winged Victory. The first four children were daughters. The fifth was a son, Henry Ware Eliot Jr. The sixth was a daughter, Theodora, born in 1885, lost in 1886. The seventh and last was Thomas Stearns Eliot. His parents were in their mid-forties, his eldest sister was already entering Radcliffe, and his youngest surviving sister already eleven.

While her youngest child was growing up, Charlotte Eliot developed a career in social work. Suffering still from that sense of deprivation because the universities had been closed to her in 1862, she was concerned to prove the value of women to society, and joined with other active women of her city in the Humanity Club and the Wednesday Club. Every American city, of course, had similar voluntary associations; and to say what these St. Louis groups pursued is to define the pursuits

of liberal American women at the turn of the century. Charlotte
Eliot herself has said it, half lightly, half challengingly, in
verses she wrote and declaimed for the Wednesday Club:

> These are the days when women must be wise
> And crown their efforts with self-sacrifice.
> Clubs shall there be, not for life's petty needs,
> Nor pride nor fashion, but for noble deeds.
> Thus organized, what may not women do?
> What *will* not, if only they be true
> To high ideals and if they unite
> With noble purpose to achieve the right?

She praises the Club's section work for science, philosophy,
economics, the arts, "current events," but goes on:

> Though culture may be our corner stone,
> We cannot exist for culture alone
> In scholarly retreat.
>
> For lo! grave problems press.
> The pleadings of distress
> Will follow the mind's sublimest flight,
> A voice from the depths disturb the height,
> When wrongs demand redress

And so the Club will, by effort and sacrifice, provide vacation
playgrounds and social settlements. It is the American parallel
to the movement that in England sent the young Fabians,
Flecker, Brooke, Attlee, Forster, Roger Fry, to the East End
and Camden Town. But in America it is a movement of women
of middle life.

The Humanity Club of St. Louis studied to "help the unfortunate." It was founded by the wife of General John W. Noble,
an invalid, unable to move out of her home. The ladies of the
Club met at her house, and set up committees for the considera-

tion of everything that demanded redress or invited interference. There is an obvious sense in which such work is busybodyness; the Hasty Pudding Club of Harvard caricatured it in the Sultana of *Diana's Debut,* who was president of the Mothers' Municipal League, of the Woman's Rights Association, etc., etc. But it is the sublimation of busybodyness. Committees devised tactics to save girls from betrayal into disreputable houses during the 1904 World's Fair, and to see that the irredeemable were turned back at the station. Committees investigated conditions in the city jails and workhouses. The Club was perturbed, for example, by the predicament of women prisoners in St. Louis, who were visible in their cells, so the Committee reported, not only to the all-male warders but to the male prisoners when these were out in the square at exercise. The Club lobbied till the male guards were replaced by female — though whether this, much as it may have alleviated the uneasiness of the prisoners, resulted in greater charity to them may be doubted — and till the jail was rearranged. The best and most sustained struggle of the Club was for the protection of juvenile offenders, boys or girls, and here Mrs. Eliot was the leading worker, and her success earned her a place in the history of St. Louis and Missouri. Visiting the courts in 1899 as one of the Club's Jail Committee she learned that two boys charged with the theft of a farmer's cart — they had driven a short distance for fun and then fallen asleep in it — were kept for four months in the town jail, among adult and hardened offenders, before being brought to trial and acquitted. The matter was debated by the Club, which asked Mrs. Eliot and Miss Mary Perry, the State Commissioner of Charities, to serve as a Special Committee for the examination of the court and detention procedures affecting juveniles. They found their city and their state completely innocent of differentiation between the child and the adult; and they saw, and confirmed by the study of procedures in other cities and overseas, that separate courts, separate places of detention, and special officers capable of care for the young, were necessary if the innocent or merely mischievous child was not to be turned into a serious offender or the serious offender to be driven beyond help. For ten years the pair labored for these reforms. Mrs. Eliot, securing a small grant-in-aid from the Trustees of the Western Sanitary Commission funds (the residue of the collections of her father-in-law and his friends during the Civil War) and adding to it from her own purse, corresponded with legislators and advisers, visited and pestered them, wrote to the press. She undertook to raise $400, to be half the salary of a Probation Officer for juvenile offenders, and raised almost $800. Gradually results were won: the appointment of a Children's Probation Officer in 1901; a St. Louis juvenile court in 1903; a separate house of detention for juveniles in 1906. Three years later the pair were still lobbying in the State House to protect their reforms against retrograde legislation and to extend them through Missouri.

This is the work for which Mrs. Eliot is usually remembered. Her family was proud of it; her husband kept newspaper cuttings about it in a scrapbook; she was proud herself, feeling that she had demonstrated that women have the instinct to uncover injustices and the strength to remedy them.

No one who does good under these conditions, and with a touch of pride in it, will escape problems. In December 1905, after Mrs. Eliot had reported to the Collegiate Alumnae Association on the successful operation of the Juvenile Court law and the probation system, the next speaker, the School Director of the Board of Education, attacked her: "The juvenile court is not a success . . ." Several women jumped to their feet with cries pro and con. "We want to hear the bad as well as the good in this matter," said one lady amid some applause. Allowance made for the imperfection of human arrangements, the balance seems to have lain with the good, and Mrs. Eliot's undertakings seem to have deserved, won, and retained almost as much esteem from the city as from her own family.

Her eldest daughter Ada (after 1905 Mrs. Alfred Dwight Sheffield) inherited her interest in social work and combined her abilities in it with both the moral passion and the business efficiency of the Eliots. She trained as a professional social worker, and very early was District Secretary of the Family Welfare Society of Boston, then Secretary of the Dependent Children's Committee of the New York Charity Organization Society, then probation officer in tough Harlem. From 1909 to 1934 she was connected with the Massachusetts State Board of Charities and from 1927 to 1939 a member of the Board of the Boston Children's Mission. In her late years when she had turned the physically exacting practical work over to younger people, she wrote three books on her subject: *The Social Case History* (1920), *Case Study Possibilities* (1922), and *Social Insight in Case Situations* (1937), presented in a style which, if the demands of her subject are taken into account, resembles her younger brother's, and is informed, like his work, with the desire to build order into her subject: to see every case in terms of principle; to diagnose the community, its failures and its duties, through the cases; to remake the community through her work.

Social work was the natural flowering of Unitarian morality, an attempt to regulate the world, and F. O. Matthiessen has accordingly used it to characterize Charlotte in his *Achievement of T. S. Eliot*. Yet it was not really centermost to her, and it was in some respects a substitute for what she had most desired of herself: success in literature. In a commonplace book, belonging to her late college or early teaching years, she has transcribed poems she likes, such as "Come live with me and be my love" and Southwell's "Times go by turns" and the Bugle Song from *The Princess*, and parodies that amuse her, such as " 'Tis the last cake of supper, Left steaming alone," and drafts for work of her own, and a translation of her own from Schiller dated March 22, 1865. You look at a photograph taken shortly before her marriage, and you see an intense girl with the face of a longing boy, her thin hair parted in the middle and brushed to shine and sobriety, her clear eyes staring — a girl you can guess to be devoted to poetry and almost ready to try to live it. Into the much later photographs some anxiety has crept; distress at the blows of life, and stubbornness in bearing it, especially as she stands at the gate of her St. Louis home the morning after the cyclone of 1896; resignation to the public disregard of her poems, and a determination, as she sits in a basket chair or bent over an old typewriter, to go on writing them.

All her life she wrote poems, and persevered in the search for editors to print them. Here and there she has jotted the names and addresses of journals — the *Independent*, 251 Broadway; the *Springfield Republican*, P.O. Box 2787 — which might have room for a stanza or two. Except for a tiny booklet, *Easter Songs*, she only found acceptance in religious journals, especially those of a Unitarian or liberal complexion, to which her married name sponsored her: *The Unitarian, The Christian Register, Our Best Words*. From time to time they published her poems, and occasionally her essays, including a series on *Hymn-Writers of the Liberal Faith*. Her delight in print is clear, for she clipped the columns and pasted them in scrapbooks for her children.

In all her work there are the qualities of a true poet. She was not concerned, as many post-Shelleyans were, with rhapsodizing or with colors, but with the shapes of stanzas and the management of metrics and rhyme. She worked to master a stanza, then passed on to experiment with another. For her son the test of a poet has been the power to innovate, and the special interest of a master like Shakespeare the restless experimentation which refused to repeat a success and made each new drama a new battle with another technical difficulty. T. S. Eliot, Shakespeare, the blind Arabic poet Al Ma'arri, belong to one class of writers. Al Ma'arri has a volume in which he performs, poem by poem, a technical feat which the rules of the verse allow but do not require. Shakespeare's approach to drama was of the same order, except that, in addition, he *invented* the difficulties which he required himself to solve. So with T. S. Eliot. And Eliot's mother had, in a minor degree, this preoccupation with form and with the extension of her technical range.

One of her experiments is *A Musical Reverie*. She marks the first movement *Andante*. Someone has died, someone already beautiful in life —

> Nay, while the soul was in the body pent,
> Thy face so shone we knew not what it meant

and now in heaven utterly pure, a "spirit beautiful beyond compare." Then she turns to a new movement, *Presto Agitato*, the tempo of distress, because she can never attain the same perfection and even when she dies God would not choose "so frail an instrument" to serve him. She does not number her next and last verse as a third movement, she is still in the cosmic spaces of after-death, but she indicates a change of pace and mood with *Poco Tranquillo*, promising herself a momentary ecstasy and consolation:

> Some time, perhaps, in pity thou wilt turn,
> To say "Poor human heart that loved me so,
> And, unforgetting, still for me dost yearn!"
> Then, though thy presence near I may not know,
> All pain will cease, all sorrow leave my breast,
> And love at last will dream of endless rest.

For all its nineteenth-century mannerisms this poem has not left me since I read it. Yet of the form it attempts there is this to be admitted, that if the pace of the sections were not specified by the musical directions, we could not experience it from the verses themselves.

Mrs. Eliot thought of her poetry and her religion together. She has a series of poems dramatizing the Disciples, poems about Paul, Peter, and St. Barnabas, and an extended poem on her favorite theme of the Emperor Theodosius subdued by St. Ambrose. A notebook, now in the Missouri Historical Society's Library in St. Louis, is filled with drafts of poems narrating episodes from the New Testament: the Annunciation, the Nativity, the Visit of the Magi, the Presentation in the Temple, the Flight into Egypt, the Purification of the Temple. Evidently she contemplated a volume or system of poems retelling the Christian story; there are signs in the notebook of a concern alike with the best historical order, the best dramatic order, and a total formal pattern. The Unitarians were lovers of Milton, whom they counted as one of themselves; some of her poems echo him (though she has her own voice, low-pitched, convincing by quietude, by a disciplined tenderness, which is her excellence, rather than by force); one has a stanza based on the Nativity Ode. Perhaps his example was often in her mind, and perhaps she spoke to herself of a complex of divine poems which would be, in sum, a great Biblical poem.

T. S. Eliot once recalled in the *Criterion* that his family respected practices and beliefs other than their own — and we have seen Dr. Eliot's reverence for the traditional rites of Christianity. In Mrs. Eliot's poems there is a sensitivity to the beauty of the antique church. "A Charade of the Seasons" — one of those poems in which there is quiver of experimental life — describes a cathedral:

> Stranger, approach! Its open doors
> Treasures of art reveal;
> Where every sense is satisfied,
> Wilt thou not pause to kneel?

> When forms of beauty fill the eye,
> Sweet music charms the ear,
> And incense fills the fragrant air,
> Must not the Lord be near?

When she writes about the Communion Table, in *Savonarola,* she uses one of her occasional triple rhymes, almost elegant, the sign of a movement of pleasure in her mind:

> For though the heaven itself cannot contain
> Its own Creator, He doth humbly deign
> In bread and wine to manifest again
> His presence to our sense.

She has an admirable sequence of poems on the Jewish Festivals: the New Year, Yom Kippur, and the Feast of Tabernacles.

Some of her poems are energized by a sense of drama, best realized when she turns, as she often does, to the lives of the saints and martyrs. She has sketched three scenes around the imprisonment and trial of Giordano Bruno. In the first scene Bruno soliloquizes in prison:

> Soul of the world! on thee doth all depend.
> Mysterious power, that mouldest to thy will!
> In the beginning seest thou the end,
> And in the end a mere beginning still.

The Inquisitor enters, and Bruno says:

> Upon my brow
> The martyr's crown will rest, and I shall die
> For truth and for the freedom ye deny.

In the second scene Bruno defends himself, telling how he loved the Church and his priesthood, but accepted the necessity of all human growth: the intervention of reason; after

which faith returns "with new and added dower." The Inquisitor tests him on the Trinity. In the third scene, on Christmas morning, Bruno prepares to die. These fragments were
published in a periodical in 1890. I do not know whether they
are excerpts from a longer work, or whether they are intended
to be complete in themselves. But it is well known that Mrs.
Eliot made a full-length drama of the life of Savonarola, in
which she found the same pattern as she had found in Bruno's.
Savonarola turns aside from the early temptations of human
life and love, then from the temptation of the Cardinal's hat:

> All earthly honours I would fain resign.
> Is this the hat I wish, a hat of red?
> If so then let it be
> The crown of martyrdom upon my head . . .

His loyal followers and priests tempt him to physical resistance
against his persecutors. Without his knowledge they have
stored weapons of defense in the cloisters of San Marco, and
despite his protests they bar the doors and arm themselves
against the Compagnacci. But Savonarola forces them to lay
down their arms and open the door and suffer his submission
and removal to prison. He is tried, and perishes. In 1926
Savonarola was published in London by R. Cobden-Sanderson
(who had published the first volumes of the *Criterion*).
T. S. Eliot wrote an introduction for the volume; and he sent
Mrs. Eliot cuttings of the reviews as they appeared.

Mrs. Eliot counted the poem which commemorates public
figures, and especially public figures who had been friends,
among the obligations and opportunities of a poet's life. As
acquaintances, respected in her circle, bowed out one by one,
she wrote formal obituary sonnets for them: for John Fiske,
James Freeman Clarke, James Martineau, Wayman Crow.
Where a newspaper report prompted her to the excitement of
the moralist and reformer, she judged it a legitimate occasion

for a poem. She read an item from the harbor jail: "Four prisoners at Deer Island very bravely rescued a boat's crew at the imminent risk of their lives. They were pardoned out at once." Perhaps those twenty-four words from the newspaper, printed as her epigraph, are more heartening than her sixty-line poem and its last couplet

> Ye who despair
> Of man's redemption, know the light is there.

She assumed that poetry is a high, virtuous vocation, which teaches and encourages its readers. But if she sometimes wrote too much, she seldom fell into the pitfalls into which the same assumption might have led others; she seldom forced or inflated her language, seldom relied on commonplace inspirational rhythms. Her work is supple, clear, quietly passionate. Only, while it never strains to the detriment of the language, it never lifts the language. It never brings a surprised recognition of the force of a word.

There are no visual images in her poems except where they are furnished by the Scriptures or the habitual vocabulary of the pulpit. In a scrapbook of hers at the Houghton Library the reader is suddenly refreshed by a clear, quick, visual image and is just about to reconsider his verdict when he realizes that the poem in which it appears is not hers. She has pasted into her leaves a typescript of her son's, the poem he wrote, *anno aetatis* 16, for recitation at the graduation ceremonies in his last year at Smith Academy, St. Louis.

Disappointed that her poems had gone almost unrecognized, Mrs. Eliot took comfort from her youngest son's literary promise. If H. W. H. Powel Jr. is right, the family guessed at an early date that T. S. Eliot had unusual abilities, and exerted all their care to foster them and guard him against bruises. Mrs. Eliot looked forward to the day when he would take his place in New York among his country's most prominent writers and perform the work she had longed to perform and win the acknowledgment she would have most desired to win.

Her dozen years between 1910 and the success of *The Waste Land* were dreary. It was wartime, her youngest son was cut off in England, his news came to her infrequently and inadequately, his publications were short and strange. She busied herself in patriotic work, knitting for the men of the battleship *Missouri,* writing letters to the press. The letters were no less energetic than in the days of her campaign for social reform, but tightly, knottily conservative: a reminiscence of the day when John Fiske sat at her dinner-table and praised Britain's record as a colonizer, pleas for the rule of law, war songs fitted to the tune of *Scots, wha hae wi' Wallace bled.* After the war she wrote in protest against Woodrow Wilson's attempt to commit the United States to the League of Nations. In her notebook of the mid-sixties she had told herself always to be ready to let the angels go so that archangels might come in; but now she held jealously to the past, to the words "over the grave of that grand old leader of the Pilgrim Fathers, William Bradford . . . 'Do not basely relinquish what the Fathers with difficulty attained.'" Perhaps the only press pronouncement in line with her old liberal constructivism was a letter in which she urged awards from the Mullanphy Fund to provide English lessons for foreign-speaking immigrants to the States.

It was a time of general suffering; of sleepless nights as she worried about her son in England; of attrition of her powers. Henry Ware Eliot Sr. died in the first month of 1919. Now she gave up St. Louis, which she had accepted loyally while he lived. The Stearnses were in New England, and some of her daughters were there, and she went to live, for the ten years that remained, in Cambridge, Massachusetts, that town of mature houses, trees, and minds.

Then in 1923 she read and reflected on *The Waste Land,* and the conservatism of age fell away. Her son had written to her before publication that he had put much of his life into it. She would not let its difficulties deter her; she read it with sympathy. The male Eliots of her generation were baffled by it; she defended it to them. She only hoped that, with its suffering and struggle, it was an interim poem and would be followed by a poem of fulfillment.

Mrs. Eliot died in Cambridge on September 10, 1929. In the previous year T. S. Eliot had dedicated to her his volume of essays *For Lancelot Andrewes*. It incorporates an essay on Baudelaire, which ends with the quotation, fifteen lines long, of "that great passage" from *Mon Coeur Mis à Nu*, in which the poet promises to pray every morning to God, and "à mon père, à Mariette et à Poe, comme intercesseurs," that he may be granted "la force nécessaire pour accomplir tous mes devoirs," and that his mother may be granted "une vie assez longue pour jouir de ma transformation."

2. "Well-Near the Centre of Our National Demesne"

A WRITER depends, Eliot wrote in 1917, on the "accumulated sensations" of the first twenty-one years. His own first seventeen years were spent in St. Louis, except for annual vacations which took him to the New England coast. In this short chapter I shall select one or two heterogeneous documents to characterize the city of St. Louis of the last quarter of the nineteenth century and the opening of this. For starting point: the years immediately following the Civil War, the years of a dream, when St. Louis saw herself as the nodal city connecting the East and West of the Union. Some historians have written that the prospect of the economic advantages that would follow a Northern triumph had swayed her to Lincoln's side at the outset of the war. That may be to confuse the result with the intentions. But, her decision made and the war endured and won, she reached elatedly for the metal prizes of victory. She was confident of a prosperous future.

Logan Uriah Reavis was the type dreamer of the hour. He devoted his celibate existence to a monomaniac hymning of his native Mississippi Valley. In 1870, already the author of five pamphlets to affirm the importance of the region by "arguments and statistics," he planned a new panegyric, *St. Louis, the Future Great City of the World*. Forty-five citizens, including Eads, the engineer, and Pulitzer, then a rising journalist and politician, petitioned the County Court to subsidize the printing and distribution of the work, which, they argued, would "add infinitely more to the material interests of St. Louis than the small sum required for its publication." The court concurred and ordered ten thousand copies to be printed in English and five thousand in German.

Reavis tells in his drab pages how he looked across the Mississippi from the east and saw over on the St. Louis shore a mile and a half of steamboats lying at the levee. That spacious, thronged wharf raised him to raptures: a thousand miles inland yet "covered with the commodities of every clime, from the peltries of the Rocky Mountains to the teas of China." Buoyed on her commerce, St. Louis would be the queen of middle America. More than that, within three generations, he forecast, she would be "the most consummate fruit of man's civilization"

> and beneath her sway will be united side by side, in the most profitable relations and on the largest scale, the producer and consumer; and they, actuated by a universal amity, will seek the most liberal compensation, attain the highest skill, aspire to a better manhood, and learn to do good.

Judge Nathaniel Holmes, writing Reavis a letter for inclusion in the sixth edition of 1873, spoke with pride of the local advances of half a decade: "the grain trade that has been created, the flour, pork, and cattle trade, the millions invested in ironworks, the railroads that have come into existence . . ."

The brochure was dedicated to Captain James B. Eads, "the man of real genius and marked fidelity to his friends, the citizen of genuine patriotism and rare public spirit, the man worthy of honor because self-made." Eads both dreamed and performed. He was the type enterpriser of the age. As Reavis' dedication shows, he had no formal education. Arriving in the city when he was thirteen, he went out to work to support his family. Shipping as purser on a river steamboat when he was eighteen, he sailed the Mississippi between St. Louis and New Orleans, and used the experience first to invent and patent a diving-bell, then to set up a salvaging business. He grew rich, gave up the river and established a glass factory, lost everything, went back to wrecking and grew rich again. When the Civil War broke out he was summoned by Lincoln to advise on the exploitation of the rivers for attack and defense, and with incredible speed built a gunboat fleet. The war over, a bill went before Congress in 1865 for a bridge to span the Mississippi. A five-hundred-feet center span and fifty feet of clearance would be required. Civil engineers condemned the project as impossible. Eads tendered a solution. His proposals were approved in 1867; he brought all his skill and ingenuity to bear in devising appliances for the subaqueous work; and the bridge was completed in 1874, a marvel of nineteenth-century engineering and his best memorial.

In 1879 Walt Whitman walked on the St. Louis levee under the harvest moon of October:

> I have haunted the river every night lately, where I could get a look at the bridge by moonlight. It is indeed a structure of perfection and beauty unsurpassable, and I never tire of it. The river at present is very low; I noticed today it had much more of a blue-clear look than usual. I hear the slight ripples, the air is fresh and cool, and the view, up or down, wonderfully clear in the moonlight. I am out pretty late: it is so fascinating, dreamy. The cool night-air, all the influences, the silence, with those far-off eternal stars, do me good. I have been quite ill of late. And so, well-near the centre of our national demesne, these night-views of the Mississippi.

Whitman had spent September traveling through Missouri, Kansas, and Colorado. He had read in the sealike immensity of the prairies and the towers of the Rocky Mountains "the law of my own poems" and a confirmation of his belief that America would give the world a new social order consonant with her landscape, and an art consonant with the landscape, the people, and their new order. One rainy day in Missouri he had tried a volume of Milton, Young, Gray, Beattie and Collins, and had given it up, except for enjoying Walter Scott. "I stopp'd and laid down the book, and ponder'd the thought of a poetry that should in due time express and supply the teeming region I was in the midst of . . ."

The central states told him "how absolutely in opposition to our times and lands, and how little and cramp'd, and what anachronisms and absurdities" many of Europe's pages were "for American purposes." Of course, when a poet urges a case against a style or a method, he seldom means to be as exclusive as his words sound and as his followers may think him. The very sentences he wrote about the Mississippi under the moon show that he knew how, at the right moment, to use an anachronism from Europe: the word "influences," lovely in the context, looks back to the Latin language, to the English Latinists from Milton to Collins whom he had lately been reading, to astrology, to the sense of the past and the atavistic. But his paramount aim as a poet was to express by a new form and a new voice the landscape of America and the aspirations it fostered. His journey from the Mississippi to the Rocky Mountains had reawakened his awareness of his purposes: to speak with America's "pure breath, primitiveness, boundless prodigality and amplitude, strange mixture of delicacy and power, of continence, of real and ideal . . ." And looking beyond his own work into the future, he prophesied the emergence in this central region of a "throbbing, vital, imaginative work, or series of works, or literature" which would at once represent and weld the Union.

Whitman stayed in St. Louis with his brother's family for the three months of that fall. He observed, with his journalistic training and his sense of politics and affairs, the city's vigor:

The points of St. Louis are its position, its absolute wealth (the
long accumulations of time and trade, solid riches, probably a
higher average thereof than any city), the unrivall'd amplitude
of its well-laid out environage of broad plateaus, for future expansion — and the great State of which it is the head. It fuses
northern and southern qualities, perhaps native and foreign
ones, to perfection, rendezvous the whole stretch of the Mississippi and Missouri rivers, and its American electricity goes well
with its German phlegm.

These material assets were signs as welcome to him as to
L. U. Reavis. He regarded the arts neither as the alternative to
human welfare nor as independent of it but as its efflorescence.
For him a free society was potentially affluent, the affluent society potentially free. Expecting America to be the living denunciation of earlier orders in which enlargement had been
the prerogative of the oligarchy, and virtues, as Blake complained, had rested on inequity, he desired America, for its
urgent first task, "to lay the foundations of a great nation in
products, in agriculture, in commerce, in networks of inter-
communication, and in all that relates to the comforts of vast
masses of men and families, with freedom of speech, ecclesias-
ticism, &c." And, he told a St. Louis reporter who called to
interview him on October 16:

> These we have founded and are carrying out on a grander scale
> than ever hitherto, and Ohio, Illinois, Indiana, Missouri, Kansas,
> and Colorado seem to me to be the seat and field of these very
> facts and ideas . . . When those have their results and get
> settled, then a literature worthy of us will begin to be defined.

That was nine years before T. S. Eliot's birth.

St. Louis was still expanding as Eliot grew up, but not with
altogether the serene conviction of Reavis' time. A census had
struck at her "great illusion." She had thought herself marked

for the ascendancy of middle America (as Henry James had noticed when, in *The American* of 1877, he reported Newman's cable "To New York, to Saint Louis and to San Francisco, those are the principal cities, you know"). The census returns of 1880 showed that she was behind Chicago. She couldn't believe it. The star mathematician of Washington University was engaged to "check the names and arithmetic of the census tabulations and to give the official census-taker the lie" —

> Faith in the approaching triumph of the Great Continental Capital had for so long been axiomatic in every mouth and on every street corner that it took some time for the bare, cold fact of Chicago's supremacy to dispel the illusion.

There followed no physical wilting, in fact a further rush of building, but a loss of some of the imaginative impetus, a loss of some of the sweetness with the illusion.

From a Chicago train on a Sunday night in November 1892, Theodore Dreiser stepped, a man dyed in drabness and passionately bitter at drabness and in love with the least touch of life. A smoky Monday morning presented "little low houses . . . the darksome character of the stores . . . Never in my life had I seen such old buildings, all brick and crowded together . . . Their interiors seemed so dark, so redolent of old-time life. The streets also appeared old-fashioned with their cobblestones, their twists and turns and the very little space that lay between the curbs. I felt as though the people must be different from those in Chicago, less dynamic, less aggressive." A store assistant revived his courage: "We have some of the biggest newspaper stories here you ever saw. You remember the Preller Trunk Mystery, don't you, and that big Missouri-Pacific train robbery last year." He found a job with the *St. Louis Globe Democrat.* For some time he was assigned to the North Seventh Street police station and its neighborhood, "a

mixed ghetto, slum and negro life." But further west he saw
another St. Louis:

> Out in the west end, where progress seemed the most vital, were
> new streets and truly magnificent residence "places," parked and
> guarded areas these, in which were ranged many residences of
> the ultra-rich. The first time I saw one of these *places* I was
> staggered by its exclusive air and the beauty and even grandeur
> of some of the great houses in it — newly manufactured exclu-
> siveness. Here were great gray or white or brownstone affairs,
> bright, almost gaudy, with great verandas, astonishing door-
> ways, flights of stone steps, heavily and richly draped windows,
> immense carriage-houses, parked and flowered lawns.

"Solid commercial figures" filled these mansions and the clubs
and hotels.

The pages of *A Book about Myself* which describe Dreiser's
year in the city catch the moment of transition from the old to
the new. The earlier city, with its vestiges of southern life and
of *France outre-mer*, was little by little dismantled. The downtown business firms ordered skyscrapers to match Chicago.
The riverboats which T. S. Eliot's father had named to himself
as he darted along the levee in 1866, and which Reavis had
counted greedily in 1870, were fewer as the freight traffic fell
to the railways. The bridge which Whitman loved as unsur-
passable was surpassed by a new bridge, thrown in the early
nineties.

Less than a decade after Dreiser had taken his short, searching look and gone away east, St. Louis was under indictment.
Legalized pillage was destroying the municipal undertakings.
Public utilities were bought and sold. The city's money was
loaned at interest, and the interest converted to private bank
accounts. Supplies for public institutions, the poorhouse included, went to private tables. The system was managed by an
Irish city "boss," Edward Butler, who protected and prolonged

it year after year by rigging the elections. His men went from booth to booth scratching ballots and "repeating" their votes to poll in his nominees. In 1900, however, he nominated Joseph Wingate Folk as circuit attorney, the officer responsible for the enforcement of law. Folk turned out to be a Becket. He took his position seriously and probed for evidence against Butler. Just when he began to dent the steel silence of the profiteers, an eastern journalist arrived hot for stories of corruption. The attorney and Lincoln Steffens met in the old Planters Hotel. Folk told Steffens everything, and in *McClure's Magazine,* October 1902, Steffens published his exposure of St. Louis, an article which in 1904 became the opening chapter of his book, *The Shame of the Cities.*

Folk pressed his indictment of Butler and the ring. He fought opposition, the lobbying of men whose rectitude he had supposed above it, all the maneuvers Butler's lawyers could devise. As he met with a measure of success, and as he offered himself for Governor of Missouri in the contest of 1904 and was elected, we may calculate in retrospect that the forces making for a clean St. Louis were, once energized by a leader, as strong as the forces intent on corruption. The Eliots were apparently involved in the resistance to Butler; at least, Henry Ware Eliot Sr.'s scrapbook contains a newspaper clipping, an announcement in which he and other gentlemen offer a reward for any information proving malpractice at the elections to be held on April 2, 1901.

But the exposures of 1902 and the following years had an effect on American opinion not to be underestimated. When Henry James drew an American businessman in 1877, he represented the virtues of an enterpriser raw but daring and pure-hearted. In 1896 those virtues appealed to an English visitor, Kipling. In *Captains Courageous* Kipling praised the hardness of American living: praised not only the dogged, narrow existence and skills of the New England fisherman, but the buccaneer ferocity of the rich speculator in San Diego. His "captains" are dual: one is the Gloucester skipper; the other is the railway builder, who has ruthlessly fought the rival magnates and is locked in a kill-or-crash struggle with the pack of them. The conservative Kipling exults in both. Throughout the second half of the nineteenth century the image of the American fighter for riches — after all, James Eads was one — shone splendidly and threw a light on wealth very different from that traditional in England's literature. For Shakespeare's Romeo, money had been the most baneful poison. For Milton, too. A definitive couplet had been written by Goldsmith:

> Ill fares the land, to hastening ills a prey,
> Where wealth accumulates, and men decay.

Wordsworth had renewed the doctrine for nineteenth-century England. Tennyson had taken it up in "Maud." But for the westward-faring American, courage was the first of the purities, and it might bring other purities into play later, and through them the wealth it had earned might do good. And so attractive was this image, springing out of the needs and opportunities of a young nation on a vast continent, that it did not perish even when the scandals of the cities called it into question. It can still be found — to quote one among probably numberless examples — in the passage celebrating Harriman, the railway builder, in Robert Herrick's *His Great Adventure*, 1913. It can be found in many Hollywood films of the last thirty years. But a sudden doubt and a corrosive dankness were thrown over it by the Folk-Steffens outburst.

The changing attitude of conscientious men can be seen in the adult Eliots of 1904. Their predecessor and model, William Greenleaf Eliot, had tolerated the nineteenth-century western pursuit of wealth. Certainly he criticized the exclusive preoccupation with "Mammon" which he found in the St. Louis of the thirties and forties. Certainly he knew that moral decay

was a possible consequence of wealth; but he did not think it a
necessary one, and he was sure that wherever it threatened it
could be contained by doctrine and discipline, by preaching
and pastoral care. "To be a millionaire," he said in his inaugural address at Washington University, "is a proud attainment
if one has learned the art of spending money to do good." He
was one of those who in 1871 urged the building of a new
Merchants' Exchange in St. Louis, and when it was built he
led the prayers at its dedication. But his confidence was denied to his sons. When Edward Cranch Eliot laid the cornerstone of a high school bearing the name of James E. Yeatman
— Dr. Eliot's old friend and fellow director of the Western
Sanitary Commission, a man who had made money in railroads
to the west, but had so regularly given it away on "worthy objects" that he died, the first citizen of St. Louis, with nothing to
bequeath but his library and a few hundred dollars — the
danger of the overvaluation of money was one of his themes:

> A famous French writer, commenting on American institutions
> a half century ago, said that the chief danger of democracy
> arises out of commercialism and the desire for money. After
> nearly forty years of internal peace this truth has become al-
> most overwhelming in importance. A student of the times can-
> not fail to see the fall in standard of public morality, and the
> lowering of public ideals of greatness and success. Many, alas!
> how many, of those who hold public office, have sought it, not
> for its honor, nor for the opportunity it affords to effect public
> good, but as a business advantage which can be coined into
> money and power, which brings money . . .

That was in June 1903, the year following Steffens' first paper,
which can be heard reverberating in these remarks. The words
"money," "business," and "commercialism" now ring harsh.

It may be possible to discern behind the climax of Charlotte
Eliot's *Savonarola* the afterthoughts of those who grieved at

the condition of decay disclosed by the 1902 scandal: when the preacher is brought into the Hall of the Grand Council to hear his doom pronounced, the poetess recalls how that grand chamber had been built, with his encouragement, to celebrate the expulsion of the Medicis, the hour of Florentine emancipation. Savonarola had composed the very words fretted on its ceiling:

> My people if this council ye preserve,
> A Government for ever firm and sure
> Vouchsafed from God, it shall for aye endure,
> And liberty and peace it shall conserve . . .

He reviews that hope and the way it has turned against him now that he is the prisoner and victim of the Council:

> I little thought the City then would turn
> So soon against me and my teaching spurn,
> But rather freedom was the corner stone
> Of righteousness and faith, and all would own
> The Christ as Lord and King. Regenerate
> The Church would be, new heavens and earth create.
> Was this but a delusion and a snare . . . ?

It is as though Mrs. Eliot contrasts the Utopian hopes of her family and all the St. Louis Unionists at the moment when Lincoln announced Lee's surrender, with the doubts that invaded them after Folk and Steffens had spoken. But her Savonarola plucks consolation from his inscription:

> That ere I die I see it once again
> Renews my hope it ever may remain
> Whate'er betide,
> A pledge of what has been and what must be
> Again restored, if ever tyranny
> Its face beneath the masque of liberty
> Should strive to hide.

A nineteenth-century spirit, who could not allow her hopes to be thwarted, Mrs. Eliot's considered response to the shock of 1902 was perhaps a militant readiness to revive the cause of Utopia.

Percy MacKaye, an advocate of a new American drama, and one whom we shall meet again, visited St. Louis in the spring of 1914 to present a historical pageant in celebration of the city's 150th anniversary. In the "natural amphitheatre" of Forest Park the St. Louis audience — T. S. Eliot not present, but Sara Teasdale there, Vachel Lindsay beside her — spent a day watching ceremonies which lacked neither pretensions nor color. In the afternoon a pageant, devised by Thomas Wood Stevens, represented the aboriginal life of the Mississippi Valley; the first settlement; Trudeau, the first schoolmaster; the Indian attack of 1780; the Transfer; Lewis and Clark; Lafayette; the arrival of the Germans of 1848 ("the singing idealists"); the Civil War; the peace. At nightfall came MacKaye's *Saint Louis, a Civic Masque.*

Its form: an agon. The antagonists: Gold and Saint Louis. Primeval figures stalk the amphitheatre: a masked, murky, yellow Mississippi; Cahokia, the Mound-Builder; Wasapedan, the Eternal Watcher, who sees the Discoverers coming:

> Out of the loins of Rome,
> Sired by olden Apollo,
> Sprang they:
> Flaunting their lilies and lions,
> Speaking with mouths of fire,
> Bearing the Cross of the Crucified,
> They wander the world!

Now begins an attempt to convert the revelations of the recent past into myth. Gold challenges the Pioneers to wrestle. Saint Louis accepts the challenge. Gold downs his first opponent, but is thrown by the second, and again by the third. He re-

treats, with a warning that he will be back. Saint Louis is not
afraid:

SAINT LOUIS
Welcome the grappling, whenever we meet!
Hail, Gold!
GOLD
(raising his sceptre, threateningly)
Long hail — and defiance.

Soon Gold rides back with the War Demons, who shout "Nike!
Nike! Kai thanatos!" Against them Saint Louis rallies a squad-
ron of World Adventurers, "clad as knights," who shout "Victory and Life." War and Gold are driven off. Saint Louis says
"Not vengeance — peace!" and lifts an American banner over
the assembly. This might be the end; but comes poverty, a
masked woman in black, with her sad family, Vice and Plague,
Dumbness and Despair and Rebellion. She complains to Saint
Louis, accusing a black hooded figure. The accused is un-
covered: again it is Gold. He robs Saint Louis of a sword and
invades the city-shrine with his Earth Spirits. Against this
heavy assault the Saint appeals for help to the brother cities of
the Union: Chicago, New York, San Francisco, Denver, New
Orleans, Honolulu, Washington. They gather like a Shelleyan
cohort. "How shall we cope with Gold?" they ask Imagination.
Imagination consults a child, Love. Love knocks at the temple
door. Gold slowly emerges, raises his sword, wavers, lets it fall,
bows and cries "Master!" Imagination returns the sword to
Saint Louis and orders Gold and the Earth Spirits into servi-
tude. Love becomes warden of the temple. Poverty and her
children are transfigured, "new clad in forms of light and gra-
ciousness."

So MacKaye tried at once to gratify the city which had employed him and given him scope to attempt his dream of the
civic drama (in which, he theorized, a community sees it-

self and gains in self-knowledge), and to tell the truth about her history; tried to face the facts of the boodle era and yet to assert an unquenchable easy optimism. He tried, as better artists before him have done in better ways, at once to remind his patrons of reality and to flatter them. One does not like to laugh at his work, still less to be censorious about it. He had a boyish courage, a refusal to stop trying, which are endearing, and which make the man interesting even when his writing is not. He had his place in the notion-spinning and scenario-spinning which worked for a new American drama. But his attempt to assimilate the social problems of the cities was too rapid and too slight. In the poetry of the greater writers who were MacKaye's juniors, there were two features which may be interpreted as a profounder response to those problems.

The first was a mood of indignation, a passion for reform, which showed in the poetry of England and America alike in 1920. Is it reasonable to connect the new tone of 1920 with American affairs of half a generation earlier? Literary historians usually relate it to the 1914-1918 war, which seems sufficiently large cause. And since the new tone and the new approach showed on both sides of the Atlantic, since they showed in the postwar poems of E. E. Cummings and Richard Aldington, whom nothing connected but their experience of the same international eruption, the usual verdict must be true. But — But there was some difference between the anger of the American poets and the British poets. The British anger was especially directed at the hypocrisy or incompetence, and sometimes both, of those in authority; and, authority being conferred in Britain, especially at that time, by the fortunes of birth, it was directed at what we now like to call the "Establishment." The American anger was against the political money muddle: against the misuse of power for the sake of money, the lack of all values but money. It was an attack on commerce and on a commerce-dominated morality and culture. In this respect it was colored, I am inclined to believe, by the events of 1902-1904. If the older, secure generation had been disconcerted by the exposures of that epoch, how much greater the effect must have been on the minds of young people receiving their first impressions of politics and society: they must have inculcated a detestation of municipal politics and a belief that the bigger world of economics and politics was only a bigger version of the municipal jungle. When, fifteen years later, the war provoked them to a skeptical scrutiny of the social order, their memories of the earlier period revived — the reactions to local gossip, items in local newspapers, revived, and possibly their reactions to Steffens. A line at the end of the *Pisan Cantos* speaks of "Stef" as if he were a mentor or a fraternal figure. Pound was seventeen when the scandals of 1902 broke. His polemic of a lifetime might be regarded as an elaborate and labyrinthine extension of his quixotic reactions to *The Shame of the Cities*. In his poetry he has converted those obsessive reactions to triumph.

In Eliot the voice of indignation was first heard in "Burbank . . . Bleistein," where sharply turned phrases caricature the commercial culture of the Midwest and set it disadvantageously against the culture of Venice. Among the phrases is "Money in furs." St. Louis had developed out of the riches of the fur trade. "Burbank . . . Bleistein" was composed at, approximately, that Armistice date when Pound was resolving to dedicate himself to the analysis of the causes of war. I take it that the aura of social criticism which invests the poem owed something to the general mood of 1918-19, something to exchanges with Pound in which the elder poet anatomized society and brought a thousand illustrations, and the particular illustration of 1902, to bear. Eliot had his reading in the Christian socialism of Péguy and in the anti-plutocratic royalism of Maurras to correlate with Pound's arguments. Three years later, in *The Waste Land*, still peopling his poetry with commercial grotesques (Mr. Eugenides) and predicating against a misshapen culture, Eliot was beginning to discover his future attitude and to display the economic shame of the cities as, at the core, a religious problem.

The second feature of the new poetry was the observance of a principle of condensation. In a "London Letter" to the *Dial*, published in May 1922, six months after the drafting of *The Waste Land,* six months before its appearance in print, Eliot attacked recent British poets and certain American poets, including Sandburg, for complementary aberrations. Both surrendered to "what people want." The English Georgians felt obliged to talk about the "green and pleasant land" of England. The American poet did not feel obliged to say that America was pleasant, he was allowed to make it infernal, but he had to affirm

> that it is big, that it is new, that it contains the germs of a colossal growth

while beneath the affirmations lay "commonplace and conventionality." In *The Waste Land* Eliot disposed of both these dogmas. He devastated the green and pleasant land and its choirs. The boys who read *The Waste Land* at school during, the next four or five years began to write during the next six or seven

> And now I pass by a forbidding coast
> Where ironworks rust
> On each headland . . .

And how did he treat the "colossal," Whitmanite dogma? He wrote of the infernal "burning, burning" of the city, but in prayer for purgation. In place of commonplace and conventionality he offered erudition and sensibility. In place of energy he offered delicacy of image. And, with Pound's editorial help, he offered, in place of size, condensation.

The principle was already in force in Eliot's early poems, and in the strophes which Pound and Eliot worked at in the late war years. It was in force (though Eliot scarcely allowed as much in his *Dial* letter) in Frost, who had perhaps been helped towards it, at a decisive early moment, by contact with Pound, then had pursued his independent way to it. In the twenties the Fugitives would recognize it and adopt it. It encouraged the choice of traditional finite forms instead of Whitman's ever extending rhapsodic continuum; brevity instead of Whitman's amplitude; elegance and grace instead of assertive energy. It meant that speed is beauty. It deplored size as a symptom of the world's disorders.

The attack on size is a point of the Triumphal March in "Coriolan." The parade mocks the veneration of statistics and warns of the destructiveness of the world of metal:

> 5,800,000 rifles and carbines,
> 102,000 machine guns,
> 28,000 trench mortars,
> 53,000 field and heavy guns,
> I cannot tell how many projectiles, mines and fuses.

In his polemic Eliot has never stopped protesting against the standard of mere size. He attacked it in some of his comments and lectures on education in the *Criterion* years, and he still attacked it in the fifties in his Chicago lectures on *The Aims of Education.* Sometimes in his polemic he forgets that quality *may* — it is not impossible — coexist with size. But in his poems nothing but gain has accrued from his insistence on condensation and concentration: the music of "Coriolan"; the rich brevities of *The Waste Land;* the compression into *The Waste Land* of a system of references to Wagner, whose own colossal system was the highpoint of the nineteenth-century taste for size.

The aesthetics and the technical consequences might be viewed as a reaction against the ideals of the Civil War victors, a reaction in favour of that legend of the south which flourished in the southern defeat. Because the industrial boom and the gigantism of the cities grew out of the victory of the north, sensitive minds retreated from the triumph. When the growth of the cities seemed, after 1902, to be synonymous with corruption, the temptation was to go into exile: to look for the urbanity of the south in old Europe. Therefore that movement which took Pound, Aiken, Eliot, Gould Fletcher abroad. Twenty years later a new generation took another course: doggedly remained at home; worked, under the incentive of the brevities, the subtleties, and the formal achievements of Pound, Eliot, and Frost, for a new American art, which they have established. (And it may be added that the whole Union has since emulated the poets: in accordance with the rule of life by which the ideology of the defeated eventually conquers the conquerors, the Union is today possessed by the legendary southern perfection: by the code of courtesy, and by "gracious living" which has lit American life with elegances that neither the plantation palaces nor Venice nor Florence ever knew.)

One or two statements which Eliot made when he revisited America in 1932 and 1933 lend some support to the interpretation of the poetry of his age as an elegy on the aftermath of the Civil War. He had been brought back, after seventeen years' absence, by the invitation to deliver the Charles Eliot Norton lectures at Harvard. He opened his lectures in 1932 with the requisite tribute to Professor Norton, from whose *Life and Letters* he selected passages bearing on the post-bellum years 1869 and 1876. "I wonder," Norton asked in the 1869 letter, "whether we are not to have another period of decline, fall, and ruin and revival, like that of the first thirteen hundred years of our era.

It would not grieve me much to know that this were to be the
case. No man who knows what society at the present day
really is but must agree that it is not worth preserving on its
present basis." The next year, opening his Page-Barbour lectures at the University of Virginia, Eliot went much further.
He began with an affirmation of sympathy for the Fugitives,
the southern poets John Crowe Ransom, Davidson, Tate, and
their friends, and referred expressly to their agrarian doctrines
and their stand on the soil and folkways of Dixie. Then he told
a story of his journey from Montreal through New England,
and thence, some months later, to Charlottesville. In the "beautiful desolate country" of Vermont he had thought of the dis-
appearance of the sheep farms. Next day he had found himself
in the "sordor"— what a conspicuously non-American word he
chose to register his angry depression —"of the half-dead mill
towns of southern New Hampshire and Massachusetts." But
south of the Potomac, which he says he had never crossed before, he found some recollection of grace, order, and "a 'tradition,' such as the influx of foreign populations has almost ef-
faced in some parts of the North, and such as never established
itself in the West."

Two years later his mood still held. In the *Criterion* of January 1935 he published an article by Canon Bernard Iddings
Bell of Rhode Island, which spoke for the Great Tradition in
education, the devotion to impracticalities, and observed that
even where it should be safest, at Cambridge and Charlottesville, there tended to be "a half concealed note of apology" for
it — and offered a historical reason:

The Great Tradition, never strongly established, was quite
easily and quickly bowled over by that new spirit which took
possession of America when once the more crude North, as was
inevitable, had conquered, in battle and by economic pressure,
the more urbane South . . .

Eliot drew special attention to that article in his Commentary that month. He had not yet given up the thought that he had expressed at Charlottesville: "The Civil War was certainly the greatest disaster in American history; it is just as certainly a disaster from which the country has never recovered." And the war settled nothing. "I doubt whether wars ever settle anything," Eliot has remarked elsewhere. And fifteen years later, in *Notes towards the Definition of Culture*, he spoke of the Civil War as a revolution which produced an expansion in wealth and a plutocratic elite. (But he now added that it was too early to make a sociological judgment on the significance of the American development).

The Idealists of St. Louis

But have I written as if the evolution of St. Louis had left the city with nothing but blemishes to exhibit to a boy growing up in 1900? That would be wrong. For a generation a movement of amateurs had made post-bellum St. Louis famous across the continent as a forum of philosophy and the arts, and in 1900 the legacy of their endeavors still endured. By its virtue she favored adventurous minds.

In the third quarter of the nineteenth century New England and Germany had met in St. Louis and ignited in a minor cultural explosion. The "frontier" New Englanders, of a serious and eager cast of mind, were already in love with German systematics. While still at Harvard William Greenleaf Eliot had read Madame de Staël on German philosophy, had discovered that far from inducing "infidelity" the German thinkers gave him reasons and a framework for his faith, had gone on to read Fichte and felt as if he were in his natural habitat. "I feel drawn as by a strong cord to German," he had written to Clarke in 1833. "I am now reading Fichte's sun-clear account of his system. English books seem too much on the surface, while

principles are what my nature craves." During the next twenty
years he was followed to St. Louis by New Englanders of a similar craving. In particular William T. Harris arrived from
Connecticut to take charge of a school. He looked, with his
"round, fair face, a massive forehead, and a mouth of almost
feminine sweetness," too slight to handle the tough western
boys; who, however, when he directed them to the gym and
showed them how to lift the two eighty-pound dumbbells like
feathers, saw that he "was able to run the school without their
help." In ten years he was running all the schools of St. Louis.
He had met Emerson in New England, he had begun to read
Goethe and Kant under the persuasion of Theodore Parker's
writings, he had a curiosity to embark on Hegel, and now in St.
Louis he happened to meet a German immigrant, Henry Brokmeyer. In 1858 Harris and two friends sat down with Brokmeyer (and kept body and soul together for him) while he
read and explained Hegel. Soon there was a small group
studying together and exchanging speculations, and Brokmeyer
started on a literal translation of the *Larger Logic*. The "St.
Louis Movement in Philosophy"! A movement is a few people
in a room. But people who carry the thoughts of the encounters with them wherever they go, who write and publish what
they think, and who attract others to the same thoughts and to
new extensions of them.

The Germans who came to St. Louis from 1824 onward were
men of high principle. The firstcomers had been attracted by
the prospect of making their home in a new democracy where
they could attempt to live the principles of equality. They
were educated men: teachers, government officials, architects,
lawyers, ministers, engineers. The stream increased after the
suppression of the liberal movement in the mid-European capitals in 1848. The German intellectuals and reformers left the
Old World for the New, and flowed through the Alleghenies to
the cities of the frontier. Fifty thousand of them in St. Louis in

1860 helped, as we have noted, to swing St. Louis to the Northern cause. In the late sixties and seventies more came from middle Europe, men who resembled E. M. Forster's Schlegel —

> the countryman of Hegel and Kant . . . the idealist, inclined
> to be dreamy . . . Not that his life had been inactive. He had
> fought like blazes against Denmark, Austria, France. But he
> had fought without visualizing the results of victory. A hint of
> the truth broke on him after Sedan, when he saw the dyed
> moustaches of Napoleon going grey; another when he entered
> Paris, and saw the smashed windows of the Tuileries . . . he
> abstained from the fruits of victory

He went to England, others went to America. Matthew Arnold during his day or two in St. Louis learned nothing about the Missouri Germans but that they had brought beer gardens with them. He was too hurried. They had also transplanted a gleam of the best Germany: music and thought, rectitude and courage and courtesy. A New Englander who came to St. Louis in 1874, James Kendall Hosmer, author of a *Short History of German Literature,* was delighted to find them in the city: "a strong German element . . . practically efficient, intellectually vigorous, pervaded with artistic tastes and the best virtues of the stock, an element which leavened and uplifted."

Henry Brokmeyer, son of a Jewish businessman, had immigrated to U.S.A. from Minden in 1844 "to obtain a land of liberty and of thought and action, and freedom from compulsory militarism." He began earning his living as a bootblack in New York, then as a laborer in a foundry. He tramped south to Memphis, and as tanner, currier, and shoemaker all in one, made enough money, and more than enough, to pay for a university education. Believing that a man must justify his existence by developing his intelligence for posterity, he spent two years at Georgetown College, two years at Brown, in campus-shattering theological quarrels with their respective presidents. Doubts of civilization possessed him, and he went west into Missouri. In an abandoned cabin in Warren County he lived alone in the woods, dividing his time between study and shooting game for food. The works of Hegel reconciled him with civilization and he went into St. Louis to work as an iron-molder, and there met Harris and agreed to lead the amateur class which became the St. Louis Movement. He served in the Civil War, was given a regiment, and applied his natural gifts as an organizer to smartening it to a crack level; was thrown into prison on charges of disloyalty; was released; and almost immediately elected as a "War Democrat" to the state legislature of 1862-64. When he and Harris organized the St. Louis Philosophical Society in the first year of peace, he became its president. In 1870 he was elected to the state senate, was lieutenant governor in 1875. In the nineties, when the victory of Chicago over St. Louis had diminished his enthusiasm for politics, he spent his old age hunting and fishing to the farther West. Evidently he was still magnificent in age, for the Creek Indians, his biographer says, called him the Great White Father in admiration for his hunting prowess, and "offered him his choice of the fairest maidens of the tribe — an offer which his Hegelianism compelled him regretfully to decline."

A much younger St. Louis German, Gabriel Woerner, has left a portrait of Brokmeyer in a novel, *The Rebel's Daughter*. Brokmeyer is the fierce philosopher, Rauhenfels ("rugged crag"), whom those who have glanced at the notes to Chapter I have heard talking, in his violent, exclamatory, sardonic style, against the Higher Law doctrine. A face like a hawk on the lookout for prey; tall; wearing, in deliberate neglect of convention, low, loose-laced shoes, dribbling socks, a ribbon for a necktie under a "modern" attached collar, a light jacket of brown holland; his voice a deep bass. A figure of Johnsonian authority, interpreting the world through Hegel: "Yes, sir! The world *is* governed

— not by speculative philosophy, but by reason, which it is the office of speculative philosophy to discover."

The St. Louis amateurs used Hegel's dialectic as their instrument for interpreting every activity. The specialist in its application to literature was Denton J. Snider. This aspiring, lovable, and in the long-drawn-out end pitiable man graduated at Oberlin, served for a year in the Civil War, then in 1864 came, a Protestant by upbringing and pagan by conviction, to teach in St. Louis at the Catholic College of the Christian Brothers. With the St. Louis Philosophical Society he labored at Hegel, and set to work writing and lecturing on Homer, Dante, Shakespeare, Goethe, and almost any other subject in the arts though these for preference. He was fond of music, met Mary Krug; they both played the flute; they married; spoke German for pleasure in their home. After seven years his wife died; he survived another half century. He wandered for two years in Italy and Greece, and brought home drafts and ideas for his books of poems of the eighties and nineties. Woerner, who manipulates dates freely, as a novelist may, singles out *The Epigrammatic Voyage* as his characteristic work, ridiculed by half St. Louis for its "conundrums," prized by one or two sympathizers for its "mythological landscapes." He lectured endlessly, pleased by his own voice, his own words. He lived in the old "ghetto" of St. Louis, hung about seedy cafés. In 1916 at the age of seventy-five he married a woman of thirty-five, and separated from her, and went back to the ashcans. He had written fifty-two books, forty of them published at his expense, one or two by small local houses; and the only phrase that answered his vanity, the type vanity of the age, was engraved on his tombstone, "A Writer of Books."

The St. Louis Movement, which Snider outlived, belongs at its most fecund to the years of William T. Harris' stay in the city, 1857 to 1880. He was an activator. He had the wit to recognize potential and the force to provide opportunities for it. As superintendent of the city schools, for example, he provided Susan Blow, when he learned of her ambition to practice the methods of Froebel, with America's first kindergarten and a school for training kindergartners. His work for the city educational system, building on the foundations which W.G.E. had laid, made the St. Louis schools, staff, and curricula the best on the continent in his time. The excellence of that system favored, we may think, the success of St. Louis in producing remarkable men in the next generation. (It is true that Eliot's family did not send him to the public schools. He went first to a Mrs. Lockwood's school, then to Smith Academy. But the good private school is always trying, at least trying, to be better than the public schools; and the new schooling which Harris bequeathed to the city must have stimulated private education. Moreover, the nurture a boy draws from his town depends on the quality of the community as a whole; and the community as a whole benefits when children, coming home from efficient schools, keep their parents awake).

Harris was an activator outside his profession as well as in it. In his enthusiasm for the arts and philosophy, riding the St. Louis streetcars with his head in his pocket Shakespeare, holding conversations and concerts at his home, founding *The Journal of Speculative Philosophy*, he set St. Louis stirring. Harris and the Germans interacted on one another and the city became a playground of ideas.

Those twenty years in St. Louis were as lively in their respectable way as the current years of San Francisco. The St. Louis Movement was mainly critical and philosophical, the San Francisco Movement is creative and theosophical; but they share a mood, share a rapture. Like the Beats the St. Louis speculatists wrapped themselves in enthusiasms, indulged in verbal pirouettes for each other's wonder, loved the aspiring, and loved the abstruse because it seemed to aspire. J. K. Hosmer's son wrote long afterwards:

This life was running into extravagances. Half-educated men, society women and girls quite untrained, were running after quite unintelligible German metaphysics, sitting at the feet of the expounders, men of magnetic qualities, out from whom went a contagion of enthusiasm which caught in simple brains even though the lessons only befoggled and bewildered.

Hosmer put it to Chancellor Eliot that the Movement was admirable but would be better for the guidance of Washington University, and naturally Dr. Eliot agreed that academic order would sober and improve it; and extension courses were inaugurated to supply the public thirst for information. The university's teachers received ten dollars a lecture, donated by a generous citizen, to steal the audiences from the Swamis and train them in astronomy, geology, mathematics, history and civics, fine arts. But although Dr. Eliot thought it wise to conduct the Movement to the classroom, its charm and real value lay in its domesticity. In the parlors the men and women were coming and going and talking of Michelangelo.

We are free to call the St. Louis Movement woolly, pretentious, comic and melancholy. Undoubtedly the gatherings were long-haired, the fireside zeal was sometimes shot with snobbery. And the end of the movement looked like a withering: the men whom St. Louis had thought "giants" dead or scattered; Horace Hills Morgan dropping away into alcoholism; Denton Snider surviving in hatred of women and personal disrepair, clinging to the seediest sectors of the town, happiest if he could talk Greek in the Greek restaurants, but gradually closing down on many subjects because "I've discussed all that in my books." But think of the best days: the weekly musical evenings at Harris' house; Snider, black-curly-haired and laughing, playing the flute with Gabriel Woerner; Harris talking of the Norse Eddas with Norwegian visitors or of the Bhagavad-Gita with a minor Indian prince who called to ask his views. Think even of

Snider in his last days, at the age of seventy-two, his mind above the squalor, writing his *Music and the Fine Arts*. The ebullience of Harris, Brokmeyer, and Snider gave pleasure to a city for half a century. If it attracted many for the wrong, snobbish reasons, it transformed some of them, touched them with real life, bestowed permanent interests and experiences. The point is, that it produced a culture, a circumambience favorable to the growth of genius.

For movements of enthusiasm, which put a city to "digging" the arts, no matter how wildly motivated, intermittent or ill-tutored the digging may be, are capable of creating. Not always in their own day, or not greatly then, but greatly a generation later. The case of Harris' *Journal of Speculative Philosophy* shows in miniature what can happen. To a reader who comes fresh to the early issues of this periodical, having learned from some history book of their significance as the first of their kind in the English language, or having read of A. J. Balfour's compliment when he showed a visitor the spines of the *Journal* on his shelves and spoke of his debt to it, what a disappointment they can be. Harris crammed the pages with abstrusifications on Rembrandt, Raphael, Beethoven, Fichte, Leibniz, *Lycidas,* Schelling, Schopenhauer, and every-thing that uplifts. He made a gallery of names rather than dis-coveries. Many words, small argument. One sees why Charles Eliot Norton wrote in 1878 that "some caution" against ob-scurity "is plainly needed at St. Louis, whence we occasionally receive specimens of dark writing that would bewilder even an original Teuton." The *Journal* is less readable today then, say, its contemporary, *The Unitarian Review,* which treated similar subjects quietly and solidly. And yet the history books are not wrong. This cloud-cuckoo-land paper had a decisive influence. It published the first articles of young men who were to be the principal teachers of philosophy in America by 1900 or 1910, Howison, Peirce, Dewey, Royce, for whom it was at once a stimulus and a medium. The St. Louis Philosophical Society's woolly desire to perform condensed into *their* performance. And in literature, just as the San Francisco Movement will eventually produce great poets and critics, the enthusiastic St. Louis Movement produced a master among critics and a master poet: Paul Elmer More and T. S. Eliot.

In the *Criterion* of December 1927 Herbert Read, who scanned and brilliantly summarized American periodicals for review pages, reported a study of St. Louis which had appeared in the *American Mercury*. For once he was not brilliant. He picked out one or two comic details, such as the panoramic-view parking lot benevolently reserved by the city authorities for courting couples, and stated: "It has been the ambition of the considerable number of famous men born in this city — to leave it. And in such departures it has usually been a case of leaving without anything like loving." Offering that joke to his editor, he missed the substance of the article, which described the creative epoch of the St. Louis of the Movement years. He might have shown how the city had been propitious to a poet growing up there in the nineties. In 1953, when it was perhaps easier to form a judgment in the case, Eliot himself told a St. Louis audience: "I am very well satisfied with having been born in St. Louis: in fact, I think I was fortunate to have been born here, rather than in Boston, or New York, or London."

3. Undergraduate Courses at Harvard

ELIOT entered Harvard in 1906, took his bachelor's degree in 1909, his master's in 1910; spent a year in Paris; and studied for three more years at Harvard from 1911 to 1914.

It was Harvard's "golden era." At the beginning of this century William James was lecturing; Santayana; Royce; Babbitt; Kittredge; and others who, if their names have sounded less persistently across the world, were almost equally royal. Great teachers, intellectual athletes with a zest for many branches of knowledge, were training their students to their own versatility.

For all the strength of his historical sense and of his desire to record obligations, Eliot has not written anything, as far as I know, to acknowledge the agglomerate quality of the Harvard of his time. He has condemned England and America in the first decade of this century as intellectual deserts, and America as the more barren of the two, "without the least prospect of even desert vegetables." But he has spoken, with respect and admiration, of individual teachers, above all Professor Babbitt. In the middle twenties when he was reviewing for the *Times Literary Supplement* he liked to select books by his former teachers: he wrote on *Founders of the Middle Ages* by Dr. E. K. Rand, under whom he had studied Latin, and on *The Renaissance of the Twelfth Century* by Dr. Haskins, whose course on medieval history he had attended; and he took the opportunity to pay a tribute to both these scholars.

I like to believe that his debt to Harvard was considerable: that the university supplied a reservoir of ideas on which he has drawn for fifty years. At the very least, it may be said that when, pursuing literary journalism under conditions of harassment and against the clock, he found himself in need of a point, he often fell back on memories of his Harvard classes. He would write, and write with a pleasure that glowed through the consciously frigid maturity (which was perhaps yet not quite mature), of Rostand, whom he had read with Dr. Wright, or Apuleius, whom he had read with Dr. Moore, or he would turn a flourish about the *Apologie de Raimond Sebond,* which he *may* have read for Dr. Schofield or while attending Abel Lefranc's lectures on the *Essais.* The material his teachers gave him, and the responses they elicited, were good enough for a powerful mind to elaborate years afterwards. More important, some of the issues under discussion by Harvard as a whole, teachers and students alike, drew his attention, and subsequently he would be aware of them and sometimes turn his effort in directions they had suggested. I am thinking especially of Harvard's passionate hope for a new drama. We shall come to that later. In this chapter I shall briefly describe several teachers whose courses Eliot followed and indicate one or two tendencies of their work which conceivably impressed a poet in the making.

Greek and Latin

Eliot has long defended the study of the classics in this civilization which is tempted to discard them. In the twenties he wrote that "neglect of Greek means for Europe a relapse into unconscious[ness]," suggesting that to abandon its study would be to consent to an ignorance of ourselves as dangerous as if an individual were to ignore the influences which formed him in childhood. In the thirties he defended it as a discipline, on the grounds that we are best educated not when we choose the subjects of study which appeal to us but when we follow those imposed by minds more experienced than ours.

At the Smith Academy in St. Louis he had started Latin at twelve, Greek a year later. He had received a gold medal for the best record in Latin, and his Latin recitation had been commended. But Greek had seemed "a much more exciting study," and

> I still think it a much greater language: a language which has never been surpassed as a vehicle for the fullest range and the finest shades of thought and feeling.

However, introduced in the same year to the *Iliad* and the *Aeneid*, he had found himself "at ease with Virgil" rather than with Homer. "The explanation I should now give," he said in 1951, "is simply that I instinctively preferred the *world* of Virgil to the *world* of Homer — because it was a more civilized world of dignity, reason and order."

He chose to continue Greek and Latin studies at Harvard. It was not a common choice, if the *Crimson* is to be trusted. The editor lamented in 1907 that most undergraduates were shunning the classical courses and missing many pleasures, historical and literary, for fear of verb drill. Eliot gravitated, as he often would in the future, to the unpopular and con-servative. Out of the eighteen courses which made up his undergraduate program, seven were classical. He took Greek literature in his first year; Greek literature, Greek prose com-position, the history of ancient art, and the history of ancient philosophy in his second; and two Latin literature courses, a general view of the poetry, and the Roman novel, in his third.

The prescribed texts for Greek literature in 1906-1907 were Plato's *Apology* and *Crito*, Lysias, Xenophon's *Memorabilia*, Euripides' *Medea* and *Iphigenia among the Taurians*, and selections from the elegiac, iambic, and lyric poets. In 1907-

1908 they were Aristophanes' *Acharnians* and *Birds,* Aeschylus' *Prometheus Bound,* Sophocles' *Oedipus Tyrannus,* and Books VI and VII of Thucydides. For Greek prose composition Eliot had C. N. Jackson, "a clear effective teacher of the fundamentals" according to one pupil, but according to another "a dry austere cold individual who never engendered any liking for the subject he was teaching." Robert H. Allen tells that, around 1914, Jackson "unbent outside of classes" to plan the staging of the *Acharnians* in Greek, but the effort "died after a few rehearsals."

For the history of ancient art Eliot had George Henry Chase. Through a quarter of a century Chase repeated his course, a survey of the remains of classical art from the Egyptians to the Romans, varying his matter very little: "You could set your watch when the Reliefs from Mantinea came on the screen. He used precisely the same slides for the same lecture year after year." He set out to give the student the facts of the field and did it, in crisp declarative sentences, with such success that a student with any sense of the visual would never afterwards be at a loss, if confronted with an unfamiliar item of classical art, to know where it must fit in the sequence. But it often struck Chase's pupils that, though he taught them the facts well, he taught nothing more: "he shared," says Professor John I. Sewall, "the peculiar blindness of the entire Fine Arts Department in failing to take any interest in the philosophical aspect of his subject. His aesthetics were shallow, conventional . . ."

George Herbert Palmer, the lecturer in the history of early philosophy, was more stimulating. Norman Foerster, who entered Harvard from Western Pennsylvania when Eliot entered from St. Louis, recalls him as

a fascinating lecturer, one of the best I've heard. He made philosophy and philosophers come alive. First came the phi-

losopher as man, then his reasons for departing from the previous philosopher, then the building up of a new edifice that
looked impregnable. Palmer spoke without notes, simply and
quietly, with perfect precision, in a human language free of
technical jargon . . .

He appears to have been gifted with gentleness and modesty.
At the age of thirty-six, already a teacher at Harvard, he read
Edward Caird's first book on Kant, wrote at once to Glasgow
and asked to become the pupil of the brawny Scot, and in fact
became his guest for six summers, marching the hills with him
(and the shaggy poodle known to Glasgow students as the *Ding
an sich*) every afternoon and reading aloud with him in the
evenings. Among many books Palmer has left a version of the
Odyssey which he regarded as "revolutionary"; a charming
record of himself; an even more charming record of his wife,
the President of Wellesley; a three-volume edition of George
Herbert, after whom he had been christened; but no book
which assembles the material of his lectures in ancient philosophy. But perhaps his themes can still be traced in *The History
of Greek Philosophy* by one of his assistants, B. A. G. Fuller.
In Fuller's pages there stand out vividly an interpretation of
Heracleitos as an aristocrat and fulminator against the common
mind, and an interpretation of the two schools of Elea and
Abdera each stimulated to the construction of a philosophical
system by the effort and the nostalgia of exile.

In Eliot's prose a passage that seems to look back to Palmer's
teaching, and to the reflections it prompted in later years, occurs in the early Dante essay when he discusses Parmenides
and Empedocles. And is there any debt to Palmer in his
poetry? May not one recurrent thought of his have stirred
first when he read the pre-Socratic philosophers with Palmer?
— the thought of the form that is within the flux and the
stillness that is within the form. It is a motif of *Four Quartets:*

> Only by the form, the pattern
> Can words or music reach
> The stillness . . .

In the moments of his life when he was most nearly "transported," the moments watching drama and ballet, the moments listening to poetry and music, the moments of sacred ceremony and devotion, his mind reached — so one dares, out of the transport of reading him, to guess — to grasp the hinter form and the hinter stillness.

The teacher of the Roman poetry course in the autumn of 1908 was E. K. Rand. In that *Crimson* apology for the classics, already quoted, the editor went out of his way to record the appeal of Rand's teaching of Horace; certainly the undergraduate journals of those years are rich in translations of Horace (one is in Irish brogue), and perhaps the profusion testifies to the pleasures of Rand's classroom. If we can judge from his books, which were written relatively late in his life, but which presumably made use of thoughts accumulated and tested in years of teaching, he talked of the poets, of Cicero, of the Church fathers, as we talk of friends, with a warm understanding, based partly on knowledge and partly on intuition, of their motives and their fears and why they missed what they missed and how they fulfilled what they fulfilled.

In afteryears Eliot appears to have looked back at the course with Rand, and possibly at more personal meetings with him in the Fox Club, with the greatest affection. The Widener Library catalogue lists a copy of *What is a Classic?* inscribed by Eliot in 1942 "for Ken Rand with diffidence." Other volumes were sent to the great old scholar in those years in which he was completing a lifetime's work: a copy of the pamphlet on the Churches of India; a copy of *Four Quartets* inscribed "To my teacher Ken Rand from his pupil T. S. Eliot." In the review of *Founders of the Middle Ages* for the *Times Literary Supple-*

ment (March 14, 1929) he described Dr. Rand as one of the foremost living authorities on Boethius and "a scholar of intelligence and wide sympathies." His one criticism of his master was that he refused to advance beyond gentle and beguiling books to a dragon-work. The review of *Founders* concludes ". . . in mentioning Dr. Rand as one of the finest classical scholars and humanists of our time we may be permitted to add that we expect from him something more substantial than this book or than his charming little introduction to Ovid, which was published a year or two ago." No weightier book came, and perhaps those who have the charm that illuminates are right to exercise it contentedly, leaving it to be transformed to the substantial by a reader or a pupil.

I imagine that Eliot must have been prepared for his doctrine of tradition and the creative assimilation of the past by lectures in which Rand showed how Virgil studied, assimilated, and transformed his poetic forerunners. In the lecture *What is a Classic?* — a lecture adroit at once in its nostalgia to delight, and its astringency to curb the complacency of, the classicists who heard it — there are signs of the recollection of Rand's teaching. It would be interesting to know whether Eliot already heard Rand speak at Harvard on the continuity of the Roman tradition into the Middle Ages, and so was prepared for his reception of the French neoclassical doctrines, or whether only later, when he had already accepted Maurras' position on the heritage of Rome, he met in *Founders of the Middle Ages* the delightful paragraphs in which Rand uncovers some of the routes by which the classics ramified into the Christian West.

When the Latin literature course was resumed in the second semester of the academic year 1908-1909, Eliot had the option between the reading of Tacitus with Professor Pease and of the "Roman Novel" with Professor Clifford H. Moore. He preferred Petronius and Apuleius.

Mr. T. S. Stensland writes about Moore:

His humility and sincerity and simplicity commanded the impression he made, and often led the casual and superficial to regard him as a "dilettante," which in the pure and literal sense, he profoundly was. I can recall his remarks, in the course of reading Catullus, to a classmate who suffered from some degree of pedantry: "Mr. Jones, what in the world are you scribbling?" "I am making notes, sir." "Well, put that damned pencil down and listen and think for a change!" Moore *lived* his classics.

In his class Eliot received the gift of Petronius, a lasting gift, as the epigraph to *The Waste Land* and the epigraph and allusions in *The Sacred Wood* show. Rivière says that the definition of a masterpiece is, that it stays in your mind forever. By that definition and in Eliot's experience "Trimalchio's Feast" was a masterpiece. And it pointed him towards a specific technique. Like certain figures in Ben Jonson and Dickens, Trimalchio demonstrated that a writer may lend his creations power by drawing them with a generous impossibility. If he makes them caricatures, gargoyles, Gascons, they will radiate "the kind of power . . . which comes from below the intellect" (so Eliot put it in *The Sacred Wood*). There was, remotely, a tradition of caricature behind Eliot: Christopher Cranch, a brother of William Greenleaf Eliot's wife, had been allured by the art and had claimed "humors" towards it. Reading Petronius with Moore, and reading him at the moment when he had discovered Laforgue and was perhaps already extending his discovery to Tailhade (who translated the *Satyricon* and is akin to Petronius no less than to Aristophanes), Eliot's sense of caricature was stimulated. Then in his first years in England he studied the art of the popular comedians and recognized the ferocity in their display. A sentence in Baudelaire reinforced his observation: "Pour trouver du comique féroce et très-féroce il faut passer la Manche et visiter les royaumes brumeux du spleen." Eliot quoted that in the *Dial* of June 1921. The names

in "Gerontion," the figure of Madame Sosostris and Mr. Eugenides in *The Waste Land,* are tinged with his sense of caricature. But they lack what Baudelaire called "le signe distinctif
de ce genre de comique": violence. In *Sweeney Agonistes*
Eliot realized the caricature of ferocity and violence and threw
the shadow of a below-the-intellect bestiality. In afteryears he
never elaborated the procedure, which means that, as he had
not done more than sketch with it up to and in the Agon, he
never fully exploited his interest. Other objectives mattered
more to him, and an artist, as he has pointed out, must sacrifice
some things to gain others. This comedy — and it is said that,
weekending with friends, he will read Dickens aloud, entering
the characters with his voice — this energetic, ferocious comedy is one of his sacrifices. Lawrence Durrell, looking back to
Rabelais, Smollett, Sterne, Dickens, and to Petronius (as the
Black Book declares), is the modern exponent of the genre.

Dante and the Middle Ages

"Prufrock," the earliest Eliot poem to reach the general public and to become famous, carries an epigraph from the *Inferno,* and already carried it when printed in *Poetry* in June
1915. Eliot's first published essay on Dante appeared in *The
Sacred Wood* in 1920. On September 27, 1929, Faber issued, in
the series The Poets on the Poets, a second essay on Dante
which is so massive that "essay" hardly seems an adequate
word. One result of this sequence, strengthened when *Ash-
Wednesday,* with its Italianate devices and its figure of the
Lady, seized the minds of readers, was to establish Eliot as the
foremost English advocate of Dante.

His interest in Dante can be related, the critics have pointed
out, to a Harvard tradition. Ticknor, Harvard's first Smith Professor, had introduced the study of the Romance languages in
1819; Longfellow had followed; then James Russell Lowell and

Charles Eliot Norton. All four had hastened to the European literatures with a voracious ardour — Pound and Eliot in *their* voracity only followed the well-established example. To read the line that James Russell Lowell wrote about Calderón, "My Arab soul in Spanish feathers," is to see how freshly the nineteenth-century scholars explored, and with what soaring feelings. They were inspired by "that sense of the past which," Eliot says, "is peculiarly American." At the center of their teaching was Dante. They encouraged their undergraduates, year by year, to go to Dante, and to go straight to him without preliminaries on grammar, to splash through him, half understanding, and wait till later to clear up problems; and the students who afterwards became teachers went on reading him with new classes of undergraduates, leading them through the same spirited immersion. Barrett Wendell has written about the process:

> In my Junior year a lecture of Professor Norton's excited in me a wish to read Dante under Mr. Lowell. I did not know a word of Italian, though; and I was firmly resolved to waste no more time on elementary grammar. [So he called on Lowell to apply for admission to the course, not hopeful of success in view of his deficiencies. At the end of the conversation he was invited to join and see what he could do.] Mr. Lowell never gave us less than a canto to read, and often gave us two or three. He never, from the beginning, bothered us with a particle of linguistic irrelevance. Here before us was a great poem — a lasting expression of what life had meant to a human being dead and gone these five centuries. Let us try, as best we might, to see what life had meant to this man; let us see what relation his experience, great and small, bore to ours; and, now and then, let us pause for a moment to notice how wonderfully beautiful his expression of this experience was . . . That was the spirit of Mr. Lowell's teaching. It opened to some of us a new world. In a month I could read Dante better than I ever learned to read

Greek, or Latin, or German . . . So in a single college year, we read through the Divine Comedy, and the Vita Nuova; and dipped into the Convito and the lesser writings of Dante. And more than one of us learned to love them always.

This essay is overmannered, but the picture is clear. And then in Wendell's *Letters* you can see the act of transmission. He has got Frederic Schenck (an acquaintance of Eliot's, incidentally) reading Dante and is encouraging him at the end of the first month; tells him to look at Arthur Marsh's article on Dante in *Johnson's Encyclopaedia;* goes on:

> The *Divine Comedy* is to me inexhaustible. I read it first in Lowell's classroom — J.R.L.'s, I mean, the most human instructor ever vouchsafed Harvard youth — in '76. What impressed me then, as well as the colossal system,
>
> > Vuolsi così colà, dove si puote
> > Ciò che si vuole,
>
> was the supreme finality of the style, and the immensely stimulating imaginative power of a thousand phrases and passages which linger still in my mind. Dante is the only poet whom I find myself constantly quoting.

In the Harvard way Eliot read Dante before he had any Italian grammar. He puzzled out the *Divine Comedy* with the help of a prose translation beside the text

> and when I thought I had grasped the meaning of the passage which especially delighted me, I committed it to memory; so that, for some years, I was able to recite a large part of one canto or another to myself, lying in bed or on a railway journey. Heaven knows what it would have sounded like, had I recited it aloud; but it was by this means that I steeped myself in Dante's poetry.

After forty years (he said in 1950) he still regarded Dante's poetry, which, like Shakespeare's, Homer's, and Virgil's, grew more communicative to him with the passage of time, as "the most persistent and deepest influence" upon his own.

In the essay of 1929 he brought his method of systematic assessment to bear on Dante with a power that makes the enthusiastic reminiscences of Wendell seem mere stammering. Yet essentially he was doing what Wendell and the other Harvard teachers did: transmitting his enthusiasm to a new generation. Elsewhere he has written that the main purpose of criticism is to rouse curiosity about a work, to send readers to it, and so to give them an opportunity to share it. The essay of 1929 was meant to send readers to Dante. But Eliot seems to have had a second, if cognate, enthusiasm to transmit in the same act: his love of the European community. "The culture of Dante was not of one European country but of Europe." The essay sketches a diagram of the European cultural system and shows Dante as its consummate representative at the moment when it was strongest. The interplay of two passions, for the poet and for the doctrine of Europe, gives the pamphlet its peculiar majesty.

For some years before he wrote the essay Eliot had been reading medieval literature and philosophy. His 1926 review of the second volume of the *History of Mediaeval Philosophy* by Professor Maurice de Wulf testifies, not least by its bibliographical references and its ardent remarks on Etienne Gilson, to his pleasure in the subject. So do the review pages and his own occasional reviews in the *Criterion* in the mid-twenties, and such occasional flashes as the comment on his old friend Bertrand Russell that his "intellect would have reached the first rank even in the thirteenth century." And he was not alone in his interest. Herbert Read, for example, who was frequently in his company at this date, was concurrently engaged with Aquinas and the medieval philosophers.

The ground for Eliot's labors with the writings of the Middle Ages had been well laid at Harvard. Partly by Rand, whose Latin, as we have seen, did not stop with pagan Rome. Partly by Charles Homer Haskins, to whom Rand dedicated *Founders of the Middle Ages:* "amico carissimo inter recentissimos medii aevi conditores principi." Eliot had elected Haskins' course in medieval history as a freshman in 1906-1907.

Like Rand, Haskins had begun as a classicist. His father, a schoolmaster at Allegheny College in the furthest rural corner of western Pennsylvania, had made him a skilled manipulator of Latin by the time he was fifteen. Before he was twenty he had gone through Baxter Adams' seminar in history at the John Hopkins University and taken a Ph.D.; and was a full professor of history at the University of Wisconsin by the age of twenty-two. He was a Dowden of history. I do not care for his writing. It is a little crabbed. None of the sweetness and urbanity of Rand, none of the urbanity, breadth, and system of Eliot, only a procession of facts. But the recollections of his students are against me. They say that he presented his subject colorfully in the classroom, and out of the classroom fired their enthusiasm for it, willy-nilly, by the prettiness of his daughter. A "glorious lecturer," who held a regular audience of several hundred students spellbound, Robert H. Allen recalls. And Eliot is against me. On August 11, 1927, he reviewed Haskins' *The Renaissance of the Twelfth Century* for the *Times Literary Supplement.* Professor Haskins, he said —

> has had long experience in lecturing to young undergraduates unacquainted with his subject. We have the right to expect from him both original and accurate scholarship and ability in popular exposition. In this volume we are not disappointed . . .

It is true that Eliot decided in conclusion that "for that general awakening of interest in the later Middle Ages of which there are signs today, this book is not quite what we want"; but he was judging there by another standard; and he had meanwhile praised Haskins' exposition of the anomaly and congruity of medieval Latin poetry ("the finest religious verse and the most brilliant blasphemous verse").

At Harvard in Eliot's day Haskins was assembling material towards his first two books on the Normans, in which he was to demonstrate, among other things, the relationship between Norman and English institutions. Work under him was good training for the dramatist of Becket: it trained him in the institutions and life of the period, as Rand's more humane training, on the verge of poetry, trained him to be the dramatist of the medieval saint and martyr. At least, it trained him to train himself by his labors of the twenties. Perhaps during this period he was fortified by the new books of his former teachers (is it significant, I wonder, that his review of *Founders of the Middle Ages* came six months before his big Dante essay?). But there is this to be added: the play which he eventually wrote about Becket is remarkable for what it deliberately does not use as well as for what it contains. Eliot abnegated the embroidery of period colors, abnegated romantic counters which he might have extracted from his sources, and of period politics abnegated all but the barest essentials. His portrait of Becket is firm because of his knowledge of the age and vital because of his passion for the age, but free from the distractions to which an equally considerable knowledge might have tempted another man.

Modern Languages

In his freshman year Eliot followed the elementary course in German, and continued in 1907-1908 with the second-year reading of German prose and poetry.

He had taken advanced French for admission. In 1907-1908

he elected French 2a, a course conducted in French by the gentle Dr. Wright and open only to men who had read 600 pages of the standard authors. The program included Corneille, Racine, Molière, Hugo, Sand, de Musset, Sainte-Beuve and Rostand.

English and Comparative Literature

Eliot followed the freshman course in English Literature given by Dean Briggs — the "seraph," as Conrad Aiken has called him — by whom at least one revelation was opened. In the opening paragraph of "Donne in our Time" Eliot writes:

> . . . Professor Briggs used to read, with great persuasiveness and charm, verses of Donne to the Freshmen at Harvard . . . I confess that I have now forgotten what Professor Briggs told us about the poet; but I know that whatever he said, his own words and his quotations were enough to attract to private reading at least one Freshman who had already absorbed some of the Elizabethan dramatists, but who had not yet approached the metaphysicals . . .

Out of that first experience there grew, not rapidly (for there is absolutely no trace of Donne in the early student poems nor amid the French voices of *Prufrock and other Observations*) but over a decade and more, the famous revolution in Eliot's experience, which he converted, characteristically, into a revolution in public taste.

A number of critics have pointed out that, though Eliot's criticism, following Grierson's authoritative edition of 1912, and followed in turn by the teaching of the Cambridge English School, did in fact revolutionize the appreciation of Donne, it did not evoke an unknown poet, nor restore a "lost" one. To indicate that Donne was a living possession of nineteenth-century

England, René Wellek has mentioned Coleridge, Saintsbury, and Gosse among his admirers; and when Ford Madox Ford wrote in 1916 about the reading which he and other young men had chosen in the eighties, he said, "Herrick moved us to ecstasy, and some of Donne." In nineteenth-century America Donne was alive at least to the same extent, and perhaps more, for the language and the literature of the English seventeenth century were revered by New Englanders as the fountain of their own. When William Greenleaf Eliot wrote a poem, when Charlotte Eliot wrote her religious lyrics, they used the accent and the forms of seventeenth-century religious poetry. But the knottier poems? and the love poems? In the second issue of Margaret Fuller's *Dial* in October 1840, Donne is named: "How can the age be a bad one which gives me Plato and Paul and Plutarch, Saint Augustine, Spinoza, Chapman, Beaumont and Fletcher, Donne and Sir Thomas Browne, besides its own riches?" Charles Eliot Norton was a collector of Donne; shortly after his death in the fall of 1908 his Library was exhibited by Harvard University as an act of homage, and the display was remarkable for its Donne items: manuscripts and early editions of the poetry and prose. In St. Louis William Marion Reedy was printing poems of Donne in the *Mirror* in 1904. Briggs read Donne to his classes because Donne was one of the possessions of Americans who cared for poetry. What Eliot did was to use Donne creatively and inspire the generation that followed him to continue and extend his usage. That was the "revolution." He did not *discover* Donne.

Other seventeenth-century figures were alive for American readers. Certain English writers of the 1930's, Beacheroft, Blackstone, Maycock and Smyth, were to direct Eliot to Huntingdonshire and so to the composition of "Little Gidding." One of them, contributing to the *Criterion*, turned a pretty metaphor about "the newly extended galleries of the academic Pantheon":

As we walk through the newly extended galleries of the academic Pantheon, pausing before the busts of Donne and Browne, of Crashaw and Lord Herbert of Cherbury, we shall look in vain for a pedestal bearing the name of Nicholas Ferrar.

But the exhibition had long been open in Cambridge, Massachusetts, and the pedestal of Ferrar was on view. One distinguished Harvard teacher of Eliot's youth, Barrett Wendell, had even mentioned the Ferrars in Cambridge, England, when he gave the Clark Lectures as Trinity's guest in 1902-1903. And we have noticed that in 1905 G. H. Palmer published the three-volume edition of George Herbert on which he had been quietly working for years.

In 1908-1909 Eliot became a member of the composition course, English 12, which Wendell had long ago developed and which was now in the hands of Charles T. Copeland, a teacher well remembered, whose character and methods have been portrayed by J. Donald Adams in a recent book. Mr. Adams' study, and in particular his pages describing Eliot's composition on Kipling and Copeland's treatment of it, make it unnecessary to say much here. It is doubtful whether Eliot expected his university to provide training in his art. He asked it rather to develop his writing by developing his mind on traditional, formal subjects and his linguistic sense on other languages, and to afford him time and books for the rest, which he would do himself. And today he doubts whether Copeland's course proved of any great help to him. But perhaps he salvaged some gains. It may have been valuable to fight for his individuality against a sharp critic. It was surely valuable, and congenial, to write the translations which Copeland, wise in this, required his pupils to submit together with their original essays. Even Copeland's histrionics may have been a little valuable — valuable even if Eliot shared the feelings of Norman

Foerster, who writes that Copeland impressed him "as a ham actor." Copeland repeatedly performed his favorite role of Copeland, and repeatedly gave public readings of Poe, Mark Twain, Kipling, Dickens. His recitals may have suggested to a hostile but perceptive Eliot that the art which is to reach an audience must live on the voice. But indeed there were other Harvard teachers to demonstrate, without even thinking that they were demonstrating it, that poetry lives on the voice. Babbit shouted poetry aloud on his energetic walks.

A group of courses of permanent value to Eliot, and perhaps of immediate importance to him, too, were those in Comparative Literature. During the year 1908-1909 Eliot followed Comparative Literature 6a, "The Literary History of England and its Relations to that of the Continent from the Beginning to Chaucer," and Comparative Literature 6b, "The Literary History of England and its Relations to that of the Continent from Chaucer to Elizabeth," both led by W. H. Schofield assisted by K. G. T. Webster, and "Tendencies of European Literature of the Renaissance," led by M. A. Potter.

Schofield has not been chronicled so amiably as other Harvard teachers of his generation, nor were the Harvardians of 1910 his unreserved admirers. His very virtue in the classroom, his smooth ease of presentation, was held against him, and so was the well-groomed appearance that matched it. The rumor ran that he wore a corset. But in his way he was a remarkable person. He had thoroughly qualified himself to teach Comparative Literature. Ontario-born, a precocious boy brought up by a gifted mother's efforts after his father's early death, he had quickly distinguished himself at Canadian colleges and at Harvard, then had spent three years in Europe. He had studied medieval literature under Gaston Paris at the Collège de France, and Old Norse at Christiana under Sophus Bugge. In Norway he had been something of a phenomenon and a social lion, and had mixed with the great Scandinavian writers of the nineties. So he knew western and northwestern Europe and loved Europe for the sake of his recollections as a visitor does who has been welcomed as an equal among scholars and writers. It is true that his *English Literature from the Norman Conquest to Chaucer,* published in 1906 and execrated by Raleigh, was not irresistibly attractive. A rather more elegant work was the volume of 1912, *Chivalry in English Literature.* This was based on the lectures which he gave as Harvard's annual visiting scholar at the Sorbonne, in the spring of 1911 when Eliot was in Paris. It praises the aristocratic tradition and its expositors, especially Malory, whom Eliot has often praised and whom (so he once said) he reads when he reads for pleasure.

Subsequently Schofield became President of the American Scandinavian Foundation, and as Chairman of its publishing program he was to encourage a series of translations from the Scandinavian classics, including the volume of Holberg comedies on which Wendell's protégé and Eliot's fellow litterateur, Frederic Schenck, collaborated with Oscar J. Campbell.

Whether by the virtues of the teacher or by his own sense of the subject, Eliot went back to Schofield for a second semester of Comparative Literature. It was the year when he was discovering himself creatively through Symons and Laforgue, and critically and as a commentator on society through Babbitt's *Literature and the American College.* Concurrently he was discovering his real interests. The three Comparative Literature courses may have seemed to him rich in material close to his affections and in methods which he could elaborate for his own purposes. And it is conceivable that the story of the spread of the literary themes and forms through Europe attracted him as a paradigm of the movement of impulses in his own mind, or at least that it gave him a sense of the interconnection of the units of the European comity and, together with Haskins' teaching and Rand's, prepared him for the doctrine of the unity of European culture.

Of Singular Charm

There was a man at Harvard who made friends on both sides of the Atlantic by what Lionel Johnson called his "singular charm." It was George Santayana. He had been born in Madrid in 1863. When he was nine years old his mother left his artist-father in Avila and moved to Boston. Santayana was educated at the Boston Latin School. Entering Harvard he chose the least expensive lodgings that the Yard or Cambridge could offer: no bedroom, no water, no heating: forty-four dollars a year. He read philosophy under Bowen, Palmer, William James and Royce; won a scholarship for study in Germany and travel elsewhere in Europe; returned to Harvard and wrote a "dull thesis" and was told that he "was the most normal doctor of philosophy that they had ever created." Forced by the academic habits of the day (scarcely any different in 1960) to pretend a speciality, he announced that aesthetics was his field and wrote his first book, *The Sense of Beauty*. Even when he had done so, and even when he had been made Assistant Professor and then Professor, he felt — whether rightly or wrongly — that the authorities looked on him askance:

> My relations with President Eliot and with other influential persons had always been strained. I had disregarded or defied public opinion by not becoming a specialist, but writing pessimistic, old-fashioned verses, continuing to range superficially over literature and philosophy, being indiscernibly a Catholic or an atheist, attacking Robert Browning, prophet of the half-educated and half-believing, avoiding administrative duties, neglecting the intelligentsia, frequenting the society of undergraduates and fashionable ladies, spending my holidays abroad . . .

But if he indeed forfeited the goodwill of the administrators, he gained the esteem of the students. The *Monthly* wrote in 1912 that he "has attained in Harvard a following which in enthusiasm and intensity, if not in numbers, is almost impossible to parallel": the students were conscious of "greatness in his presence," of "completeness and grandeur."

After taking Palmer's course in ancient philosophy, Eliot followed Santayana's "History of Modern Philosophy" which was the natural sequel and complement. In his first graduate year, beginning in September 1909, he elected Santayana's more advanced course, "Ideals of Society, Religion, Art and Science in their Historical Development."

Santayana had the gift for explaining every philosopher with lucidity; not quite with that ease of Bertrand Russell's, in which the most difficult systems are restated plainly in a familiar vocabulary; but a more sympathetic lucidity in which the personal rhythm of the thought is kept. He was "critically sceptical" and regarded systems of philosophy as inventions for evading the absurdity of the world, an absurdity which he accepted "compulsorily and satirically"; yet each of them he could present with sweetness and trace their congruency with love. Philosophers completely different in orientation and degree of insight he could present to their best advantage. He detested Herbert Spencer, yet he would present him with justice. He had been most influenced by Spinoza, and of him he spoke and wrote with the most glowing feeling. Possibly some of T. S. Eliot's very appreciative references to Spinoza look back to Santayana's teaching or to reading done under his inspiration. In his writing Santayana was never banal and yet never dark. At his best he was clear, fearless, benign, almost godlike. The testimony of the *Monthly* suggests that his talk in the classroom equaled his writing. (However, a young poet possessed of the glimpse of an entirely original and different concept of style may not have concurred in the prevailing view.)

Santayana was committed to beauty. His religion of beauty had grown out of the Spanish Catholicism into which he was born. He early rejected the dogmas of his Church, but never its rituals; for beauty's sake he cherished "the Christian epic and all those doctrines and observances which bring it down into daily life."

On inheriting a legacy in 1912 Santayana left Harvard. The university hoped that his absence would not be long. But it was permanent. He undid his mother's immigration to America, recrossed the Atlantic, and lived, as he had always desired, a wandering scholar in Europe. The lectures published in 1920 as *Character and Opinion in the United States,* while they are full of affection, tell of a dourness in American life, a lack of completed beauty. In a contribution to the *Dial* of June 1922 he examined a new book on American civilization and drew the conclusion that America slays her poets. "The chronic state of our literature," he quoted "is that of a youthful promise which is never redeemed," and he commented:

> The fate of the Harvard poets in my time — Sanborn, Mc-Culloch, Stickney, Lodge, Savage, Moody — was a tragic instance of this. If death had not cut them all off prematurely, would they have fulfilled their promise: I think that Moody, who actually accomplished most, would have succeeded notably . . . but even so, it might have been at the expense of his early poetic colour and disinterested passion for beauty . . .

And even William James, Santayana went on, even William James, who had responded to America's intellectual stimulus and had cut into rough, new ground, "even he would have found it uphill work to cultivate beauty of form, to maintain ultimate insights, or to live in familiar friendship with the Greeks and Indians." For once Santayana's pure clarity became absurdity in that neat, fallacious phrase (at that very hour Marianne Moore was showing that a poet could live with the Greeks and Indians, that is, with a perfectionist technique and with her country's history). But he may have confirmed

the fears of some of his expatriate readers who doubted whether
their abilities could prosper at home.

President Charles William Eliot (1834-1926)

When Eliot entered Harvard, its president, C. W. Eliot, a
third cousin once removed of his grandfather, was approaching
the end of his term of office. It had been a long and remarkable
term. From the day he assumed his appointment in 1869 he
had set out to remake the university. He decided to equip his
students not so much with a general and theoretical training as
with a practical training for the professions and government,
and began his reforms in the professional departments. The
Medical School was turning out textbook-examination doctors
who were killers. He invaded it, broke the embittered opposition of the old stagers, and revolutionized it. The Law School
had no standing. He reformed it by appointing Dean Langdell
and supporting his introduction of the "case system," and enjoyed the fruits of the step when Langdell's first graduates
went into practice and soon applications to join the School
flowed in from all over the continent. The Eliots have been
brave in defense of ideas, and President Eliot's imposition of his
policy was in its way beautiful. To his forcible conduct as
planner of programs and employer of men was largely due the
golden quality of the Faculty in 1900.

Besides endowing the university with quality he endowed it
with size. It is debatable whether this was his intention. In
two articles which he contributed to the *Atlantic Monthly* on the
eve of his appointment he had spoken against the emphasis on
mere size. In 1894, reflecting on what he had achieved in
twenty-five years, he made a distinction between his educational ideals and the building he had been bound to do in the
realization of them. But he shrewdly saw that posterity would
be inclined to ignore the distinction:

I have privately supposed myself to have been pursuing certain educational ideals; but so many excellent persons have described the fruits of the past twenty-five years as lands, buildings, collections, money and thousands of students, that I have sometimes feared that to the next generation I should appear as nothing but a successful Philistine.

To a small group of living critics he appeared so too. John Jay Chapman rent him tooth and claw. In October 1909 Chapman wrote a typical article for *Science* arraigning the Harvard Corporation and the recently retired President on the charge of commercialism: Harvard had become simply an agency to advertise itself, raise money, place its men in employment; it cared for nothing but publicity and business, witness the ex-president's Five-Foot Shelf of Classics, and for gigantics, witness the Stadium performance of *Joan of Arc* by 1300 players. Chapman summoned the University back to its studies, and urged, to that end and the recovery of its influence, the ejection of businessmen from its Corporation and the substitution of scholars. He did not win a very sympathetic hearing. The president had only been going the way majority America was going, and going it supremely; he was its supreme exponent. The *Crimson* editor defended him, indignantly repudiating Chapman's charges and his advice. But a handful of teachers, students, and observers sympathized with the attack.

Especially he went the way America was going by establishing the "elective system" at Harvard. It is the system that prevails in most American universities today. It relieves undergraduates of the necessity of pursuing, though not of the opportunity to pursue, the old disciplines; it puts a wide range of subjects at their disposal and invites them to choose for themselves which to follow. It is the reflection of the democratic doctrine that everyone, confronted with a choice, is capable of making the best choice, or that the aggregate of choices will be for the best, or that, if a mistake is made once, people will have enough sense to recognize it and choose right next time. President Eliot did not invent the system, but he had announced his liking for it in the *Atlantic* articles, and so exactly did it represent him, and he it, that many persons through the United States regarded him as its inventor.

Brought up in the atmosphere of Boston Unitarianism, the president was a perfectibilist. He believed that the world was striding towards the light. He called his time "the happiest age the world has ever known."

After vacating the presidency in 1909 the patriarch appeared before Harvard's Summer School of Theology to enunciate the seven propositions of the "Religion of the Future"; (1) "the religion of the future will not be based on authority, either spiritual or temporal," for "the tendency towards liberty is progressive, and among educated men is irresistible"; (2) "no personifications of the primitive forces of nature"; (3) "no worship, express or implied, of dead ancestors, teachers, or rulers"; (4) "the primary object will not be the personal welfare or safety of the individual in this world or the other . . . but . . . service to others, and . . . contributions to the common good"; (5) It "will not be propitiatory, sacrificial, or expiatory"; (6) It "will not perpetuate the Hebrew anthropomorphic representations of God"; (7) It "will not be gloomy, ascetic, or maledictory." T. S. Eliot was attending the Harvard Summer School that year, though taking Fine Arts, not Theology, when this new revelation burst on the public ear.

T. S. Eliot evidently sided with the president's critics. He differs from him on almost every public issue. He has attacked the concentration of university administrators on numbers and size: "American universities, ever since Charles William Eliot and his contemporary 'educators,' have tried to make themselves as big as possible in a mad competition for numbers." He has attacked the elective system. "No one can become really educated without having pursued some study in which he took no interest — for it is a part of education to *learn to interest ourselves* in subjects for which we have no aptitude." He meant, his old president's anathema notwithstanding, that the student should take Latin and Greek whether he liked them or not. Just as the president loved the elective system as the corollary of democracy, the poet deplores it as the corollary of democracy. His view is that "natural and unregenerate man," left free to choose, is unlikely to make the right choice. His conception of religion is the opposite of the president's "religion of the future," and depends on authority, tradition, on a Johnsonian sense of the terror of death, on a severe askesis. His preferences in literature are unlike the president's, who, when he edited the Five-Foot Shelf of Classics included the complete works of only two poets, Burns and Milton, honoring the latter because, as he said at the Milton Tercentenary exercises at Harvard on December 8, 1908, "he was the apostle of civil and religious liberty." Possibly T. S. Eliot's silence regarding the agglomerate quality of the Harvard of 1908 is that he still sees it, in retrospect, as predominantly tinged by the ingenuous, hard-working, tradition-defying hopefulness, the left-wing Unitarianism, of President Eliot. In 1926 when he reviewed Maurice de Wulf's book on medieval philosophy, he hinted that a change was taking place at Harvard and rejoiced in the new attention to scholasticism in "this former stronghold of Unitarianism."

Barrett Wendell (1855-1921)

C. W. Eliot represented a prevalent view of his time: that good and sane men are liberal-minded. T. S. Eliot has fought against the assumption, following the lead of two anti-presidential teachers: Babbitt and Wendell. Barrett Wendell once asked Professor Merriman: "In all the twenty-five years you

have known me, Roger, have you ever heard me utter one liberal sentiment?" Merriman: "Not one, sir." Wendell: "Thank
God!"

Born in Boston, Wendell had grown up subject to illness,
consequently lacking the American muscle, for which he compensated, in due course, with a lordly and ferocious temper.
While still an undergraduate he traveled widely in Europe
from Pall Mall to the Kremlin and made love to the Old World.
In New York he had been a fervent theatregoer, and never lost
the habit, except in the European cities, where the street scenes
were so intoxicating that he cried, "who can go to the theatre?"
In England the speech cadences intoxicated him and he picked
up an English accent, high-pitched, and wore it, with English
mannerisms and tailoring, for the rest of his life. In the Gil-
bertian sketch by T. S. Eliot's brother, Henry Ware Eliot Jr.:

> The atmosphere of London is so well suggested there,
> You'd think you were in "Rotten Row" instead of Harvard Square.
> How palpably inadequate my feeble talents are
> To tell what Harvard culture owes to this, its guiding star!
> Coherence, Mass, and Unity in Barrett are combined
> To edify the vulgar, and abash the unrefined.

He became a Harvard instructor in 1882 and was soon, by his
fire and bawdy, attracting a hundred and fifty men to his English Composition class. He taught English Literature, American Literature, for the introduction of which subject, now so
important, he pioneered, and World Literature, until failing
health compelled him to retire in 1917. In his twenties he had
worked eagerly at novels; subsequently he neglected his own
creative writing, but did the next best thing: encouraged young
writers. Robert Herrick was one of his protégés; later Frederic
Schenck, whose premature death caused him grief. And he undertook critical and historical writing, which postures but is
vivacious, and within the vivacity there is an elegiac note.

In his fifties, when T. S. Eliot knew him, he had settled down with satisfaction to playing the public role of reactionary, the "last of the Tories." There was an inner man who was no Tory; who had a hidden river of humanity, like Matthew Bramble's; who also saw facts clear and who, visiting Egypt, had recoiled with "Mohammedanism is a smack between the eyes for anybody who believes in conservation and authority." But in his own country he thought he perceived a value in playing the autocrat. At the least it forced people, especially students, with whom he was mainly concerned, to remeasure their values. Did his example encourage Eliot on the way to the conservatism and royalism he was to acquire from the French?

Wendell's fulminations against the assumptions of his time foreshadow in their arguments and the turns of their rhetoric some of the editorial Commentaries in Eliot's *Criterion*. Wendell writes in 1913:

> We are living in an age of less liberty and less; every extension of suffrage makes the individual less free. Such bonds diminish all sense of responsibility. It was evil that many were once slaves of few, if you will. It is worse evil that now we are bidden believe that all should be the slaves of majorities — whatever their whims . . .

There is a gleam of cheeriness in the acerbity because Wendell is enjoying himself; and it may be felt that Eliot's early Commentaries, by contrast, lack cheer and are tight-lipped. So in April 1924 when he expressed his hatred for modern politics with their "meanness of spirit, that egotism of motive, that incapacity for surrender or allegiance to something outside of oneself." But gradually the Commentaries learn to combine, now and again, pleasure and purpose. After he has sharply attacked a British General Election, that of 1929, as a "waste of time, money, energy, and illusion," Eliot thinks again and returns to the attack, not less incisively but more gaily, with "Second Thoughts on the Brainless Election":

> The Labour Party is a capitalist party in the sense that it is living on the reputation of the thinking done by the Fabians of a generation ago (we do not know whether any Fabian veterans are still thinking or not). The names of a few men of brains (though not necessarily of sense) still lend it a sunset glory. The Conservative Party has a great opportunity, in the fact that within the memory of no living man under sixty has it acknowledged any contact with intelligence . . .

and he encourages the Conservatives with the assurance that if their party has a muddled record, its long history can, the moment an agile mind works on it, be manipulated into a tradition. Nevertheless, he adds, it's a safe bet that they won't do any thinking.

In Eliot polemic always has far and away the precedence over exhibitionism, while in Wendell the exhibitionism preponderates. But under the performance Wendell, too, was serious. He saw around him in New England and in his university's president the engaging perfectibilist view of man. If the popular view were right, he wrote in 1893, then democracy would solve human problems. "But if human nature should after all prove damnable, democracy may turn out to be a less certain panacea than we have been accustomed to believe." He became the historian of the Unitarian theological revolution in New England, but only the better to discern virtues in the gloom of the old Calvinist convictions.

At the turn of the century, Wendell completed a chronicle of New England thought and its consequences for American Literature. It was published in 1900 by Scribners in New York and in 1901 by T. Fisher Unwin in London. Wendell called it *A Literary History of America,* but it was sometimes retitled in common parlance "A Literary History of Harvard College" —

a gibe which indicates its popularity. Eliot knew it, and ten years after he had left Harvard was recommending it to the readers of the *Athenaeum* as the best survey of the background from which Hawthorne sprang. Throughout its pages rings an avowal of "national inexperience." Wendell had invented the phrase in *Stelligeri;* and now he plied it, complaining that England had steadily developed her national experience, New England had not. "A great national inexperience," the sum of American history, stunted the literature and arts of the United States. One or two writers had overcome the defects of their environment by making them the very material of their writing. Hawthorne, "self-searching," "permeated with a sense of the mystery of life and sin," "typically Puritan," had done this. Yet even of Hawthorne it had to be conceded, as some of his critics had insisted, that his localization for almost fifty years "to isolated, aesthetically starved New England . . . may very likely have made literature the poorer."

Eliot accepted the general verdict on American inexperience and the particular application of it to Hawthorne. His *Athenaeum* review of April 25, 1919, incorporated the verdict in a paragraph on Hawthorne, Poe, and Whitman, which is at once an astringent criticism and a moving lament:

> . . . all pathetic creatures, they are none of them so great as they might have been. But the lack of intelligent literary society is not responsible for their shortcomings; it is much more certainly responsible for some of their merits. The *originality,* if not the full mental capability, of these men was brought out, forced out, by the starved environment. What the Americans, in point of fact, did suffer from was the defect of society in the larger sense . . . Their world was thin; it was not corrupt enough.

This must have sounded to the British reader like Eliot's own fresh thoughts on America from the expatriate's vantage point, but it was a repetition of Wendell's thesis, only strengthened by the appearance of a new conception, to be developed afterwards in the essay on Baudelaire, of the significance of "corruption."

Wendell added that the national inexperience was being rapidly supplanted by experience. He was right, and, as the change developed, the profuse American Renaissance of this century set in. But it was easy for his first readers to miss the addendum and hear only the bourdon of his verdict on the past. And an ardent student, rising from the *Literary History,* might well think that if the capabilities of a Hawthorne had remained undernourished and imperfectly fulfilled in the thin purity of the American emotional climate, he would avoid that starvation and give his powers the opportunity to grow in the Old World.

It is a curious fact that President Eliot had foreseen at the first perusal of *A Literary History of America* that it might disconnect a young man from his loyalties. He wrote to Dean Briggs on March 13, 1901:

> Wendell's new book is highly interesting and meritorious . . . [But] He implies that moral purity — national or individual — is the accompaniment, or the result, of an experience undesirably limited . . . If he be right, will not the courageous youth or nation say — give me the large, rich, various life; I prefer Voltaire to Dr. Holmes.

Wendell did not precisely drive his most courageous youth to Voltaire, that is to godlessness, but he drove him to Voltaire's Europe, to Pascal and Racine, to the old Church with its "experience" and its system in which the experience is harmonized as it is expiated.

4. The Young Writers of
Harvard — and the Shore

ELIOT was not a very conspicuous figure in his first three years at Harvard. He was no leader, no public focus, like the political Walter Lippmann. Reading the undergraduate journals of the time, one does not encounter his name often, except in the professedly literary *Advocate,* and even there he appeared a quiet, minor talent. William Chase Greene writes: "he was recognized as able and witty; not influential, at the time; rather aloof and silent; I used to tell him he reminded me of a smiling and quizzical figure of Buddha." The Eliot family motto is *Tace et fac.* Eliot worked assiduously, grew silently.

Harvard had all the usual complement of student poets in his time. The kind of work which occupied those who seemed to their friends and teachers to be destined for the main stream of literature, indeed to be already sailing there, may be gathered from the following sample of contributions printed in the *Harvard Monthly* in 1910: Edward Eyre Hunt adapted *Sir Orfeo,* William Chase Greene translated a Ronsard sonnet, Alan Seeger translated Canto XXVI of the *Inferno.* Greene, a distinguished classicist who, as a Rhodes Scholar at Merton, was the first American to win the Newdigate Prize, the subject that year, 1913, being *Richard I before Jerusalem,* recalls that Tennyson and Browning were his chief models in the Harvard period. A Tennysonian elegance, a fluency in oration and in rhapsody, and sometimes a consciously noble attitude, mark the work of the Harvard poets of this order. And it appears that Harvard in general regarded this order of poet as the most admirable; for when the class of Eliot's year proceeded, in accordance with the annual custom, to elect a Class Poet for its graduation ceremonies, the rival candidates were Edward Eyre Hunt and Alan Seeger. Hunt polled 335 votes, Seeger 123. Eliot was nominated for the position of Class Odist, whose task is to write a short, shapely, orthodox tribute to Fair Harvard. R. MacVeagh was the rival candidate. Eliot took 304 votes, MacVeagh 158. Whereupon, summoning the Unitarian hymnbook and his sense of propriety, Eliot produced the self-subduing, conformist piece that the occasion demanded.

Agreeable as were the verses which the "fluent" school produced, they justify Eliot's contention that English poetry in his day could not renew itself from the old stock, and throw into relief his perspicacity in transplanting the late French ironists.

Was there no one but Eliot experimenting in the mode which he found by emulating Laforgue? Had not other men observed the appeal of the "fourmillante Cité," of dingy streets, factories, and wharves, and tried to use it in their work? Was there not a "gaslight cult" among some young writers? William Chase Greene, in a generous answer to my inquiries, thought not: "I don't recall any 'gaslight' or Prufrock idiom among our contemporaries, except so far as Eliot was reaching in that direction." It is hazardous to suggest, against his testimony, that there was more than an occasional experiment in search of the style which Eliot developed. Perhaps it cannot be done. I will simply refer to three passages in the student journals of the day and leave readers to decide whether these may belong to one family.

The first, a piece of criticism in the *Harvard Monthly,* July 1909, defines a worthwhile poetic sensibility by pointing out its absence in Lafcadio Hearn and his consequent oversweetness:

Hearn could not see finer things in the sordid dirt and clamor of New York; he could not, like Whitman, transform the crowded Brooklyn ferries into vast realms of poetic possibility. He could not even see the beauty of northern winters. "I hate cold!!!" he exclaimed, and his physical fear prevented his knowing the delights of snow and gray sky and north wind.

Norman Foerster was the writer, and his analysis foreshadows the standard of "cold beauty" which Pound and Eliot learned from Yeats a little later. It recognizes, too, the potentiality of the modern cityscape for poetry while indicating that an American poet, Whitman, has already shown how the poetry of the city may be written.

The second document is a short drama by Hermann Hagedorn. Three years Eliot's senior, a hard-working, prolific poet, he was constantly going from subject to subject and method to method — without ever producing pages that compel a reader. Santayana, criticizing his *Troop of the Guard* in 1909, justly noted his skill in imitating the pomp of Milton and Shelley and justly complained that the result was merely "archaistic." But the volume included, together with the retrospective verses, a short play, *Five in the Morning* (it had been performed at Harvard when the Dramatic Club gave an evening of new one-act plays on May 18, 1909). That, said Santayana, "belongs, in its plot and characters, to a living art with a public function." Hagedorn called it "a tragedy of modern life in blank verse." The locale was New York's East Twelfth Street; the characters clerks in the downtown stores and a hack writer. Its dialogue was not poetically very active:

> What do you know of human drudgery?
> The same walk to the subway every day,
> The same gray streets, the biting shriek of the cars
> Wheeling about the curve at Union Square,
> The wan, tired faces and the same dun sights —

and the evolution of its plot was melodramatic; and its author dropped it from a later edition of *A Troop of the Guard.* Yet it *was* an experiment. It tried, as did the plays of the young Harvard dramatists who worked with Ibsen as their model, to see the harsh realities of the American metropolis of that age, and it tried, as they did not, to do it in poetry. The historian will see a connection, however faint, between that passage which is aware of the faces of the clerks in Union Square and the passage in *The Waste Land* which describes the faces of clerks streaming over London Bridge to offices in the City; he may even see a connection between Hagedorn's feeble attempt to dramatize the rooms of the poor and Eliot's crackling dramatization in "Sweeney Agonistes."

The third document is C. V. Wright's review of John Hall Wheelock's *The Human Fantasy*, a volume of poems which Houghton Mifflin published in 1912. Wheelock had preceded Eliot at Harvard by two years. While still an undergraduate, the reviewer says, he had written:

> Look — on the topmost branches of the world
> The blossoms of the myriad stars are thick,
> Over the huddled rows of stone and brick
> A few sad wisps of empty smoke are curled
> Like ghosts languid and sick.

— a stanza which displays in its third and fourth lines how the sensibility of the "Preludes" was at work in Harvard before the "Preludes" were written, and in its second and fifth lines how effete images and rhythms still prevailed, and how writers could not identify and separate the useful from the useless among their resources. Is the stanza *representative?* In *The Human Fantasy* there are few other examples of poetry touched with the sensibility of the city. But C. V. Wright had no doubt, when he wrote his review for the *Monthly*, that the book belonged to a school of realism (that is, he explained, of an intense curiosity about the commonplace):

All the singers of Manhattan praise the picturesqueness of streets and factories with a certain childlike wonder in the fact they have been the first to discern, that these things are really picturesque . . . It is conceivable that they have never read Villon, but there is still Browning and James Thompson in their own tongue. I find Union Square and the Statue of Liberty a little overworked in their verses . . . Messrs. Towne, Stringer and Wheelock explore the slums like voyagers bound for some exotic country.

It was assumed by an older generation that the country was lovely, the town stale; the assumption has now been reversed:

The moon is beautiful because it is rising over housetops, the setting sun because it silhouettes the black spires of old churches; a star is a pretty thing but a lamp-light is a work of art.

Wright remarked that the method could not properly be called "realistic": what it attempted was to symbolize the sadness of humanity. The best results were distinguished by the note of poignancy. But this distinction was insufficient for great art, as a comparison with Baudelaire would show: Baudelaire, whose cadences the poets of the school often borrowed, raised himself above a merely humanitarian sympathy for men: "To this great saint and cynic life justified itself in every detail." With that last remark Wright anticipated Eliot's subsequent writing on Baudelaire. More, he grasped as a theoretical point what Eliot in the "Preludes" and "Prufrock" (none of them yet published) had grasped in practice: that while compassion was a part of the gaslight sensibility —

I am moved by fancies that are curled
Around these images, and cling . . .

— it should not be allowed to dominate, lest it blur the power to

describe objects sharply; and that the poet should push past it
and work for a hard, cold power:

> Wipe your hand across your mouth and laugh;
> The worlds revolve like ancient women
> Gathering fuel in vacant lots.

Wright suggested that Henley was a forerunner of the school,
a suggestion that may be worth the investigations of a critic.
We may also think that John Davidson influenced it. Eliot has
recently recorded how much Davidson influenced *him*, alike
by his diction and by his subject matter (he endowed his thirty-
bob-a-week clerk with dignity and he "could look with a poet's
eye on the Isle of Dogs and Millwall Dock"). And Eliot was
far from being the only Harvard man reading Davidson; in the
student journals of his time there are several reviews of the
Scot's work and discussions of it. Another influence was Arthur
Symons, who had experienced the direct stimulus of those
French poets Eliot was to discover with his help, and who had
looked at London with the eyes of the French Impressionists.

During the last hundred years the painters have led the arts.
In the early seventies of the nineteenth century France had
felt the sensibility of the city and the need to express it, and had
developed a technique for it. Some British painters began to
acquire the same technique ten years later. Painters in America began to strive for it in 1900. Shortly before the appearance
of the passages just quoted, the dingy life of Baltimore, Philadelphia, Pittsburgh, New York, the washing on the roofs of tenements, had become the subject matter of the "Apostles of Ugliness." The exhibition at the Macbeth Gallery in New York in
1908 caused a minor furore, the Armory Exhibition in New
York in 1913 a major furore. A portion of the Armory Exhibition circulated through the public galleries of the eastern
cities, including Boston. Some of the Harvard men must have

been aware of the new cityscapes of the painters, whose adventures may have accelerated the experiments of the young writers — if it be thought, on the rather slight evidence of these documents, that such experiments were in train.

Supposing that there was a general reaching towards the kind of poem which Eliot was the first and the only man to succeed in writing in pre-1914 Harvard, all the more, rather than the less, praise is due to him. Where other men stumbled in a mist, he grew quickly to see his objective; and where they experimented feebly, he advanced firmly.

Before and After the Reading of Symons

The poems which Eliot contributed to the *Advocate* up to the end of January 1909 show little or no trace of interest in the "realists." In one respect, their care for elegance of diction, they might be said to be nearer to the work of the Harvard Tennysonians. But with a difference: Eliot willingly foregoes any largeness, any expansiveness, which might seem to claim public attention. Instead he aims at unity and coherence, and is content to write a poem of very small compass if within the small compass he can produce the result. He is content to do a modest thing well as the best way to learn to do a greater thing well. His power of self-containment and discipline is already strong. And already, the poems show, he has the desire to innovate, to perform the experiments which must follow the experiments of his forerunners: in his first *Advocate* poem the rhyme scheme shows it, in the second some delicate metrical effects.

The first poem is a song, "When we came home across the hill," published on May 24, 1907. K. G. T. Webster, an instructor assisting Professor Schofield in the Comparative Literature course, reviewed it in the *Crimson* of May 28: "Mr. Eliot's 'Song' is pretty and suggestive in its vague way. In general,

Advocate poets — as well as others — should consider that
sense hurts no poem."

Eliot had to wait almost a year and a half before the *Advocate* printed him again. "Before Morning" appeared on November 13, 1908. It is composed of two quatrains, each closing
with the line

Fresh flowers, withered flowers, flowers of dawn

in the metrical subtlety of which the poet evidently took pleasure — and indeed there is subtlety throughout the poem.
B. A. G. Fuller reviewed it in the *Crimson* and failed it: "one
is jolted, not impressed." Even with these juvenilia, from
which the nineteenth-century lyric has not yet been shed, Eliot
was, apparently, already "jolting" his readers; already the contemporary ear sensed, as we no longer can in a case like this
where the movement away from the old norm is slight, a disregard of the fluency which his predecessors had demonstrated
and a readiness to be angular in order to explore new possibilities. Fuller misapprehended, as more famous and professional
reviewers were to do with later work, innovation for infelicity,
not perceiving the gains.

"Circe's Palace" appeared twelve days later on November
25. The title suggests that Eliot was attracted by the Renaissance theme of man's reduction by seduction. The imagery
belongs to the furniture of a very different period: its blood-
stained, fanged petals, its panthers, python, and peacocks belong to the romantic agony in its last phase. But here too there
is at least a sketch towards one of Eliot's innovations. The
two seven-line stanzas move each from highly colored, "deca-
dent" statements to plain, terse statements. And, attempting
the feat of a statement that arrests by its plainness Eliot is
stimulated to the discovery of one of his permanent images:

> And they look at us with the eyes
> Of men whom we knew long ago.

The theme of *recognition* is to recur in the mature Eliot: in the City offices of *The Waste Land* ("There I saw one I knew") and in the great terza rima of "Little Gidding."

Two poems were published in the *Advocate* of January 26, 1909. An eight-line song has a first verse of splendid, full, Tennysonian images —

> A great white bird, a snowy owl,
> Slips from the alder tree —

but falters in its second verse. A sonnet describes a portrait: Eliot meditates on the lady it shows him, trying to plumb the mind behind the features and suspecting a lamia in those depths; but in the final couplet escapes from romantic agonizing by turning to a detail the painter has used to light her —

> The parrot on his bar, a silent spy,
> Regards her with a patient curious eye

— and brings in a new, piquant tone.

In December 1908, Eliot had made a transforming discovery, by picking up, in the Library of the Harvard Union, Arthur Symons' book on *The Symbolist Movement in Literature*. If he has sometimes spoken of the limitations of that work (he told H. W. H. Powel Jr. that its criticism was "execrable" and that it made its impact on him by its quotations), he has also cordially acknowledged his debt to it, most strikingly in the *Criterion* of January 1930 when he reviewed Peter Quennell's *Baudelaire and the Symbolists:*

Mr. Quennell has done for his generation what Arthur Symons did many years ago with his *Symbolist Movement in Literature*.

I am not disposed to disparage Mr. Symons's book; it was a very good book for its time; it did make the reader want to read the poets Mr. Symons wrote about. I myself owe Mr. Symons a great debt: but for having read his book, I should not, in the year 1908, have heard of Laforgue or Rimbaud; I should probably not have begun to read Verlaine; and but for reading Verlaine, I should not have heard of Corbière. So the Symons book is one of those which have affected the course of my life . . .

And through Eliot the book affected the course of English poetry. "The poets of whom Mr. Quennell treats," he was able to say in 1930, "are now as much in our bones as Shakespeare or Donne."

Many passages in Symons seem to have caught his attention. There is a rather remarkable page in which Symons attempted to imagine the birth of a poem in Mallarmé's consciousness: first, sensation; then, rhythm; then thought, concentrating with extreme care lest it break the tension; then, stealthily and diffidently intruding, words, each one of which "seems, the clearer it is, to throw back the original sensation farther and farther into the darkness." Whether simply because his own experience is similar, or because his perception of his own experience has been sharpened by the memory of this passage (retained at a profound level even when apparently "forgotten"), Eliot's account of the formation of his poems is comparable with this, and his reflections, in *Four Quartets*, on the poet's struggle with words may be tinged with it.

Above all, the book set him on the way to Laforgue. He has on several occasions described the decisive part Laforgue played in his development. In a talk given at the Italian Institute in London in 1950, he put it that Laforgue "was the first to teach me how to speak, to teach me the poetic possibilities of my own idiom of speech," and explained:

Such early influences, the influences which, so to speak, first introduce one to oneself, are, I think, due to an impression

which is in one aspect, the recognition of a temperament akin
to one's own, and in another aspect the discovery of a form of
expression which gives a clue to the discovery of one's own
form. These are not two things, but two aspects of the same
thing.

Symons' chapter on Laforgue, while short, was vivid. It included an account of the poet's character which may help us to
say what kind of "temperament" Eliot identified in Laforgue.
He was, according to Symons, the most reticent of reticent men,
of whom we know nothing "which his work is not better able to
tell us." He preserved his inviolability under a disguise; and
the disguise he chose was the vestiture, sober and correct, of a
clergyman, complete with umbrella; and the pose he wore was
politeness:

> He has invented a new manner of being René or Werther: an
> inflexible politeness towards man, woman, and destiny.

To a young man the acquisition of the dress and behavior of
his heroes is the first step towards acquiring their strength; and
Eliot has retained and elaborated something of Laforgue for
the mask he wears in public. But, as the sentences which he
spoke at the Italian Institute emphasize, he did not have to alter
himself for the purpose. There was an element of this Laforgue
already in him; it was easy to progress to the pose from the urbane dandyism, the perfection of dress, manners, and accom-
plishments, which was the Harvard style in his time and in
which he excelled.

On the incentive Symons provided, Eliot went, in December 1908, or New Year 1909, to Schoenhof's and ordered the
three volumes of Laforgue, which he thinks he may have been
the first man in the United States to possess. He plunged into
the French Symbolists as Harvard was accustomed to plunge
into Dante, delighting in them before he could accurately con-
strue. Next he worked to know them better by translation and

paraphrase. J. Donald Adams reports that he wrote a translation of Mallarmé for Copeland in March 1909. Only, I wonder
— simply taking into account that a student who has to perform classroom tasks week by week has limited time for his individual explorations — whether he was able to devote all the
effort he desired to Laforgue until the spring examinations were
over in May.

The first three poems to reflect his discovery, and to attempt a
new "form of expression," appeared in the *Advocate* eleven
and thirteen months after the reading of Symons. E. J. H.
Greene has said that Symons precipitated in Eliot a *crise de
conscience poétique,* basing his judgments on "Nocturne," "Humouresque," and "Spleen," their contents and methods. In
"Nocturne" Eliot imagines himself as dramatist or puppeteer
presenting the traditional encounter of Romeo and Juliet.
Since lovers always say the same things, or sing the same banal
tunes to cover the same silence, he kills his Juliet and so pre-
serves the puppets from the falsity of swearing "Love forever"
and awards them "The perfect climax all true lovers seek" — a
witticism which is the climax to the acid sonnet. "Humouresque," with the acknowledgment "(After J. Laforgue)" for
subtitle, illustrates Eliot's point that Laforgue taught him the
poetic possibilities of his own idiom of speech. Various locu-
tions are tried: the low-pitched "I rather like"; some tightly
packed phrases; the marionette's smart colloquialisms such as
"The snappiest fashion since last spring": each of which vari-
eties we may suppose to belong, more or less, to the Ivy college
speech of 1909-10. And both poems, and "Spleen" which followed, suggest that Eliot had noted Symons' observation on
the asentimentalism of Laforgue, in whose art "sentiment is
squeezed out of the world before one begins to play ball with
it." The *crise de conscience poétique* meant that diction and
rhythms redolent of Tennyson were no longer acceptable to
Eliot and that a poetic idiom must be made from his daily,

living idiom, and that the attitudes of the nineteenth-century
English poets were no longer acceptable, though poetry could
be made out of the very act of analyzing and exposing them.

No cityscape or gaslight, if we except the fleeting glance at
New York and gas, is to be found in those first three poems
"after Laforgue." Laforgue had in fact written irresistible evocations of the "gaz jaune et mourant des brumeux boulevards,"
and these Eliot was to emulate in the "Preludes," "Prufrock"
and "Rhapsody on a Windy Night." But Symons' chapter had
not commented on this aspect of Laforgue; it had only told
Eliot of the *drôle* pose, the piquancy, the drypoint.

Is it permissible, for the sake of charting Eliot's success in
the reform of English poetry and the lack of success in the efforts of his gifted contemporaries, to rough out a very over-
simplified version of the steps he took in 1909? As follows. He
had conceivably realized in 1907 and 1908 that a few of his
contemporaries were groping for a poetry of the city; he had
certainly — we have his word for it in E. J. H. Greene's book —
read Baudelaire in 1907-1908 and had met *his* compelling
images of the city. But even Baudelaire had not aroused him
to the intuition of a form and a voice in which he could
make poetry of his own knowledge of the city. As long as he
lacked them, he could not attempt it. Then Laforgue came to
him, revealing form, voice, stance. In the experiments which
were his first response he was chiefly concerned to practice
the voice and the dryness, working from the hints he had
been given by Symons, and indeed employing the material Symons had given him, for Symons had quoted "Encore un de
mes pierrots mort." When he had done that, he realized that
Laforgue had used certain metropolitan sensations beautifully,
and, feeling surer of his power and unafraid of beauty now
that he had made his initial essays in his new idiom, he incorporated the metropolitan vision into his poetry. An excellence of "Prufrock" is that it combines the elegant posturings of

the poet-in-disguise (and the self-criticism that accompanies it) with the evocations of fog and dinginess. He did what his contemporaries had been groping to do but could not.

For they had tried to communicate sensations without inventing a new form equal to the work. They had felt the potentialities of the city, and had thought that existing rhythms, existing stanza shapes, would quicken simply because the material was new. They had failed, just as one or two gifted pre-1914 poets in England had failed: Flecker, putting his observations of Camden Town into old stanzas, and on the Bosporus wishing in prose that he might be invigorated by the sight of a London gasometer, but never finding a form to say it in verse; Rupert Brooke, by great dexterity, almost transmuting fresh, domestic sensations into a piquant art, but retarded by his nineteenth-century equipment from doing all he might have done.

In effect, using his formal approach, and succeeding, Eliot demonstrated that a poet's business is not just reporting feeling, but extending feeling, and creating a shape to convey it: is, in other words, *creating*, and *creating verse*.

While he was practicing his new verse during 1909, Eliot published two articles in prose, which suggest, in the one case by excitement and speed, in the other by an adagio pace and a fine flavor, that all his powers were advancing simultaneously.

Prose

Eliot was appointed to the Board of Editors of the *Advocate* in January 1909. There was nothing precocious about the elevation. Rather more precocious among the editors were Conrad Aiken and William Chase Greene, who, a year younger than Eliot in academic standing, were already on the Board.

It was an *Advocate* custom to review the publications of literary figures who had made their first excursions in its own pages.

Such a publication appeared in the spring of 1909, and Eliot claimed it for review: *The Wine of the Puritans* by Van Wyck Brooks.

As a freshman Eliot had been aware of Van Wyck Brooks, then in his final year and already conspicuous. After graduation Brooks had gone to England and won early success as a writer; in 1908, for example, he was writing for the *Contemporary Review* to explain the life and ideals of *Harvard;* and the first of his long line of books, *The Wine of the Puritans,* was accepted by Sisley's in London and Mitchell Kennerley in New York.

It is a fascinating document to the student of expatriation. Its author strikes at the shortcomings of American life, but has a faith in their amendment; loves Europe, but recoils from the dangers of loving her. He says that no American artist has become effective without European training; that the ideals of American life, such as to "maintain the appearance of prosperity when we have not the reality" and to " 'get together' . . . because we aren't together, because each of us is a voice crying in the wilderness," make it hard for the artist to tolerate his country and to work as belonging to it; yet he also says that no American artist will be great till he absorbs American life. Attracted though he is by life in Europe, he condemns the expatriate life as the last and worst element in the American condition of distraction and divorce. After he has praised by several telling and pleasant anecdotes the excellence of French public life and private taste, arising from the partnership of intellect and tradition, he still advises the American artist not to overvalue tradition, rather to absorb his native life, for "in all its vulgarities and distractions and boastings there lie the elements of a giant art." It is a torn as well as a clever and brave book.

Eliot's review appeared on May 7. Drawing on an image which has appeared with force in his poetry, from the sensa-

tional opening of "Prufrock" to the mature lyric on "the
wounded surgeon" in "East Coker," Eliot qualified *The Wine*
as a surgical exposure of "the reasons for the failure of American life (at present)." "The more sensitive of us may find ourselves shivering under the operation." The book demanded the
attention, he said, of those "double-dealers with themselves,"
Americans divided in allegiance, their hearts in the Old World,
their bodies detained in the New by business or socialities or a
sense of duty — "the last reason implying a real sacrifice." For
such readers it would be a "definition of their discontent."

It is easy to understand that this book was significant to a man
who had recently found the French Symbolists and was assimilating their poetry of dinginess. Brooks confirmed that the
artist needed the seediness, the ugliness of his contemporary
life, not the veneers with which a would-be prosperous society
screens the seediness. The American artist in Europe, said
Brooks, frequented the "mean streets" with relief. That quick-
ened Eliot to look for the equivalents of Ashcan France in the
American scene, the broken spring in a factory yard, the
smells in passageways. It may have helped to put the first two
"Preludes" and "Prufrock" in motion.

A poem subsequently written by Eliot in England performs a
feat which Brooks predicted American art would one day accomplish (implying, by the very act of prediction, that it was
scarcely possible in 1909). Some American artist who rejected
the temptations of Europe and stayed at home would at last
raise the commonalities of the native scene to art; in particular
he would find richness in the names of his towns and use them
so as to distill it:

> I think a day will come when the names of Denver and Sioux
> City will have a traditional and antique dignity like Damascus
> and Perugia — and when it will not seem to us grotesque that
> they have.

Eliot quoted the prediction in his review in the *Advocate.* Some seven years later he composed "Mélange Adultère de Tout." There he declared himself, with energetic and pleasing geographical tic-tac, a wanderer, a dilettante in Brooks' special sense of the word; and, to give the clearest evidence of his cosmopolitanism, he said it in French. But he integrated, not Denver or Sioux City, but a Midwestern place-name of the same order, into his poem and partnered it with Damascus:

> J'erre toujours de-ci de-là
> A divers coups de tra là là
> De Damas jusqu'à Omaha.

Having made that desperate and delightful bid, he relaxed his claim and ended the poem dead on the coast of Mozambique. He has since written other answers to Brooks: the poems of place, poems of "spots of soil," which are the most superb of his century. The places he has celebrated are both English and American.

Warnings that excite you and recur in your memory are disregarded at peril. You may flout them if you are prepared to toil to overcome the peril all your life. Eliot's work is, from one point of view, determined by his lifelong struggle against the warnings and challenges of books. Among the books is this of an immediate Harvard predecessor which he happened to review at the age of twenty. A special warning lay in the passage in which Brooks penetratingly said that the expatriate will be "unduly concerned with perfection of technique, ignoring the ruder elements of life itself which come to him — more and more rarely — bluntly clamouring to be expressed." The young Eliot who read that already had a fastidious concern with technique. It has constantly grown. But I fancy that, nourishing it, he has often heard in the recesses of the mind some half-echo of Brooks' warning that it might come to ex-

clude a creative contact with life, and has strenuously labored
to keep his contact with living things.

In the *Advocate* is the second of the two pieces of prose
which bespeak a new Eliot. He has been in the Peabody Museum at Salem examining the portraits of the old merchant leaders, the "plebeian aristocracy," of New England, whose "sombre
faces, with an inflexible contraction of the lips" suggest na-
tures difficult and unyielding, formed by religious principle
and the interminable struggle against what he has always
thought of as the narrow resources of New England. He takes
pride in his descent from then, but is happy not to be their contemporary. Then he turns to old woodcuts of ships. Altering
the names with a poet's felicity he describes three of them:
"The '*Ajax*,' two hundred ton brig, entering Algiers under full
sail with a thundering salvo from the city; the ensign very
large, triumphantly shaking out its thirteen stars from the
end of a yard-arm. Or the '*Poor Richard*,' off the coast of
Africa repelling pirates; the native feluccas very small in contrast; or the '*Samuel Adams*,' passing a sea-serpent in the Bay
of Biscay." He thinks of Salem harbor at the height of its prosperity a hundred years earlier, its China fleet, the ships coming
home, the shawls, the ginger jars, the carved ivory their captains brought back. The images are vivid, the language is full
of flavor. Eliot has perceived the capabilities of English anew
in the light of his reading of French. He captures sensations
by describing the things he sees.

Dean Briggs, reviewing "Gentlemen and Seamen" in the
Crimson, complained of "imperfect workmanship" and a "tendency to moralize." Neither verdict says much for the Dean's
powers of criticism. Perhaps there *is* some tendency to moralize,
but the moral tone arises from the observations and the feeling
and convinces by virtue of them. A judgment which Eliot
made in later years is relevant: "The first condition of right
thought is right sensation — the first condition of under-

standing a foreign country is to smell it, as you smell India in
Kim." The Atlantic Coast sensations which are the source of
"Gentlemen and Seamen" were deeply ingrained in Eliot, and
have since been the source of some of his best poetry.

It may be timely to say something of his knowledge of the
New England coast, the more so as he probably found the leisure to read his three volumes of Laforgue, brood on them, and
experiment with them while spending his long vacation at Eastern Point in the summer of 1909.

Cape Ann

The Eliot family loved the coast that runs north and northeast from Boston. William Greenleaf Eliot, devoted to his
work in St. Louis and determined to stick to it, never forgot that he was born in New England and gave himself the
refreshment of the sea summer by summer. Usually he took
his family to Hampton Beach. Occasionally he crossed to
Europe and his greatest pleasure was watching the sea during
the voyage. "O my God, how wonderful are thy works," he
wrote during a crossing in 1847, "how beautiful thy garments
in which we see thee. None know thee who have not seen
thee here." In the last summer of his life he was sent to inland
New Hampshire, to benefit from the air of the mountains, but he
regretted it: "Oh, I so longed for the seashore." Charlotte Eliot
left St. Louis every year as soon as the heat struck and carried the children to the Massachusetts or Maine coast, most
often to Gloucester. In 1895 they were staying at the Hawthorne Inn. In 1897 they were at Eastern Point, the East
Gloucester house which Henry Ware Eliot had now built for
the family's summer home.

The house, raised on the crest of the moors, was large, as it
needed to be for the big family. Like the other Point resi-
dences, it had spacious porches around the ground floor, and

on the face of the upper floors many angles and casements (and on the roof a "widow's walk") to command the open Atlantic to the east, the shore of Massachusetts to the south, and Gloucester harbor to the west:

> From the wide window towards the granite shore
> The white sails still fly seaward, seaward flying
> Unbroken wings.

To accord with the style prevailing on the Cape, Henry Ware Eliot Sr. built in timber; only he brought in his best brick for the magnificent fireplaces and chimneys. In the garden there is a protrusion of weather-smoothed rock, which the present owners, Mr. and Mrs. John Cahill, call "The Whale's Jaw." Beyond the rock Henry Ware Eliot planted trees, and today they add to the green luxuriance that pairs in summer with the granite of Cape Ann. Bird songs fill the garden. Behind the house are the lank grasses of the moor. When T. S. Eliot revisited Eastern Point a year or two ago he told the Cahills that his memories of the house were among the happiest of his life.

Photographs of the nineties show Eliot on the beach near the Hawthorne Inn with his nurse and his Boston cousins, the two charming Hinkley girls, and at the house with his parents and sisters. One shows him, a boy of nine or ten, in a broad-brimmed hat, standing on "The Whale's Jaw" and planting a huge American flag on it, his face alight with gaiety and pride. Those of the next decade are yachting pictures. In 1909, wearing a soft white yachting cap, he is handling his brother's "little boat," the *Elsa*, and his father and mother are passengers. Five or six years earlier his mother had engaged a retired mariner to teach her sons sailing, and, a man who expects proficiency of himself, the young T. S. Eliot became proficient with boats. "He used to take me sailing in his catboat," recalled his *Advocate* friend, W. G. Tinckom-Fernandez, "and he could handle the sail with the best in Gloucester harbor." Summer by summer he lived the Gloucester holiday life, learned to know the waters around Cape Ann, the paths across the headland, the language of the boatmen and fishermen, the habits of the fishing community.

I fancy that it is in Eliot's nature to seek the work of any fellow artist who has shared his keenest experiences — as if his own experience, once compared with the other man's, becomes the brighter to him and more distinct; and that in early days, loving the harbor of Gloucester, he was attached to one or two books that reported its life. For example, *Captains Courageous.* In the years when Kipling was living in the high green of Vermont beside his American wife's family, the Anglo-Indian felt the sea pulling at him, set his friend Dr. Conland to digging up tales of the Atlantic fishermen, made trips to the coast and strolled the wharves and met the seamen. Into the writing of *Captains Courageous,* his gift to America, he put all he could grasp of the talk, the manner and outlook, the techniques of the Gloucester fishermen. And how much he grasped in a short time! With what an acute sense he described the hauling and bailing and the gutting of fish, and with what wonderful mimicry he gave the talk! Eliot evidently enjoyed it; and even more enjoyed the discovery that the mimicry was not quite perfect: he heard the people of Gloucester complain that it sometimes confounded their speech with the dialect of Cape Cod ninety miles further south! Eliot remembered their discrimination for years and mentions it, with the tone of pleasure, in a *Criterion* Commentary.

Eliot had also steeped himself in another annalist of Gloucestermen, and one who, he remarked "with all respect," knew them better than Kipling. James B. Connolly had published *Out of Gloucester* in 1902:

> The Gloucester seining fleet had been cruising off Georges Bank, when one of those New England north-easters came swooping down on them.

That opening sentence carries you straight into the story. The prose is cleared of adjective and adverb to do its work and nothing but its work, like the ships it describes — and like Kipling's prose, for Kipling used to go over his text paring and baring it. Now and again verses thread the story, and they are just as trim:

> She's the schooner Lucy Foster,
> She's a seiner out of Gloucester,
> She's an able, handsome lady,
>   She can go . . .
>
> She can sail to set you crazy,
> Not a timber in her's lazy,
> She's the handsome Lucy Foster
>   And she's go-o-ing home.

Later volumes were as good: *The Seiners* of 1904; and *The Crested Seas* of 1907 with its song:

> I know a girl in Calinore,
> Vessels sail right by her door;
> She has sweethearts by the score,
> Never a lock on her front door.

And the less tangy but lovely Gloucester berceuse:

> Home to his sweetheart your father is sweeping,
> Home through the gale his brave vessel is leaping, —
> Home through the foam of the turbulent ocean,
> Over the shoals, over the knolls, over the wild western ocean to thee.

But I must not quote more of these attractive verses, lest they assume more than their place in Connolly, the essential substance of whose writing is a prose fitted to the toil of the sea and the courage of its toilers.

Connolly was himself a captain courageous. With a hard upbringing, first a clerk, then an Army surveyor, he did not enter Harvard till 1895, when he was twenty-seven. The first modern Olympic games were announced for the spring of 1896. He wanted to compete, asked the university for leave of absence, and when it was refused walked out. He went to Athens, set the triple-jump record at the opening of the Games, and was the first Olympic champion of modern times.

He never returned to Harvard as a student, but one day in 1907, invested with his legend, he visited the Harvard Union as a guest to give an evening lecture. There he described, as he does in his books, the hardihood of the men in their fisher calling. Why do they stick to a dangerous existence for seventy-five dollars a month, he asked: they would rather have the zest of it than a fatter, duller life.

In 1928 Eliot persuaded Faber and Gwyer to publish an English edition of one of Connolly's books under the title *Fishermen of the Banks,* and wrote a preface, in the prose of "Gentlemen and Seamen," only planed and made easier by the experience of twenty years. Gloucester, Eliot said in that preamble, "has the most beautiful harbour for small ships on the whole of that coast," and into a few words, largely reminiscences of Connolly's other books, he braided one or two personal memories: the fish on the drying racks behind the wharves; the sailors who told their stories, which are Connolly's stories, as they lounged "where fishmen lounge at noon" at the corner of Main Street and Duncan Street.

Gloucester is still beautiful. On a bright day the bay from the mainland to the south point of the Cape is flecked by bobbing yachts, buoys and pennants. When a northeast storm shows, the fishing vessels come in by twos and threes for shelter. Beyond the wharves a short sandy lane runs between peeling houses to the beach: brown-faced, thin-cheeked Mediterranean old men and women sit on the porches, salt-brown youngsters go down to the boats, you hear Italian, and you

think you are in Sicily. Nowadays in late June the Italian fishermen celebrate St. Peter's Fiesta and the Blessing of the
Boats with dory races, seine-boat races, and walking the greasy
spar; this was instituted only in 1931, and Eliot cannot have
seen it, at least not in his early days; but of course it was not
beckoned out of the void; the fishermen have at this season
long made their annual devotions to the deity that controls the
waters. The Portuguese seamen of Gloucester celebrate St.
John's Day in June. On the hillside the Portuguese have their
church, a replica of a church in the Azores, an exotic among
the neat New England churches. Here the ship's boy Manuel,
in *Captains Courageous,* used to light candles to the Virgin:
"She is very good to fishermen all the time. That is why so few
of us Portugee men ever are drowned."

Gloucester is on the south side of Cape Ann. Some miles away
on the north side is Ipswich Bay. A guidebook author in the
nineteenth century, sitting on his veranda in fair weather,
counted five or six hundred schooners of the mackerel fleet.
The Salvages, bare rocks, just protrude their heads from the
water. On a halcyon day they are, the nineteenth-century author thought, "a brooch on the bosom of the sea," or, Eliot
thought, merely a monument or a seamark to lay a course by.
But in the sombre season . . . An early chronicle of New England tells of Thatcher and his family and friends wrecked on
the night of August 11, 1631: travelers who had embarked at
Ipswich for Marblehead, among them "one Mr. William Eliot,
sometime of New Sarum." Mr. Eliot was not an ancestor of the
poet, as far as I know, but if a poet meets his own name in a
tragic context, he suffers a momentary act of identification.

In 1910 it must have seemed that no poet had yet made great
poetry of the Cape and its beauty and peril. Longfellow had
written about the "fog-bell on a rock-bound coast" in the popular "Wreck of the Hesperus." The Reverend J. G. Adams, on a
July Sabbath in 1851, had written

> On sunlit spire, and roof, and shore,
>   And sail that stains the dark, blue sea
> And red horizon spread out o'er
>   That emblem of eternity —
> I read thy brightness, God of Love

which is sung sweetly enough, and is, in New England terms, the innocent song of the parson under Milk Wood; but it sees only the fairness of life, and the sea also tells of mystery and terror. One American had translated the experiences of the coast into great pictures. Winslow Homer, after he settled at Prout's Neck, Maine, had recorded, in his heavy but powerful oils —

> the fishermen sailing
> Into the wind's tail, where the fog cowers.

But a supreme literary monument was wanting. Eliot raised it over thirty years later when he wrote "The Dry Salvages." That poem depends on his memories of the Cape and of the tide that sweeps round the deep curve of Ipswich Bay, on his memories of Kipling and Connolly (since books are frequently intermediaries in his realization of his world in art), on the respect he has long felt for the people whom Kipling and Connolly describe

> forever bailing
> Setting and hauling, while the North East lowers
> Over shallow banks unchanging and erosionless

and on a protracted, profound consideration of the nature of human experience. Eliot thought of his ancestors and their pilgrimage from an old to an unknown country, and, resisting any temptation to make a pageant, elicited their eternal significance, and the eternal significance of his own reversal, completion, and renewal of their journey. "The Dry Salvages," with its vision of the arterial river at St. Louis and the coast of New England, is at once a local and a national masterpiece, and, with its vision of human reaching-out and human patience, it is an international masterpiece. It is the greatest of his poems and among the great poems of his time.

Its fourth movement, for example, is at once Eliot's private prayer, that, having chosen to "fare forward," he may be forgiven for the choice and protected, and that all who have made the same choice or another may be forgiven and protected; and it is the prayer of the fishermen of Gloucester: of the Portugee, Manuel, or of Captain Mesquita, who was saved from the Atlantic in a fishing disaster of 1900 and every Trinity Sunday through the afteryears consecrated a crown in the Church at Gloucester. *Figlia del tuo figlio* requires us to think of Dante and of all that Eliot has taught us to associate with him, and connects the poem with Gloucester's Mediterranean stock and their religious heritage. And besides *being* a prayer, this movement *designates the function* of prayer in human conduct; the anthropologist in Eliot as well as the religious sufferer writes "The Dry Salvages" as a study of the human pattern. And I hope I have not forgotten that the poet, in the sense of the man combining words into music, writes the prayer.

If Eliot had died in 1940 we might not have guessed him capable of this consummation, or even that the local material for it was assembled in his mind and of such intense importance to him. It had made appearances, but momentary appearances. I can recollect how in schoolboy readings of *The Waste Land*

> the evening hour that strives
> Homeward, and brings the sailor home from sea

possessed me; and I turned to the note about the "longshore" or "dory" fishermen, and found that fascinating too, perhaps because "dory," to my English ear, was an unknown word and, by false association, a golden one; but the lines fondled me, even without the note, as they do still. Today, in the light of "The Dry Salvages," they are seen to be New England lines, and the glow in them to be the glow of Eliot's feelings for his coast. There is, however, another element present — the allusion to Sappho — to augment their vitality. Often Eliot doubles his richness in this way. Often . . . But occasionally in the later work there are beautiful images which are exact memories of things seen when he was young:

> The salt is on the briar rose,
> The fog is in the fir trees.

In East Gloucester in July the wild roses climb on fence and low seawall and wherever they can find a hold; the salt moisture clings to them and creeps through the trees. When he summons this memory to "The Dry Salvages" he adds nothing to support or enrich it; and now the marvel is that the lines are perfectly local and exact and yet, perhaps by Eliot's concentration on catching the images in their sharp purity, seem to catch the eternal form and the stillness.

Popular Themes Called to Service

If his Atlantic poetry and its salty images, the salt on the rose, have grown with his sympathy for the fishermen doing one of the world's basic labors, they have also been fostered by a pleasure of the lucky. Eliot has named yachting as one of his sports. Many Harvard boys enjoyed their liveliest days sailing off the coast. Moving out of college to work in and about Boston and to mature into city elders, they still sailed. When Arnold Bennett browsed round the city in 1912 he praised its bookshops, more per acre than anywhere else in the world except in Aberdeen, but at once added that its yacht clubs were better. "And for one yacht club I personally would sacrifice many bookshops." They took him to *the* Boston Yacht Club, the ipsissima, with its "acute and splendid nauticality." It stamped Boston, he congratulated them, "as a city which has comprehended the sea."

The Harvard boys sailed and they wrote about their sailing. Hermann Hagedorn included a yachting poem in his *Poems and Ballads* of 1912. J. G. Gilkey had a poem, "The Drifting Bell-Buoy," in the *Harvard Monthly*, May 1909. Some of the best *Advocate* short stories in Eliot's time were written by yachtsmen about yachting. Thorvald S. Ross of the class of 1912 would not have called himself a vates. His future was managing a light industry, nursing it through the depression, reconstructing it afterwards. But he loved boats and the coastal waters. He had been becalmed in fog that smeared his binnacle light to a blur, had watched ice crust on his rigging and settle two feet deep on the deck. He put into his stories what he had experienced, and the result is that if you start reading them, you read them to the end. And in reading them you know the perils and beauties of the Atlantic.

A yachtsman, incidentally a writer, could do that with the material. What could a poet, incidentally a yachtsman, do? In *The Waste Land* the images of sterility suddenly give, to disclose an image of perfection, of the life of discipline which must replace the futile life, and which means delight with discipline; and this is a sailing image:

> *Damyata:* The boat responded
> Gaily, to the hand expert with sail and oar.

And later comes *Marina*, with that yacht image for the creating soul and the physical delight of the creative act (like the handling of a yacht and the rhythm of its movement) and the psychic revelations of the creative act (like reach after reach of the granite islands opening up).

To consider what the mature poet did with this theme so popular with his university friends, the subject of their most attractive writing, is to be drawn towards a generalization: that it is a feature of his art to have taken material that was lightly bandied, with pleasant but passing results, by his contemporaries, and to have made serious and lasting poetry out of it.

What he made of the sailing and sea poetry of his time was so grand that the metamorphosis took many years. Another Harvard practice, which he adopted and refined much more rapidly, was the satire of Boston society. The undergraduate journals teem with skits on the mother-city and its Brahmins, against powerful mothers and subdued fathers and against their unfortunate daughters "expected to wear gloves and to talk of nothing but Dickens and Swinburne, Chateaubriand and Lamartine." In 1909-10 he appropriated a segment of the satire on the bluestockings and transformed it and raised it to criticism and self-criticism (for who is most at fault, the lady or her admirer?) in "Portrait of a Lady." At Oxford in 1915, resuming poetry after a silence, he looked back at Boston and in a few succinct lines nostalgically captured and destructively ridiculed its authoritarian ethos in "The *Boston Evening Transcript*" and "Aunt Helen." On publication in 1917 these two poems were at once recognized by the Harvard men of that year — so one of them, Dr. Kenneth Robinson, tells me — as perfecting the art of local iconoclasm at which class after class had aimed.

In Eliot's comic poetry there are characteristic touches which connect it with an art much cultivated at Harvard: musical comedy; the burlesques of the Hasty Pudding Club and the less celebrated but comparable productions of other groups, such as the players of the Architectural Department. Eliot has said that he did not attend the Hasty Pudding evenings, and possibly he did not regard their entertainments with any special cordiality; so if I suggest that he integrated anything of their methods or style with his own, I suggest that he did it quite unconsciously. The spoofing rhymes were in the air. Every Harvard man knew their lilt, their aura, even if he never witnessed a production (just as Oxford men know the OUDS style whether they are OUDS or not). The lyrics were witty, elegant; they were the efflorescence of the current dandyism. Are there not traces of the lilt and the spoofing in *Sweeney* and the *Practical Cats?* Traces of the burlesque names in Grishkin, Krumpacker, Lady Klootz, Mungojerrie, Rumpelteazer? There are vestiges, metamorphosed, of the choric refrains (for the Hasty Pudding scenarios had originated in opéra bouffe) in one of the most effective devices of Eliot's dialogue: a phrase repeated, thrown from speaker to speaker: "I'd be bored" . . . "You'd be bored"; "The only man I ever met who could hear the cry of bats." "Hear the cry of bats?" "He could hear the cry of bats." The point of the device is to use the poetry of authentic conversation: Eliot simulates the echo habits of our talk; to that extent, he is a realist, or rather, distills from realism; but he also delights the ear with a half-memory of traditional choric effects, than which nothing could be less realist and more formal. Above all, there is an affinity, a distant connection, between the Hasty Pudding style and Eliot's comedy, in the music which remains with a man when he leaves the theatre or rises from the book. The after-music of Eliot's comedy is a very rare experience, and I may appear to lose the sense of fitness in comparing it with that of the student frolics. But indeed the point is, that from a very flimsy (yet very gay and effective) kind of writing, which was within the power of many young men, an exceptional genius developed a method of unusual beauty. Eliot has done with Harvard's traditions what he has done in a more important way with Britain's popular theatre and music hall: used it for great purposes, in accordance with the prescription he laid down in an article in the *Dial* in 1923: "Fine art is the refinement, not the antithesis, of popular art."

Critics have lately been calling attention to that formula, and we are beginning to appreciate that the assumption of twenty-three years ago, which admiringly and fearfully detected an austere erudition behind every line of Eliot, has to be amended. Of course the remarkable erudition *is* at work, and Eliot has educated my generation by displaying it, and displaying what it may do for a poet and what a poet may do with it. But often — and often when it is best — his work looks to the classics of the foreground, the common stock of entertainment, and particularly light entertainment: *Alice in Wonderland*, Lear (E. rather than K.), Fitzgerald, Kipling, Conan Doyle, Gilbert and Sullivan. Its affiliations with so much popular literature may help it to live with the common possessions in the popular memory. But it must be added that Eliot's employment of light material, light allusions, the light manner, is nearly always double, contrapuntal. Against the comedy he sounds notes of danger and eternity.

5. A Year of Diligence

"THE whole man must move at once," said Addison, in a phrase which Hofmannsthal loved to quote. All Eliot's powers advanced at once early in 1909 after the discovery of Laforgue and the sight of himself-to-be in that fellow mind, which, as he told the Italian Institute, was like an admired elder brother's.

In the exhilaration with which the sense of sudden growth endows a man, he resolved (if my imaginary picture of him is right) to understand the intentions and methods of the masters in every creative field. Reviewing *Egoists*, in the *Advocate* of October 5, he praised James Huneker:

> . . . he is a musician; plays himself, and has written an interesting life of Chopin; has written also a volume on contemporary European drama, and can speak intelligently on art.

He would acquire an equal versatility.

Enjoying his intellectual athleticism, he attacked his academic courses with a steely passion. He had taken his bachelor's degree in three years (at a time when men often spent four) but without scoring a conspicuously high mark. During the two terms, 1909-10, he completed the work for a Master's degree in English literature with all-round distinction. To read the list of his courses is to feel the sparkle of pleasure: Neilson's Comparative Literature 18, "Studies in the History of Allegory"; Neilson and Robinson's English I, "Chaucer"; Baker's "Drama

in England from the Miracle Plays to the Closing of the Theatres"; Neilson's English 24, "Poets of the Romantic Period";
Babbitt's French 17, "Literary Criticism in France with special
Reference to the Nineteenth Century"; Santayana's Philosophy 10, "The Philosophy of History: Ideals of Society, Religion,
Art, and Science in their Historical Development." He pursued them diligently, in the full sense of the word.

Irving Babbitt (1865-1933)

So many courses in English literature, only one in French.
But that one, given by Babbitt, provided, of all the courses of
the year, the most powerfully formative experience.

Like Wendell, Babbitt was a Tory, a critic of President
Eliot, an influence in strengthening T. S. Eliot against the assumptions of his society. But Wendell was fiery-frail, an actor, an exotic, an ape of Europe; Babbitt a lover of Europe, but
the typical American, all muscle and force. He preached the
ordered control of energy, especially his nation's energy, but
he lived and taught as the nation's free energy incarnate.
In boyhood he had learned to depend on himself; sold newspapers and scrapped with his fists in the streets of New York City;
done farm jobs in Ohio. As a young man he had worked a spell
as a cowboy in Wyoming; pulled a rattlesnake out of a hole by
its tail; rifling an eagle's nest, fought the eagle, and afterwards
carried the talon scars on his hand for life.

He graduated at Harvard in 1889, taught two years in Montana, joined Sylvain Lévi's Sanskrit and Pali courses in Paris
and continued the languages back at Harvard in Lanman's
library, where he found a fellow student in Paul Elmer More.
Harvard appointed him to its French Department in 1894, and
rising by slow steps — some have said too slow in penalty for
his criticisms of the administration — he spent the rest of his
years there.

Literature and the American College, which Eliot knew and

regarded as an important book, was published by Houghton
Mifflin in 1908, though only a part of the writing belongs to
that date, some of the chapters having already appeared in
magazines, one as early as 1896. The subtitle to the book was
"Essays in Defence of the Humanities"; and in the opening
pages Babbitt particularized his understanding of the word
"Humanitas" by showing how the Romans fell into misuse of
it and were recalled to order by Aulus Gellius: *"Humanitas,*
says Gellius, is incorrectly used to denote a 'promiscuous benevolence, what the Greeks call philanthropy,' whereas the word
really implies doctrine and discipline, and is applicable not to
men in general but only to a select few, — it is, in short, aristocratic and not democratic in its implication."

In the essays, as at the table around which his small class
then met, Babbitt denounced the drive for size, the criterion
of numbers, quick industrialization, the criterion of wealth.
"We [in America] seem certain," he wrote, "to break all records of bigness, but unless that bigness is tempered by quality
we shall sprawl helplessly in the midst of our accumulated
wealth and power, or at best arrive at a sort of senseless itera-
tion." From the assumption of human perfectibility, and by
the illegitimate equation of growth with improvement, his
fellow citizens had come to suppose "that each decade is a gain
over the last decade, and that each century is an improvement
on its predecessor." In rebuttal he told this parable: that one
Sunday evening, walking along a country road in a remote
part of New England, he passed a farmhouse and saw through
the window the members of the family around the lamp, each
one bending over a section of a "yellow" journal. "I reflected
that not many years before the Sunday reading of a family of
that kind would have been the Bible. To progress from the
Bible to a comic supplement would seem a progress from religious restraint to a mixture of anarchy and idiocy." He attacked contemporary society for "the quantitative life" adul-
terated with "moral impressionism."

The American college, Babbitt implied, followed the trends he deplored, adopting the mores of industry and concentrating on size, quantity, and success by the extrovert's standards, whereas it should impose discipline and restore reason and taste.

We have seen that when John Jay Chapman attacked the prevalent ideology in 1909, he evoked very little support. The majority of people, even in an intellectual center like Cambridge, were satisfied with the current conception of progress. Individuals like Chapman and Babbitt were isolated. But in their very isolation they looked redoubtable; and students who appreciated intellectual heroism were won to Babbitt by his craggy loneliness. Eliot has put it: "His outspoken contempt for methods of teaching in vogue had given him a reputation for unpopularity which attracted to him some discerning graduates and undergraduates." Later to champion Joyce and Wyndham Lewis because he admired their acceptance of unpopularity, Eliot was enchanted by Babbitt's uncompromising assault on the popular. And, as we have noticed in examining his reactions to President C. W. Eliot, he has never ceased to maintain a polemic, against the overconcern for buildings and numbers and against the weakening of the disciplines in modern education, which continues the polemic of *Literature and the American College.*

Babbitt's polemic was not merely destructive. In place of the prevailing values of the time, he offered the values of certain nations at certain moments the most propitious in their history, and doctrines by which a writer might assimilate and communicate them. Eliot, coming to him in that receptive year, heard at his table and read in his book the doctrine of classicism and the complementary doctrine of tradition.

Whoever would write or know how to judge writing should study the Greeks, Babbitt said. Their work in all the arts was judicious, moderate, humane. He quoted Goethe: if "we are looking for masterpieces we must think neither of the Chinese

nor of the Servians, nor of Calderon nor of the Niebelungenlied
but must turn to the ancient Greeks, for in their work is found
the model of man in his true beauty." Goethe had carried his
modesty too far when he had said that, if the masterpieces
that exist in Greek had been known to him when he was a
young man, he would never have written a line; "but how grateful just a touch of it would be in the average author of today."

Literature and the American College is in fact a primary
document of the neoclassical movement in English. There, in
1908, Babbitt urged young writers to the cultivation of the classical spirit, and characterized it:

> The classical spirit, in its purest form, feels itself consecrated to
> the service of a high, impersonal reason. Hence its sentiment of
> restraint and discipline, its sense of proportion and pervading
> law.

Eliot's response can be illustrated by a passage in the *Criterion*
in January 1926: explaining the "classicism" for which his periodical stood, he said that this did not mean that living art
should be measured by dead laws (for in England he had
heard the thunder of men, schooled in Greek and Latin, who
were the deadly enemies of new art, and he must not comfort
them), but it meant that "there is a tendency — discernable
even in art — towards a higher and clearer conception of
Reason, and a more severe and serene control of the emotions
by reason." Babbitt's voice is audible in Eliot's.

It may seem to us that Babbitt's words and Eliot's, noble
and elevated, were as vague as some of the grandiose pronouncements of Whitman. They were. But I suppose that they
took their precision from the palpably contrasting tendencies of
their days. A young writer in 1909 might well conceive an
image of strength by reflecting on Babbitt's pronouncement
and keeping it before him as he practiced his verses or his
criticism: Norman Foerster might develop that sense of a cold

bracing beauty which appears in his criticism of Hearne; Eliot
might see a general principle behind the asentimentalism
which Symons had shown him in Laforgue, and might begin
to think of "the firmness, the true coldness, the hard coldness
of the genuine artist" for which he praised Hawthorne in 1919.

Above all, the classicism of Babbitt instructed Eliot in concentration on the essentials. The instruction is implicit in *Literature and the American College,* where the author approves
of the Greeks for their unfailing discrimination between what
is peripheral and what central in human experience, and ex-
plicit in *Masters of Modern French Criticism,* published in
1912, and embodying his teaching of the preceding year,
where he quotes Chateaubriand's praise of the ancients: "Ils
ne savent travailler que l'ensemble, et négligent les orne-
ments." By exalting Chateaubriand's comment to a rule, Eliot
has achieved a purity and power in his work. We have noticed how *Murder in the Cathedral* gained more than it lost by
his refusal to admit period ornament, period color. Perhaps the
heightening of his sense of the requisite, the strengthening of
his will to surrender everything else, was the greatest service
Babbitt performed for him.

But a service almost equally important was to introduce
Eliot to the theory of the living past. Babbitt hated the overvaluation of originality. His famous attacks on Rousseau,
which were also attacks on Petrarch and Bacon, turned on the
charge that he had overvalued his differences from other men,
and, by his success in glorifying his own weaknesses, had induced writer after writer to seek to be different in life and art.
The writer whose work would be permanently satisfying would
know what he shared with his predecessors, not his differences,
and would depend on the past, not break from it. The supremacy of Greek literature had lain in "the balance it maintained
between the forces of tradition and the claims of originality,
so that Greek literature at its best is a kind of creative imita-

tion." The Greek hoped "to become original by assimilating tradition." Modern literature often failed by its "enormous repudiations" of the past. "There is needed in the classics today," Babbitt decided, "a man who can understand the past with the result, not of loosening, but of strengthening his grasp upon the present." Eliot soon hailed the work of Ezra Pound because he found him such a man; when he reviewed *Quia Pauper Amavi* in 1919 he wrote:

> Mr. Pound proceeds by acquiring the entire past; and when the entire past is acquired, the constituents fall into place and the present is revealed. Such a method involves immense capacities of learning and of dominating one's learning, and the peculiarity of expressing oneself through historical masks. Mr. Pound has a unique gift for expression through some phase of past life. This is not archaeology or pedantry, but one method, and a very high method, of poetry.

The first of the essays with which Eliot revolutionized criticism and the practice of poetry, "Tradition and the Individual Talent," began to appear in the *Egoist* at almost the same date. That essay was the organization of Babbitt's traditionalism and the traditionalism of Maurras and Benda into a cogent whole, the immediate fusion fired by the work of Pound. It was also a chart for his own poetry: for *The Waste Land,* in which he himself appeared as a man the more strongly grasping the present for his understanding and creative assimilation of the literature of the past.

There was, Dr. W. P. Kinne has pointed out to me, a tradition of tradition at Harvard. When Eliot was Babbitt's pupil, the crucial American debate, whether the nation's art should be utterly independent, or whether it would only be rich if it grew from the traditions of Europe, was already seventy years old. Whitman had been the magnificent exponent of independence. We have heard him meditating on his hopes in Missouri, fortified by a geography vast beyond West European comprehension. But in Cambridge, a generation earlier, Longfellow had debated the issue and had given the best of his sympathy to the other side. James Russell Lowell, inheriting the Smith Professorship from Longfellow, had inherited with it, and intensified, the devotion to tradition. Babbitt had absorbed Lowell's teaching. And Babbitt had combined the lesson with the lessons of the French neoclassicists, and brought to its promulgation not a donnish quietude but, paradoxically, the ruggedness of independent America. Eliot received the lesson from Babbitt. And Eliot went to the French to whom Babbitt directed him, immersed himself in their neoclassicism, immersed himself so thoroughly that it was practically a rebaptism in the doctrine; and then, with the excitement of Pound's work to impel him, and his philosophical training to provide the means, decisively systematized the theory of tradition in his essays and decisively demonstrated it in his poetry; through both of which a Harvard taste crystallized into an English literary counterrevolution and, shortly, into a world movement.

A Babbitt needs an Eliot, and an Eliot a Babbitt. Other Harvard men sat at Babbitt's table, and other Harvard men and men elsewhere read *Literature and the American College,* but either they did not see the force of what they read, or did not see that it had to be restated to be transmitted — or, if they saw the need, they did not know how to do it. Eliot saw all the implications and worked out what to do and did it.

Together with his debt to Babbitt for the first disclosure of these essential doctrines, Eliot has some debt to him for lessons in the art of controversy. Babbitt and Eliot both impress us, as we read them, by their coherent method: they begin by breaking down their subject into its divisions and subdivisions and so clearing away ambiguities; and when they have established their categories, they place their material in the scale of human values, and draw consequences for our conduct. They are *marshals,* and watching them we feel that we are watching reason in action.

After I had made this comparison, I remembered Eliot's remark in *The Sacred Wood* that Babbitt's important books "would be more important if he preached discipline in a more disciplined style." Which is sad, if there is indeed, as my ear still infers, a family resemblance between the style of master and pupil. But the verdict, engendered by those occasional immoderate and hyperbolical flights in Babbitt's prose, is not on the whole justified. Eliot himself corrected it when he read *Democracy and Leadership,* which he listed, in 1926, as one of the books which exemplified the severe and serene classical spirit. Possibly when Eliot wrote the *Sacred Wood* essay, his memory of the printed page had become confused with his memory of Babbitt's classroom technique, notorious for its energetic, versatile discursions and surprises. The confusion of memories, however, may have done good: it may have led Eliot to impose stricter discipline on himself, in order to improve on his master. And he has done this. Of the two he is the more restrained and ordered. But though he excels Babbitt, he excels him in the methods that he learned from him.

Throughout Babbitt's lifetime Eliot remained attentive to his work. When the Professorship of English Literature at Oxford fell vacant in 1922 on the death of Sir Walter Raleigh, Eliot suggested in his "London Letter" to the *Dial* that Babbitt would be a good successor. The proposal went unheeded. In the later twenties, when Babbitt's pupils, the Humanists, claimed the interest of America and the civilized world for their views, Eliot, disagreeing with their allegiance to the "ethical will" as against his own faith in revealed Christianity, opened the pages of the *Criterion* to them and to their critics alike. Some of the criticism of Humanism he wrote himself, with the result that Babbitt complained, "He begins his letters

'Dear Master,' but he attacks me whenever he writes about me." In fact, Eliot cannot be said to have "attacked" him; he disputed with his teacher, but as one who shared common ground.

In his latest days, as Warner G. Rice tells in the volume of essays commemorating Babbitt, the Old Master felt that his disciples had abandoned him. It was his greatness and tragedy that he attracted the strongest pupils and helped them to find, in combat with him, their bent and their proper beliefs, to which they moved away, whereupon he saw himself deserted and left to front the worsening world singlehanded while "Art after Art goes out and all is Night."

Neilson's Essentials

William Allan Neilson had been trained in the exacting University of Edinburgh, and then had seen his hope across the water and taken advanced degrees at Harvard in the early nineties. By assiduous publication he had quickly risen. Associate Professor of English at Harvard in 1904, he had gone to Columbia as Professor in 1905, and that had titillated the zeal of President Eliot, who had brought him back to Harvard as Professor the next year. He stayed till 1917. Then he became president of Smith, where he presided for the next twenty-two years.

There are not many ideas, nor much fun in his writing. His Lowell lectures on *The Essentials of Poetry*, given in 1911, and preluded by an acknowledgment to the Harvard students who had exchanged ideas with him and tested his opinions in class discussion, do not reveal the essentials or say what poetry is, only praise "imagination" as the quality he preferred in it. One may sympathize with the difficulty of saying what poetry is; but there are teachers who can throw light on it by their peripheral gymnastics — read Neilson and then read

Empson. His book on Burns is all quotation, which is very agreeable, but some commentary might have been attempted. He was a bit of a prude or pretended to be. Yet Eliot elected two of his courses. He was an Associate Editor of the Harvard Classics. Yet Eliot appears to have forgiven him that.

It may be that the appeal of the literature which he was appointed to teach was so great that Eliot did not mind if the teacher was dry. To a man reading *Gawain and the Green Knight* in one class, Chaucer in another, and Byron in a third, dryness was not an offensive fault; it could not come between him and the poem.

Did Neilson read Byron's *The Island* with his class in the romantic poets? His discussion of it in *The Essentials of Poetry* suggests so. In the published lectures he used it to illustrate the poetic imagination working at a mediocre level. Its second canto, where "both human and external nature among tropical savages are held up as exhibiting a condition far superior to civilization," struck him as vulnerable to criticism. He quoted a score of lines on the daughter of the southern seas, "lovely, warm, and premature," and half a dozen on "The cava feast, the yam, the cocoa's root." "A little rational consideration," he said, would have shown Byron that the island couldn't really please him. "One cannot imagine this spoiled child of civilization, this connoisseur of sophisticated pleasure, finding any prolonged satisfaction in an existence whose content is typified by the picture of a native pair, as free from subtlety as from clothing, strolling by a tepid beach under a tropical sunset, eating unsyndicated bananas." So the destructive song in *Sweeney Agonistes:*

> *My little island girl*
> *I'm going to stay with you*
> *And we wont worry what to do . . .*

It would have bored Byron in a week, said Neilson. So Eliot:

> I'd be bored.
> You'd be bored.

But Eliot's refrain is not precisely concurrent with Neilson's remark. Neilson believed in civilization and genuinely supposed the island boring. Byron said, with some passion, that civilization was boring. Eliot works from Byron's position — works far from it on the basis of his reading in anthropology. In W. H. R. Rivers he read how civilization had deprived the Melanesians of interest in life and they were dying of boredom. In *The Waste Land* he displayed boredom as a blight of civilization; and the lyric in *Sweeney* is a continuation of his display.

Eliot has told, in the essay which he contributed in 1937 to Bonamy Dobrée's symposium *From Anne to Victoria,* how Byron was an infatuation with him at the age of sixteen. Presumably his appeal had diminished by 1909. Yet the poet who posed as an English sporting dandy may still have seemed an interesting figure to a student who was studying another poseur, the primmer dandy, Laforgue. Certainly there were passages of Byron which continued to ring in Eliot's mind for many years. Donna Julia's letter, "You will proceed in pleasure, and in pride," seems to sound in the "Portrait" behind the lady's "You will go on"; a piquant phrase from *Beppo* serves as an epigraph to *The Sacred Wood;* the second canto of *The Island* may be connected with the island blues of *Sweeney Agonistes;* the same canto perhaps supplies, from its phrase

> . . . the sordor of civilisation, mixed
> With all the savage which Man's fall hath fixed —

that peculiar word "sordor," with which, near the opening of *After Strange Gods,* Eliot expresses his dismay at the manufacturing towns of New England. Much more gaily in the Charles Eliot Norton lectures Eliot quotes from *Don Juan* to clear *Ash-Wednesday* from any design against the creed and morals of his land, and assures the Harvard men of 1932 that

I don't pretend that I quite understand
My own meaning when I would be *very* fine . . .

It was only fair that, so much of Byron enduring with him to please him, and to please us through him, he should in 1937 call the critical world back to an appreciation of Byron's poetry. Grover Smith, apparently guided by the 1937 essay, has half hinted that Byron's attraction for Eliot lay in "a burden of blight and guilt," characteristic of the protagonists they both invented. It may be so. But an equal force in the attraction may have been this: that Byron was the only English poet to be at once a dandy and a man with a variety of practical interests, and the only one to raise dandyism to comic poetry.

Neilson was sensible enough to see that poetry must include comic poetry, and he determinedly took "Humor in Poetry" for one of his Lowell lectures. But the very "in" of the title betrays his difficulty. By the test of his experience he could not believe what his shrewdness told him, that poetry could be comic. There could be comedy *in* the work of a poet, but he really thought that the moment it came in, the "imagination" went out. When Byron swung from the sweetness of the gondolier to

Sweet is revenge — especially to women

he found that "we descend from poetry to satirical humor." I suspect that the Laforguian Eliot already fretted at the distinction in class. His own comic poetry was just putting on feathers. He was making, and would make, and perhaps would make the more keenly to prove Neilson mistaken, a comic poetry which was, in his Professor's phrase, "true imaginative poetry." Byron's idiom, the easy, sane, delighted deflation of himself and his society, helped him, though he had to find new forms and rhythms to accommodate it. The same idiom served him for some of the side thrusts in his polemic.

There was a long-term problem, about which Neilson had

nothing exceptional to say, but said what he could at the right time. He remarked that meter prepares the reader to realize the content of the poem more intensely, as heat prepares wax to take the impression of the seal. He quoted

> Go button your boots with a tiger's tail,
>   Comb down your golden hair;
> And live for a week upon bubble-and-squeak
>   On the steps of a winding stair

and commented that nonsense verse gave strictly a musical pleasure, or a pleasure at the same level "as the rhythmical beating of a drum." "There is a point, indeed, where it is difficult to distinguish the pleasures derived from verse and music respectively." Eliot (who used the title "The Beating of a Drum" for his *Athenaeum* review of October 6, 1923) was much exercised by the problem. For thirty years he would speculate on it, probing further than Neilson; thinking of a future medical analysis of the nervous complexes, of diagrams of the nervous impulses produced by rhythms; attempting to apply the drumbeat measure to seize the nerves of the *Sweeney* audience; refining the beat in the speech cadences of the later comedies; trying to work out the relationship of music and poetry, to locate some of the overlaps, some of the differences, and to exploit both.

The Stage and the Wrong Stage

In George Pierce Baker's course Eliot examined those fundamental works of English drama, the medieval mystery plays and the Moralities, from which he was eventually to elicit "the living past," creating *Murder in the Cathedral.*

Baker's predominant concern was less with the quality of a play as literature than with the theatrical craft which the playwright brought to it. To read his book on *The Development of Shakespeare* is to realize how well he could illuminate the business of the stage. His analysis of the exposure of Aumerle in *Richard II* —

> The scene shows . . . theatrical as contrasted with mere dramatic skill. Note the sure feeling for the emotional possibilities of the two incidents, the discovery of the indenture and the departure, which leads Shakespeare to "hold" them, as the technical phrase runs, by looking at them through the eyes and feelings of each participator . . . It is specially evident in the climax gained by having York so long hold back the exact nature of what he has read in the indenture, and in the frenzied cry of the Duchess to Aumerle as the servant enters to receive the orders of the infuriated Duke: "Strike him, Aumerle!"

— genuinely helps a student to see the theatrical structure of the scene. Or his commentary on Mercutio gasping out phrases against the pain of his wound — how well that shows that the poetry is actor's poetry, the speech of action! If the nineteenth-century poets had gone through Baker's classroom, they might have written the poetic plays they wanted to write.

Behind his analyses there was always the intention that young playwrights should benefit. It was his delight to recognize and interpret the craft of the masters, his purpose to put it at the service of American drama. For he believed that a drama to match the Old World's was about to be created in America. This was not his private dream. It was a movement. It was not even Harvard's private movement. But Harvard men were foremost in it. Of the graduates of the nineties, now adult and struggling with life, William Vaughn Moody was attempting the Promethean theme; approaching it through Shelley; not gifted enough, or not practical enough, to guess the technique of the transposition of the Greeks, which Paris would discover; but still, making his attempt. Edward Knoblauch, more practical, and better fitted for success than poetry, had written

The Shulamite. Percy MacKaye, brought up almost in the prompt-corner, for his father was the actor and theatrical innovator Steele MacKaye, was trying his hand at every genre: the classics versified, in *Sappho and Phaon;* history, in *Jeanne d'Arc;* prose comedy, in *Mater;* and he was theorizing and haranguing in article and lecture, convinced that "the Renaissance of the Drama" was breaking.

The men ten years younger, undergraduates or recently graduated, hoped that the privilege of founding the drama would be theirs. They were encouraged by the good fortune of E. B. Sheldon of the class of 1907. His play of the tenements, *Salvation Nell,* met with quick, heady success in 1908. Perhaps he was the expected restorer of the drama, some enthusiasts thought. But if not he, why, every ardent young man had a bid to make.

The Yard in Eliot's day was "play-mad." So said the *Advocate,* and the pages of the *Crimson* repeatedly confirm it. "Of course, we all write plays," said Paul Davis in an article, "Toujours Dramatics," in the *Advocate* of June 1, 1908. A New York literary agent, who listed among her clients Maeterlinck, Sudermann, Hauptmann, Schnitzler, together with numerous local names which have faded, judged it worthwhile to buy a quarter page in the *Advocate:*

A L I C E   K A U S E R

1402 Broadway   New York City

The Largest Play Brokerage
in the world

Plays by new authors produced this season include "THE BARBER OF NEW ORLEANS" by *Edward Childs Carpenter,* "THE BATTLE" by *Cleveland Moffett,* "A MAN AND HIS MATE" by *Harold R. Durant,* "SALVATION NELL" by *Edward Sheldon,* "THE STRONGER SEX" by *John Valentine,* and "THE UNBROKEN ROAD" by *Thomas H. Dickinson.*

One of the documents of the hope for an American drama is the novel, *His Great Adventure*, by Robert Herrick. The hero fails as a playwright, succeeds as a business tycoon, uses his financial success to found a national theatre for new American playwrights. His theatre meets the opposition of vested interests. It aims at low prices, no boxes, so society cuts it and the theatrical agents and the press blacklist it. But at last it wins the public with the hero's own story, *His Great Adventure*. At supper after the glorious first night the company toasts "The American Drama!"

Baker gave an immense impetus to the movement by offering to translate enthusiasm into skill. In 1903 he began to teach the girls at Radcliffe "English 46. The Forms of Drama. Practice in Dramatic Composition." In 1905 Harvard's English Department agreed, over the resistance, but unfortunately not the dead body, of Kittredge, to sponsor a similar course for its graduates, Course 47. It was in abeyance, on account of Baker's visit to the Sorbonne, during Eliot's first two undergraduate years, but from 1908 onward it was drawing recruits. As W. P. Kinne has shown in his book on Baker, the milling playmakers welcomed it, agreeing that they must learn their craft and confident that in the result they would fulfil their ambitions and revolutionize the stage. Lee Simonson proposed a Harvard Dramatic Club, and Sheldon took up the plan and announced a charter in March 1908:

> to devote at least half the year to the production of plays written by the undergraduates themselves. It is needless to dilate upon the splendid chance this offers to those interested in dramatic composition. It is hoped that Professor Baker's course in "The Technique of the Drama," to be given next year, will supply a large share of this material.

and the first production came indeed from Course 47, *The Promised Land*, a play with a Zangwillesque theme by Allan Davis, presented February 1909.

A month later an editorial paragraph in the *Advocate* congratulated the Club on its enterprise and ex-Harvard men on their New York and Providence productions:

> . . . the American theatre will receive, let us hope, more plays
> of a kind she has had in several recent instances, written by
> craftsmen trained to the profession, who carry on the good tra-
> dition of the stage. This is the sea mark of our utmost sail. The
> drama is open to corruption as is no other human institution;
> and now as always it needs playwrights of intelligence to guide
> it.

Here one is prompted to a question. Intellectual Harvard as a whole, the literary *Advocate* in particular, approved of the efforts towards a new drama and of Baker's contribution. Eliot was to devote a lifetime to restoring the poetic drama. In 1909 he was eligible for Course 47. Why did he not choose it? Baker's summons to the workshop was the counterpart of the contemporary English rediscovery, by Granville-Barker and others, of Shakespeare the stage technician, and if anything it was a more vital counterpart because it addressed itself to potential writers. Why did Eliot neglect the opportunity to practice craftsmanship, taking, instead, a long, lonely, dogged way forward without Baker's help?

Was it that Baker encouraged plays in which the predominant political accent was liberal and in which the task of drama became the advocacy of humanitarianism? When Henry Arthur Jones lectured at Harvard in November 1906 he praised the university and Baker for doing what antiquarian Oxford failed to do, undertaking the teaching of drama, and urged them to foster a theatre which would be "a school of counciling, fearless, uplifting truth." E. B. Sheldon's *Salvation Nell* and *The Nigger* belonged to the school of philanthropic commentary on current social problems. Of plays of this tendency Baker approved, and was to approve increasingly as he got older. He had a sense of the sadness of man's treatment of man; he felt that one of the functions of drama in his time was to present the human predicament naturalistically and move the spectator to reflection and reform. Some of the plays that resulted were low-level versions of Ibsen — or of what Ibsen appeared to be. The young Eliot and his contemporaries saw Ibsen with the same eyes: saw only the surface of his plays. The difference was that his contemporaries liked what they saw; Eliot took a doubtful, censorious view of it. (In 1937 he was still censorious. By 1954 he had reread Ibsen and saw deeper, and repudiated his earlier remarks.)

Or was Eliot repelled by a concurrent tendency of the men around Baker? Baker's friend and admirer, Percy MacKaye, who spoke to Harvard audiences twice during Eliot's years, and who, though he did not command more than a handful of listeners at his first meeting, was almost rapturously reported in the student journals and commended by Professor Neilson, prophesied "the Drama of Democracy" — a drama as uniquely American as the independent American poetry Whitman spoke for. "The Drama of Democracy" was not a phrase to win the poet on whom Babbitt had just prevailed, nor were some of his predictions well framed for fastidious ears: ". . . huge Satire and the vast guffaw of Folly will chant harmonious; shrill wit, twanging a lightening bow of verse, shall rattle his barbs of melodious mockery; and Reason, standing in the wings, will smile his sweet serene smile philosophical . . ." In a sonnet, which the *Harvard Monthly* printed in October 1909 MacKaye addressed Baker, said that Puritanism had starved poetry and the stage in America, yet —

> Yet not so now at Harvard; there betakes
> him now the scholar-player, with his Muse
> (that deathless wench, the Mermaid) and renews
> his vows, and breaks his fast, and is restored
> by our own Baker. — May the loaves he bakes
> soon pile a feast at Master Shakspere's board.

And what about MacKaye's own drama, prolific at this time? As long as he contained his ebulliance, he could write, pleasingly, if thinly. But he had that post-Civil War craving, of which Babbitt complained, for size and quantity. He was big with a dream of pageants: pageants projecting the history of communities, the community itself participating and so growing in self-knowledge. At Gloucester in the summer of 1909 he produced *The Canterbury Pilgrims:* fifteen hundred Gloucester citizens, descendants of the Puritans, adopted "the garb and spirit of Chaucer's 'Merrie England.'" This was a preliminary essay; more was pending. The next years were to provide opportunity on opportunity, as anniversaries, centenaries, bicentenaries, and tercentenaries followed each other, for mass pageantry. We have seen MacKaye unrolling his "Civic Masque" for the St. Louis celebrations of 1914. Baker was involved in similar undertakings. Baker drafted a gigantic plan for Oregon, not put into effect, and for Plymouth's tercentenary festival of 1921 he wrote *The Pilgrim Spirit,* which was put into effect under his personal direction (and now he styled himself "Pageant-Master"). Eliot probably did not see any of these experiments. But with some disdain he differentiated, in his *Dante* of 1929, between "what are popularly called pageants" and "the serious pageants of royalty, of the Church, of military funerals."

Ideological questions apart, it may be that Eliot's disregard of Baker's workshop lay in a feeling that it might teach craftsmanship but could not teach words. Twenty years later Eliot was to say to the Friends of Rochester Cathedral: "Naturally clever craftsmen are not, I think, usually apt to be anything more . . . The man who has something more to give can, I hope, usually learn the craft by sheer doggedness." He has since paid tribute to F. Martin Browne and to the actors who have helped him to acquire theatre craft. But, clearly, he felt that the first thing for a poet to do was to cultivate his words and his knowledge of human behavior; the rest would follow. The language of the Workshop scripts was without subtlety or energy. The longer Baker taught, the more obvious his verbal deficiency was to become. His anthology of 1920, *Modern American Plays*, shows that he would accept dull writing. And possibly even in his sense of action he was too ready to compromise with the hackneyed. In 1926 Eliot's complaint against the unregenerate theatre of England and America was that it lacked beauty of phrase, thought and image, lacked the unity "of thought, word and scene, of visual and aural rhythm" which is the distinction of "classical" drama.

Whether any of these points of difference from Baker actually occurred to Eliot in 1909, I cannot know. But they are at least aspects of an essential difference between two ways of working for a revival of the drama: the way Eliot's most ambitious contemporaries were going with Baker's encouragement, and the slow and ultimately efficacious way which Eliot took.

On one major issue everybody at Harvard in 1909, whether the playwrights desiring a trade, the men with a heart aiming at a neo-Ibsenist drama, the conscious Americans planning a powerfully American theatre, or Eliot choosing poetry and tapping for the living past — on one issue everybody learned a lesson from Baker. He saw and said that, if drama was to be revived, it must be done on the commercial stage. The best minds must reach Broadway. In *The Sacred Wood* Eliot recorded his agreement, that the revival of poetic drama could not be accomplished through "the small public which wants 'poetry.'" Eventually Eliot carried his new poetic drama to the West End and Broadway; and without any sacrifice to mediocrity.

There were other lessons in Baker's books — and I suspect that he let them fall in his classroom, too — which were not widely adopted. But perhaps one man noticed them; at least, certain of them correspond with the theories which Eliot developed as scaffolding for his first plays. Baker pleaded for a dramatist to "give us fresh, interesting treatment of old psychological facts." *The Cocktail Party* does that, and so, only a little less obviously, do *The Confidential Clerk* and *The Elder Statesman.* Baker said, "Read the liturgical tropes to see what drama is." Eliot recognized that the liturgical and ritualistic character of drama must be restored, and worked out techniques for its restoration.

Even some of the suggestions made by Percy MacKaye in the pre-1914 years of enthusiastic theorizing can be correlated with Eliot's later theorizing and practice. MacKaye had observed in his Harvard lecture of 1908 (and the *Advocate* had reported) that, while poetry was the best medium for a playwright, Elizabethan blank verse would not do, and had argued for a fresh consideration of the "natural cadences of emotion in speech which are allied to music" and the adaptation of these cadences to poetic drama. His *Sappho and Phaon* begins with an induction in which a four-beat line is rather neatly handled to bring the verse nearer to speech. And a point which he emphasized in his design for the "civic" theatre, that the audience should *participate* in the performance, bears a resemblance to Eliot's subsequent theory of participation. MacKaye seems to have oscillated between the notion that the audience, even in their seats and their habitual clothes, would feel themselves involved because they watched their communal history re-enacted, and the notion that the audience must dress and perform the crowd scenes and so realize their history. In either case we may think his view a little too circumscribed by the context of local history from which it arose. Even so, is it very different from Eliot's conception of audience participation, which arose when he heard the English music-hall audience join in the chorus with Marie Lloyd?

A day came when Eliot even wrote a pageant: *The Rock.* But where Baker's pageants and MacKaye's had been ambitious in structure and meager in poetry, Eliot's pageant, devised by E. Martin Browne, aimed at a lively simplicity in structure while providing the opportunity for rich poetry in a number of choruses. Although *The Rock* is treated rather slightingly by critics, it has memorable passages. The passage about Nehemiah, the passage on the Crusaders and the brief exploitation of the boyish but deep-seated English pride in Richard I, are poetry such as no other man of 1909, with the exception of Pound and Ford, could have written.

If Eliot was not the American dramatist whom Harvard awaited, he was the awaited restorer of the poetic drama. To this extent it may be said that the Harvard of his hour helped to determine the course of his ambitions. He found himself in the "play-mad" tumult. He gave the appearance of staying aloof — W. C. Greene's word applies. But he must have been aware of the furore; after all, he was not only reading but helping to edit the *Advocate* which continually reported the hopes of the movement, the adventures of the movers. Now and then a phrase in his later work echoes the vocabulary of the playmakers: reviewing *All God's Chillun Got Wings* in 1926 he said that he did not share the enthusiasm for O'Neill, or for Pirandello, as the author of "a renascence of the drama." He heard the Harvard debates on the New Drama and the New Dramatist, refused any facile assent, any show of competition. But he set himself, consciously or unconsciously (we shall not know which, unless some day his letters, or other documents, of the time are published), to working out an adequate theory for a revival of the poetic drama. It was a labor of years. A student journalist wrote that when the dramatist arrived in the Yard, he would not pass unrecognized; too blithe a promise; the dramatist had to learn by immense work and many circuits to clear the blocked connections between poetry and the stage; and could not be known till he had learned. Twenty-five years passed before Eliot completed his first play, forty years before he captured Broadway. Eliot was a model of persistence and patience.

His triumph in *The Cocktail Party* was to beguile the public with a new genre, modern poetic comedy, which, attempting the unity of "thought, word, and scene, of visual and aural rhythm," was free of all sign of the attempt, free of weight and solemnity. And I am inclined to trace Eliot's first glimpse of that objective to hints thrown out by the Harvard debaters. Baker advised his students not to neglect farce. MacKaye rhapsodically prophesied a new comedy. Eliot *may* have noticed their advice. But the hints I have in mind are those of various shrewd contributors to the *Advocate,* who warned that the way to lose an audience was to be obviously serious: the public didn't love Ibsen but songs, and, above all, comedies with songs: "À bas Sudermann, Ibsen and Jones! Vive Gilbert, Sullivan and Gus Luders. For further confirmation enquire at the box-office." In 1912, when Frederick Wilmot offered a prize of a hundred dollars for either a comedy or a playlet of half an hour's duration, the *Advocate* advised the competitors to ignore the alternative and stick to comedy, preferably comedy written to the pattern of *Charley's Aunt:* "Let us first make a few masterly little comedies, and then we can attempt more serious things." It has been noticed that Eliot's poems are dramas. But what kind of dramas? Sometimes comedies. Of course, comedies with implications. The faces of humanity in trouble are corrugated into grimaces; and Eliot's comedies are comedies in this sense. They are comedies with tragic and religious implications. "Prufrock" and "Portrait of a Lady" already look forward across half a century to *The Cocktail Party.*

6. Some Gifts of France

By the spring of 1910 Eliot had decided to spend the coming academic year in Paris. He explained to his family that he wanted to study the particular genius of France. The prospect was not welcome to his parents. His mother could not bear to think of him alone among a people in whom she had no confidence. She shared the view of France general among the Unitarians of her day. "We recognize," Isabel Francis Bellows wrote in the *Unitarian Review* of January 1883, "that we have much to learn from France in art, in literary style, and in good manners," but what can really be said for a nation which alternates "from Catholicism to the wildest rationalism," values wit, humor, and art above morality, industry, freedom, and sends *Camille*, Offenbach's "indecent burlesques," and Zola's novels to redeem Americans "from our half-savage estate"?

What in fact do young Americans do in Paris? When Conrad Aiken arrived from Italy and came hurrying to find Eliot, the two poets indulged in nothing more enervating than a *sirop de fraises*, then up to the attic to discuss their new writing and the discovery of *Bubu*. Nothing there to alarm a parent. Nor were there any evident perils in Frederic Schenck's experience, as told in his article for the *Advocate* of December 21, 1910, describing the Paris reunion of four Americans. They talked about the heroism of the Parisians in the floods, about three new restaurants, about "every dramatic event of the past winter from *Chantecler* to Fursy's latest song," and then, the conversation veering, they found, in the perspective of three thousand miles, that they loved nothing so much as the old buzzards, the hard leathery men of Maine and Texas.

Looking at 1910 in terms of weather, politics, and wages, the French called it a bad year, a year of floods and a long railway strike. *Figaro's* cartoon on December 30 showed 1911 shrinking back in the wings and a manager trying to persuade her to go on: ". . . n'ayez pas le trac comme ça! . . . Celle que vous remplacez était si exécrable que vous n'aurez pas de peine à être moins mauvaise! . . ." In the New Year of 1911 the Seine floods were worse than their predecessors. The winter persisted into April. On April 21 the trees still stood in black icy lines down the avenues. The orchards were blighted. In the last week in April, when Rilke arrived in Paris from his North African journey, it was snowing. Then all burst out. On May 10 Rilke wrote to Marie von Thurn und Taxis that the lilacs were almost over, the red and white thorn peopled with blossom, and "tomorrow or the day after tomorrow the blossoming cities and towers will stand in the full greenness of the chestnuts," and he was going to exhibitions of Ingres, Rembrandt, and Persian illuminations, and out to Marly where Maillol was showing his sculptures in his primitive garden.

With the last sentence and the name of Maillol we get a glimpse of the intellectual excitement of the hour. For an ampler look at it, we might turn to the *Evocations* of Henri Massis, a book Eliot recommended in 1934 when, happening to open the pages (the book was not a new one), he felt refreshed by its narrative of the Paris of his youth. Refreshed and yet chastened; for it made him wonder whether he and his contemporaries were offering newcomers the significant, various enlivement and enrichment that the French of 1910-11 had offered his generation:

Anatole France and Remy de Gourmont still exhibited their learning and provided types of scepticism for younger men to

be attracted by and to repudiate; Barrès was at the height of
his influence, and of his rather transient reputation. Péguy,
more or less Bergsonian *and* Catholic *and* Socialist, had just become important, and the young were further distracted by Gide
and Claudel. Vildrac, Romains, Duhamel, experimented with
verse which seemed hopeful, though it was always, I think, disappointing; something was expected of Henri Franck, the early
deceased author of *La danse devant l'arche.* At the Sorbonne,
Faguet was an authority to be attacked violently; the sociologists, Durkheim, Lévy-Bruhl, held new doctrines; Janet was the
great psychologist; at the Collège de France, Loisy enjoyed his
somewhat scandalous distinction; and over all swung the spider-
like figure of Bergson. His metaphysic was said to throw some
light upon the new ways of painting, and discussion of Bergson
was apt to be involved with discussion of Matisse and Picasso.

"Un présent parfait," Eliot called the epoch when he made
another and comparable mosaic of memories for *La France
Libre.* A whole book should be written on Eliot's debt, which
is a debt of all of us, to the Paris of the five years before the
Great War.

When that book is written, a considerable chapter will belong to Bergson. This topic I am not equipped to touch, however lightly, and must be content to leave to those who will do
it justice. Only in passing I will quote, as an indication of
Bergson's impact on the young people who flocked to hear him
at the Collège de France, a passage from Camille Vettard.
Listening to the lectures some four years before Eliot heard
them, he found the philosopher's "affirmations and construc-
tions" dreary and fugitive; but the display of the critical and
destructive faculties filled him with astonishment:

> Je ne connais pas de critique plus acérée et plus décisive que
> celle qu'il a faite soit du *scientisme,* de la prétension de réduire
> le monde à un vaste réseau d'équations differentielles, soit de
> la *cristallisation* de l'intelligence dans les "catégories héritées."

And this shock of astonishment awakened Bergson's audiences to unpremeditated undertakings:

> Ce faisant, il a adressé un appel à nos facultés d'invention, de création, et, en même temps, dissipant les "clartés apprises" . . . il nous a induit à reprendre contact avec les choses. Et c'est par ce qu'il galvanise nos facultés de perception que son oeuvre nous donne si souvent cette impression de nouveauté et de fraîcheur, de vue non livresque et directe du réel . . .

By demolishing a clutter of assumptions and claims, especially the claims for scientific law as allowed by the nineteenth century, Bergson cleared a space in which work and play could begin afresh; and if he liberated the human mind, as some observers feared, for experiments in anarchy, he also created the conditions in which the new conservatism might grow by reaction and make its own use of the leveled space.

The main concern of this chapter is to notice the objectives and hopes of several writers whose adventures Eliot observed during his Paris year and a little later; and if of one writer more particularly, then of Alain-Fournier, to whom Eliot went for practice in French conversation. I shall take Fournier and his friend and brother-in-law, Jacques Rivière, as an index to the taste of young Frenchmen of the same age as Eliot, and shall occasionally suppose that Fournier spoke of his literary interests to Eliot in their conversational exchanges.

Provincial greathearts, Fournier and Rivière are still to be met as Eliot knew them, in their four volumes of letters to each other. At the age of seventeen they were members of the same class at the Lycée Lakanal in Paris, to which they had come, Fournier from Solange, Rivière from Bordeaux, to prepare for higher studies. They were brought together by a sudden spontaneous enthusiasm when they heard a master read Henri de Régnier's *Tel qu'on songe*. Their joint exploration of literature began from that moment (it was the end of 1903).

They examined writer after writer together, training themselves for a creative and critical life as strenuously as Eliot, and the more consciously because they were French. Separated in 1905, they depended on letters for the communication of their discoveries — and thus they have provided us with what is, in effect, a map of the enthusiasms of the first decade of the century. We see them analyzing Rouault; confessing their doubts of Wagner and their admiration for him; reading *L'Immoraliste* and learning the salvation of scandal; reading Dostoyevsky; pushing into English (Fournier passed a season in grayest Chiswick), steeping themselves in Kipling, studying Wells, Hardy, Wilde. They were as intoxicated with Paris as any foreigner, because it was the capital of literature, and because their eyes selected from its attractions the "coins de rues éclairés, la nuit. Trottoirs déserts. Maisons, boîtes alignées avec leurs recoins, leurs lanternes . . ." — the seedy beauties discovered by the recent poets they and Eliot were adopting for models. Naturally, they had found the models a little earlier than he could, three thousand miles from France. At the date when he was submitting Tennysonian lyrics to the *Advocate,* they were turning the secondhand books on the quays for copies of *Ermitage,* the *Revue de Paris,* the *Revue Blanche,* for early work of Jammes, Claudel, Barrès, Ghéon, and for the twenty years dead Laforgue.

Laforgue and Transparency

Vincent Cronin, in his brilliant note on Eliot and the French, has suggested that only a foreigner could think of Laforgue as advanced in 1910; that in Paris he must have seemed already a little outmoded. Possibly; but he was still a cynosure. In the review pages of the early numbers of the *Nouvelle Revue Française,* the reviewers often remark his influence on young poets. Rivière and Fournier can be seen, in their correspondence

from 1905 to 1910, in the act of finding him and forming and
re-forming their attitudes. In 1905 Fournier excitedly adopted
him. Some months later he wavered, describing him as less
a master than a friend, pitiable "à cause de toutes les petitesses
dont il n'a pas su se dégager — à cause aussi de toutes les
choses dont il a cru qu'elles 'étaient arrivées': Paris, le moder-
nisme, le progrès, la poésie tuée par le progrès . . ." Then he
settled down to a steady appreciation. Epigraphs from Laforgue stand above some of his own poems. In the first
exchanges of 1905 and 1906 Rivière resisted Laforgue; complained that he was "pleurard et pédant"; preferred Maeterlinck and Barrès. But he yielded a little to Fournier's advocacy,
and, weighing Rimbaud and Laforgue against Verlaine, admitted that they were "plus poètes malgré tout, plus spontanés,
plus amples, plus visionnaires."

In a letter of January 22, 1906, Fournier attempted to say
what it was in Laforgue that seized him:

> Ce que j'ai cherché tout de suite avec passion chez Laforgue, et
> que j'ai trouvé, ce sont par instants, comment dire? des vers, des
> bribes de phrases qui étaient l'expression parfaite et poignante
> de quelque chose. Une vision, une impression sentie qui m'allait
> droit au coeur, en retrouver une autre à moi. J'avais l'impres-
> sion, à ces trouvailles (comme je voudrais l'avoir pour tout ce
> que j'écris) que ça n'était pas écrit comme le reste, tant c'était
> précis et senti. Peut-être étais-je si vivement et complètement
> saisi par l'impression, que j'en oubliais la vision même des mots
> et des lettres?

One poem, he said, sustained this effect from start to finish:
"Dimanche." The effect of this experience of Laforgue, and of
his skill, which was almost genius, in watching his own reaction
and generalizing from it, was that he now had an objective to
pursue in his writings: to describe whatever he described so
precisely and, strictly speaking, *sensationally*, that the reader

would experience it as if without the intervention of words
and page. The same point was still in his mind in a rather
different exchange with Rivière in 1910. On March 30, that
year, Rivière had arrived by an independent route at the intuition of a style which would persuade by its clarity:

> Je pense au style qu'il faudrait avoir la force d'écrire et que
> personne n'aura jamais le courage d'employer. C'est à peu près
> celui de Matthieu.

Fournier replied by quoting a phrase of Laforgue, "le style . . .
du français de Christ," and said that he too was seeking it.

Fournier's conception of the *impression sentie* was very close
to Eliot's later conception of the *transparent style*. In a lecture
at New Haven in 1933 Eliot said that he had "long aimed" at
transparency: "to write poetry . . . so transparent that we
should not see the poetry, but that which we are meant to see
through the poetry, poetry so transparent that in reading it
we are intent on what the poem *points at*, and not on the poetry." Now there is a passage of Joubert, quoted by Babbitt,
which emphasizes the danger that style may convert the reader's interest to itself and so distract him from reaching the object, to which it is meant to be merely the road. Conceivably
Babbitt's exposition of the French critics prompted Eliot to
the first inklings of the principle of transparency. But I would
like to think that Fournier first revealed it in their conversational reconnaissances; or, if not, that his experiences en-
dorsed Babbitt's teaching. I would like to suppose that, when
the two young poets compared their discovery of Laforgue,
Fournier analyzed his reactions as he had analyzed them to
Rivière, and that Eliot never forgot the lessons of the narrative.

Fournier was reported missing on the battlefront in the
second month of the Great War. He left, besides a few stories,
articles, and soft-fog-impressionist poems, one complete work,

the novel, *Le Grand Meaulnes*. It was in preparation while
Eliot was his pupil and companion (and the stage in which
a writer is contending with his material and method is sometimes the stage at which he says the most illuminating things
about it, at least if he is in the position where he is obliged to
talk and teach). It was published at the end of 1912. It is
predominantly a rural novel, which identifies the countryside
at once with youth, irretrievable, with an old, noble regime,
irretrievable, and with a pure dream, irrealizable. It is a
descant, sung by the France of 1910, on a poem of Baudelaire's:

> Mais le vert paradis des amours enfantines,
> Les courses, les chansons, les baisers, les bouquets,
> Les violons vibrant derrière les collines,
> Avec les brocs de vin, le soir, dans les bosquets,
> — Mais le vert paradis des amours enfantines,
>
> L'innocent paradis, plein des plaisirs furtifs,
> Est-il déjà plus loin que l'Inde ou que la Chine?
> Peut-on le rappeler avec des cris plaintifs,
> Et l'animer encore d'une voix argentine,
> L'innocent paradis plein de plaisirs furtifs?

Those two stanzas spoke to Fournier's generation. In 1907 Rivière found them echoing in his head, found himself saying
them aloud, after he had risen from reading Baudelaire. In the
autumn of 1910 Gide quoted them in his essay on Baudelaire
in the *N.R.F. Le Grand Meaulnes* was a vision of *l'innocent
paradis* and a parable of the vain attempt to recover it. Gide,
who first read the novel twenty years after its publication,
complained that the narrative is too long and tends to evaporate
in the later chapters. These weaknesses are real; as Gide saw,
they are almost implicit in the theme; all the same, *Le Grand
Meaulnes* leaves a reader with scenes and sensations he is not
likely ever quite to forget: the image of the mansion, the
rhythm of its antique festivities; the contrasting images, the

washing drying on the hedges, the rough wind, the fire-lit
room and the child, in the wonderful two pages that open the
marriage chapter; sensations of the schoolhouse, the village,
the country lanes. To that extent Fournier succeeded in writing
as he had wished and producing *impressions senties*.

Charles-Louis Philippe

In 1932 Eliot wrote a preface to an English translation of
Bubu de Montparnasse, the central work of Charles-Louis Philippe, which he read on arrival in France in 1910. As he looked
back at it after twenty-two years, he located its excellence
in its *impressions senties*. He did not use that phrase, but he
wrote in terms that remind us of it and of his own ideal of the
transparent style. Philippe's strength, he said, was to record
directly, without trying to be *un homme de lettres;* and in
Bubu, where he was at his best, he conveyed the sights, sounds,
pressures, and smells of the Boulevard de Montparnasse.

Bubu had been published in 1900; its author had died in
1909. In 1910, Eliot noticed, he was still "none too well-known"
even in his own country. But he had begun to reach his readers. Fournier first got hold of *Bubu* in 1908, and his immediate reaction was adverse. A bad book, he wrote to Rivière:
like Maeterlinck at his worst ruminating the fate of public
women. Three years later Rivière was defending it. He saw,
prevailing over the shortcomings, two notable qualities: the
originality of writing a novel about strictly simple people
"qui ne se dédoublent pas, qui ne se regardent pas"; and the
courage of representing the lives of prostitute and parasite:
"Jamais nous n'aurions eu le courage, nous, de traiter un pareil
sujet, s'il nous était venu! Tout ce que nous aurions craint,
toutes les excuses que nous nous serions trouvées. 'C'est trop
facile! C'est trop sentimental!' etc." And evidently Philippe
gradually persuaded both men; and gradually he invaded

Fournier's sensibility. Although *Le Grand Meaulnes* shows that his best gift lay in purity, in the far, clear voice of *l'innocent paradis*, Fournier began to experiment in the atmosphere of evil and its flowers. His story, "La Dispute," an alternate version of an episode in *Le Grand Meaulnes*, described an "odeur de sang corrompu, de femme malade," rising from the bed of the quarreling lovers. He played with fancies for a new novel, the urban counterpart of *Le Grand Meaulnes*, to be set in Paris instead of the countryside. From sketches, from the Paris chapters of the rural novel, and from glimpses of the city in the correspondence with Rivière, one can guess how he would have filled it with the taste of fog, the shining squares of windows, rain-wet benches, the violence of street quarrels, the intimations of a repugnant secret. It would have been an extension of *Bubu*, only softened — perhaps weakened, perhaps refined — by his compassion and by his delicacy.

During the early years of the *N.R.F.*, which had been launched in February 1909, the editors paid considerable attention to Philippe, evidently regarding his work as important. They devoted one issue exclusively to him; they published the *Lettres de Jeunesse* serially, the installments appearing during Eliot's year in France. Is it coincidence, or the sign of a general debt to the sensibility of the time, that "Prufrock," on which Eliot was engaged in Paris, displays the materials, colors, and mood of some striking sentences in the *Lettres?* Philippe tells of the pleasure, the mirror-pleasure of authors, of communing with his own composition, with the Marie he has created:

Il m'est si doux le soir de fumer la pipe en pensant à elle . . . Je me promène par ma chambre, j'ouvre la fenêtre, je vois le reflet rose du gaz sur le ciel et le haut de Notre-Dame et je pense aux pensées de Marie, et je l'ai là à côté de moi, et je me lis mes phrases et je leur souris . . .

That passage betrays the Philippe who wrote *Marie Donadieu*
to be, unlike the Philippe who wrote *Bubu*, a conscious *homme
de lettres;* but even so, the roofscape and skyscape are winsome
examples of urban beauty, and they may have penetrated Eliot
and passed into "Prufrock," and there become roofscape, street-
scene, and the smoke that rises from the pipes of lonely men in
shirtsleeves leaning out of windows.

In another letter Philippe bursts out with a strident impressionism:

> La Seine est un fleuve affreux, jaune sale, vert sale, souillé de
> mille immondices, et elle a l'air vicieux comme une de ces
> Parisiennes pourries et bien habillées que je déteste plus que
> toutes choses. Pendant qu'on respire le parfum des fleurs à la
> campagne, on respire à Paris l'odeur des égouts.

Eliot had too much respect for the neoclassical warning against
"viles couleurs éclatantes" to imitate that closely. Yet it is a
passage likely to have caught the eye of an unimmunized Puritan, consciously exposing himself, Wendell's *Literary History*
in mind, to the aura of European corruption. Certainly Eliot
found *égouts* (which he no doubt encountered elsewhere as
well as here) a desirable property for his poems; they recur in
his work of this period: "the cat which flattens itself in the gutter," "you heard the sparrows in the gutters," "poking the peev-
ish gutter." But later in life, when the gutter, pipes, and lamp-
light had been dropped from his poems, he may still have
remembered Philippe's passage, or not so much the passage as
the experience of Philippe's violent image of the Seine merging with the river within him, the Mississippi at St. Louis, and
the confluence of the two visions, Philippe's and his own, may
have generated the energy for passages of "The Dry Salvages."

Even in the first process of assimilating the material and
methods of the Paris of 1910, Eliot simplified and tranquillized
them. Grover Smith has pointed out a possible connection be-

tween a phrase in Philippe's *Marie Donadieu,* "des odeurs de filles publiques mêlées à des odeurs de nourriture," and

> Smells of chestnuts in the streets
> And female smells in shuttered rooms.

If the English passage is really indebted to the French, how well the poet has reorganized the material. And what Eliot did with the French sensibility in the course of ten or eleven years is clear if we compare the dingy beauties of the "Preludes" and "Prufrock" with the dingy urban beauties of *The Waste Land.* The whole of *The Waste Land,* as a cry and a prayer for the modern metropolis, depends on the city sensibility of the French, and represents an ultimate fulfillment of it in one direction. But the details of *The Waste Land* refine superbly on the French details from which they grew. The image of the typist's underclothes drying in the sun's last rays is more surprising, more exact, more uncompromising and everyday, than the softly lit images of lights and windows in Philippe's *Lettres* or in "Prufrock." And if we invite still later works to the same comparison, the process of refinement appears the sharper. The *ifs,* which throng Fournier's poems, occur once in Eliot — suddenly, momentarily — in *Ash-Wednesday.* The fog of the French poets and "Prufrock" becomes in *Marina* the purer coastal fog through which the woodthrush sings, and that in turn becomes "The fog is in the fir trees" in "The Dry Salvages." The end is utterly simple and perfect. But in putting it this way I may seem to belittle the early methods, and that I would not do. Certainly we have to praise Eliot for an advance: for advancing from the sensibility of 1910 which he shared with a number of other creative minds to a new sensibility, to which he alone has awakened the world. It is a remarkable thing to have done this; to do it is perhaps one of the distinctions of a great poet. But seen in the longer perspective, the work he did in 1910 is no less beautiful than the work of later years; in all his styles he gives us something that we would not wish to be without.

Claudel

Rivière and Fournier were enthusiastic readers of Paul Claudel. In a reply to E. J. H. Greene, Eliot said that Alain-Fournier prescribed Claudel's *Art poétique, Connaissance de l'Est,* and the early plays for their lessons. This sounds a positive beginning. But he added that after 1911 he read Claudel little and without attention, and Greene thought the addition decisive and left Claudel unconsidered in his admirable thesis on French influences on Eliot. But could *any* incipient poet in Paris that year, reading the *N.R.F.* in which *l'Otage* appeared serially, and studying Claudel for lessons, emerge from the process uninstructed?

Rivière had first come across Claudel's name in the *Mercure* in 1906. After a long resistance to the announcements of *l'Arbre, l'Agamemnon d'Eschyle,* and *Connaissance de l'Est,* he had opened a copy of *l'Arbre* in a bookshop, and "tout debout je lus, au milieu du bruit, les premières pages. Elles me donnèrent une impression d'étrangeté et de vastitude incomparables." He read the five hundred difficult pages in a week, not understanding all of it, but "cela est pour moi une des choses les plus passionantes, les plus profondes et les plus belles que j'aie jamais lues. Oh! mon ami, cela est vrai que c'est plus grand que Dante." He saw a danger in the style: it gave the effect of a translation, for the thought seemed to struggle for expression. But there, on reflection, lay the truth of the style: "La pensée n'est pas cet éclair dont parlent les gens pour qui Zola ou Faguet sont les penseurs. La pensée est une chose obscure, pénible, s'efforçant avec lenteur et peine, pareille à la germination" — which is a just reaction to the effort and the marvel in Claudel. Fournier was deep in *l'Arbre* and *Tête d'Or* at the beginning of 1906, and found him superb in "les immenses laïus sans raison apparente, les images très précises, brutales toujours, belles souvent, qui arrivent encore sans raison apparente." In April Fournier was a little less sure: the weight of Claudel's incomprehensibility was depressing his enthusiasm. But a week or two later he took up *La Jeune Fille Violaine* and reread it in an evening at his school desk, pausing over every difficult line till he had accounted for it: "Je lisais à haute voix, je parlais selon les indications des lignes, je prenais les attitudes lorsque c'était plus difficile, et je comprenais tout." The first reading of *Violaine*, he says, is an astonishing and *âpre* experience, but *Violaine* read a second time is a precious event renewed, and now when the book is put down, the story, the ideas, recede but the lovely phrases stay and call out in the mind: "Voix-de-la-Rose cause dans le soir d'argent."

How permanently Claudel lodged in Fournier's mind can be seen from an incident of two years later. Early in spring, 1908, Fournier was summoned to army maneuvers in the forest of Maisons-Laffitte. In charge of sentries, he roused himself in the middle of the night, called the relief, and led the men through the dark of the wood, slithering over plashy earth. He was only half awake, irritable, disgusted. But suddenly

qu'on entend, sur les plus hautes branches, un rossignol. Puis un autre, au plus profond du bois. Ravissement. Appel. Rire et plénitude de l'espoir. *Eucharis m'a dit que c'était le printemps.* C'est sa voix au fond du jardin. *Voix de la Rose chante.* Et c'est comme une cruche fraîche qu'on avale, l'été, c'est un éclat de rire dans le bois, ce sont comme des coups de serpette sur des branches de lilas pleines de pluie, puis l'égouttement de leur rosée dans la buée de deux heures du matin, la nuit où le printemps doit venir!

The phrases from *Violaine* that he and Rivière quoted to each other two years back had become part of his life — as poetry will become part of the life of a young man who reads with all his powers committed to the dramatizing.

It would have been hard to sit opposite Fournier in 1910, to explore poetry with him, and to examine Claudel under his guidance, without receiving some stir from this passion.

These lines from the second act of *l'Otage:*

> Et me voilà, gardant à la fois l'amour de l'ordre
> et l'instinct de la précaution,
>   Avec le nez du chien de chasse qui reconnaît
> son gibier.

or Sygne's speech in the first act:

> La valeur de chaque terre étudiée et de chaque coin de chaque terre, le prix du blé et du vin, et de la pierre à bâtir, et du plâtre, et du bois, et de la journée de femme et d'homme.

These "paragraphs," and many others which one might quote from Claudel, bear a pictorial resemblance to the paragraphs of certain of Eliot's choruses — the seventh chorus and the final chorus of *The Rock*, for example, and the chorus "I have smelt them" and the final chorus of *Murder in the Cathedral*. There is a structural resemblance in the succession of images. There is sometimes, and this is more intimate, a likeness of kind between the images of the two poets. When Eliot writes of

> Our brains unskinned like the layers of an onion

his image has the joint strength and humility of the earth and the household in Claudel's way. His paragraph

> I have lain on the floor of the sea and breathed with the breathing of the sea-anemone, swallowed with the ingurgitation of the sponge. I have lain in the soil and criticized the worm . . .

has the "vastitude" that Rivière found in Claudel, Claudel's sense of the organic life of all creatures on the face of the globe. Claudel will gather a group of images which represent, with a sort of authoritative compassion, with a note which seems to say "This is harsh, but it is good," the basic toil of man. Eliot does it, too, in *The Rock* and *Murder in the Cathedral.* And in those two plays Eliot's vocabulary is often startling, magistral, and yet right, as Claudel's is.

Eliot has passed through a cycle of interest in internal rhyme, mastery of it, and discontinuance of it. Some of the rich and ecstatic passages of *Ash-Wednesday* depend on it. In *The Rock* it is used elaborately. In *Murder in the Cathedral* it has its moments

> What sign of the spring of the year?
> Only the death of the old: not a stir, not a shoot, not a breath

but is used sparingly. Perhaps it is the more effective when used sparingly, for if it charms the ear, and if, in a building drama, like *The Rock,* it seems to mortice and miter, it can soon cloy (though more quickly for a reader than for a listener). I point out this sequence with the thought that here too there may be a resemblance between Eliot and Claudel. Claudel is, when he wishes, a master of internal rhyme:

> Que j'entende seulement dans le clair-de-lune une voix
> de femme éclatante,
> Puissante et grave, persuasive et suave . . .

The lines are from his "Cantate à trois Voix," and were quoted in Henri Ghéon's long, explanatory review in the *N.R.F.* of June 1913. I choose them because we know that Eliot possessed a copy of that issue of the *N.R.F.*; the copy now stands, his signature on the cover, in the stacks of the Widener Library.

Henri Ghéon called attention to a characteristic of Clau-

del's verse: a *bondissement intérieur,* a sudden movement
forward, a sudden *gaie et pure chanson.* That compelling effect also occurs in Eliot: "And the lost heart stiffens and
rejoices . . ." Even more rapidly than internal rhyme, it is liable to forfeit its effect if it is ventured too often, and Eliot
has been reserved in its use.

Had Eliot never read Claudel, the resemblances — the most
decisive of which is the pictorial shape, this being not merely
pictorial but expressive of a rhythm, a great and powerful
phrasing — would be coincidental: two minds working in the
same age, both attracted to order and authority, both sensitive
and humane, and independently finding the same mode of
speech. But since Eliot read Claudel in 1910, by which date
Claudel had formed his style and he had not, it is most
tempting to believe that, no matter how much he resisted
Claudel and declined to study his later work, he learned from
him.

There was a new poet appearing in the *N.R.F.* who had also
apparently learned something from Claudel:

> La tête du poisson ricane
>   entre les pis du chat crevé qui gonfle — vert ou
> mauve? — Le poil, couleur d'écaille, est misérable,
> colle,
>   comme la mèche que suce une très vieille petite
> fille osseuse, aux mains blanches de lèpre.

The Caribbean colors are the poet's own, perhaps the movement, too, but the paragraphs suggest Claudel (and is it fanci-
ful to think that the *mains blanches de lèpre* recall Violaine?).
The poet, at that date using the signature Saintléger Léger,
was St-John Perse. In his mature *Anabase,* which Eliot translated in the mid-twenties, the pictorial organization of his
pages still suggests how he had built on Claudel, though the
voice and the myth are entirely his own.

If Eliot owed something to Claudel, why did he turn away and neglect his writing after the 1914 war? Presumably through the influence of two powerful critics. Pound was attacking Claudel for "fake-bigotry" in 1918; attacking him as "ninth-rate" in 1927. Benda, who may have influenced Pound's attitude, made a series of assaults in *Belphégor*. Benda's severe, cold, and imposing view we shall consider shortly. Perhaps it was the decisive influence in Eliot's long disregard of Claudel.

The disregard was long, but not final. In 1960, introducing Michael Hamburger's edition of Hofmannsthal's poetic plays, Eliot named Hofmannsthal, Yeats, and Claudel as "the three men who did most, in the same age, to maintain and re-animate verse drama — in German, English, and French respectively."

Jacques Rivière

In the critical essays of Rivière, whom he visited once in Paris, and of whom he must have heard a great deal from Fournier, Eliot recognized a fault from which he himself was free and a power that he had not himself attained. The fault? Rivière was "a little too partial." Copeland had been struck by the harshness of the undergraduate Eliot, who was the perspicacious observer of error and inadequacy and their ruthless delineator and proud of it. Rivière always found the virtues in writing. Rivière's central experience had been the moment of his mother's death when he was ten. She had summoned her last reserves to live till he came home from afternoon school and say goodbye to him. His piercing sense of her love for him had ripened his capacity for love. In his essays and reviews he could never be pleased to score over his subject by indicating faults, even though he had all the French skill in detecting them and would do it when the case obliged. Rather he extended his reserves to discover and cherish merit. He was supreme in his sympathy.

With the readiness to find beauty went, Eliot thought, a slightly confused indiscipline, the lack of a theoretical foundation, and only with maturity did precision come to reinforce Rivière's suppleness and finesse. But in the same obituary tribute in which he made this point, Eliot acknowledged, with a concession which itself is a legacy from Rivière —

> Pour un esprit comme le mien, trop disposé à mesurer toutes choses selon des règles d'une conception dogmatique qui tendrait de plus en plus à devenir rigide et formelle, la méthode critique employée par Rivière est une excellente discipline.

That is, Eliot needed the discipline of Rivière's "indiscipline"; his courage in entering a work without preliminary examination of his equipment, in experiencing it on his nerves; his gift for seeing the intellectual consequences of the experience. Eliot loves art no less excitedly than Rivière. But as a critic he finds it easiest to communicate his excitement in the disguise of justifying and correcting it. Gibbon, before he wrote a chapter of history, used to walk round the garden reviewing all he knew about the topic in hand. Eliot, before he sits down to report on a writer, reconsiders his theoretical position on the kind of work his man writes, and places the man in relation to the theory. He is committed to the Whole. The authority of his page is due to this procedure. We feel the compass and control of his mind. But the method is highly schematized, and there may be moments when we recoil from it. Moreover, Babbitt and the neoclassicists said that criticism organizes works of art in a hierarchy of values, and he has worked to establish the hierarchy for his century, with the penalty that sometimes he has appeared to be what Rivière called, speaking of contemporary critics in general, a *marchand de valeur*. Is this to admit that, though he descried the merits of Rivière's indiscipline, he was unable to assimilate them? No example of uncharted voyaging, however felicitous, could wholly change him, so deeply rooted is his critical procedure in his Puritan temperament; but indeed he not only saw, with his sense of the excellent and his modesty, the felicity of Rivière and the perils of his own formalism, but strove to be a little freer, and sometimes succeeded.

Diction, Pitch, and Measure

In a study contributed to the *N.R.F.* in December 1910, Rivière analyzed Baudelaire's diction. Claudel had once said that Baudelaire's style was "un extraordinaire mélange du style racinien, et du style journaliste de son temps." From that position Rivière went on to consider the range of Baudelaire's vocabulary — nothing excluded, he said — and the intent of his deployment of it: now he would deliberately choose a feeble word; now he would take a bizarre word, and by assimilating it control it and remake it. "Il cherche d'abord les termes les plus éloignés; puis il les ramène, il les apaise, il leur infuse une propriété qu'on ne leur connaissait pas." Baudelaire's poetry represented the collaboration of all the words of the language:

> Les plus rares y sont pris avec les plus familiers,
> les plus humbles avec les plus hardis. Mais plongés
> dans le sur et délicat mouvement de l'ensemble,
> aucun ne surprend . . .

Again and again in his criticism Eliot has examined the way in which the poet struggles for a diction at once his own and his readers', a diction which both draws from the reservoir of the living language and supplies the reservoir; and sometimes he has made his best poetry out of his attempts to define "the sentence that is right." I do not want to seem to suggest that Rivière's article was Eliot's first summons to the problem, nor the first hint he received of the "easy commerce of the old and the new." It seems possible that an earlier forerunner of Eliot's definition was the sentence of Sainte-Beuve describing ". . . un style nouveau sans néologisme, nouveau et antique, aisément contemporain de tous les âges . . ." But this much may be said: that some of the best minds in Paris in 1910 were actively aware of critical and technical problems which were to preoccupy Eliot and were formulating solutions comparable with those at which he eventually arrived.

André Gide, in an article printed the month before Rivière's, claimed that a beauty of Baudelaire's poetry lay in the moderation of his pitch. Laforgue, who had advanced to his own peculiar soliloquizing half-voice from the study of Baudelaire, had observed that Baudelaire "se raconta sur un mode modéré de confessionnal et ne prit pas l'air inspiré," and had praised it as a great innovation. Gide quoted Laforgue with approval but added that Baudelaire had, in fact, a predecessor: Racine. Corneille and Hugo used all their voice, but Racine and Baudelaire "parlent à mi-voix; de sorte que nous les écoutons longuement." Thus France possessed a tradition of the moderated pitch, and a contemporary writer might renew it — and at this point Gide cited Barrès:

> C'est par les *Fleurs du Mal*, peut-être, que nous reviendrons à la grande tradition classique, appropriée sans doute à l'esprit moderne, mais dédaigneuse des viles couleurs éclatantes et de toutes les sauvageries plastiques, convaincue que l'intellectuel s'honore d'être discret, et rêvant d'exprimer en termes clairs et nuancés des choses obscures et toutes les subtilités intimes.

If Eliot read the article, he must have been struck by this quotation which chimed with Babbitt's call to classicism, and by the whole argument, which made clear to him that Laforgue had taught him the use of his own speech — the low-pitched, understating speech of New England — by demonstrating the development to a fine point of a classical tradition.

Gide also spoke of the music of Baudelaire's poetry and emphasized that a poet represents otherwise indefinable emotions by the specific musicality of his verses. If this does not sound very unusual, it is because critics, and Eliot foremost of them, have been at pains to repeat it for fifty years. It must be among the considerations Eliot has kept in mind in his protests against the translation or paraphrase of poetry which is often tendered as a substitute for criticism. What prose cannot do, and the poet can only do by the utmost manipulation of language in obedience to rhythm, it is absurd for the critic to try to do in prose.

In *La Grande Revue,* a periodical scarcely equal to the *N.R.F.* but possibly of interest to Eliot because Fournier published in it, there appeared on May 10, 1911, an article by Jules Romains, "La réforme technique du théâtre en vers." It was Romains' contribution to a current controversy ("Cette question a été vivement débattue depuis un mois"). In the course of his argument he made the same point which Eliot later made in English: a masterpiece exhausts a form. Because Racine used alexandrines and rhymes every poet-dramatist had felt obliged to use them. In fact, Racine's form could no longer be useful precisely because it had been perfectly used: "Tout chef d'oeuvre *épuise* dans une certaine mesure la technique qu'il emploie." Playwrights faced the question which confronted composers after Beethoven: to accept a technique already fully exploited, or to create a new technique?

What medium might serve a new French poet for his plays? Romains contrasted the comic effect of this line

Qu'on se hâte, là-bas, de fermer la portière

which constrains a normal phrase into an alexandrine, and the normal phrase carried directly in an octosyllabic line

Fermez la portière là-bas!

"Les mots familiers, dans le rythme familier" were no more comic on the stage than in the street, and he recommended their adoption, together with the four-beat line which lent itself to them. For passages of abnormal excitement the beats might be increased or decreased (not line by line but mass by mass, since "chaque rythme, pour être effectif, pour imposer sa présence à l'oreille et à l'esprit du spectateur, doit agir par masse"). Nine-syllabled verses might be suitable for incertitude; ten-syllabled, cut by the caesura, for pathos; five-syllabled or seven-syllabled for tension. Very occasionally the alexandrine might be interposed for solemn declarations, lyric bursts, epic evocation.

No rhymes at all ("sinon pour effet local"). The constant use of rhyme in dialogue produced *physical monotony*. The use of rhyme in the past had been harmonic; the new poet must develop in his own way "toute une famille d'*accords.*"

It is interesting to compare the article with the theorizing of Percy MacKaye, and with his experiment in the four-beat line for the induction of *Sappho and Phaon*. On both sides of the Atlantic poets were struggling for a poetry closer to speech. But it was one thing to recognize the need; another thing to invent the answer. MacKaye's attempt and Romains' both seem slight. To compare the solution Eliot found forty years later, to listen to his dramatic poetry which is apparently conversation, yet which is ballet, too, an exquisitely delicate beat sounding through it, is to realize how resourceful and supple his mind is, and with what concord the theoretician and the nervous creator have worked together in him.

Quatrains

In England in the Great War years Pound and Eliot came to the conclusion that

the dilutation of *vers libre*, Amygism, Lee Masterism, general floppiness had gone too far and that some counter-current must

be set going . . . Remedy prescribed "Émaux et Camées" . . .
Rhymes and regular strophes.

Result: Poems in Mr. Eliot's *second* volume not contained in
his first "Prufrock" (*Egoist,* 1917), also "H. S. Mauberly."

Other examples may have combined with Gautier's to guide
Eliot to his anfractuous quatrains. In Paris he had read, he told
E. J. H. Greene, a volume of André Salmon. Among Salmon's
poems are a number of quatrains in the hard, piquant style:

> C'est une blonde au front ridé
> Dont les seins aux pointes fleuries
> D'onguents et de fards sont bridés
> Par un vieux corset de féerie

and

> Rosine est seule. Un peu de bleu
> Autour des yeux. Un peu de rose
> Sur la joue et dans les cheveux,
> Bijou convulsif, une rose.

Some of Salmon's verses, and the pages of such a magazine as
Soirées de Paris, founded in 1912, with Apollinaire, Billy, Dalize,
Tudesq and Salmon himself on the editorial board, show that
the French had addressed themselves to the formal exercises,
and to the sculptured, almost cubist, effects which these
favored, some time before Pound saw the advantages of the
method for English writers. This is not to detract from the importance of Pound's suggestion. So unfamiliar was the hard
style in the England of the day that the shock produced by the
experiments was tremendous. And Eliot himself had apparently not realized, until Pound made the suggestion, that the
style he had met in France could be practiced in English.

I wonder whether Eliot's curiosity about Salmon had been
first aroused by some pleasant sentences of Henri Franck's in
the *N.R.F.* of September 1910. Reviewing *Le Calumet* Franck
pointed out that Salmon derived from Laforgue. This, I sup-

pose, would have been enough to claim Eliot's attention for the volume. The review begins:

> Un rossignol chante la nuit, dans un bosquet de Prague, mais non loin d'un café bien éclairé, où l'on joue des danses de Brahms.

When Eliot was at work on his strophes, were many thoroughly buried and apparently "forgotten" pleasures of the Paris year mobilized and laid under contribution? And did this scene, by which Franck sought to characterize Salmon's sensibility, blend with many other, and perhaps more important, associations to constitute the scenario of "Sweeney among the Nightingales"?

It may be that even much flimsier work, work of which he could not particularly approve, had something to suggest to Eliot in his state of Parisian receptivity. In *Figaro* of January 30, 1911, under the rubric *La Vie Littéraire*, Marcel Ballot reviewed a book of poems, *Par Vents et Marées*, by Mme. Lucie Delarue-Mardrus, a lady who had already published four volumes of poetry and four novels and had another novel in the press (and was to be represented in later editions of an anthology Eliot had used at Harvard, *Poètes d'aujourd'hui*). Her febrile poetry lacked innovatory techniques, hardness, sharpness . . . but it was poetry of the coast and the "pèqueux d'Honfleur," and tried, said Ballot, to give a voice to the "pauvres bougres" who live from the sea and die on it:

Pour eux, elle dira "l'Oraison" à Notre-Dame-de-Grâce

> Tout ce peuple salé lève vers toi les yeux,
> Sainte Vierge de mer, madone un peu sirène . . .

et le dévot "Chant de bourrasque" et le "Refrain de la cloche de brume" au rythme si obsédant, au si anxieux appel; pour eux elle chantera le plaintive "Ballade du pêcheur noyé," dont le corps, ramené par le flot, va reposer en terre sainte, mais "dont l'âme reste à la mer" . . .

Honfleur is a French counterpart of Gloucester. Did the review strike a casual American reader? Did he, seeing what Mme. Delarue-Mardrus had done and what she had failed to do, glimpse what he might do with her subject?

Classicism and the French — 1913

Although he had sometimes wondered whether it might be agreeable to settle in Paris permanently and write in French, Eliot returned to America on the completion of his year, and in September 1911 was back at Harvard beginning the preparatory work for a doctorate. To keep in touch with the French, he subscribed to the *N.R.F.*, and continued to learn from them through its pages. The issues of the first half of 1913 appear, to an observer who reads them today with the advantages of hindsight, particularly distinguished. I shall speak of two articles of that time in the belief that they may have been significant to Eliot.

One was a study of Charles Maurras, whose work Eliot had already encountered in 1910. He was the fierce critic of the nineteenth century and hated the industrial plutocracy and the intellectual anarchy to which he maintained it had given rise. He looked back with regret to the order and harmony of the France of the sixteenth and seventeenth centuries. He was possessed by a grand image of Europe's civilizing tradition: it had originated in Greece, emigrated to Rome, marched with the legions into France, ramified with the Roman colonists alike into Spain and up the Rhine; it was best preserved in France, and the health of Europe lay in its development around the French massif. In his book of 1905, *L'Avenir de l'intelligence*, which Eliot was to name in 1926 as an example of the classical spirit in full play, he drew a terrifying picture of the mind reduced, if the trends of the nineteenth century persisted, to total servility or hungry isolation; and then offered, in three last missionary pages, the hope that the dangers might be forefended by the "Counter-Revolution" — this is the book's ultimate word. A counterrevolution might bring about a fourth *moment privilégié*, a successor to the perfect moments of Greece, Rome, and classical France. His doctrine of the *moment privilégié* was adopted by Eliot, and indeed, we may say, cherished by him, for it is evident that meditation and love have gone into the definition, or redefinition, of it given in the *Criterion:* a moment precious in the eye of God for the balance it strikes between the eternal and the temporal. For many years, certainly for thirty years, Eliot continued reading Maurras' books and elaborating his thoughts; he has constantly affirmed his respect for him; and to a pamphleteer who urged in 1928 that Maurras led his disciples away from Christianity, he answered: "Upon me he has had exactly the opposite effect."

The author of the *N.R.F.* study of 1913 was Albert Thibaudet, by birth a Burgundian, by profession a teacher of philosophy and occupant of a chair at Geneva. A writer who surveyed in the course of his life a hundred topics from Thucydides to Bergson, and who was a figure genial in his affection for food and wine and the arts, Thibaudet interpreted Maurras' "aesthetic of the three traditions" in his customary style: sympathetically, as if from inside, but with a descant of corrections and addenda. His article was worth Eliot's reading.

Here in the discussion of Brunetière was an interpretation of seventeenth-century man who "vivait sur deux registres, et naïvement et puissament: celui du monde, celui de la religion." Here, cogently summarized, was Maurras' legend of the high points of the cultures of Greece, Rome, and France, and his claim that France "après Rome, plus que Rome, incorpora la règle à l'instinct, l'art à la nature, la pensée à la vie." Here was a statement of classicism, more beautiful than Babbitt's: "Le secret de la culture classique est justement dans une force consciente qui discerne, hiérarchise, discipline." Here was a justification of the process of "hierarchizing": that it leads, not to the dismissal of all but the writer at the apex, but to the clarification, and therefore to the accentuation, of the interest of the writers lower down the pyramid. Here was Maurras' doctrine of the institution: "Par elle l'homme s'éternise; son acte bon se continue." And there was attached to this article, in an editorial footnote which connects the second installment with the first, a formulation of the three traditions as *classique, catholique, monarchique* — pointing to Eliot's famous description of himself, in 1928, as classicist in art, Anglican in religion, royalist in politics.

From Maurras Eliot imbibed encouragement for his Jamesian foible, his love of converse with the aristocrats. (No one, he says, in an unexpected, significant application of it, can understand Confucius without a long frequentation of the best Chinese society.) Thibaudet pointed out that the word classic is associated with rank, with the Roman *classici,* and with the standards of conduct and the urbanity that are at once the hereditary possession and the responsibility of families of rank. Powerful originality may be the prime requisite of the poet, but it must be accompanied by a transforming felicity, which may be called, as we please, either classical or aristocratic:

Il y faut certain recul d'antiquité; il y faut une politesse, une modération, une mesure, une pudeur, par lesquelles l'excellent se présente sans s'offrir, se dévoile sans s'imposer; il y faut le commerce avec les grands, avec ses pairs, je veux dire la marque des autres classiques, le signe qu'on les fréquente, qu'on est reçu chez eux, et qu'on rapporte un peu de leurs paroles et de leurs présents; il y faut sur la générosité d'un coeur ardent et d'un sang riche la visible discipline de l'honneur; il y faut enfin cette chance, cette bonne fortune, cette εὐτυχία que demande le Grec [Aristotle], cette heureuse rencontre d'un temps propice, d'une langue fraîche, d'un prince au nom fait pour désigner un siècle et l'ordonner comme un État. Il y faut tout cela, et, si l'on réfléchit, rien de tout cela n'est exceptionnel dans l'humanité. C'est de cela même que sont faits une classe noble, des *classici* politiques, une saine aristocratie.

This was perfectly attuned to Eliot's temperament; and he took it as a touchstone in questions of art and social organization alike; and he ignored Thibaudet's comment, made in restraint of Maurras, that it was applicable only to art. (Yet for all his maintenance of the social tastes of James under the disguise of the rectitude of Arnold, he has recognized, fought for, and published men outside the charmed circle: Joyce, D. H. Lawrence, James Hanley, A. E. Coppard, Dylan Thomas. And he has continued to respect and champion them if, like D. H. Lawrence, they were not merely born outside it but willfully insisted on remaining outside it and hating, and discouraging the acquisition of, its graces. Part of Eliot's excellence is his capacity to defy his predilections.)

In the eyes of the neoclassicists, the nineteenth century had placed an inordinate value on the uninhibited representation of the passions. With characteristic generosity Thibaudet said little about their destructive critique, and lent his powers to eliciting the beauty inherent in their call for order. All art depends on the passions. But the mere representation of passion is not yet art. "Rien n'est vraiment notre ouvrage, qui n'ait été conquis sur nos passions, qui ne les ait ployées à un ordre . . ." Thibaudet differentiated three ways in which the passions may be directed into art:

they may be mastered by the will;

they may be broken, annulled, and buried by "la juste nécessité" and the serene laws of order;

they may be sublimated in intelligence and become radiance, pardon and peace.

The third is the way of lyric and is the glory of romantic poetry at its best (and here Thibaudet went beyond Maurras and corrected him). The first two ways are essentially dramatic: Corneille used the first, Racine the second. Under the guidance of the French neoclassicists, Eliot has long taken the view that "a good poem, for instance, is not an outburst of pure feeling, but is the result of a more than common power of controlling and manipulating feelings." It is interesting to consider *The Cocktail Party* in the light of Thibaudet's analysis. *The Cocktail Party* is a tragedy (and in saying this I am not forgetting that the title page calls it a comedy) of the mastering of the passions. We are human observers of the events, and few of us are celibate, fewer saints, and it is natural for us to grieve for Celia's lost relationship with Edward. But in the light, and what we feel to be the rebuke, of her religious sublimation, we blame our grief, and perhaps it stays repressed and rankling and misunderstood. Thibaudet's argument can put us on the right terms with it. We were meant to feel the human grief; Eliot himself felt it; unless it is felt, the classical quality of Celia's choice goes unvalued, and the very drama goes unappreciated. As Thibaudet saw, the struggle to master passion is the stuff of drama, and every success in mastering it is tragic as well as triumphant, for something is lost in the subordination of passion even though something greater is gained. Eliot's assimilation of the neoclassicist teaching into his theatre demonstrates that a theory may sometimes lead to a work of art. It is rare; the course almost always runs the other way, that is, the writer educes his theory from his practice; but sometimes, when a mind like Eliot's is at work, this reversal of the familiar order may take place and a high beauty result.

Thibaudet made the point: "Une littérature classique ne saurait naître d'une autre dans la même langue." A new Western classicism might spring up in France by a new return to the Greeks, or elsewhere by the fertilization of another language from the French. If Eliot saw that passage, he must have been delighted by its confirmation of his experience. Fertilization, Thibaudet went on, does not mean imitation: ". . . nul art ne prête moins à l'imitation que le classique." The genuine neo-classicist has to acquire the spirit of classicism. So Eliot urged: if the severe and serene control of the emotions by Reason "approaches or even suggests the Greek ideal, so much the better: but it must inevitably be very different." Thibaudet offered one technical hint for the practicing neoclassicist: "le caractère le plus exquis et le plus profond d'une langue classique c'est de maintenir un certain équilibre entre la langue parlée et la langue écrite qui se trouvent présentes l'une dans l'autre, bornées et disciplinées l'une par l'autre." This is the definition which we have heard Gide and Rivière enunciating in 1910, providing Eliot with a principle by which he was to re-examine the English poets and the progress of English criticism and which he was to honor in practice with a perpetually renewed struggle. And he has been anxious that critics should recognize that a poet composing is principally occupied with diction, and should occupy themselves with it when they judge a poet; therefore his appeal for "more attention to the correctness of expression, to the clarity or obscurity, to the grammatical precision or inaccuracy, to the choice of words . . . of our verse."

An important article by Rivière, *Le Roman d'Aventure*, appeared serially in the *N.R.F.* of May, June, and July 1913. This famous essay is impregnated with the spirit of the new classicism. Symbolism had done all it could for the time being, and should be avoided. It was time to give up private communication and cultivate universal appeal, to give up ambiguity and practice clarity. The writer should observe Descartes' four principles: (1) take nothing for true unless you know it; (2) analyze and synthesize the elements of your thought; (3) survey the field thoroughly; be sure you have missed nothing; (4) leave nothing incomplete. "Ce sont les grands principes de l'honnêteté littéraire (et peut-être aussi de l'honnêteté morale)," said Rivière. He added, with a characteristically supple check on his own thought, that the artist has not quite the same concerns as Descartes: "nous exigeons de cette oeuvre, non pas qu'elle soit vraie, mais qu'elle soit belle."

Most striking is a passage in which, turning to music, Rivière recommended the renunciation of the nineteenth-century symphonic method by which emotions were collated, accumulated, and intensified into crises. Bach had carefully separated emotions and had expressed each in its purity. The new classicist should imitate Bach in his regularity, in his *propreté magnifique*, in his *formes fixes et définies*. And the poet? —

> dans un beau poème, il n'y a jamais de progression; la fin est toujours au même niveau que le commencement . . .

We may question whether this will be found applicable to every good poem. But it described what the French exponents of the short poems in quatrains — *formes fixes et définies* — were already doing, and what Pound and Eliot would be doing four years later. And it was a remarkable forecast of what would happen, alike in poetry and music, during the next forty years.

When Benda attacked the *N.R.F.*, and almost everybody else, for "émotivisme," Rivière replied, in an article of 1919, that even before the war the periodical had worked "à défendre et à faire valoir les vertus intellectuelles en art":

> si quelqu'un a travaillé à désembourber la littérature du symbolisme, à la faire sortir du lyrisme pur et inarticulé, à rendre de la faveur aux genres qui exigent du raisonnement, de la composition et de l'artifice, c'est bien nous . . . Quand l'art intellectualiste, aujourd'hui en bouton, se sera complètement épanoui, on s'apercevra que nous en avons été les précurseurs véritables . . .

The issues of 1913 justify him.

Benda

Julien Benda was often wrong. He said that the great art of
the past had mirrored, unlike our own, the disinterested intellect; whereas it includes the gross and beautiful flattery of
Mutanabbi, the partisan Protestantism of Spenser, the money-
making stage strokes of Shakespeare. He said that art had always neglected man's struggle for the very staple of life;
whereas it includes, side by side with their conflicting pleasure
in the energy of life, the humanity of Chaucer, Fielding, Van
Gogh. He said that true art was always unpopular, whereas the
mixed crowd in the Globe held its breath when Brutus and
Cassius were at sword points.

He was often wrong, but even when he was wrong he was
magnificent. His diamond attitude, hard and clear, compelled
Eliot. Eliot has always honored the noncompromisers of his
time: Babbitt, the quixotic Pound, the truculent Wyndham
Lewis, the lonely and self-assured Joyce, and Benda — Benda,
to whom isolation was so much the essence of virtue that he
rounded on other neoclassicists, like Maurras, and exposed
their faults, and branded in advance his own friends and followers who would "clap the hand to the sword-hilt, strike the
Castilian attitude, and shout 'I am a classicist!'" (Of these
men and of Eliot we may say the same thing: that it helps an
artist to feel embattled against the world; it helps him if he discovers one or two friends committed to the same struggle; it
helps him if he can see in them not only his allies but his competitors, not only his competitors but his critics, not only his critics
but his superiors, by whose merits he is chastened and incited.)

Eliot praised the "formal beauty" in Benda's work. Benda's
paragraphs are terse, pure; reading them one has an intuition
of the rational, intellectual aesthetic which they advocate. In
1911 some of his work was appearing in the *Cahiers de la Quin-*

zaine, with which Eliot was acquainted, but whether he read it there, or whether it yet made an impression on him, I do not know. Babbitt did not include Benda in the list of critics appended to *The Masters of Modern Criticism* in 1912. In 1913 Gilbert Cannan translated *L'Ordination* as *The Yoke of Pity.* But Eliot gives Pound the credit for making Benda known to the Anglo-Saxon world. And it is understandable that Pound admired the cold, beautiful force of Benda's work and recognized how salutary it might be to English criticism. *Belphégor* appeared in 1918. Looking back ten years later, Eliot remembered how "some of us recognized [it] as an almost final statement of the attitude of contemporary society to art and the artist." He named it in that *Criterion* of January 1926, which any commentator on the neoclassical movement in English must repeatedly quote, as one of the living examples of the trend towards classicism. In 1929, presumably with his encouragement, the house of Faber published an English translation by S. J. I. Lawson, and Babbitt contributed an introduction.

According to the subtitle, *Belphégor* was an "Essai sur l'esthétique de la présente société française." As Eliot pointed out in *The Sacred Wood,* and Babbitt in the introduction to the translation, if the examples of the "Essai" were French, its strictures applied everywhere in the western world. Under the epigraph "Le charme de sentir est-il donc si fort?" it was an attack on the modern immersion in feeling, the modern abdication of the intellect. Like Babbitt, Benda criticized his contemporaries for

la haine de l'intelligence . . . qui se manifeste surtout dans leurs goûts et doctrines esthétiques, dans leur incroyable proscription — consciente et systématisée — pour tout ce qui dans l'art leur paraît une intervention de cette fonction.

Like Babbitt he implied that an aristocracy sought or at least cared for the prevalence of the human reason, and that democracy was "en quête du seul sentir." In literature and the arts he resisted what he thought to be the adulteration of understanding by an interest in the genetics of the work. We should concentrate on the work "tout fait," not on the work "en train de se faire":

> Il faut contempler le beau dans lui-même, en ignorant la créature mortelle qui l'a produit.

Already the author of two destructive studies of Bergsonism, he attacked the cult of the indistinct, the denial of outline to objects. He attacked the musicalization of the arts, the exploration of the entirely unintellectual recesses of the soul. He attacked the predominance of the theatre, alleging that in the theatre the word, by which the human mind may discriminate, is in perpetual danger of subordination to action, which is nondiscriminating. He attacked the contemporary love of surprise, which led to the invention of the character whose mark is inconsistency, and recalled the precept

> Et qu'il soit jusqu'au bout tel qu'on l'a vu d'abord

He attacked the overvaluation of originality and invention, and gave higher place to "arrangement" and "composition."

Through the more polemical essays of *The Sacred Wood* the spirit of Benda plays. But it is not yet well assimilated. A phrase in which Eliot attempts to define Benda's role is telltale: "He is the ideal scavenger of the rubbish of his time." The word "rubbish" is not the right word; too strong, too much asperity in it, too little appreciation. Although Benda is ruthless, he lets it be seen that he knows (and, despite his polemic against feeling, that he feels) the beauty of some of the work he sweeps away. He must sweep it away because it represents a dangerous excess; but were it present in moderation, were it used under con-

trol . . . He is really not the scavenger but the surgeon. Eliot
in due course was to ascend to the same level. (He was to
point out, for example, that heresy is only "the overemphasis of
a part of the truth"). Again, Benda knew, said, and sometimes
proved in practice, that persuasiveness, lightness, irony are the
proper weapons of the controversialist. Eliot was to develop
these tones, and often in recent years he has proved himself of
all the controversialists in English the most supple and elegant,
the most winning; but in *The Sacred Wood* he was not yet so.
He was *formidable,* and that perhaps served him best in 1920
and enabled him to cow the opposition and inaugurate a revolution. But that is not to possess all the virtues. Conrad Aiken,
remembering the early years of the *Criterion,* has said that
from time to time a literary "assassination" was deliberately
planned and executed. Though striving for the higher things,
the first thing Eliot acquired from Benda was the art of assassination. He exercised it on some of his earlier enthusiasms:
Bubu, once loved, he now looked on with rebuke.

Included in *The Sacred Wood* is the essay on "The Possibility
of a Poetic Drama," two paragraphs of which censure Claudel
and censure him, together with Maeterlinck and Bergson, for
mixing the genres and for confounding clarity and substituting
"emotional stimulus." These are the faults for which *Belphégor*
pillories the age. The paragraphs are an attempt to do in English exactly what Benda was doing in French.

It was with these paragraphs in mind that I suggested on another page that Benda's influence was responsible for Eliot's
neglect of Claudel. Benda counted Péguy and Claudel among
his successful contemporaries — that is, among the contemporaries he deplored: for success in his eyes was a proof of high
standards forsaken and impure techniques pursued. He attacked Claudel in *Belphégor;* accused him of a typically twentieth-century "thirst for totality," of a deliberate outrage of the
common sense of fitness, of an emotional wantonness. In one of

the "Notes," which contain some of the most interesting passages of his book, he complained — without naming Claudel, but he must have had Claudel in mind — of the modern literary Christians who made the Christian mystery mysterious, whereas the great teachers of the seventeenth century stressed the clarity of their religion: "la non-agnoscibilité du dogme chrétien." I fancy that for a long time Eliot could see Claudel only through the haze of these strictures, and could not recognize merit in his profuse invention, the resolutely bizarre and shocking turns of his drama, the far-ranging language, his compassion for the human lot, his sense of responsibility.

I fancy, too, that the same note, entitled "The Literary Exploitation of the Christian Mystery," provoked Eliot to thoughts of greater consequence: that it helped him to discover his own way of writing Christian drama. Since the last years of the nineteenth century dramatists had been seeking to write modern miracle plays. The new understanding of miracles, which accounted for them in terms of the consent of the sufferer, and which seemed at first to explode the conception of divine intervention, then seemed again to recognize it, favored the resumption of the miracle play (and of the miracle as a mainspring of the novel). Björnson led the way before the nineties, with *Beyond Human Power*. Claudel's first version of *Violaine* was written as early as 1893, his second in 1898, and, when Eliot reached Paris, he was recasting the play as *L'Annonce faite à Marie*. In London in 1917 Yeats saw *L'Annonce faite à Marie* and was excited to an intense reconsideration of the psychology of miracles and the opportunity they afforded the dramatist. From *The Player Queen*, written for Mrs. Patrick Campbell, who had excelled in the English production of *Beyond Human Power* in 1901 — from that hard-to-complete composition onward, Yeats struggled with the miracle play, his efforts culminating in *The Herne's Egg*. Eliot took part in the movement with Becket and Celia; took his part in it after long reflection, and modified, almost transformed, the genre; for in effect he wrote miracle plays from which the miracle and its literary exploitation have been withdrawn. His dramas examine the psychology, record the struggles, of martyr and saint. They make the audience feel the pain and shock of a martyr's death (that is why Celia's death at Kinkanja is so terrible, because an audience which is to understand the meaning of a martyrdom, and of the religion which it represents, must renew its consciousness of the pain of testimony). But they do not make the mystery an *obscurity*, nor take it beyond a believer's comprehension, nor declaim over it. With a subdued voice they imply that they are telling of familiar things — things which the audience may have forgotten or omitted to meditate, things which may surprise and hurt as they reawaken, but essentially things familiar, belonging to the Christian doctrine and traditional experience.

Of course, to write dramas at all was in a sense to defy Benda, who insisted that the theatre was meretricious. But Eliot has been trying to write plays not unworthy of a writer he and Benda both respect: Racine. He has been attempting to revive not only poetic drama but classical drama; and he labors, as Benda demanded that an author should, to maintain the supremacy of reason in them; and he succeeds; his audience feels the constant presence of an ordering intelligence. Whether the result can entirely be called "serene" is another matter. Eliot seems to perceive, as he looks at reality, a horror which would destroy us all if he described it by more than a hint. But he also seems to perceive the organization and architecture of the universe and to reflect it and its strength.

The fencing dialogue of his plays and the expository speeches are classical after the prescription of Babbitt and Benda. They "multiply distinctions." So with Becket's speech "Now is my way clear." So continually in the conversation of Harcourt-Reilly. So when Edward and Lavinia try to see their difficulties and make their halting but real self-discoveries. Eliot's plays progress by acts of discrimination, such as Benda loved.

There were aspects of Benda and of Maurras which Eliot ignored. Both of them were addicted to a sexual metaphor in their judgment on art and society. Work which they liked was masculine, work they disliked feminine. Benda complained that contemporary society was ruled by women, to whose taste their businessmen husbands deferred; consequently, the weaknesses of contemporary art might be called feminine as reflecting the preferences of women. Babbitt, introducing *Belphégor*, cordially agreed, glancing at the role of women in his own country. Thibaudet referred to the distinction, and accepted it, in his *N.R.F.* article of 1913: he cited the Acropolis (the usual example with all the neoclassicists, including Matthew Arnold) as the supreme instance of a Greco-French aesthetic of masculine harmony, and opposed it to the barbarian aesthetic of character, "that is, the feminine aesthetic, which aspires to personality rather than beauty, exaggerating instead of correcting and beautifying." But Eliot, I think, has nowhere imitated the comment on society and nowhere employed the metaphor. Again, while at first encounter he enjoyed the neoclassicist attack on hybrid art, progeny of a mixing of the genres, and we have seen him joining in it to criticize Claudel, and although in 1928 he translated the essay in which Maurras wrote "Those who wish to display in French the graces of the Teutonic or the type of sensibility which is proper to the Slav are wasting their efforts, and when they succeed in forming a fashion they are criminal," he seems to have grown doubtful about it in due course. Might not his own work in borrowing from the French, thoroughly though he had assimilated the French voice to his own, be branded under their indictment? We are all mongrels, he pointed out eventually. And he could not really accept Benda's attack on the musicalization of literature. No one was more conscious than he of the importance of the stirring of the oldest human memories, the oldest impulses, alike through music itself and through the "music" of poetry. Rather than abandon or diminish the musical function in his work, he engaged, as he matured, in new experiments in musicalization: in "Coriolan"; in *Four Quartets*. *Four Quartets* might be open to censure as hybrid art. He must have known that. But he was prepared to fight his masters to produce a masterpiece.

Eliot has said that a man of ideas likes ideas to fight against. The excellence of Benda was to provide a fund of such ideas. In *Précision,* sections of which were appearing in periodicals between 1930 and 1937, when Gallimard issued the book, Benda complained of a major deficiency in western literature:

> On peut dire que, depuis le théâtre d'Eschyle jusqu'à celui de Dumas fils, depuis les romans de Longus jusqu'à ceux de Marcel Proust, les personnages de la littérature occidentale, qu'ils soient des héros, des rois et des reines, des hommes d'Etat, des bergers et des bergères, des bourgeois et des bourgeoises, et même des gens du peuple comme dans nos mystères du Moyen Age, sont agités de passions politiques, sociales, morales, religieuses, amoureuses, fort peu de la passion de l'homme luttant avec la nature pour assurer son existence.

One answer to that is the sestina of "The Dry Salvages," where Eliot uses those deeply ingrained images of Connolly's fishermen of Gloucester to describe man's struggle with nature for subsistence, and forces the issue ("Can literature fittingly represent life?") by employing the most artificial of literary forms to embody the humblest, hardest struggle of men and the sea. A little earlier, in the choruses of the women of Canterbury, scrubbers and sweepers —

> . . . with the hand to the broom, the back bent in laying the fire, the knee bent in cleaning the hearth . . .

he had raised the lives of the poor of England to poetry.

Modes of a European Master

Discussing Marianne Moore in the *Dial* of December 1923, Eliot ranked her with five poets — American, English, Irish, French, German — who interested him most at that date. He did not name the poets, and so left a pleasant puzzle to readers of this generation. Some three years ago he said, in answer to an inquiry, that by the American poet he no doubt meant Pound; by the Irish, Yeats; that he thought Valéry must have been the French poet; and that the poet of the German language was probably Hugo von Hofmannsthal, since, to the best of his recollection, he had not yet begun to read Rilke.

Hofmannsthal had astonished middle Europe by the poems of his schoolboy years, published under the pseudonym Loris. With the pure, fluid German of the lyrics and short lyrical dramas which he wrote up to his twenty-second or twenty-third year, he won to his allegiance alike the older writers and the young in the classrooms. Rudolf Borchardt has told how, in a college reading room, he came by accident on a copy of *Pan* which contained passages of *Das kleine Welttheater*, and, as soon as he had read the first lines, seized a sheet of paper from his briefcase and began to copy them; copied them all, took them home, and by nightfall knew them by heart; and gave up everything for a while to pursue Hofmannsthal's work and to collect information about him. The poet might have remained content with the style he had evolved, the work he had done. Certain critics have wished as much and have said "If only he had died then!" But "there was in him much of the valour of the explorer." Raoul Richter told him in 1896 —

wie der reifende Mensch die Fülle über die Uberfülle stellen lerne, die fromme Zufriedenheit über die schweifende Sehnsucht —

and Hofmannsthal turned from his lyrical accomplishment in obedience to the law of maturation. In 1901 he fell into the year of silence, the document of which is *Lord Chandos' Letter:* a young English nobleman, brilliant, creative, a glass of fashion and mold of form, a Hamlet or a Sidney, explains why he will write no more: invaded by realization of the hypocrisy of language as commonly used, and its utter insufficiency to express the ecstasy with which dumb things speak to him, he will write no more. Working out his crisis with the aid of the *Letter,* Hofmannsthal went on to twenty-five years of writing, and especially writing for the theatre. "I want to dramatize everything I come across," he said, "even the correspondence between Schiller and Goethe, or the *Linzer Tagespost."* Play after play came from him. Among the first plays of his new period, *Elektra,* which he had published in 1904, appealed to Richard Strauss, who composed, between 1906 and 1908, an opera which, from the hour of its first performance in January 1909, appalled and fascinated its audiences, appearing to exalt the horrible and monstrous "jusqu'au paroxysme." There followed the famous collaboration of Strauss and Hofmannsthal which led to *Der Rosenkavalier, Ariadne auf Naxos, Die Frau ohne Schatten,* and other operas.

Hofmannsthal's *Elektra,* in English, reached America in 1908, when a translation by Arthur Symons, foremost in making known to the English-speaking peoples the art of Hofmannsthal as of so many other Continental writers, was published by Brentano's in New York. On February 1, 1910, the Strauss opera, in a French translation, was sung for the first time in New York by the Manhattan Opera Company, and late in March it was taken to Boston. But I do not know whether Eliot was aware of Hofmannsthal's name as yet.

In Paris the name was more familiar. Hofmannsthal had made the acquaintance of Gide and other writers in a visit of 1905. Lugné-Poë's company performed *Elektra,* not the opera but the play, translated by Paul Strozzi and Stéphanie Epstein, in 1908.

In the autumn of 1910 a correspondent, Charles Bonnefon, reported to *Figaro* on the condition of the German stage. He described the naturalistic revolution of 1889 and numbered Hofmannsthal among the naturalists:

> All these authors have jettisoned antiquity and its every rule
> . . . The groan at the beginning of the last century was "Who
> will set us free from the Greeks and Latins?" The German au-
> thors have accomplished the emancipation. Undisciplined, un-
> haltered, with the innocent recklessness of very young theorists,
> they have bestirred themselves to climb the heavens. I would
> not claim that they have led us very high so far. But their gym-
> nastics have been interesting.

If a pupil of Babbitt saw that, it may have seemed discouraging news. As an account of Hofmannsthal it was, of course, misleading. Far from rebelling against antiquity, Hofmannsthal was practicing, in *Alkestis, Pentheus, Elektra, Das Gerettete Venedig*, that renewal of the classical tradition that Babbitt was concurrently recommending to the young men at Harvard.

Lugné-Poë again presented *Elektra* at the Théâtre Femina in December 1910. Perhaps he hoped to exploit the excitement spreading among the journalist-critics and their readers at the reports of a new Strauss-Hofmannsthal opera in rehearsal at Dresden.

It was *Der Rosenkavalier*. Great secrecy invested it — the promoters imposed, up to the very hour of the opening, complete silence on the cast — with the result that the press of Europe crepitated with rumors. A book and score as sensational as *Elektra* were expected, and the lodgings in Dresden were bespoke three months in advance.

When the new opera was performed on January 26, 1911, it turned out to be entirely different than anyone had imagined.

It was a creative renewal of a European tradition of comedy and sentiment. After the first act the curtain had to be raised a dozen times, a dozen times after the second act, and twenty-one times at the end. Music critics of every capital had traveled to Dresden for the event. Their reports were appearing during the next week. Some of them carped, some were exhilarated, some mixed censure and enthusiasm. What the public absorbed from them, almost regardless of their censure, was an enthusiasm such as had seized the Dresden audience. A dormant element in the Continental sensibility seemed to be reawakened, and urban Europe delighted in its restoration.

Figaro's report from Robert Brussel filled three columns on January 27 and three on January 28. There is a difference between the first hearing of a masterpiece, at which, driving out the emptiness or the erroneous guesses in the minds of the audience, it establishes images which will stay in the public experience forever, and the subsequent hearings for which we arrive with the collective image already present to us, and we cannot have the shock and delight of the incursion of the work, and thus in one way we cannot know it, but we take other beauties out of it instead, extending or subtilizing our knowledge. In a report like Brussel's the first revelation can be half recovered, we can half repossess the first moment "où Sophie inconsciente et transfigurée, s'incline devant le chevalier comme devant la statue du dieu Eros lui-même et lui baise la main." The enthusiastic paragraphs afford us, like the pages of a diary, something of the living experience. They also proceed to make critical points, which must have struck readers in 1911 and which are still relevant. Brussel questioned the plausibility and the propriety of the quasi-vaudeville entanglement in the third act. But, he said, if the piece was not always that of "un dramaturge très habile," it was certainly that of a true poet. He praised the elegance with which, re-creating the culture and mores of eighteenth-century Vienna, Hofmannsthal had infused the work with an "ambiance mondaine . . . faite autant de subtilité italienne, de charme slave, que de politesse française." And he saw how Hofmannsthal had invented, out of the sensibility at once Austrian and European which determined the details of his plot, a piquant new diction:

> un dialogue chatoyant où milles langages et jargons se mêlent; un dialogue en verité charmant de diversité, de timbre, et d'accent.

With that sentence he entered into the spirit of Hofmannsthal, who himself loved the language of the libretto. A month or two later, defending himself against critics less percipient, Hofmannsthal pointed out that if, to catch the spirit of the society he described and the peculiarity of the characters, he had "invented" his diction, he had invented it in a very strict sense, by finding it — identifying it — where it was still current, in the speech of his own day: "Die Sprache ist in keinem Buch zu finden, sie liegt aber noch in der Luft, denn es ist mehr von der Vergangenheit in der Gegenwart als man ahnt . . ." He had extricated it from the very air. Although it was, as one critic averred, an imaginary eighteenth-century Volapük, it was yet, by the supple discrimination of its author, an essay towards the "familiar speech" for which the poet-dramatists were looking: familiar and yet unexpected and fine, antique and yet fresh, highly charged though simple.

Hofmannsthal had the impression, as his correspondence shows, that he and Strauss were a misunderstood and over-criticized pair. He exaggerated (though this was fortunate, since it led to those forays in which he used for weapons his deft analyses of his own work). During the winter and spring of 1911 *Der Rosenkavalier* received twenty-eight performances in Dresden, and was presented in Nuremberg, Munich, Bremen, Frankfurt, Prague, Berlin, Vienna, Budapest. Mainly cities of middle Europe; but the Scala saw it too. Throughout the season newspapers and periodicals everywhere were filled with accounts of libretto and score. There *were* disputes over the merits of poem and music, and a nice seeking and weighing of the imperfections of each. But the disputes, which have never stopped, were and are a pleasure of the opera; and the critical exchanges made the year all the more enlivening to young men forming their views of art and their own designs. It is possible to imagine that for those young men who thought that masterpieces must overcome initial opposition, the disputes, the attacks by the Italian critics after the Milan production, the charge, current chiefly among those who had not seen it, that it was sensual and depraved, and the rumor of the Kaiser's disapproval (he traveled to the Dresden performance, but said, as he got back into the royal train, "Det ist keene Musik für mich"), redeemed the opera from what might have been the odium of its immediate success.

In June Eliot was in Bavaria, and there, as he recollects, he read Hofmannsthal for the first time. I do not know whether he rose from the reading with a sense of emulation. He has said, speaking of other English writers to whom he could not yet react very deeply in 1911, that a young man's feeling for poetry is strong but narrow and tends to exclude writers from whom he cannot learn the use of his own voice — and that only the French poets could help him at that time. In the light of that explanation one fancies that, reading such perfect work as the stanzas in terza rima on our dreams —

> Das Innerste ist offen ihrem Weben;
> Wie Geisterhände in versperrtem Raum
> Sie sind in uns und haben immer Leben.
>
> Und drei sind Eins: ein Mensch, ein Ding, ein Traum.

— he may have envied Hofmannsthal his good fortune in finding contemporary German so ready an instrument, capable of

carrying immediately experienced images in traditional forms,
and yet have turned away despondent of applying Hofmannsthal's techniques in English where the familiar forms and
rhythms had grown wearisome.

Yet a poet can scarcely read another, especially a near-con-
temporary master, without learning something, and I sometimes wonder whether the traces of Hofmannsthal may show
just lightly on Eliot's 1911 work. It is said that he was completing, or correcting and perfecting, "Prufrock" that summer.
Edmund Wilson pointed out twenty-five years ago that the
closing sequence of "Prufrock" comes from Laforgue. So it does,
but not quite "line for line" as Wilson claimed. The last eleven
lines are somewhat different from anything else in the poem,
Eliot being — then and sometimes later — sufficiently romantic
in temperament to work for a heightened ending to his poem.
Although they predict the timidity of old age, they claim
glimpses to which the poets and the mystic aspire. Echo Laforgue they may, but also, like the peroration of *The Waste
Land,* they echo de Nerval's *El Desdichado:*

J'ai rêvé dans la grotte où nage la sirène . .

And it may be that they reflect, in the shapeliness and glow by
virtue of which they suggest the glory of those glimpses, the
shapeliness and luminosity of Hofmannsthal's *Terzinen.*

But ten years later, by which time he knew something of the
range of his own voice and was confronting new problems, he
began to find Hofmannsthal an example. Hofmannsthal's attempts of the first decade of the century to renew the Greek
drama must have seemed important to a poet who had been
challenged by Pound to remold the *Agamemnon* and who was
deeply engaged with the general problem of the drama, and
the particular problem of the poetic drama, in England. And
perhaps more important were the complementary modes with

which Hofmannsthal had come to maturity, at once fulfilling
his nature and evoking answers from his audiences, in 1911:
comedy and the Morality Play. *Der Rosenkavalier* was produced at the outset of the great year, *Jedermann* at the end.
By these two works Eliot has identified Hofmannsthal to a later
generation, in the preface written for the recent bilingual edition of the *Poems and Verse Plays*. After the collapse of the
Austrian Empire in 1918 Hofmannsthal advanced simultaneously the practice of both modes: he wrote his Viennese prose
comedy, *Der Schwierige,* and a morality play, in poetry, for
Salzburg — *Die Salzburger Grosse Welttheater*. In a later
chapter I hope to draw comparisons between these works and
the plays with which Eliot fulfilled his own mission in the
theatre.

And there may be a case for comparing the note of nostalgia
in the two poets. Hofmannsthal is a famous master of nostalgia.
It is not only that he made himself the poet of a vanishing Austria, and of the graces associated with it as it disappeared (just
as a legend of the graces gathered about the defeated South); it
is also that the note of nostalgia was one of the instruments by
which he performed what he thought was a dramatist's work:
distinguished between "the heart that beats, the heart that
freezes." Eliot also is a master of nostalgia: if less obviously, it
is because he has reserved the note, as he has reserved the
bondissement intérieur, using it seldom lest it lose its beauty by
familiarity. In "Prufrock" it is to be heard in the sudden response to the perfume of a dress and the down of light brown
hair. In "La Figlia che Piange" there is French clarity, American observation and reflection, and perhaps the shapeliness of
Hofmannsthal, perhaps his nostalgia. In *The Waste Land* there
is more than one moment of profound nostalgic beauty: the
sudden turn, "Yet when we came back, late, from the Hyacinth
garden," must be one of the most beautiful passages in this
kind in English. And the sledding scene in the opening se-

quence of *The Waste Land* is touched with the quality of a passage from Hofmannsthal. Eliot built it, a critic has shown, from a passage in a book of memoirs; built it by a favorite method of great writers, which is to shape another person's ephemeral page into a fresh, living drama. I would only ask whether Hofmannsthal's work as the poet and dramatist of a vanishing, aristocratic Europe may not have exercised Eliot in the sensibility on which the passage depends, and helped him to commemorate a lost epoch.

7. Eleven Years: and a Poem for Europe

BACK at Harvard in September 1911 Eliot enrolled in Lanman's Indic Philology course. Babbitt and Paul Elmer More had followed it seventeen years earlier. Perhaps Babbitt's example was an incentive to Eliot. Perhaps an image of India, evoked by Kipling, had long been attracting him. Perhaps his interest was part of that general recourse to Asia which Disraeli had foretold in *Tancred* —

> . . . the spiritual hold which Asia has always had upon the North . . . seems to wane at present, but it is only the decrease that precedes the new development

— and which in 1911 was a tendency of Western thought.

America had been hankering for ancient India for three-quarters of a century, rebellious against the rulings of Puritan theology. To a people on a frontier, the unknown interior lying just beyond their doors like a crystal, the occult is tempting; and because it was tempting, it was rigorously suppressed in the New England colony. The witch trials put an abrupt check on dabbling. Wendell vindicated them on the grounds that they preserved the national sanity. But there was an awkward contradiction entailed in the suppression. In a Puritan nation every man seeks the disclosure of the divine for himself. Suppressing the witches, the New England communities disavowed a principle of their religious experience. As the frontier receded, and as the spirit of inquiry was rehabilitated by the American Revolution and the French Revolution, the suppressed impulses disgorged themselves in a burst of speculation and experiment. The New England Transcendentalists pursued the literature of the Orient, and exulted in a mode of thought which devalued the material progress around them. Simple, bold spirits practiced the trance, detaching themselves from this world of cities and wealth, for contact with the spirit world and its wealth of priestly power. At Chittenden in the hale air of Vermont, Colonel Olcott examined the Eddy brothers, received Madame Blavatsky, founded the Theosophical Society. The craving for esoteric knowedge, involving the rummaging among the few available texts from India, spread rapidly among persons uninformed or half informed but very eager. Edgar Lee Masters knew one of them, Tennessee Claflin Shope, in Spoon River:

> Before Mary Baker G. Eddy even got started
> With what she called science
> I had mastered the "Bhagavad Gita,"
> And cured my soul . . .

and the St. Louis Movement had explorers of orientalist theosophy among its members.

The hybrid movement exasperated opposition. One form it took was pragmatism, patient or impatient. Another was Pound's rejection of India as formless, "obnubilated" (and I have heard Robert Frost criticize Indian art in rather similar terms). Another was the serious, hard study of the subjects which the movement had appropriated. This was Lanman's kind.

Charles Rockwell Lanman, born in 1850, had learned Sanskrit at Yale under William Dwight Whitney, then had gone to Tübingen to study the Veda under Whitney's German master,

Rudolf Roth. When he was thirty President C. W. Eliot had
called him from the Johns Hopkins University to lead Harvard
Indic studies. In a productive, energetic life he scoured India
for books and manuscripts and brought them home to Harvard.
He edited the journal and proceedings of the American Oriental Society and planned and edited the Harvard Oriental Series.
At the outset of his Harvard career he wrote a *Sanskrit Reader,*
designed not only for his classroom but for the amateur student: "It is especially *the requirements of unaided private
study* that I have taken constant pains to meet" (his italics).
"Numerous enquiries for such a book have been addressed to
me by persons very remote from any of the higher institutions
of learning." He hoped that the work would help "to save the
literature from undue depreciation and from exaggerated
praise." Later he said of his Harvard Oriental Series that it was
"especially timely now, when so much of the widespread interest in Buddhism and other oriental systems is mis-directed by
half-knowledge, or by downright errors concerning them."

For two years Eliot studied the language in Lanman's library
and during the second year he read Indian philosophy under
the direction of James Haughton Woods, a versatile man who
had taught history, philosophy, anthropology, and comparative
religion, who had traveled in India and Japan, and who was at
work, while Eliot was his pupil, on his *Yoga System of Patanjali,*
to be published in 1914.

In his radio talks of 1946 on "The Unity of European Culture"
Eliot recalled:

> Long ago I studied the ancient Indian languages, and while I
> was chiefly interested at that time in Philosophy, I read a little
> poetry too; and I know that my own poetry shows the influence
> of Indian thought and sensibility.

It will one day be an attractive study for a comparatist who en-
joys the necessary knowledge of both ancient Indian poetry

and the traditions of English literature to define the influence of which Eliot speaks: to say whether his metrical innovations owe anything to the meters of Sanskrit, whether the internal rhymes which are rich in his middle period were encouraged by the internal rhyming which is said to be elaborate in certain Sanskrit poets, and what images were fostered by his reading of the early poets and philosophers. There are two outstanding passages in which he explicitly incorporates memories of his reading in Sanskrit literature: the final section of *The Waste Land* with its red glimpses of Indian landscape, its myth of the thunder god releasing the pent-up rivers, and its three interpretations of the thunder as three complementary commandments or keys to life; and the middle section of "The Dry Salvages" with its dramatic allusion to Arjuna's dilemma, whether to advance to the battle against his kin, and his decision to "fare forward" after he has heard Krishna expound the duty of man. These two passages alone would justify the terms Eliot spent in his Sanskrit course, for they bestow on English something no other writer has given: dramatic material from the Sanskrit tradition, and presumably a tincture, at least, of the style and sensibility of the works on which they depend. By Eliot's intermediacy these touches of India have become part of the living system of English thought. The identification of other passages where Eliot's memories of Sanskrit have been at work, we have to await from the critic with specialized knowledge. Meanwhile, I fancy that the ceremony of the libation at the end of the second act of *The Cocktail Party* may be such a passage. Early Sanskrit literature, according to those who have described it for the Western world, is a religious literature, of praise, prayer, and sacrifice to the gods. The two years devoted to it probably did much to foster Eliot's conviction that ritual was the beginning of art and must remain a living power in art. Now *The Cocktail Party* is the work in which all Eliot's slowly evolved theories of poetic drama are used with perfect tact and success; among them, the theory of ritual; and that theory is successfully practiced in the libation ceremony. No wonder if, writing the scene, Eliot caught some echo of Sanskrit poetry. "The words for the building of the hearth," "The words for those who go upon a journey" — one would not be surprised to find such titles in the index of an anthology from the Sanskrit.

Eliot has naturalized into English from the Indian literature and the Indian sensibility little, and perhaps nothing, that is decorative. He denied himself the saffron paste, the sesamum seed, the açoka blossom, all the touches of pleasure that the Hindu landscape justified but that would be obviously exotic in a Western poem; all with the exception of images *already* naturalized in the Western imagination and languages: the unfolding lotus of "Burnt Norton," for example. Perhaps he was kindled not by images of indulgence but by the austere language of old hymns, prayers, runes, and that led him first to the burned coloration of

> Rock and no water and the sandy road

and then to poetry almost without adjectives:

> REILLY: Let them build the hearth
> Under the protection of the stars.
> ALEX: Let them place a chair each side of it.
> JULIA: May the holy ones watch over the roof,
> May the moon herself influence the bed

where he found the words right for exciting a modern theatre audience to the same feelings — feelings of chill and awe, when the flesh creeps in the presence of the elemental and eternal — that the antique words and rhythms excited in him.

At the date of *The Waste Land* Eliot made an austere, cauterizing poetry out of his response to the spirit of asceticism in

Buddhism. He gave the title of "The Fire Sermon" to the third
part of the poem; and his note advises the reader to consult the
English text in Henry Clarke Warren's *Buddhism in Translation,* which had been published as the third volume of Lanman's Harvard Oriental Series in 1896:

> All things, O priests, are on fire. And what, priests, are all
> these things which are on fire?
> The eye, O priests, is on fire; forms are on fire; eye-conscious-
> ness is on fire; impressions received by the eye are on fire; and
> whatever sensation, pleasant, unpleasant, or indifferent, orig-
> inated in impressions received by the eye, that also is on fire.
> And with what are these on fire?
> With the fire of passion, say I, with the fire of hatred, with the
> fire of infatuation; with birth, old age, death, sorrow, lamenta-
> tion, misery, grief, and despair are they on fire . . .
> Perceiving this, O priests, the learned and noble disciple con-
> ceives an aversion for the eye, conceives an aversion for forms,
> conceives an aversion for eye-consciousness, conceives an aver-
> sion for the impressions received by the eye . . .

The preacher reiterates how he conceives — strange word in
this place — an aversion for every sense and the impressions it
supplies. A Western reader may feel an aversion for this conquest of life by the annihilation of life, together with some respect and a recognition of the efficiency of the escape for those
who thoroughly undertake it. The ascetic in Eliot, who claimed
the ascendancy in him when he wrote *The Waste Land,* and
remained long in the ascendancy, responded to the Sermon;
urged purgation and self-denial, detachment from the world.

Eliot has not long ago complained that his critics tend to
judge him only by what he has done at some conspicuous early
stage of his development. He preached the Buddhist askesis in
the early *Waste Land.* He preached a new askesis, the Buddhist
renunciation in Christian guise, in his essays on education in

the late twenties and thirties, urged it by the example of Becket
and the examples of Agatha and Harry, urged in "Little Gidding" the cultivation of "detachment From self and from things
and from persons," and in *The Cocktail Party* again described
the saint's renunciation of the world.   But in *The Cocktail Party*
a tremendous change occurred: an acceptance of humanity.
He made a distinction between the opportunities of the saint
and the opportunities of the common man, and admitted a
decent value in the latter. Buddha had called renunciation the
abandonment of "the household life" and the election of the
"houseless" one. "The household life" covers what the common man values most. It is worthless, said Buddha, a source of
inevitable sin and thus of the prolongation of the agony of the
incarnate soul. By a moving concession in *The Cocktail Party*
Eliot made himself the champion of the household life as well
as of the self-sacrificing martyr. The household, he said there,
is, for all its lacunae,

> a good life. Though you will not know how good
> Till you come to the end . . .
> > > In a world of lunacy,
> Violence, stupidity, greed . . . it is is a good life.

The Confidential Clerk examines that limited but real excellence of household relationships more closely. *The Elder Statesman* allows it, too, though it also allows for the malcomprehension and pain of family life.

So there have been changes from the conspicuous *Waste
Land* asceticism. The figures of Krishna and Arjuna in the
middle movement of "The Dry Salvages" stand for the resolute
pursuit of life; they warn that whatever we are doing at this
moment is what we are doing in eternity, and require us to consider whether we are doing what we would like to be doing in
eternity, and, if not, to amend ourselves; but they say that we
must accept the duties of living. In *The Cocktail Party* the

psychoanalyst makes his regular farewell to his patients in words that can be as true for the discriminating pursuit of life as for its renunciation, according to the belief of the man who receives them. They are the words of the dying Buddha to his priests: "Work out your salvation with diligence." Before he had met that sentence in Lanman's class or Warren's book, Eliot had met it in Babbitt, on whose mind it was engraved. He had certainly seen it in Babbitt's *Literature and the American College;* he had probably heard him quote it. It is majestically recalled in Paul Elmer More's memoir of Babbitt. Repeating it to his theatre audience and his readers, Eliot has put it into wider currency in the West. The words which seized More and Babbitt once they met them in their studies with Lanman, and remained with them as a perpetual source of strength, evidently seized Eliot and rang in his mind, and he has put them at the disposal of all of us for our strengthening.

After the spring of 1913 Eliot withdrew from the Sanskrit courses. He has volunteered an explanation in his Virginia lectures. "Two years spent in the study of Sanskrit under Charles Lanman, and a year in the mazes of Patanjali's metaphysics under the guidance of James Woods, left me in a state of enlightened mystification." He would have been able to penetrate the difficulties only by "forgetting how to think and feel as an American or a European: which, for practical as well as sentimental reasons, I did not wish to do." He turned to concentrate on European philosophy. In June 1913 he bought a copy of F. H. Bradley's *Appearance and Reality* at the "Coop" in Harvard Square.

There is a paragraph in Conrad Aiken's *Ushant*, humorous and magnificent, in which he describes the doctoral thesis on Bradley, completed in 1916, as marking the most radical point Eliot reached: there, says Aiken, he halted and took a homeward way, which brought him to Canterbury. What conception of Eliot's outlook at that extreme point lies behind Aiken's leaping figure? Does not Aiken mean that the Eliot of 1913-1916 valued more highly than ever before or ever since

> the very world, which is the world
> Of all of us, — the place where, in the end,
> We find our happiness, or not at all!

except that where Wordsworth speaks of "happiness," Eliot perhaps thought of "fulfillment"? Dr. Anne C. Bolgan has examined Eliot's philosophical writing, and, if I understand her, interprets his view of 1916 as a belief that a man must fulfill his potentialities in action, and that by doing so he may extend God's creation. Dr. Bolgan quotes from Eliot's contribution to the *Monist* of October 1916:

> soul is to body as cutting is to the axe: realizing itself in its actions, and not completely real when abstracted from what it does.

By placing it against that passage we may see the point of the sentence in *The Sacred Wood* in which Eliot recalls Rudolf Eucken:

> No one who had not witnessed the event could imagine the conviction in the tone of Professor Eucken as he pounded the table and exclaimed *Was ist Geist? Geist ist* . . .

Eucken was visiting professor at Harvard in the academic year 1912-1913. He came with a great reputation (he had received the Nobel Prize for Literature in 1908) and as the champion of the "spirit," the inner life, against the monopoly of the outer life with its oscillation between meaningless work and meaningless leisure. But he went far beyond the needs of the criticism of an insufficiently spiritual era. He constructed an "independent spiritual life . . . superior to all time and to all change." "This life," said one of his English translators, "must be conceived of as something quite distinct from the human intellect and from every kind of merely human psychic life." The word "merely" is telltale. Though it was not quite true, what an opponent contended, that Eucken preached the inner life with never a word to say about its manifestations in art, religion, and the family, the total effect was almost as desiccated. Eliot's reaction to the boom of *Geist* through the classroom was an insistence on the endeavors of men as the reality on which all abstractions depend.

It seems significant that Eliot recoiled from Eucken with that "radical" reaction in the year in which he decided to withdraw from the study of the metaphysics of India. Eucken slighted the works of man, the Fire Sermon renounced the sensations of man. The withdrawal from Indics was an act of radicalism, in the sense of Aiken's metaphor, no less than the rejection of Eucken.

Aiken says that Eliot reversed the direction of his thought. But *Ushant* was written in the early fifties before the end of Eliot's development (and, for that matter, dare we in the early sixties yet speak of "an end"?), and Aiken was unable to foresee how change would be followed by counterchange. In the youthful strength of 1913 that part of Eliot which sympathized with the world had overcome another self which hated the senses. A very few years later, however, in the postwar world with its difficulties he took up the lessons of the Fire Sermon and the Christian saints and preachers, and became the poet of renunciation. He most influenced and modified his contemporaries as a highly original and intense poet crusading against the senses; though the poetry was most intense, and he compelled his audience most, when the beauty of the world momentarily broke through despite his renunciation, reclaimed him momentarily for the experiences of earth. But then, tentatively in "The Dry Salvages," decisively in *The Cocktail Party,* there came the further change which we have noticed. The new mood has persisted in the plays of the fifties. The Eliot of 1913 and 1916 has been resuscitated. Only, a balance has been struck: the self that loves the senses is no longer in battle with a self that fears them; the latter has altered into a self who, while he believes in a supreme experience beyond the senses, allows the claim of life.

A Californian Philosopher

At Harvard Eliot must have been aware of the Professor of the History of Philosophy, Josiah Royce, and he appears to have done work under him during either the first or the last of his graduate years. "That extraordinary philosopher," he subsequently called Royce — a tantalizingly reserved phrase.

John Jay Chapman tells how, conducting round Cambridge a lady who collected celebrities and insisted on examining a Harvard specimen, he sent his undergraduate son to explain "the exigencies of the occasion" to Royce and to fetch him at all costs. Royce came, took his stand against a high chair, and, without removing his coat and muffler, lectured for an hour on the German mind from Odin to the Kaiser. The point is, not that Royce was able to improvise beautifully, but that he complied with the request to do it. He thought of himself as the traditional sage-in-employment: the philosopher at the Caliph's court, the theologian at Charlemagne's, the man whose business it is to dispense information and interpretation on request. Chapman thought of him as the embodiment not of historical but prehistorical understanding:

> The legend about him among the students was that he was the first man born in California; and it was a strange place for him to choose, for his appearance suggested Asia. No country in Europe seemed old enough to have produced this type of super-

man, the gnarled cavern sage who was wiser than Europe, more
abstract, more Himalayan. I believe that if only he had never
been taught to read, Royce would have been a very great man.

The "red-headed boy" had come east from California to join
President Gilman's first score of brilliant fellows at Johns Hopkins University in 1876. In 1882-83 he substituted for William
James at Harvard, and he remained in Cambridge for the rest
of his days. "He's the best man going," Santayana has his young
hero say in *The Last Puritan* — the best man although he's an
idealist.

One or two passages in Eliot's poetry and certain motifs in
his polemic seem tinged with the influence of Royce's teaching.
As a child in a Sierra Nevada settlement in 1860, Royce had
been fascinated by a miner's grave and the rotting pine props
in an abandoned digging, fascinated by the puzzle of these
signs of human effort and human decay shining like contradictions of the sunlight that played on them. To reconcile the
contradictions, the grave and the fire of vitality (which remind
us of Eliot's contrapuntal art), he had invented a new "proof"
of the existence of God, a proof that began with the datum of
error. If error exists, as common sense, and the grave and the
abandoned digging, show it does, there must be a truth from
which it differs; and the existence of truth implies that someone
knows the truth; and since to know the truth thoroughly and
supply the corrective to every possible error involves omni-
science, there must be an omniscient mind or universal thought.
When Eliot wrote his "miracle-play," he affirmed the existence
of God by the same argument. "The darkness declares the glory
of light" is Royce's answer to the puzzle of the grave in the sunlight. Similarly Royce argued that "as soon as you try to deny
. . . propositions, you implicitly reaffirm them by your very
attempt at denial." The same logic, the same theology, and almost the same words, stream into Eliot's final chorus:

> Those who deny Thee could not deny, if Thou didst
> not exist; and their denial is never complete,
> for if it were so, they would not exist.
> They affirm Thee in living; all things affirm Thee
> in living; the bird in the air, both the
> hawk and the finch . . .

and the hunters and the hunted and the sunlight and the grave.

In 1908 Royce published his *Philosophy of Loyalty*, and as he went on with his work during the next six years "the depth and vitality of the ideal of loyalty" seemed to become ever better known to him. The philosophy of loyalty hinged on a philosophy of the community:

> Loyalty . . . is the willing and thoroughgoing devotion of a self to a cause, when the cause is something which unites many selves in one, and which is therefore the interest of a community. For a loyal human being the interest of the community to which he belongs is superior to every merely individual interest of his own.

The individual should find himself in subordination to the community. Some of Royce's critics questioned the adequacy of that view. E. A. Singer, in an engaging essay of 1915, pointed out that "merging oneself into something big may not be just the same as reaching for something high" and suggested that the group mind has amoeboid, tigerish characteristics. But passages in Eliot's prose indicate that he was impressed by Royce's doctrine. So, for example, the sentence in *The Sacred Wood* concerning "the mind of Europe — the mind of his own country — a mind which he [the poet] learns in time to be much more important than his own private mind." The dashes and imprecision in the sentence evince some uncertainty on the writer's part but he seems to be upholding the paramountcy of the group over the individual, and of the larger group over the units that comprise it. His frequent references to the poet's duty to his language, among them the line of 1942 in which he writes, echoing Mallarmé, that the poet's function is to "purify the dialect of the tribe," testify to the conviction that the work of the poet is performed for his community.

During Eliot's graduate period Royce was much occupied with the issue which he calls *The Problem of Christianity:* the Church, or the "Beloved Community," as an ideal community: ideal if its members could respond to its challenge, "Create me":

> "Create me," — this is the word that the Church, viewed as an idea, addresses to mankind.

And, out of his reflections on loyalty and the Church, he was developing the theme of atonement.

Man is free to oppose the divine will, Royce said, and the evidence of history is that, from time to time, an individual does wittingly oppose himself to the divine will. When he does, he must find redemption through atonement, and his atonement heals ("at-ones" in the earlier English usage and in Royce's) the cleft his defection has struck in the harmony of his community and of the universe. Just as error points to God, this great disobedience may enrich God, for the expiation which it makes possible is a creative deed, transformed by which the world is better than it would have been had the divine order never been resisted. The sin of Peter is a sin against the light, but how much richer is creation for the drama of the sin and the atonement. It may be that Royce's teaching helped to guide Eliot to that intense concern with atonement which has sounded in *The Waste Land, The Family Reunion,* "Little Gidding." Or it may simply be that Royce and Eliot formed their outlook from the same sources, yet there are such likenesses that it is tempting to think that the teacher at least hastened the pupil in the way he was going.

Royce deplored the lack of a sense of sin. "The modern man," he said in *The Problem of Christianity,* "is one who does not believe in hell, and who is too busy to think about his sins."

Throughout the twenties Eliot said the same thing. Above "The Hollow Men" he copied the phrase from Conrad's *Heart of Darkness,* "Mistah Kurtz — he dead"— meaning that the figure of evil has disappeared from life, and thus all values have disappeared. He held up Baudelaire as the edifying contrast to modern man: Baudelaire performed and wrote of acts of sin in knowledge of the sin; sinned, therefore, with dignity, not inanely; was capable of atonement. In *The Cocktail Party* the proof of Celia's differences and her vocation is that she feels "a sense of sin." "This is most unusual," Reilly tells her, probing for her meaning, encouraging her to find it; and she finds that "I feel I must . . . *atone —* is that the word?"

In the Harvard College Archives there is a notebook in which Royce has sketched his program of teaching for his course Philosophy 15 in 1908-1909. Now that is a little earlier than Eliot's work with him; I quote the passage, however, because it shows how he was accustomed to introduce the concept of "ritual" to his students (and we know from the preface to *Savonarola* that Eliot wrote a paper on ritual for his eye). Under the heading "Correlation of serial and cyclic orders" Royce has jotted down:

> . . . Any serial order determines possible cycles [repetitions of series, reversals of series]. Any cyclic order may be transformed into a serial order: a given series and a given cycle may be set in oneone correspondence, if they are numerically similar forms.
>
> Examples from chronology, ritual, ceremony, and recurrent processes of all sorts. Trigonometry as a science of cyclic orders. First glimpse of the concept of Rhythm . . .

In 1923 when Eliot defined "ritual" as "a set of repeated movements" he was looking back to his hours with Royce.

Philosophy or Literature?

Eliot's success as a philosopher almost decoyed him from literature. Little record of new experiments in poetry on his part in the years between his return from Paris and his arrival in England. He served as an Assistant in Philosophy in the academic years 1912-13 and 1913-14. He figured in the transactions of the University's Philosophical Club and was its president for the years 1913-14. Among the diverse personalities he afterwards located in himself in "Mélange Adultère de Tout," the Germanic philosopher

> Surexcité par Emporheben
> Au grand air de Bergsteigleben

was ascendant. In the spring of 1914 he decided to go to Germany to complete his training, as many leading American teachers of philosophy had done. The Harvard authorities, who regarded him as a potential light of their Department of Philosophy, planned to advance him rapidly when he came home.

The outbreak of war cut short his stay in Marburg, and he made his way to England, found a haven at Merton, which welcomes American poets, and there continued his reading in philosophy for a year. He completed his doctoral thesis on Bradley in April 1916. Two months later James Haughton Woods wrote to him from Harvard that the Division of Philosophy accepted it "without the least hesitation" and that Royce acclaimed it as "the work of an expert." "Please let us be reassured," added Woods, "that your interest in Philosophy is as strong as before." Whatever Eliot replied, and whatever he thought the right reply, it is evident in retrospect that, though he continued to write on philosophical questions for another year or more, he was returning to poetry.

He was rescued from the Bastille of philosophy and recalled to his natural life as a poet. But he has always valued the training he received among the philosophers. Various critics provoke his comment that he would admire them more if their work had been strengthened by a philosophical technique. Of

Babbitt: "His mind was in one sense profoundly philosophical; he had an intuitive apprehension of certain — but not all — essentials. But of philosophical technique he had none; and in his writings you will find no coherent system, but some apparently important inconsistencies." Of Matthew Arnold: "the greatest weakness in Arnold's culture was his weakness in philosophical training." His own prose writing impresses, and one may even say subdues, the reader with its philosophical order. More important, his poetry is sometimes modified by the habitually philosophical procedure of his thought, and comes in the result with a distinctive texture, hardly precedented in English. A word about this later.

But what rescued him for poetry? A large part must have been played by the influence, personal and immediate, of Ezra Pound. Pound's achievement, which will be celebrated as long as English literature is read, is threefold: he has composed an immense body of poetry, which comprehends and brings alive for us the utmost in beauty that many civilizations have attained, and which includes passages that possess us and stay with us once we have read them; he has ejected an immense flow of criticism, the pages of which are full of suggestions which a man could spend a lifetime pursuing, and any one of which might, if studied, improve a poet's versifying or a reader's pleasure (I have just looked, for example, at his essay in the *Criterion* of April, 1934, and have been excited by the passage in which he differentiates between the staccato and legato styles in English poetry); and, believing that a writer, or other creative artist, is of value to the world, he has striven with all his energy, all his knowledge, all his practical resources, to help potential makers to develop their gifts. His contributions to *Poetry* in the two years preceding Eliot's arrival in London show him consciously, urgently, looking for poets, nursing talent wherever he saw a spark of it. In a survey of the English scene dated London, December 10, 1912, he began with Yeats

as the only poet worthy of serious study; made a point or two
about Padraic Colum; turned and said, "I would rather talk
about poetry with Ford Madox Hueffer than with any man in
London" and praised three poems in *High Germany;* noted
Richard Aldington among the young men, and observed "a
gleam of hope" in him, "but it is too early to make predictions";
referred to some men of the nineties who contributed to the
charm of London: Wilfred Scawen Blunt, Ernest Rhys, Victor
Plarr. The last words of his article:

> In fact one might name nearly a hundred writers who have
> given pleasure with this or that matter in rhyme. But it is one
> thing to take pleasure in a man's work and another to respect
> him as a great artist.

As soon as he read the poems Eliot had been storing for three
or four years, he recognized his artist. The letter to Harriet
Monroe on September 30, 1914, says so. And his enthusiasm,
the steps he took for the publication of "Prufrock" and the "Portrait" and then of poems of the Oxford year, and his urging and
advice towards new work, must surely have encouraged Eliot
to resume writing.

During the years 1915 to 1920 (when Pound left England)
Eliot benefited, as he recalled in a contribution to *Purpose* in
1938, from Pound's "criticism of my poetry in our talk" and
from "his indications of desirable territories to explore." In
1920 he wrote, without naming Pound but quoting the phrase
with which he was to dedicate *The Waste Land* to him, that
"there is no more useful criticism and no more precious praise
for a poet than that of another poet:

> 'Fu miglior fabbro del parlar materno . . .
> e lascia dir gli stolti . . .' "

It is remarkable and moving that two Americans who had independently turned from their home to Europe and the Euro-

pean traditions to find their art, came nearer to it each by working on the other. It is remarkable, too, how, working on each other, they remained free of each other; and especially remarkable that the younger man, who had published only a few poems in a college magazine, learned from the older man, who had spectacular publications to his credit, without falling into imitation of him. In the short, clear appreciation of *Ezra Pound: his Metric and Poetry* which he wrote, without signature, for Knopf in 1917 Eliot shows a close acquaintance with the several styles in which Pound had experimented up to that time, and a delight in them; yet there is little or no trace of them in his own work of the war period. Eliot listened to Pound's ideas, examined the models Pound suggested, but completely assimilated them to his own needs and capabilities, and the work they influenced came out of the process his own.

Pound had ready for Eliot the gallery of monitors, the battery of technical effects, that he had accumulated in his rush towards beauty through several languages. Especially active in his mind at the time were lessons which he had learned or elaborated some in the company of Yeats, some in the company of Ford Madox Hueffer — whom I will call by his adopted surname, Ford.

Ford's lesson was: to say it naturally and briefly. He defined literary virtue as "the fewest possible words on your page." Pound took that up: speed is beauty. If Pound has filled volumes, it is because he has had so many points to make, not because he has made them wordily. He has made them elliptically. Eliot appears to have accepted the advice, which ran with his predisposition. He overcultivated brevity for a period: it helped towards the excellence of the 1915 poems about Boston; it was too powerful, and too lonely a power, in the strophes.

Pound mated Ford's doctrine of brevity with lessons which he had drawn from Flaubert. His teaching in 1916 can be re-

constructed in some detail from his letters to Iris Barry. He
tells her to learn from Flaubert, as de Maupassant had learned:

> . . . consider the excellent example which Flaubert set us in
> sitting on De M's head and making him write, and De M's excel-
> lent example in doing what he was told . . . In describing such
> and such a concierge in such and such a street so that Flaubert
> would recognize *which* concierge when he next passed that way
> . . . Consider the wagon full of young ladies in "La Maison
> Tellier."
>   That is the way to write poetry.

The fewest words, then; but the precise words to visualize the
object beyond possibility of misidentification. This he taught
Eliot; to whom it was not absolutely new, for Alain-Fournier, as
we have seen, had maintained that the writer's aim should be
to show the object as if the words were not there; but perhaps
Eliot did not realize, till the same advice came afresh through
Pound and Gourmont, that it was Flaubert's precept. The Vignettes in "A Cooking Egg" and "Sweeney among the Nightingales" were early experiments with the recipe: economical, precise, vivid. The difficulties in those poems come from the lack
of explanatory connections. We are not told why the scenes,
the people are described, nor how the person and scene belong
with one another. But each image is perfectly precise and
identifiable. In *The Waste Land* Eliot is rewarded for his exercises in the technique: the sequence of vignettes is still unex-
plained, the connections still omitted; but the total rhythm
holds the vignettes together; and how wonderful these are, beginning with the "Marie, Marie" episode, through Phlebas the
Phoenician, to the travelers who are aware of another traveler
with them.

Pound's approval of the Flaubert method is complementary
to the view, developed in discussions with Yeats from 1913 to
1916, that poets were missing the effects they desired — of
"beauty," of "astonishment"— by invoking "beauty" and "as-

tonishment" in the abstract, instead of describing the scenes and events that give rise to them. Pound recommended the practice (of which Imagism was only the extreme form) of precise reporting of the object. One way of guarding against imprecision was to avoid not merely such words as "beauty" but all abstractions. He combed Yeats' poetry for abstractions, and found more than Yeats had expected or thought possible; and the two men agreed to write entirely without them. Eliot must have heard of their rule from Pound. It must have been salutary to a man who, if he was a born poet, had spent the recent years among philosophers. No doubt it guarded him from that wrong kind of abstraction which anticipates the effect a verse is meant to have, and so weakens it. But he did not apply the rule too literally or rigorously, for that would have been to abnegate an unusual linguistic resource which his work in philosophy had developed: the language of the vignettes (which represent *his* variety of imagism) is ironically and vigorously bookish; calls on language which might not have surprised the eighteenth-century but would have surprised the nineteenth-century poet; sometimes calls on a technical abstraction of the philosophers:

> And even the Abstract Entities
> Circumambulate her charm.

Perhaps in the poems of the twenties, *The Waste Land* and *Ash-Wednesday*, there is an avoidance of abstractions, just as there is the cultivation of the vivid, perfect pictorial image suspended in a perfect music. But Eliot's habit of thought favored the use of abstractions, and by 1939 he developed a method of employing them, of which this is one example:

> Accident is design
> And design is accident

and this a more striking example:

Internal darkness, deprivation
And destitution of all property,
Desiccation of the world of sense,
Evacuation of the world of fancy,
Inoperancy of the world of spirit.

There the abstractions are not really of the order Pound feared. They are unexpected; they are a powerful attempt to express the lack of sensation, the lack of care about sensation; they have, one might almost say, the sensation of nonsensation. It is part of the originality of the *Quartets* that the poetry is sometimes the poetry of a philosopher (including the Indic philosopher), and abstractions are used as only a man both an expert poet and an expert philosopher could use them. This use of abstractions, highly expressive and provoking thought and emotion, became possible after the training in abstention that Pound had encouraged. Sometimes it happens that a poet learns how to use a mode of speech purposefully by depriving himself of it for a season.

In the same years immediately preceding the 1914 war Yeats and Pound had also developed the conception of "cold beauty." As we have seen from Norman Foerster's essay on Hearn, the search for a bracing, northern beauty was already afoot in 1910. Yeats performed the work sometimes required of a great poet, in that he first found and registered the voice for which the young men were longing. The poetry of *The Cold Heaven* and *The Fishermen* is a repudiation of that submission to the emotions which Babbitt was attacking in the classroom, and a model. Pound with his usual energy set about transmitting the lesson: one cannot be at the mercy of emotions while composing. Eliot noted — and approved — the opinion; and a saving coldness in the approach became one of his tests of an artist's capacity. In 1917 he used it, perhaps insufficiently coldly, to measure Jean de Bosschère, who, he said, abstained from emotions and words which appeal to them, and so produced an ef-

fect of "intense frigidity which I find altogether admirable."
He applied the same test to Hawthorne two years later and
justified him by it:

> He had . . . what no one else in Boston had — the firmness, the
> true coldness, the hard coldness of the genuine artist. In con-
> sequence the observation of moral life in "The Scarlet Letter,"
> in the "House of Seven Gables," and even in some of the tales
> and sketches, has solidity, has permanence, the permanence of
> art.

So, while he has said that the poems of Yeats were not helpful
to him at that stage of his life, he responded to Yeats' cold
beauty as it reached him through Pound; and later, in his *Journey of the Magi*, he created it, and in all the Ariel poems. It is
notable that Ford accepted and worked by the same standards.
Part of Ford's praise for a poet is

> your flawless cold words
> Shall hinder
> Our poor mortality.

That poem of Ford's belongs to the postwar era. From Ford's
earlier "leaflet" of 1912, *High Germany*, Pound had singled out
three poems: "The Starlings," "In the Little Old Market-Place,"
and "To All the Dead." "I do not expect many people to understand why I praise them," Pound added: the average reader
was likely to be deceived by Ford's lightness of touch and
easy attitude. But Pound understood the technical seriousness
which underlay the apparently careless meandering: the art
which underlay the artlessness. Ford was intent to sound like a
man talking, intimately but entirely naturally, to a close companion or to himself. The poems move with a light chattering
rhythm, observe scenes and quickly sketch them, call up brief
sharp memories. If Pound brought these pieces to Eliot's notice,

Eliot evidently found nothing there that he could as yet emulate. But eventually, when he began to work out a style for his Aristophanesque melodrama, it may be that he benefited from Ford's pioneering with the poetry of contemporary speech. I shall revert to this suggestion in the chapter on drama.

Contact and Conquest

And perhaps the pleasure and friction of living in another country helped to recall Eliot to poetry: at first the amusement of a stranger, when everything, even British cookery, damp bedclothes, and the hats worn by the wives of Oxford dons, entertained; then the sense of communion which a visitor may feel as he moves among another nation's landscape and memorials and gradually desires no longer to be a visitor but to embrace and give. The London moments in *The Waste Land* are informed with that feeling. From one or two excursions in his miscellaneous prose we may guess how he arrived in London looking for images acquired in his early reading —

> Sherlock Holmes reminds us always of the pleasant externals of nineteenth-century London . . . I wish that Messrs. Murray would bring out another volume with the old illustrations: I cannot even remember the name of the artist: but I remember the hansom cabs, the queer bowlers, Holmes's fore-and-aft cap, Holmes in a frock coat after breakfast, Sir George Burnwell when he took down "a life-preserver from the wall." But in the Sherlock Holmes stories the late nineteenth century is always romantic, always nostalgic, and never merely silly.

— and how he sympathetically discerned the images behind the façade of the London of 1916 and 1920. Sometimes his eye sought and found the London of Conan Doyle or Dickens; sometimes sought and found the London of Lancelot Andrewes, whom he was already reading before April 1921. The

London churches, he wrote later, are "as precious as any of the four hundred odd churches in Rome." He has striven for the preservation of the churches whenever schemes have been mooted for changes in the City which would obscure them; the editorial commentaries in the *Criterion* several times defend them against encroachment; and as early as 1921, before the *Criterion* existed, he was saying:

> To one who, like the present writer, passes his days in this City of London (quand'io sentii chiavar l'uscio di sotto) the loss of these towers, to meet the eye down a grimy lane, and of these empty naves, to receive the solitary visitor at noon from the dust and tumult of Lombard Street, will be irreparable . . .

The physical City helped to gain Eliot for England and the Anglican Church; possibly it helped to regain him for poetry.

It was not unknown for the brighter Englishmen of the post-1918 epoch to decry the interest of London and call her dowdy compared with Paris. Raymond Mortimer reported to the *Dial* in 1922 that in Paris he might see the windows of Bernheim full of Derain and Matisse, and on three successive nights attend three different plays flawlessly performed at the Vieux Colombier. In London he asked for an art periodical and was given the *Studio*, asked for a critical magazine and was given the *Mercury!* One advantage of London "for the last few years" had been that Diaghilev had found his warmest welcome there, and "One could go every other night to his Ballet and never be bored; and one went. All London became *balletomane* . . ." — but even this advantage had recently diminished, for the balletomanes liked their fare soft, and had let the critics kill *Le Sacre du Printemps*. But Eliot, while he would no doubt have conceded each of these points, apparently did not concur in the implied conclusion, that a man in search of the arts or a creative or a satisfying life should abandon London for Paris. Even from intellectual as well as physical London he drew sustenance. He did not sentimentalize. It pleased him at moments — pleased the stern young critic and reformer in him — to pillory the shortcomings of his adopted neighbors: their mental laziness, for example: he would suddenly jump on "the British writer, who shrinks from working overtime or at weekends"; or he would reflect that "there is in contemporary English literature a very great deal which I cordially detest." Of course, we might speculate that the very flaws were stimulating to Eliot: that they gave him a lot to do, with scarcely a rival to challenge him. But I rather believe that he found something positive in the scene to require his respect, even his enthusiasm. In a recent reminiscence he has said that the post-1918 years, when Murry was editing the *Athenaeum,* Bruce Richmond the *Times Literary Supplement,* and there were auxiliaries like *Art and Letters* and the *Calendar* to provoke thought and provide a forum, were "the high summer of literary journalism in London in my time." As early as 1917, in his book on Ezra Pound's poetry he had attributed the growth which took place between the writing of the early verses and of *Ripostes* as a gift of London. Pound had spent three years in London when *Ripostes* appeared in 1912:

> The effect of London is apparent: the author has become a critic of men, surveying them from a consistent and developed point of view; he is more formidable and disconcerting; in short, much more mature.

To recognize the part a city plays in the development of a friend is not to admit that it did as much for oneself; but I fancy that very often Eliot records the movements of his own mind by discerning and recording comparable movements in another, and that this is a case in point.

Eliot in his first half-dozen years in London rapidly assumed the leadership of English letters. A critic has written of the period as if it were characterized by hardship and therefore by meager results. There is a simple sense in which it *was* a phase of hardship: a young man, brought up in an affluent home, now responsible for a wife and desiring to enjoy London with her, must have found inconvenience in the limited income and in the long hours of preparation, commuting, and labor, entailed in earning it. But it was essentially a period of triumph. Eliot conquered intellectual London as brilliantly as Dr. Johnson. Area by area by area he took possession of it. He began by penetrating the professional philosophical periodicals. By January 1917 he was, according to Pound, "in touch with various papers here and sees what is going on." Eleven months later he was reading his poems among Gosse and the Sitwells, the old Spender and Garvin, in a drawing room in Mayfair; and Arnold Bennett, hearing "The Hippopotamus" there, told his diary "If I had been the house, this would have brought the house down."

As each volume of his work appeared, his conquests advanced. So strikingly new, and so definitive of the style in which it innovated, has been each successive volume he has published, that it has made an immediate impact, and has excited opposition (from those who resented a new style and denied that a new style could be a style at all) and emulation (from those awake to new beauty, but better able to follow than create). This has been true from his earliest days in England. After *Prufrock and other Observations* the sensibility of "Prufrock" gradually pervaded the work of other poets. "Street Meeting," a poem by John J. Adams, published in *Coterie,* Easter 1920, meditates:

> Speaking without thinking, one would say —
> Is it you? How strange! — That sort of thing. —
> "Is it cold," or "It is good weather today" —
> Or "This street affects me as unpleasing . . ."
>
> And if I chance to meet
> One who bears within the grey soul of this street,
> One is the grey street prowling among men —
> What then?

Then came the strophes in the Hogarth Press *Poems*, 1919, and *Ara Vos Prec*, 1920. Grover Smith and other critics of today have trounced the strophes. Overseverely. They are unlovely. But they were meant to be. Having denied themselves all charm, all yielding, they bear the consequences: no one will delight in them. But they have become part of this century's poetic history, in the stream of which they stand like "bold anfractuous rocks," and their almost instantaneous effect when they appeared in print was to set every young poet with a spit of rock to him simulating their form and emulating their performance. Robert Nichols' cameo of Sinclair, for example, appeared in *Coterie* in December 1919:

> Sinclair's looks can never lie,
>   He is well shaved, has curved lips,
> His nose is straight, so is his eye,
>   Also he boasts substantial hips . . .

"So" and "also" are cruder sutures than Eliot would have admitted — Eliot who had remarked that syntactical variety was part of Gautier's skill — and the imitation missed the subtleties and went for the emphases:

> Sinclair would make his muslin choice, —
>   Spring and his father say he must:
> Corah has ankles and a voice,
>   Nancy has French and a neat bust.

In the same issue of *Coterie*, Herbert Read invented a character, Huskisson, who wants to do a Waring from London and his business and domestic successes

> To Amazonian forests bilious and lush
> Where the gobbling boa-constrictor glides,
> And pachyderms twist their enormous tails
> In the middle of absurdly big backsides

and remind us of the Brazilian jaguars and the divine hippopotamus. Huskisson follows his bent and

> Over the rolling savannas he strides,
> Essential shagginess

Hippopotamoid savannas and Sweenoid shagginess. It is Eliot
Assorted. John J. Adams also practiced more than one Eliot
style: together with his "Prufrock"-like contribution to *Coterie*
of Easter 1920, he had a poem, "Profiteer Williamson pursues
Culture," which derived from the strophes and specifically
from "Sweeney among the Nightingales":

> The orange and vermilion lights
> Twinkle among the indigo trees.
> Williamson in violet tights
> Converses with the blonde marquise.

Louis Untermeyer, a clever observer, not very sympathetic to
Eliot, drew attention, in a review of the Knopf edition of
Eliot's *Poems* in 1920, to the retinue of emulators, and quoted
Robert Nichols' "Spring Song" and Osbert Sitwell's "The Dusky
King of Malabar."

While incubating and hatching the strophes, Eliot prepared
the first critical essays which were to take possession of their
readers and find continuators with equal speed.

At the same time he was acquiring the acquaintance and
admiration — and perhaps imbibing the psychic energy for
strophe and essay from the acquaintance and admiration — of
various men and women who cared for literature, alike gentlemen readers of the old school, such as Charles Whibley, and
the writers and painters of Bloomsbury, who, being not quite
forty, still viewed themselves as the devastating young. By
1922, as we have all been pointing out to each other since the
publication of *A Writer's Diary*, the great Virginia Woolf was
calling him "Great Tom."

Eliot won Bloomsbury by his quiet power to wield words like rapiers, to compare and correlate the most distant studies, to compare and correlate the newest literature and the oldest, to destroy and revive and legislate. Copeland had characterized him as a harsh critic, implying that he should mitigate his severity. But he gained by it in England. Urbanely and ruthlessly he brought his harsh judgment to bear on the contemporary practitioners of the Word, the professional critics, the professional creators, the amateur disputants at cocktail party and houseparty. After all, they were very clever but frivolous; they made it their boast that they believed nothing; and that left them easy victims to the man who argued, no less dexterously than they, with an authority he was determined to impose. At the head of *The Sacred Wood* in 1920 he printed Remy de Gourmont's sentence:

> Eriger en lois ses impressions personnelles, c'est le grand effort d'un homme s'il est sincère.

and he can be seen in an engaging photograph, reproduced in the sixtieth birthday book, elevating his impressions into laws at Garsington Manor, sober and definitive, while Lord David Cecil, Anthony Asquith, Leslie Hartley, and Edward Sackville-West listen. It is the charm of the English intellectuals that they do not elevate their impressions into laws; they are happy to coast on the stream of pleasure wherever it takes them. But in the presence of a lawgiver their deep-ingrained English morality, from which fortune so long seemed to have delivered them, acknowledges its master.

Looking back at the years of conquest across the space of a quarter of a century Eliot deprecated, with modesty and humor, the formidable reputation he acquired:

> In my earlier years I obtained, partly by subtlety, partly by effrontery, and partly by accident, a reputation amongst the

credulous for learning and scholarship, of which (having no further use for it) I have since tried to disembarrass myself.

But indeed the reputation was justified, if not for the qualities which he disowned in that later statement, for the demonstration he provided of the working of a mind concerned for society, and for literature as a high function of society, and of the duty of such a mind to explore the various fields of knowledge and to indicate co-relevant aspects of them. Making that demonstration, Eliot prompted young England to an emulous effort to the mastery of many branches of knowledge and to the correlating of diverse interests to a common end. The present-day teachers and critics of English literature, who, initially devoted to literature, extend their interests and think of themselves as sociologists and direct their earnest efforts towards the health of the whole culture to which they belong, and do so very valuably, owe something to the example Eliot set in his first London decade and afterwards in the *Criterion*.

It has been imputed to Eliot an unpardonable blemish that those first London years were made pleasant for him by friendships with men of the old school. An American, coming to England free of the narrowness that is involved in the war between the establishment and the unestablished, could make friends with both sides, and benefit intellectually and spiritually from an acquaintance with both, without any loss of virtue. Besides, there are men in England, born into the establishment, who are free of it and above it. This fact did not escape Pound when he

> with decency, knocked
> That a Blunt should open

and

> gathered from the air a live tradition
> or from a fine old eye the unconquered flame.

And it did not escape Eliot. Of course Eliot loved what he saw in the old eyes. He saw there the rich experience which Wendell had preached and which he had traveled far to find. He welcomed it without any surrender of his literary integrity. He kindled that mature eye to respect by arguing and writing for his own view of literature, not by deferring. "He has successfully irritated almost every one of the older professional critics," said a compiler who called himself "Recorder" in *Chapbook* No. 12, June 1920. That was why the old loved him. They loved literature and its rebellion. The best days of Whibley's life, on which he drew for sustenance ever afterwards, had been his days in Paris among the poets (did that first draw Eliot to him? — he had seen Mallarmé plain). In the young American he saw his French theorists of the Word again.

It could be maintained that Eliot's progress through Mayfair, Bloomsbury, Garsington pampered his Jamesian side: erected a foible into a law, drafted for him by Maurras, that the poet, as he must build on tradition, must meet the tradition on the lips of the "best people." Yes, but with two important qualifications. First, he was not the man to relax into simple, uncritical satisfaction in any gathering, no matter how representative of wit, charm, or history. A sentence in his Byron essay is suggestive: telling how the last cantos of *Don Juan* are at the head of Byron's work, because Byron genuinely hated hypocrisy, and the house party gave him the opportunity to make poetry of it, Eliot says:

> He was right in making the hero of his house-party a Spaniard, for what Byron understands and dislikes about English society is very much what an intelligent foreigner in the same position would understand and dislike.

The man who wrote that must have been alive to the weaknesses of the circles amid which his faculties expanded; and later in writing *The Family Reunion* he succeeded in making poetic drama of his knowledge, and his knowledge of Byron's knowledge; and in *The Cocktail Party* he again succeeded, and better, though there, if the weaknesses of men and women in society are sharply displayed, there is a certain glow in the comic writing which eliminates acrimony. Secondly, Eliot endeavored to know another England. He was intent to reconnect the poet and the people, and could not be the poet of reconnection unless he found and understood the ordinary man. But this was difficult. Temperamentally it must, I suppose, have been as difficult for a philosopher-poet to meet the people as it was easy for him to captivate the elite. But he tried. He tried by eavesdropping. His quick, mimic's ear listened for the London voices in street and vehicle, pub and ABC. He tried by frequenting the music hall, and became the observer and analyst of working England by analyzing the art of Little Tich and Nellie Wallace; and the process slowly extended his own art. He caught something of the temper of the people: the wants, the skills, the doggedness. It pleased him to be able to pick out regional characteristics. So, writing for the *Dial* in June 1921, he explained the Lancashire mind through the Lancashire comedian, who, he said, "is at his best when unsupported and making a direct set, pitting himself, against a suitable audience."

But almost the only direct contact he could have with the greater England of the people was through writers who had come from working or middle-class families: Middleton Murry, D. H. Lawrence, A. E. Coppard. Though his "whole soul" could never be with them, he moved the frontier of his sympathies out towards them. It is instructive to reflect on his relations with Middleton Murry: his appreciation of Murry's invitation to him to serve on the *Athenaeum* in 1919 and the printing of his contributions there; his later reciprocal care to print Murry's contributions and review Murry's books in the *Criterion;* his readiness to indicate common ground between them, his readiness to respect differences. Possibly Murry's equipment was improvised and defective compared with his; yet he recognized the courage that lay behind the improvisation and the worth of work conducted under difficulties. He strove to learn from colleagues nearer to the body of England, and he learned a little. Only, contact with literary men sprung from working England is a very uncertain way of making contact with working England; everything in the situation makes them insufficient representatives.

All the handicaps considered, it is remarkable how much Eliot managed, within the first few years, to learn of the country with which he gradually linked himself. He manifested a capacity to go beyond the limitations of the visitor, and, for that matter, the limitations of the resident who is often anxious to insulate himself in lifelong habits. The conditions of wartime London helped. War does something to heighten a sympathetic sense of each other in people who might otherwise practice a mutual disregard. Eliot was to be a Londoner in two wars. Under the bombs of the second war his sympathies were to be shaken and remade and extended, and his art extended and deepened with his sympathies and his reflections on history, and he was able to write the last two *Quartets* and then go on to the successful plays of which he had dreamed. The London of the second world war produced those results; the London of the first world war and the glimpses it gave of people, suffering, and courage led to a first remaking of his mind and the heightening of his poetic powers, and *The Waste Land* was the result.

The Poetry of Askesis

In *The Waste Land* Eliot spoke with the voice of the lonely prophet in a corrupt city. To read the magazines of 1919 and 1920 is to see that he was not alone in the impulse to lament the desolation or disorder around him and to cry, as the prophet traditionally does, for a new sense of the antique laws; he was only isolated in that he was the first to find a voice and a form for the cry. The post-Armistice years were a period of denunciation of a society which had the recent war and the postwar confusion to its discredit. Richard Aldington pledged:

> O, I could charm the high gods
> With a more than Aristophanic levity
> Deploy before their histrionic cachinnations
> The biggest fraud in history;
> O, I could play hell with this epoch
> Had I still three friends in the world
> Untainted by moral cowardice,
> By respect for institutions.

And sometimes the energy that would dismantle a bad world felt strong enough to furnish a more satisfying one: Wyndham Lewis announced a New Renaissance in the first issue of *Tyro*. There was a general ferment. Was not Eliot's *Waste Land* the conspicuous work to which any movement, that is to pass from the first condition of tangled impulse to the second stage where it assumes a direction, must give rise?

Harold Monro inclined to that view. When "Recorder" summed up the literary events of 1922 for *Chapbook* No. 33, he did not mention *The Waste Land*, apparently unaware that a masterpiece had appeared: "The year 1922 has not been particularly noteworthy in poetry . . ." Monro, his editor, intervened in the next issue to make the deficiency good. With a pretended naïveté he called attention to the poem, said it was perplexing, resumed its central argument, and then:

> Those poor little people who string their disjointed ejaculations into prosaic semblances of verse — they pale as one reads *The Waste Land*. They have no relation to it: yet, through it, we realise what they were trying, but have failed, to represent. Our

epoch sprawls, a desert, between an unrealised past and an un-imaginable future.

When he had lived six years in England, Eliot interpreted England and Europe with *the* poem of the postwar struggle for re-orientation. It is sometimes possible, in the process of cultural exchange, for a man who has lived a little while among people not his own, examining them with a curiosity that ever the more approximates to love, to become their spokesman and to say for them what they cannot succeed in formulating for themselves.

Eliot wrote the work under the stress of illness. Six years of strenuous double-living — wage-earning faithfully and effi-ciently pursued, intellectual conquests pursued at the same time — had exhausted him. But a poet's breakdown is often the moment of creation. To let slip his hold on the day is to slip free of the day's hold on him; he gathers all that he has experienced into an innovative act.

He wrote at a time when two technical suggestions had come to his notice. Whether he took them up consciously, or whether the impression they had made on him on the eve of illness determined their use without any conscious scrutiny and decision on his part, they appear to have contributed to the method of his poem. One derived from *Le Sacre du Printemps;* the other came from Pound.

In the summer of 1921 Eliot saw *Le Sacre du Printemps* in London, was involved in the warfare over it that almost sepa-rated friends, watched Diaghilev surrender to the Philistines and withdraw it after three performances, and defended and interpreted it in his "London Letter" to the *Dial.* Its mu-sic, he told the *Dial,* metamorphosed the "rhythm of the steppes" into "the scream of the motor horn, the rattle of machinery, the grind of wheels, the beating of iron and steel, the roar of the underground railway, and the other barbaric cries of modern life." It brought home the continuity of the human predicament: primitive man on the dolorous steppes, modern man in the city with its "despairing noises"; the mind of the one a continuation of the mind of the other, the essential problem unchanging. Eliot's interpretation of Stravinsky suggests that a theme of *The Waste Land* is the unchanging predicament of man, and the unchanging remedy; and that Eliot realized that the theme required the capture of the frightening barbaric sounds, and (since poetry combines music and pictures) of the frightening or poignant images of man's environment; and that he equally realized that if he could capture these effects he would create the contemporary literature which no writer in English had yet created: he would bring a literature which had not yet had a Stravinsky, and lagged behind, level with European music. In another *Dial* letter, written two months earlier, he wrote a sentence which throws further light on the method: he pointed out that contemporary, as contrasted with earlier, ballet was at once more sophisticated and more simplified; and "what is needed of art is a simplification of current life into something rich and strange." The last words echo *The Tempest*, the alchemical drama which *The Waste Land* echoes. In *The Waste Land* Eliot worked by bold, simplifying strokes to metamorphose the despairing sounds, the desperate sights, of his world into the rich and strange.

It is notable that Rivière, writing essays on Stravinsky eight and ten years earlier, had come to conclusions about the new music similar to Eliot's: had shown that "son audace . . . se marque par des simplifications"; that his strokes are "franches et sommaires"; that he never runs away from the banal, but "il l'accepte, il parle avec sa voix, il se sert de tous ses avantages." With Stravinsky's deliberate incorporation of banalities, and the harrowing beauty won by the sudden bold acceptance of the noises of common man, may be compared the intervention of Mrs. Porter's ballad or the tale of Lil in *The*

Waste Land. To Rivière the sudden appearance of material
without preparatory, and therefore mitigating, leads or transi-
tions was an essential of the method of Stravinsky's ballets. He
said "L'oeuvre est entière et brute, les morceaux en restent
tout crus; ils nous sont livré sans rien qui ne prépare la diges-
tion; tout ici est franc, intact, limpide et grossier." The words
might describe the organization of *The Waste Land.*

In the *Dial* of January 1921 Pound commented on Cocteau's
Poésies 1917-1920. He claimed that Cocteau, inheriting from
the *école de Laforgue,* wrote the poetry of the city intellect, a
poetry which reflected the intersecting pluralities of the city:

> The life of a village is narrative; you have not been there three
> weeks before you know that in the revolution et cetera, and
> when M. le Comte et cetera, and so forth. In a city the visual
> impressions succeed each other, overlap, overcross, they are
> "cinematographic" . . .

In Eliot's city poem the visual impressions "succeed each
other, overlap, overcross . . ." As the original draft of *The
Waste Land* on which Pound performed his Caesarian operation — that is, did the "cutting" — has disappeared, we cannot know to what extent the "cinematographic" technique was
already in play in Eliot's version, to what extent it was imposed by Pound at the final stage. My supposition is that the
original already brought the technique to bear, not because
Eliot was interested in cinema (for he seems to have been resistant to it as an art form until the late date when he sanc-
tioned, and participated in, the preparation of *Murder in the
Cathedral* for the screen) but because, with the help of
Pound's sentence in the *Dial,* he perceived that the technique
was right for communicating the rhythm of London where the
eye passes moment by moment from green to drab, from grim
to nostalgic; and that Pound, when he saw the draft, approved, only thought that Eliot had not pushed the process far

enough: Pound had perceived the essentials of cinema, and cut with ruthlessness and taste to complete the poem's cinematographic form.

The Waste Land is a work in which the poet, like some of his predecessors, writes simultaneously about his own illness and the world's illness, of which his own is a reflection. He records and condemns his own "despairing" state and prescribes a discipline for his cure and for the healing of the city civilization of which he is the representative.

This brings us to the use he made of Jessie L. Weston's *From Ritual to Romance*. Miss Weston finished the book in Paris in October 1919 and the Cambridge University Press published it in 1920. Eliot seems to have read it rapidly, perhaps skimmingly (for one or two pages of his copy, Grover Smith found, remain uncut), but with that extraordinarily swift insight which has marked his pursuit of anthropology and the cognate sciences. Some of its material filled his mind and crossed into his poem; the material on the doctor was still mobile in him three decades later when he wrote *The Cocktail Party*. What he does not say, in the note in which he acknowledges his obligation to her, is that he used her material with a defiance of her argument. For Miss Weston showed that the story of the Grail, as old in its essentials as the *Rig Veda*, and older, tells of the dead earth restored by the magic of human lovemaking. A drought falls on a kingdom, and will persist until a young man abandons the chastity in which he has been reared. When the boy has been sought, found, tempted, and won, and his marriage with the king's daughter consummated, the spell is broken and the refreshing rain comes.

At a far remove Wagner took this story, saw the essentials even while he retained the Christian conditions, and instilled the story with a special meaning for his art, and for the European arts of his time. His Kundry is not the wounded king's daughter. She is the servant of destruction, the seductress, sex as sin; yet she is the tormented lover of the good, the helper, who flies in exhausting self-sacrifice to the orient for restoring herbs. She is the art of the nineteenth century: Baudelaire's; Wagner's. As compared with her late Renaissance forerunners, Puck and Ariel (Shakespeare's projections of *his* art), who put a girdle round the earth in forty minutes to fetch their magical herbs, she is a dark spirit. Through her, Wagner said that his work was at once voluptuous sin and a straining devotion to the good. Kundry is the genius of redemption and restoration. By capitulating to her kiss, the hero is flooded with a world-comprehending sympathy: the King is restored, the waste land revived.

But Eliot adopted a different stance. His poem refused the myth of the kiss of comprehension and the blameless sin: Kundry's kiss was not a cure for civilization's blight, but a symptom of it. *The Waste Land* is an ascetic, correcting response to Jessie Weston and Frazer, whom Eliot regarded with an intense admiration as one of the great men of his age; it is as though the poet says "You have disclosed the mind of the past; but we cannot be content with that mind; though we continue it, we must struggle to a higher level." And as between two contrasting "higher levels" which the nineteenth century had invented, Wagner's and Tennyson's, he chose the latter — even though he had once said that Tennyson, against Malory, was "Chaucer retold for children." The tones of the other school, a Wagnerian thunder and excitement, can be heard in his poem, but they have been taken into the service of the sermonizers. We might compare the use made of the Grail legend by a commentator called Ernest Bradley, who published a pamphlet on it in the Geneva series (the series in which Eliot's mother's *Easter Songs* appeared) or by the designer of the panels in the Boston Public Library, where Kundry is the Loathely Damsel and the Grail is achieved by a virgin knight. But to suggest these comparisons is not to try to score off the poem. Indeed it may be part of its brilliance that it rescues the "moralizing" view of the ancient myth from men who could not moralize without falling into milk-and-water and embodies it in an art as fierce as Wagner's or Baudelaire's.

This brings us back to the mood of the post-1918 years. It was a mood of anger with disorder and failure. Men wanted to be condemned, that they might be pushed into the effort to readjust and reconstruct. *The Waste Land* made its impact, and was taken up in language after language, because it found the tones and, as we like to say, a "myth" for the condemnation. It said in the terms of the Grail story that we are blighted and in terms of our feelings that we are bored. Eliot read in W. H. R. Rivers how civilization had brought blight and boredom to Melanesia, and he showed the boredom of blight in civilized London, alike in the typist's bed-sitter, where love-making, which should be fertilizing and significant, is automatic and "now that's done: and I'm glad it's over," and in the homes of the rich:

> "What shall I do now? What shall I do?"
> "I shall rush out as I am and walk the street
> With my hair down, so. What shall we do tomorrow?
> What shall we ever do?"

He castigated our living death and he proposed renunciation and discipline for our redemption.

Meanwhile an alternative literature, which sustained the doctrine of the kiss of comprehension, was claiming England and Europe. In England it had begun twenty years earlier with Forster's first novels and tales — work entirely delicate and terse, yet urging, out of the purest conviction, that the blight of civilization was to be healed by the earth and the air and by the free play of impulse which the elements would release if we let them. It grew through D. H. Lawrence, angry with men who had lost the honesty of earth. The literature of the primitive impulse has been more pervasive and abundant than the opposing literature of discipline which Eliot started with *The Waste Land*. But both literatures have had their magnificent triumphs, and the new generation of the fifties and sixties begins its work with the advantage, and the puzzlement, of having been shaped by both.

Wendell once characterized the native trait of American literature as the absence of lubricity. Up to the first world war the trait was certainly marked. After 1918 there was an equally certain reversal of it and lubricity burst out in all directions. Not a novel without it since then; and Wendell's definition reads like comedy in the present age. But Eliot left the United States while the tradition prevailed. It prevails in him. But of course his poem does not make its effect by an *absence* of lubricity, but bids for a permanent abstention from lubricity, bids for the containment of our passions, and dramatizes sexual experiences so that they seem painfully undesirable. "The whole poem," said Geoffrey Tandy in 1938, "is . . . fiercely anaphrodisiac . . . Anything more savagely moral (in the contemporary and limited sense) than *The Waste Land* I have yet to read."

Eliot's poetry of the nonsignificant seduction, and of the battered Lil and her abortion, encouraged some striking essays in the anaphrodisiac art during the next twenty years. There is an example in a writer who much admired Eliot and whom Eliot admired, translated, and published: Ramon Fernandez. A powerful critic, Fernandez was occasionally a novelist, and among his novels was *Les Violents* of 1935. Pauline, the wife of an industrialist, deliberately crosses the town to the room of a workman and gives herself to him. At each touch her body quivers and he interprets the spasms as pleasure. But they are spasms of protest, and she wants only to have it over — *qu'il vienne, qu'il vienne, et que tout soit fini*. Fernandez isolates all her reactions, not for clinical or "documentary" curiosity, but to define her repulsion and to make us share it. In other writers, who do not share Eliot's outlook as closely as Fernandez, the anaphrodisiac lineage shows at moments. Lawrence Durrell is often the poet of pleasure, not of *askesis*. Yet the adulterer in *The Black Book* who thinks of the absent husband throughout the compulsive adultery is in the tradition. Graham Greene, although he has many pages of pathos, where the sympathy is with the human habit of love, also has occasional pages in the anaphrodisiac tradition: that, for example, in *The Heart of the Matter* where a young airman takes without passion ("no time like the present for a prang"), but puts his jacket on again because "you're not enthusiastic."

At the end of *The Waste Land* Eliot picks, from the crowded Dante gallery, Arnaut Daniel for his pattern-figure. Daniel had traveled to the margin of civilization, ultimate England; he was an innovating poet: in these respects he was Eliot's mirror. He had hammered out his innovations to provide later poets with forms for their masterpieces: in this respect he was Eliot's ideal. Above all, he was the proper monitor for the anaphrodisiac poem because, the most illustrious love poet of his day, he leapt into the fire, *willingly*, to burn away his lusts.

However, to talk of the outlook of *The Waste Land* and to translate it is to miss much of its poetic interest and lose sight of some of its beauties. *The Waste Land* helped Eliot to reorganize himself for another eight years of work; it helped younger men to organize for another thirty: it set in motion the moralist poetry of men like Auden. And if those whose background and whose attitude to life were very different from his were organized by it, the reason lies less in the force of the views he professed than in the originality and beauty of the poetic techniques with which he found words and rhythms to profess them. The conquest was a technical conquest. But one result of technical conquests is likely to be that the technician inculcates his views with his craft.

The Waste Land *and Joyce*

The Waste Land and the issue of the *Criterion* in which it was first published formed the node of an exchange between Eliot and Joyce.

Eliot had no predispositions in favor of Irish writers. Harvard had been mildly stirred by the Abbey Company's troubles in Boston during the visit of 1911 and the return visit of 1913. Some student critics came away from the theatre delighted by the charm of the playing: by the authenticity of the handling of pipe and matches in *The Rising of the Moon* (much as, attending the Habima plays in the 1944 period, when the actors were veterans, I felt I could watch Mesqin forever washing his hands over the bucket in the desert). But Eliot, warned by Babbitt against the nonclassical literatures, and those tributaries which may tempt a man away from the main stream of the Western development, resisted Irish art, and especially the Abbey plays which depended on a provincial dialect. Then, through Pound and through the ladies of the *Egoist,* he became aware of Joyce. He had a near view of the last stages of the struggle for the *Portrait of an Artist* and the public reception of it. He read the novel, found in Joyce an Irishman who shared his prejudices against the Irish literary renaissance, and who reflected as he did on the history and value of words, on the differences between the market usage and the literary usage, on the possibilities of relating the spoken and the written speech.

The attacks on the *Portrait,* Pound's defense of it, Miss Weaver's sympathy for it, braced him. Then at the *Egoist,* where in 1917 he replaced Aldington (called up) as Assistant Editor, he saw the first chapters of *Ulysses.* He followed the struggles of the American *Little Review* to justify the printing of Wyndham Lewis and Joyce. He was roused to championship.

Besides acquiring the sense of crusading, which may be the indulgence of a sense of virtue, he was filled with ideas by *Ulysses*. He realized, and later was to make this point and argue from it, that the prose of the new "roman d'aventure" might be poetic; that Joyce's prose must be read with the same care as poetry: the words might be savored, absorbed, directed to the voice as song, to the limbs as movement and touch; and that the images might act in the mind like dramatis personae on a stage. The early chapters of *Ulysses* seen at the *Egoist* office, and later chapters which Joyce sent for his opinion, he read as poems. He told Joyce certain chapters were "superb" and "I have nothing but admiration, in fact, I wish, for my own sake, that I had not read it." This was not merely to compliment Joyce by confessing envy; he meant that some of Joyce's images, some of his rhythms, had invaded his own. Every poet fears swamping by the genius of another, and Eliot feared that Joyce's work, overpowering in its immensity, would color his own for the immediate future. What he had avoided in his close encounters with Pound he might incur with the distant Joyce.

He had too much individuality to be swamped, but did he not hearken after Joyce for a period, during which he wrote *The Waste Land?* Ellmann has intimated that the principal effect of his reading of *Ulysses* was that he dared, indeed was forced by emulation, to undertake an innovatory work. Melchiori and Grover Smith have suggested that the poem has debts of detail to *Ulysses:* the dog, the canal and the gasworks, the drowned man. I would add the suggestion that the narration in the public house, "When Lil's husband got demobbed . . ." is another debt. Molly Bloom's soliloquy had moved Eliot as a great achievement. He must have wanted to write a comparable dramatization of the popular mind. In the result the Lil sequence is very different from Molly's soliloquy. Joyce presented human squalor more thoroughly than anyone before him, but transfigured it, and his chapter is the praise of life.

Eliot made his women witnesses to the breakdown of society, and the narration tells of the misery of life without values. The contrast is part of the total contrast between Joyce and Eliot. Joyce, whom Eliot thought arrogant at a first meeting, had begun as a despiser of anyone but the artist, and of almost any artist except himself, but had steadily grown into the poet of democracy, the Irish Whitman: abnegating the role of god or prince and sympathizing with the common man through whom alone we know the capabilities of humanity. In *Finnegans Wake* he constituted himself the poet of all men. Eliot steadily believed that only in the best men do we glimpse the strength and capabilities of humanity, and that the rest must humbly limp behind. Yet under the stimulus of Joyce Eliot made a bid, and made it with striking if crude success, to express the common man.

Up to 1922 Joyce appears not to have been much interested in Eliot's poetry. He was always ready, however, to reciprocate the interest of his apologists, and when he had received Eliot's praise of *Ulysses* he looked more carefully at Eliot's work. Whenever he applied his interest to poems, his literary intelligence generally told him true. His ear caught the music of *The Waste Land*, he saw both the novelty and the durability of the style. When he parodied the poem in a letter of 1925, he did it with affection and felicity (perhaps a diminuendo felicity, the end crumbles a little). Evidently the poem had entered his blood. He must have noticed even in his first reading how it absorbed some of his images and his structural devices. Then Eliot reviewed *Ulysses* in the *Dial* of November 1923 and claimed that Joyce had invented a new use of "myth," which was diffused throughout his novel by the manipulation of "a continuous parallel between contemporaneity and antiquity": the technique had "the importance of a scientific discovery," and others would adopt it in their independent ways. In fact, *The Waste Land* was the first independent foray with it. The allusions to the Rhinemaidens and Tristan, the metamorphosis of the collapse of Wotan's Rainbow Bridge into the fall of London Bridge and the modern city world — these devices recall Joyce's use of Homer and Wagner. Joyce was pleased at the emulation, which implied the highest admiration, and recognized that it had led not to mere repetition but to new work by an original mind. Not so mighty an imagination as his own, he may have thought, but a strong, disciplined mind, and — this was capital for him — a mind that had heard a new music and had assembled the words to sound it.

Now began a reciprocal creative borrowing. Open to *The Waste Land* for these reasons, Joyce talked — I imagine — its *Tristan* snatches to himself, and they kindled his feeling for the opera. They reminded him that Isolde was a Chapelizod girl, reminded him of Evelyn Innes visiting Chapelizod to understand the role in Isolde's own seascape and Irish weather; and they stirred once more, since *Tristan* is the glorification of an adulterous love, the unappeasable pain which was the spark of his most determined writing (because the pain could be tamed and tolerated only by writing). He had read *The Waste Land* where it was first published: in Vol. I, No. 1, of the *Criterion*, an issue of immediate interest to him because it contained the English text of Valéry Larbaud's pioneer lecture on *Ulysses*. Among the other contributions to this number he found, placed just before *The Waste Land*, a long essay by T. Sturge Moore: "The Story of Tristram and Iseult in Modern Poetry." It deplored the failure of modern writers to exploit the potential of the legend. Hypersuggestible, as he was to be for the next fifteen years, Joyce responded to *The Waste Land* stimulus and Sturge Moore's challenge, and in the next spring he drafted the Tristram fragment, the second of the work-studies that led to *Finnegans Wake*.

Eliot remembers Joyce as his friend. Friendship is not always the same thing as companionship; it may be at once less and more. Meeting seldom, and perhaps formal and reticent when they met, Eliot and Joyce communicated at the level below speech at which writers know and give to each other. Increasingly they lived in each other's meditation and supported each other. Even without this intimacy, Eliot would have defended Joyce in his criticism and stood by him as a publisher; but the interior communion lent depth to all he did. In crisis Joyce wrote his difficulties to Eliot rather than to a more familiar person, and Eliot returned the confidence.

Faber

For twelve years Eliot had watched other men's exploits with magazines. He had seen the *N.R.F.* seize at one swoop the leadership in French intellectual life. He had seen Pound energize the *Egoist* and *Poetry,* had assisted the *Egoist,* and seen it crumble before he could do more than use it as a medium for his first larger critical experiments. (Had the *Egoist* not been there to publish it would he have ventured "Tradition and the Individual Talent," an essay which fitted the style of no existing organ?) His player's view of Murry's run as editor of the *Athenaeum* had proved how an editor with initiative elicits new writing and new ideas that might go unattempted without him. Above all he admired the work of the revived New York *Dial,* edited by Schofield Thayer and managed by Gilbert Seldes whose undergraduate writing, already bold and supple, he had seen when a Harvard graduate assistant. In fact, the *Dial* was in one particular his closest model: more than the early *N.R.F.,* which was a little stupid on literature other than French and nineteenth-century Russian, the *Dial* was aware of Europe, printed chronicles from London and Paris, Austria and Germany, and invited Europe's best living writers to its pages.

Every young poet is likely to think he would wield the editorial power better than the men he serves. And Eliot did it at least as well as the men he had watched.

How he used his magazine to pursue his convictions and make men share them, and how it led towards his fulfillment, including his fulfillment as a poet, is the subject of the next chapter. But perhaps a word may be said about Geoffrey Faber, whose publishing house, which Eliot joined halfway through the twenties, has published many of the most interesting volumes of poetry of the last thirty-five years and kept the *Criterion* in being when the quarterly was in danger of extinction at the end of 1925.

Faber sprang from north country clergymen, absorbed in the traditional tasks and pleasures of their calling, and some of them "enthusiasts," Oxford apostles and poets. He received the classical training of the English public school, a training which, he has himself remarked, remained virtually unchanged throughout the nineteenth century; and it made him, as it made many young men of the pre-1914 generation, a man dedicated to poetry, an elegant and supple manipulator of words, but a manipulator of words entirely in the mode of the public-school lovers and translators of the classics, a mode so limited that English was dying in it (whereas a young American lover of words in 1910, though he might be far less dexterous, had a new language, with no obvious limits to it, fresh to him, and all was open if he had the curiosity and the nerve for the unattempted). Taking a double first in classics at Christ Church, he entered the Oxford University Press, and worked to master publishing and practice his verse.

A year later the war broke out and claimed five years from him. He has said that those exhausting years damaged the creative ability of his generation; that afterwards he could write only intermittently. His energies turned to business. From 1919 he studied law for two years; became a director of the brewing house of Strong; then acquired a small publishing house, and made it thrive.

To those who met him only briefly in the late forties and

fifties he appeared at one moment all autocracy, conservatism, severity, at the next moment all charm, humor, and liberality. It was a little hard to see in the powerful face the poetry-lover and poet. But they had not perished. To read the preface to *The Buried Stream* was to find the poetry-lover, to read some of its poems or those of earlier volumes was to find the poet. When he began writing he loved the conception of beauty fostered by the classical curriculum of nineteenth-century Rugby and Oxford. His first volume, *Interflow*, 1915, named the Odyssey, the odes of Sappho, Catullus, Virgil, Milton, Shelley, and Browning as his touchstone. In 1918 Eliot, reviewing his second volume, noted its "fine heroic taste," which meant, I think, that it aspired too much to the sublime. Faber went on loving the sublime, the old beauty. But here was his amplitude: his tastes running to the past, he recognized divergent tastes. At an early date he said:

> There are many poems which are not beautiful at all, but drab and ugly or horrible or forceful or even humorous, but which are, nevertheless, unmistakably poetry

— which showed him ready to acknowledge the men of the new temperament, whether or not they were ready to acknowledge him. And three taut, self-incriminatory sonnets, dated 1940, show that, though he never learned the idiom of the new "intolerant" poets whom he published, he learned in their company to write without the unreal elegance of public-school classicism and under pressure of emotion to write his feelings without affectation and with their full force.

For a quarter of a century the work of the Faber publishing house (first Faber and Gwyer, then Faber and Faber) has been marked by vivacity, which has arisen from Faber's capacity to act on his instinct for the Different Man, and for the capacity of the different men to enjoy the Different Faber. Settling down to publishing, Faber prepared to undertake, together with safer kinds of books, literature insecure and wayward. Seeking coadjutors, he recruited Richard de la Mare towards the end of 1925, T. S. Eliot in 1926; later Frank Morley, W. J. Crawley, George Blake; rather later still, Morley Kennerley. The team published with an originality that made everything new and fresh, and yet with a discretion, a certainty, that has made almost everything of lasting value: the Faber monographs on ceramics edited by W. B. Honey, who contributed to the *Criterion;* the Faber books on the Indian arts and Indian thought; the Faber Poets.

8. The Editor and His Contributors

ELIOT launched the *Criterion* as a quarterly in October 1922, almost lost it when his sponsor withdrew in 1925, resumed it over the Faber imprint in 1926, made it a monthly in 1927, cut it back to a quarterly in June 1928, and then issued it steadily until New Year 1939.

Yeats told *Poetry*'s guests at a cocktail party in Chicago that the way to treat a man of genius was to endow him and leave it to him. Viscountess Rothermere endowed Eliot and left the *Criterion* to him, and then, when she withdrew, the Faber board endowed him and left it to him. No other editors or advisers were named on the *Criterion*'s pages. For twenty years it was his autocracy. Allen Tate was eventually to call it a model: "The great magazines have always been edited by autocrats."

But the autocrat imposed on himself the law of free inquiry, free debate. He kept in mind how Péguy had opened the *Cahiers de la Quinzaine* to articles of "truth" regardless of the party affiliations of their writers. He found space for John Gould Fletcher to attack Pound and himself; for MacAlpine to attack the "extravagant and pretentious" books of Major Douglas; for Vasudeo Metta to oppose the assumption that the Greco-Roman-European was the only worthwhile civilization. He printed Ramon Fernandez in defense of Gide, Proust, and Shaw, though in preceding issues he had trounced Shaw and placed Proust low in the order of writers; and he printed his own translation of Fernandez's protest against the detractors of Humanism, of whom he had been one. What he most cherished he would most readily hear examined and even opposed; in fact, his autocracy was exercised in determining that what he cherished should be pressed on the public attention by controversy. To deal with heterodoxy he cultivated an Olympian tranquillity. Occasionally his feelings burst through: for example, his exasperation with the "stupidity" of Freud's *Future of an Illusion*. But as early as 1923 he published Rivière's *Notes on a possible valuation of the theories of Freud,* and later Thomas Mann's tribute to Freud and Philip Mairet's critical valuation.

With his intellectual range he saw the bearing of distant subjects on each other, and the result was a periodical which surveyed literary developments throughout Europe and America, music and the visual arts as well as literature, politics and philosophy, anthropology and psychology. His review pages, which he considered the most important and to which he allocated increasing space as the *Criterion* matured, dealt, to take an example from 1931, with *History as Direction;* Jeans's *The Mysterious Universe;* Hugh McDiarmuid; *Sound and Meaning in English Poetry;* John Gould Fletcher's *Europe's Two Frontiers;* J. M. Robertson on Shakespeare; *The Social Control of Sex Expression;* Coleridge as a philosopher; Liddell Hart on the 1914-18 war; Gerard Manley Hopkins; *The Philosophy of the Good Life;* Newman; Henry Adams; Thomas Aquinas; Goya. He encouraged men who shared his versatility. He had Robert Graves reviewing anthropological works at an early date; ten years later, the young Charles Madge.

It could not have been evident to a reader of the first issue that the scope would be so wide. The contributions were immediately noninsular, but they were not immediately extra-literary: Saintsbury on "Dulness"; a Dostoyevsky document,

"Plan of a Novel," translated by Koteliansky and Virginia Woolf; Sturge Moore on the legend of Tristram; "The Waste Land"; May Sinclair's story, "The Victim"; Hesse on "German Poetry of Today"; Valéry Larbaud's lecture in exposition of *Ulysses*. It declined the fireworks of self-conscious avant-gardism, and soberly printed two old and respected writers, and yet sent into the world the poem which was to determine the course of poetry in the next twenty years, and the first constructive account of a novel which was to modify the course of fiction. The next three numbers were of the same character. A pamphlet, inserted in the July 1923 issue to announce the second volume for the autumn, put the emphasis on literature. The contributions would not be "a fortuitous concourse," Eliot explained, but would each represent "something which the CRITERION wishes to support." What did it wish to support?

> The CRITERION aims at the examination of first principles in criticism, at the valuation of new, and the re-valuation of old works of literature according to principles, and the illustration of these principles in creative writing. It aims at the affirmation and development of tradition. It aims at the determination of the value of literature to other humane pursuits. It aims at the assertion of order and discipline in literary taste.

The ambitious phrases hold out the possibility of the exploration of subjects cognate with literature, but literature comes foremost.

Yet while Eliot was defining his plans in those restricted terms, he began in the next number to go beyond them. The complexion of the more familiar *Criterion* first shows in Charles Guignebert's "Concerning the Devil." Then in February 1924 the scope broadens to include F. W. Bain on Disraeli, Lévy-Bruhl on "Primitive Mentality and Gambling," and J. B. Trend on "The Moors in Spanish Music."

When he published his next manifesto, to introduce the new

Criterion with the Faber and Gwyer imprint in January 1926, he pointed out that "even the purest literature is alimented from non-literary sources, and has non-literary consequences" and that he could not restrict himself to literature. Some readers had complained of the extraliterary contributions, but he felt bound to take cognizance of contemporary work in "history, anthropology, archeology, and the technical sciences" and anything else which should also "be operative on general ideas." He hoped that when the volumes of the first ten years came to be bound they would represent the development of the keenest sensibility and clearest thought of the decade; and "Even a single number should attempt to illustrate, within its limits, the time and the tendencies of the time."

With that he clarified his plans for a periodical of the widest range. A year later he justified to himself and his readers the encouragement of views that challenged his own: the *Criterion* was a vehicle

> not for the haphazard opinions of a miscellaneous group of "writers," or for the opinion of an individual, or for the drilled opinion of a school or order, but for the various divergent or even contradictory opinions of a widening group of individuals in communication.

In June 1928 he said the same thing again: the *Criterion* was concerned with everything that could be examined in a critical spirit, and the contributors were united not by a common adhesion to a set of dogmatic principles but by "a common interest in what we believe to be the most important ideas of our time" — an interest which allowed "the widest variation in attitude and tendency."

At approximately the same post-Armistice date when Pound addressed himself to the analysis of the causes of war, Eliot had reread Matthew Arnold and seen him, with eyes opened by Pound's activities, as a man engaged in battle with and for a sick and wasting civilization: Arnold seemed the less complete poet and less complete critic because he attempted a task not his own, but

> he wasted his strength, as men of superior ability sometimes do, because he saw something to be done and no one else to do it. The temptation, to any man who is interested in ideas and primarily in literature, to put literature into the corner until he has cleaned up the whole country first, is almost irresistible.

That paragraph in the introduction to *The Sacred Wood* glows at once with Eliot's knowledge of Pound's campaign and with his own "temptation" to the same mission. What Arnold had done, what Pound was undertaking, and what Maurras was professing in France, evidently stirred him. *The Sacred Wood* itself and the early numbers of the *Criterion* suggest that he tried in 1920, and still in 1923, to concentrate on literature: to resist the temptation to waste his strength. But though "interested . . . primarily in literature," he accepted the risk of sharing Arnold's fate, and after 1923 moved towards a crusade for "une renaissance intégrale de la vie publique," and by 1926 was committed to it.

In 1925 he discussed Arnold in the *Criterion:* no critic, he repeated, but some of his prose "a perpetual inspiration"; and he quoted the passage:

> We have not won our political battle, we have not carried our main points, we have not stopped our adversaries' advance, we have not marched victoriously with the modern world; but we have told silently upon the mind of the country, we have prepared currents of feeling which sap our adversaries' position when it seems gained, we have kept up our communication with the future.

He quoted it with exultation. He would attempt Arnold's work again.

His first approach was through politics. Good government must put civilization right. He understood "good government" in the light of his reading of Maurras: the re-establishment of a hierarchy, privilege and responsibility. There were British politicians of the past who had been disposed, if any truth underlay their legend, to govern heroically. Some of these, Bolingbroke, Disraeli, Curzon, he proceeded to rehabilitate, not by essays of his own but by a series of articles from his contributors. He hoped to raise a spirit of emulation in Britain and inspire a vital new Toryism.

But the articles tended in their conclusions to be cries of Ichabod rather than battle cries. Disraeli, in Bain's portrait, saw at the close of his life a hopeless vision of chaos to come. And when Eliot turned from political textbooks and inner fantasies to the political parties bleating around him with profuse promise and incoherent performance, he saw little likelihood of any revitalization, certainly none of a kind that he would welcome. As a commentator on current policies, elections, legislation, he found himself entirely in Arnold's position: never able to approve, but constantly criticizing, dissecting, attempting to expose the fallacies behind the catchwords of all the contemporary factions. The *Criterion* was driven from the new-Tory constructivism, which had been its star, to the defensive task of undercutting the enemy's position. Arnold once praised Newman and the Oxford Movement for helping to mine the ground "under the self-confident liberalism of the last thirty years." Eliot quoted that with approval. Eventually he put it that his business was "to arouse dubiety": to pose the Socratic questions which arrest a sincere listener and bring assumptions under reconsideration.

By 1931 he was saying that politics must take second place after religion. He was not willing to give up his quixotic conception of a new Toryism, but he announced a platform which would have been unfamiliar to Curzon and the other heroes: it should "refuse to identify itself philosophically with that

'Conservatism' which has been overrun first by deserters from Whiggism and later by businessmen," and it should "erect its philosophy on a religious foundation." For the next eight years the dominant concern of the *Criterion* was theology. Looking back when he wrote his "Last Words" for the issue of January 1939 he acknowledged that, and explained it clearly:

> For myself, a right political philosophy came more and more to imply a right theology — and economics to depend upon right ethics: leading to emphases which somewhat stretched the original framework of a literary review.

Though it might be impossible to remake the world as the City of God, the serious man should strive for it without pause.

He combined Arnold's doctrine of the Remnant with his religious-political doctrine. The Remnant is the saving minority, by whose efforts grace is diffused through a civilization. He rallied the twentieth-century Remnant to a civilization-saving mission, in preparation for which he urged a rigorous training of a monastic character. It is significant that in the final issue Philip S. Richards studied Maritain's hope of the Christian city which might arise, after a long interim, from the ruins of the European war, and exhorted Christian intellectuals to concentrate, for purposes of survival and for the distant building of the city, "in intense *nuclei*, like the monastic orders." The monasteries of Eliot and his friends were in the world, not withdrawn from it. They were comparable to the societies of illuminati to which Hartcourt-Reilly, Julia, and Alex belonged, and the societies of trainees which Celia joined.

The *Criterion* of the late years, then, was dedicated to organizing the Remnant for the world's emergency. Eliot was concerned to advocate (through contributors, rather than through his own writing) what he regarded as the right theology; and to probe, cautiously but irrepressibly (and through his own commentaries rather than through contributors), the political commitments of his contemporaries, testing these by his theology.

One of his contributors, George Every, wrote in 1938, evidently thinking of the *Criterion* in England and Allen Tate in America, that the "theological revolution has certainly begun, not only at Rome, Geneva, and Canterbury, but in Kentucky and Russell Square." History must still decide whether this claim was or was not too ardent, whether the developments that excited it were or were not too scattered and too few to constitute a major movement, and whether commensurate consequences have resulted a generation later. Meanwhile, a reader of literature may say: that in deciding that a man may not *partly* adopt a religion, but that if he is genuinely religious he must apply his faith at all times and in all contexts, Eliot aligned himself with a powerful tradition of the English writers, who have repeatedly attacked the separation of belief and practice or the cultivation of a Sabbath self apart from the daily self.

The Eliot of the thirties liked not so much the word "religion" as the word "theology," with its connotations of system and discipline. The quotation from St. John of the Cross at the head of *Sweeney Agonistes*, and the poetry of *Ash-Wednesday*, speak of an earlier concern with mysticism. But in 1935, when he wrote an obituary tribute to Orage, he spoke rather frigidly of that admirable editor's mysticism, then rebuked himself for the remark, which, he said, must smack of the reformed drunkard's horror of intemperance. Apparently he had called himself away from the mystical absorption of the mid-twenties, as if it were too yielding and self-indulgent, and had resolved that faith is best observed as a discipline and a debt to society: daily it must be applied to the exigencies of the world.

But for a man to declare himself a Christian, or anything equally serious, is not to afford himself an easy solution of all problems. He has to ascertain the proper application of his faith in every case, and there are cases where the forces of good and ill on either side will seem almost evenly distributed. Clear-sightedness for action and in action is hard, Eliot said:

> That balance of mind which a few highly-civilized individuals such as Arjuna, the hero of the Bhagavad Gita, can maintain in action, is difficult for most of us even as observers.

The poet of "If and Perhaps and But" he called himself in the "Five Finger Exercises," as if his demurrers proved that he was the *impossible* Mr. Eliot. But they arose — and I assume that he knew it with a touch of pride — from the seriousness of his convictions: from his effort to decide where his support should be given; and from the cultivation of the dubiety of Arnold so that every appeal that the milling factions make to us he might strip of its pretensions and judge on its naked merits.

His dubious probing has never meant that he was cold, but that he was painfully concerned for the right answer. In 1938 he pointed out that "the detached observer . . . is likely to be anything but a dispassionate observer; he probably *suffers* more acutely than the various apostles of immediate action." The sentence was written about Wyndham Lewis, but it sounds, like so many of Eliot's judgments on other men, autobiographical too.

Eliot's Europeanism

It is easy for an American, brought up in a federation of states, to see what Europe lost by the separatism of its nations. It is easy for him to see Europe as a unity and a community. It is also as natural to him to range from European country to country as it would be at home to pass from state to state, and with the same pleasure that he travels his own continent he makes the continent of Europe his playground. Eliot became, more distinctly and powerfully than any other writer in England, an exponent of the values of Europe as a whole.

When Europe disintegrated and lay broken at the end of 1918, the collapse evoked the healer in some of the great artists of the time. *The Waste Land* is informed with grief for the disordered continent. The note to lines 366-70 quotes Hermann Hesse: "Schon ist halb Europa, schon ist zumindest der halbe Osten Europas auf dem Wege zum Chaos." Saint and seer weep at the outburst of Dmitri Karamazov's drunken song, said Hesse; and *The Waste Land* is the poet's weeping for a ruined heritage. The famous opening page of *The Waste Land* is like a parable to regret an earlier Europe, as Eliot had briefly seen and savored it in 1911. Eliot resolved to lend his strength to the restoration of the European tradition. I do not know whether he saw Hofmannsthal's question-and-answer manifesto for the postwar Salzburger Festspiel:

> Was leistet und vollbringt jeder Gönner und Förderer des Unternehmens?
> Er stärkt den Glauben an ein Europa, wie er die Zeit von 1750 bis 1850 erfüllt und erhellt hat.
> Liegen heute solche Zeiten nicht auf ewig hinter uns? Wer glaubt noch heute an Europa?
> Diesen Glauben mit deutlichen Worten zu verleugnen, hatte niemand den Mut. Herder und Napoleon haben diesen Glauben besessen; Goethe und die französische Revolution begegneten sich in ihm. Er ist das Fundament unseres geistigen Daseins.

A comparable purpose inspired the *Criterion.*

Through its pages he designed to communicate the new thought and work of Europe to his countrymen; to communicate his thoughts to Europe, seizing the attention of the Remnant in every country by his continental consciousness; and, as a result of the reciprocal process, to advance Europe's sense of a common tradition and of its yet unexhausted potentialities as a cultural unity. He pointed out when he looked back at the magazine in 1956, that it

> was only one of a number of reviews similar in character and in purpose, in France, Germany, Switzerland, Spain and elsewhere; and my own interest in making my contemporaries in other countries known in England, responded to the interest of the editors and contributors of the other reviews.

He named Gide and Larbaud, Hofmannsthal, Curtius, Ortega y Gasset, as men attempting the same work: "No ideological differences poisoned our intercourse; no political oppression limited freedom of communication."

He led off at once in the first number with contributions from Hesse and Larbaud. During 1923 he published work by Curtius, Pirandello, Benda, Marichalar, Valéry, Hofmannsthal. In 1924 he added Hauptmann, Proust, Cavafy. By 1926 the names of Alberti and Lorca, Rilke, Denis de Rougemont, and Maritain, were made known to his readers. It was a remarkable international procession, subsequently to be matched by the procession of new young English writers, the discoveries of the thirties.

The names would be a snare if the articles were not worthy of them. Occasionally Eliot had a disappointment. Hesse's commentary in the first issue was flat, and Eliot did not represent him again. But on the whole the articles were as noble as the names. They may be classified as of two kinds: primary statements by writers like Hofmannsthal, Croce, and Maritain; secondary articles in which critics discuss the work of the writers. It is significant of the character of the magazine that the secondary articles are the more vital: Marichalar's essay on Ortega, Max Rychner's essays on Rudolf Borchardt and Stefan

George. After the first two or three years, when such critics began to realize that Eliot was inviting them to contribute in exposition of the European spirit, their discussions became highly conscious in their emphases of points dear to the editor. Here, for example, is Rychner tracing the vein structure of the European tradition in the background of Stefan George:

> By birth and descent George is a Catholic, a son of the Rhine, whose "Roman atmosphere" he extols. The buildings of the colonies of the Roman Empire were among his earliest youthful impressions; the vines of the Rhine, of which he sings, were planted by the Roman colonists. And it was along the Rhine that Christianity first penetrated into Germany . . .

He shows George as European classicist, a poet who regretted the Reformation which deprived Germany of the sensuosity just blooming, and who struggled to compensate for the loss with a new humane order. He is playing to his editor, but he is not falsifying his subject or his feelings, rather is better aware of them for his editor's passion. A good editor always does something like this to his contributors. A little later there came an occasional contributor who attempted, so it looks at this distance, to slip what was fundamentally an opposition contribution into his paper by using the editorial vocabulary and so exploiting the editorial interest, and Eliot accepted, either because the sleight deceived him, or because, seeing through it, he still thought the article of merit. But usually he fostered real passion and understanding.

At the outset, influenced by Maurras and the doctrine of the Greco-Latin culture and its transmission through France, he cried exaltedly that England was "Latin." Some of his friends were more cautious and their remarks were corrective. J. B. Trend, for example, discussing Busoni's *Faust* in the *Criterion* of September 1927, Trend shot at a tangent to deplore the "self-satisfaction of some Latin minds, quite content to abide by the law, once it has been laid down — by themselves":

> The exclusively Latin spirit leads to dictatorship; the Greek
> spirit and the Northern to liberty, idealism, exploration and dis-
> covery.

Next year Trend insisted that the Englishman is born Teuton
and bred Latin, and shares the advantages of his hero, Busoni, who was born Mediterranean and bred Northern. Ten
years later, a "Spanish Chronicle," contributed by Marichalar,
told how Ortega imagined Europe as a swarm in which there
are many bees but only one flight: "The multitude of European
forms constantly emerging from their radical unity and falling back into it in order to impart to it a new force, this is the
greatest treasure of the West." Eliot's view grew to be somewhat similar to Ortega's.

Around 1927 he was much exercised by the question of peripheral England's place in the European comity. Just as he
described the virtue of the Church of England as its spirit
of moderation and mediation, he began to suggest that Britain
by geography, history, and temperament was the ideal cultural mediator. A mediator between the components of the
European complex. And a mediator between Europe and a
large part of the world outside Europe. There were debates
current to prompt the claim. In the London *Times,* André
Siegfried asked Britain to make a choice between her European affiliations and her affiliations with the English-speaking
countries of the Commonwealth and the United States. To this
challenge Eliot referred in the *Criterion* of March 1928, and
replied that Britain should "persist in that policy of *media
via* which she had pursued for several centuries":

> To our mind the peculiar position of Britain is this: that she is
> on the one hand a part of Europe. But not only a part, she is a
> mediating part: for Britain is the bridge between Latin culture

and Germanic culture in both of which she shares. But Britain is not only the bridge, the middle way, between two parts of western Europe; she is, or should be, by virtue of the fact that she is the only member of the European community that has established a genuine empire — that is to say, a world-wide empire as was the Roman empire — not only European but the connection between Europe and the rest of the world.

He imagined Britain selecting from the values of Europe and carrying whatever was worthy of adoption to the more recent civilizations. The interfusion would be effected through the medium of the common language, English.

In retrospect, when he wrote "Last Words" in 1939, and when he wrote the 1956 tribute to Curtius, it seemed to him that the hope of reconstruction of the war-stricken European culture had waned very quickly: that as early as 1926 "there were fewer writers in any country who seemed to have anything to say to the intellectual public of another." But whatever the practical opportunities for its immediate realization, the ideal was evidently still alive to his mind after that. He clung to it during the Second World War and still said that the European organism must be concerned in any civilizing development. After 1945, as after 1918, he spoke earnestly of Europe: he gave his three broadcast talks, "The Unity of European Culture"; and his conception of a genius in which the whole Continent shares and by which it knows itself shines through his Hamburg lecture on Goethe.

A Reciprocal Process

When the Czech crisis of 1938 proved that a European war could not be escaped and that, for who could know how long, European communications would be severed, he decided to discontinue the *Criterion*. He set matters in order to close down, and the last number appeared in New Year 1939.

The strenuous labor of the periodical through seventeen years must have limited Eliot's time for his own creative writing. When at last the trays were empty and the files stacked away, he wrote "East Coker," his first wholly successful poem since *Ash-Wednesday,* and then two more Quartets and then the comedies. It looks as if that sudden progress was made not only because he now had more time and more energy for his own work, but because in his relations with his contributors he had learned new lessons.

The influence of the editor on his contributors is obvious. Less obvious but at least as important is the influence of the contributors on their editor. Eliot was scrupulous beyond the custom of periodical autocrats. This does not mean that he badgered his authors for revisions and refinements. It means that he read and meditated on everything that went in. To study the files is to feel the play of one mind in every issue, and the continuity of thought from one issue to the next; to see how he found in his contributors the provocation for new contributions and sometimes the names of new contributors, whom he approached with commissions right for their aptitudes and his pages; and how sometimes the themes or the perceptions of the articles penetrated his mind, lodged there, irritated, and pearled years later in a passage of his own. This is true alike of the earliest and latest contributors, but perhaps the earliest led him to his most remarkable discoveries. Except for that rapid, two-year application of Laforgue to English, he has generally needed a long time to use the suggestions that have interested him.

Some Themes of the Plays

In one of the earliest issues there is a contribution, "Alcestis and Savitri," which makes a point that the editor retained for twenty-five years and then put to use in *The Cocktail Party.*

Stanley Rice presented, and answered by a comparison with the *Mahabhárata*, the usual objection to the dithyrambic Heracles:

> . . . how, it is said, can we recognize in this drunken reveller the semi-divine hero of Greek legend? He comes into the house with importunate demands for service, calls for wine, and drinks himself into a semi-maudlin state, "crowning his head with myrtle sprigs" and "howling discordance," and later giving the servant a sermon of drunken solemnity on the vanity of human life.

The article must have attracted the editor, when it reached him, as a comparative study which correlated his two warring interests, the Attic and the Indic; and it is not surprising if this vivid passage brought the Heracles of Euripides into sharp focus in his mind.

Alcestis was brought to the editor's attention again in two later issues of the *Criterion*. In July 1937 Guy Manton reviewed *Alcestis* in the translation of Dudley Fitts and Robert Fitzgerald, and *Ion* in H.D.'s version: the pattern-plays of *The Cocktail Party* and *The Confidential Clerk* discussed together! Then, in January 1938, came F. McEachran's "A Pattern for Reality," which tugged at Eliot as anthropologist, Christian sociologist, and dramatist. *Alcestis*, McEachran said, represents the elevation to tragedy of the dynamic of the seed, which "is both hero and victim. It triumphs in defeat by producing more life." He showed how Shakespeare, Dante, the Christian religion, the Mass, reproduced the same pattern at higher levels. His exposition was a challenge to Eliot to find a new Christian dramatization of the Alcestis myth; the method that resulted will be touched on in the next chapter.

Eliot was able to make his adaptation of *Alcestis* when he had learned to look on clinical psychology not as the "dubious science" he thought it when he discussed May Sinclair's *Harriet*

Frean in 1922, but as a genuine guide to the perplexed. From 1929 he had been asking reviewers to assess major psychological works for the *Criterion:* in July 1929 Alan Porter wrote animatedly on Jung's approach to "the living dead" who "must be set free from their tombs" — the very words for the rescue of Alcestis; in April 1930 E. L. Grant Watson explained Alfred Adler: "It is the *defect* and the accompanying conflict that genius can turn to achievement"; in January 1932 the same writer described Wilhelm and Jung's *Secret of the Golden Flower.* Eliot had feared that psychology might be only a new palmistry, a new Sosostrism; then that, even if therapeutic, it might be a rash intruder on religion and a heresy; but now, under the influence of his contributors, and opening his mind, as he has always tried to do, to the truth, and also, as he has always tried to do, working hard to bring his observations into line with his belief, he wrote in his editorial commentary in April 1932 that

> the chief use of psychology (apart from curing people, if it does) seems to me to be to restate old truths in modern jargon which people can understand; and if psychology helps people towards truth which they cannot apprehend when put in simple theological language, so much the better.

There was still a frown implicit in these lines, but it relaxed into acceptance of the psychologist. Harcourt-Reilly submits to religion, acts in the name of religion — no heresy founts from him — and confesses with humility that he speaks more than he knows:

> And when I say to one like her
> "Work out your salvation with diligence," I do not understand
> What I myself am saying.

Nevertheless, he imposes an immense authority. A practicing analyst remarked to me, after one of the early performances of the play, that he is far, far too august and godlike. But after all he is the semi-divine Heracles — the dithyrambic Heracles, rollicking with irrational strength.

The passages in the *Criterion* which seem to foreshadow *Murder in the Cathedral* occur much nearer to the date of the play's composition than the passages which look towards *The Cocktail Party*.

In 1928 John Masefield wrote a festival play for Canterbury, *The Coming of Christ*. Eliot was not present at the perform-ance, but read the text, and found a tinsel replica of the Wakefield shepherds, feeble poetry, and feeble doctrine, and said so in his *Criterion* Commentary in June: "We venture to counsel our spiritual pastors, that they should see to it either that they employ artists who are definite in their theology, or else who are really good artists." The man who criticizes an-other's work is always likely to be bidden do it better, and, if he is as sincere as Eliot, he is almost bound to challenge himself to do it better. Seven years later, after *The Rock* had proved him sound in poetry, was it? or theology, was it? or both? to his spiritual pastors, he was given his opportunity. He took it and celebrated the metropolis of his Church and England's best-known saint.

Eliot had printed in the *Criterion* of October 1927 an anony-mous review of Sidney Dark's biography of Becket; in that of November 1927 an anonymous notice of Herbert Read's *Eng-lish Stained Glass* (a book which contains illustrations of the glass in Canterbury and a three-page account of the passage in *The Golden Legend* about the courtship of Becket's parents); and in that of October 1932, F. Wormald's review of *Thomas à Becket in Art* by Tancred Borenius. There are three feasts of St. Thomas, Wormald pointed out: on December 29 the Church commemorates his martyrdom; on July 7 the transla-tion of his bones to a magnificent shrine; and on December 2 the Regressio S. Thomae, "the return of the exile to Canterbury

in 1170." Eliot arranged his play so that the martyrdom of
December 29 provides the climax. He found no place to honor
the Translation, not merely because it took place fifty years
after the martyrdom, but because it was part of the glory towards the overvaluation of which the most dangerous Tempter
encouraged Thomas, and from which Thomas successfully
averted his eyes. He opened his play with the Regressio:

> For good or ill, let the wheel turn.
> The wheel has been still, these seven years, and no good.
> For ill or good, let the wheel turn.

I do not know whether Eliot saw Borenius' book itself, or only
Wormald's notice. Borenius had hints to offer suggestive to a
dramatist. He mentioned Becket's "vividness of speech." He
pointed out that "there arose . . . quickly a tendency to establish a parallel between the last days of St. Thomas and the Passion of Christ." But the review alone without the book may
have been sufficient to implant suggestions for the design of the
cathedral play. And it is possible that Eliot was the more alert
to its suggestions because he received it, read it, and sent it to
the printers on the eve of his return to America after seventeen
years' absence. Matthiessen, with his sensitive judgment, felt
that Eliot's re-encounter with America in 1932 and 1933 was
decisive in heightening his self-knowledge and recruiting his
powers, so that he was eventually able to proceed to works
larger than he could accomplish before.

Some Themes of the Quartets

Already quoted earlier in this chapter is the sentence from
one of the editor's Commentaries in which he speaks of the balance of mind which "a few highly-civilized individuals such as
Arjuna" can maintain in action. It is a sentence which shows
the thought and the imagery of "The Dry Salvages" astir in

Eliot. A number of passages in the issues of the *Criterion* published in the thirties point, rather similarly, to the emergence of the themes of the Quartets.

In that issue of October 1932, assembled just before Eliot's return to America, there is a very striking Commentary. He has been reading Curtius' *Deutscher Geist in Gefahr*. "The Permanent," Curtius noted and deplored, "has come to mean Paralysis and Death." Eliot reflects on this observation. The antithesis between change and permanence, he says, is at least as old as pre-Socratic philosophy, "and metaphysics has struggled with its conundrums ever since." In 1910 the popular William James and Bergson equated change with value and permanence with valuelessness; and the equation has not been abandoned in the shifts of fashion, has only acquired a new vocabulary which sets the "static" against the "dynamic" to the advantage of the latter. Against the fallacies of his time Eliot maintains that the task of each age, each art, each individual is to try to adjust "the delicate relation of the Eternal and the Transient." There have been men and societies "precious in the eye of God" for finding the adjustment. We must always strive for the perfect society on earth, while conscious of the "inadequacy of these ambitions and ideals." We must know that natural man can never be perfect, and must affirm "that perfection is as nearly attainable for any man here and now as it ever will be in any future place":

> That there can be no art *greater* than the art which has already been created: there will only be different and necessarily different combinations of the eternal and the changing in the forms of art. That men individually can never attain anything higher than has been already attained among the Saints; but that in any place, at any time, another Saint may be born. Such a just perception of the permanent relations of the Enduring and the Changing should on the one hand make us realize our own time in better proportion to times past and times to come: we are

now inclined to think of our own age and moment as hysteri-
cally as people did in the year 1000. And on the other hand it
should help us to think better of our own time, as not isolated
or unique, and remind us that fundamentally our individual
problems and duties are the same as they have been for others
at any time — and equally our opportunities.

The Commentary looks forward alike to Eliot's subsequent
prose works, *The Idea of a Christian Society* and *Notes towards
the Definition of Culture,* to his drama (for *Murder in the Cathedral* is the study of a saint, and *The Cocktail Party* shows a
saint of our time), and to *Four Quartets.* The statement that
there can be no *greater* art than the art already created, only
"different and necessarily different combinations" which may
be equally great by revealing the same secret, looks forward to:

> what there is to conquer
> By strength and submission, has already been discovered
> Once or twice, or several times, by men whom one cannot hope
> To emulate — but there is no competition —

And the problem around which the whole Commentary re-
volves, the puzzle of the Permanent and the Changing, the
Eternal and the Transient, is a theme of the Quartets as a
whole. It is at the front of the poet's mind when he begins
"Burnt Norton":

> Time past and time future
> What might have been and what has been
> Point to one end, which is always present

and when he suggests, by his rhythm and imagery, the simultaneous excitement and bafflement of man trying to catch at
fleeting time and hold the vision which he feels lies behind the
movement. It is in his mind at the end when he commemorates
Little Gidding, a community "precious in the eye of God" for
the adjustment of the Eternal and the Transient.

The first of three *Criterion* contributions which drew attention to Little Gidding appeared in October 1932: an essay on Nicholas Ferrar and George Herbert by T. O. Beachcroft. Beachcroft said that the round of services at Little Gidding showed the influence of Andrewes — a remark which must have engaged Eliot's attention — and he pointed out that Ferrar chose, at the moment when office and opportunity were open to his abilities, "to abandon every worldly interest for a life of self-effacement, whose sole end was religious devotion."

In 1938 the Society for the Propagation of Christian Knowledge published A. L. Maycock's book, *Nicholas Ferrar of Little Gidding.* Bernard Blackstone reviewed it for Eliot in October. The orthodoxy of Little Gidding, he said, looked like flagrant nonconformity to many seventeenth-century contemporaries: "Less eccentric persons, at the furthest extremities of the kingdom, did not sleep the better . . . for knowing that a taper was burning through the night in the oratory where Nicholas Ferrar was keeping vigil." But Blackstone complained that literature and modern literary criticism had neglected the community. He feared that "the prim little church, the tombs of Nicholas and John, the fish-pond into which the Puritan soldiers once flung a shining eagle," would be left "to slumber in peace for another hundred years."

Then Blackstone's own book followed, his Cambridge edition of the Ferrar papers, selected to illustrate "in a greater degree than has hitherto been possible the life and work of a saint of the Church of England." Eliot asked Charles Smyth to review this for the *Criterion.* The review was sparkling, describing, among other things, the human frailties of the Ferrars, which imperiled the delicate adjustment of the community (and that Eliot ignored, as no doubt he was right to do, measuring the triumph). But the review also took on a somber hue in a paragraph gathering some of the solemn pronouncements on the immediacy of death which ring through the early seventeenth-century writers.

If literature had indeed neglected Little Gidding, as Blackstone said, the neglect was soon over. Bringing the chronicle of the community into *Four Quartets*, Eliot has rewritten it into the English nation's memory, and made it known and prized beyond England. And here was a case where his contributors helped to prepare his mind for the work — and perhaps Blackstone most by that very remark that literature, which had let the story of the saint slumber, would let it slumber "for another hundred years." I imagine Eliot taken by the more challenging phrases of his contributors, struggling with them, discriminating what he might use, what he must rebut: sometimes he used them by rebutting, as here; sometimes by a thoughtful restatement of them.

A story which appeared in a very early *Criterion* may have still echoed in his memory when he wrote "The Dry Salvages"; it was certainly in his memory ten years after its publication. And perhaps the distinguished writer who contributed it had helped him, in his first decade in London, to form his standards and perceive his ends. She was May Sinclair. She had been publishing since 1895, had impressed the critics, and worried the Puritanical among them, with *The Divine Fire* in 1904. In 1907 when the sophomore Eliot was reading the *Advocate* he had perhaps noticed a review of a new book of hers, *The Helpmate*, which "P.D." characterized as the ultimate in psychopathic fiction. She had courage in literature, which rushed her to the confrontation of sex ahead of other novelists, and courage in life which sent her to the Belgian battlefields with the Red Cross in 1914. In London in 1916 Eliot found that the people he most respected respected her. A feminist and progressive, she was admired by the *Egoist* group. In the *Egoist* of September 1918 Jean de Bosschère extolled her work for "charity and grace." Later she was to be a co-sponsor with Pound and Aldington of the Bel Esprit circular on behalf of Eliot. When she died in 1947 she left Pound her pewter cigarette box, her Aristophanes and her Greek anthology, and any other book he might choose from her library.

She was primarily a novelist and poet, but in 1917 she entered the field of philosophy and religion with her *Defence of Idealism*. It had something to say about Bradley, whom Eliot had studied for his Ph.D. thesis, and it appeared at the time when he was still professionally intent on philosophy. In the *International Journal of Ethics* in July 1918 it was reviewed at some length by M. W. Robieson, while Eliot reviewed E. D. Fawcett's *The World as Imagination*. There is a fairly reliable rule in the study of literary genetics, that young writers, maybe all writers, notice work if it appears between the same covers as their own. Robieson commented, in general, that her conclusions "are plainly intended to be in harmony with those of Mr. Bradley," and he praised, in particular, her chapter on The New Mysticism, and judged that "nothing that she has written is more interesting than the contrasts she draws between eastern and western mysticism . . . The defect of the latter, which it overcomes only very occasionally in the case of great mystics like Lady Julian of Norwich, is its persistent asceticism . . ." For May Sinclair attacked Christian asceticism as "unclean and profane in its repudiation of the earth," but she called Lady Julian "that most exquisite and lovable of all mystics, whose love of God was not greater than her love of her neighbour, who saw 'that each kind compassion that man hath on his even-Christen it is Christ in him.'" She found that the Christian mystics, "admirable psychoanalysts as they were," lacked the psychological theory and practice which the Indian mystics possessed; and they failed, but for one or two exceptions such as Lady Julian, to achieve a perfect and safe detachment from the world. Similarly the religious poets of the west failed by comparison with those of the east. Western religious poetry was seldom written by poets, was not supremely devotional, was a horrible tangle of material and carnal imagery; it imagined the throne of God, but never arrived; and it never appeased "your finer metaphysical hunger."

In 1922, when the *Criterion* was under flotation, May Sinclair's writing was much in Eliot's eye. The New York *Dial*, his immediate model, was employing her: in the number of February 1922 she reviewed H.D.'s *Hymen*, and said — which was bound to please a poet who had the unprecedented *Waste Land* in readiness — that the poet is entitled to expect the lover of familiar beauty to make an effort to receive new beauty. During the summer he read her own attempt at new beauty, *Harriet Frean*, and discussed it in his "London Letter," datelined August and printed September: he was doubtful whether it justified the psychoanalytical novel, a species that rested on a "dubious and contentious science," but he found the Aristotelian pity and terror in it, and he prophesied that she would rouse these emotions even more powerfully if she passed in her next work from the psychoanalytical to the supernatural. In the first *Criterion* he published her story "The Victim," a study in the transfinite. Shortly afterwards he published her story "Jones's Karma," and her poem "The Grandmother."

In "Jones's Karma" she put the reading she had done in preparation for the *Defence of Idealism* to creative use. A Guru, guest in an English house, is asked to explain how a man's will is free yet his fate determined, and answers with a parable. Jones made three decisions, each wrong and disastrous. At the moment of death he clearly saw the sequence of errors and willed that in his next incarnation he should make the opposite decision at the three moments of choice — which he was able to do, as he had willed it at the moment of death. Even so, the result was disaster. Though he had willed his amendment, he had looked only at the details of the sequence, not at his whole self; had exercised his will on the inferior thing.

Whether or not this is a too simplified rendering of Indian subtleties Eliot was better competent to judge than most of us.

It sufficiently satisfied him, seemed sufficiently to constellate the riddle of human conduct, to detain his mind. We know that by a very striking and specific allusion to it nine years later. In the *Criterion* for July 1932 he discussed Queenie Leavis' *Fiction and the Reading Public.* Reflecting on the gap between the serious writer and the larger public, he said that poetry was a permanent need of man, that drama too was a permanent need, and that poetry might revivify the drama. Then, by a sudden transition, he spoke of the experience of

> St. Peter when the cock crew. This kind of determinism is essential to Buddhism as well as to Christianity; but whether "determinism" is the right word for it, I leave unsettled. See *Jones's Karma* by May Sinclair, in the *Criterion* for October 1923, p. 43.

This abrupt movement of thought sets us speculating. It appears that Eliot was at once: questioning whether it was possible for a Peter to avoid his guilt; thinking that the question afforded the proper material for drama; and looking on Peter's situation as fundamental or "archetypal," of eternal validity, recurring again and again under different aspects — and all the more, therefore, the proper subject of drama.

The "unsettled" question of 1932 haunts the slow movement of "Little Gidding." At the end of "Jones's Karma" the Guru said:

> "When you talk of free-will and bondage you talk of the pairs of opposites. You are free and you are bound also. It is according. But so long as you affirm the reality of the pairs of opposites you are subject to illusions."
> He paused.
> "Notwithstanding, there is a path of perfect freedom. When it is indifferent to a man whether he is himself or not himself, whether he lives or dies, whether he catches the cholera or does not catch the cholera. Thus he escapes from desiring and un-

desiring, from the pairs of opposites, and from the chain of
happenings and the round of births."

This is a persuasive passage, even when read in isolation, and
as the product of the story it is highly persuasive. Could Eliot,
when he came to look at it from the standpoint of a Christian,
completely reconcile it with his faith? At one end of the scale it
overlaps with Dante's repose in the peace of God's will. But at
the other end it will not meet the Christian obligation to make
certain choices. The Guru's indifference is freedom from the
obligation to choose. The Jesuit indifference, to which Father
d'Arcy drew attention in his review of *Eyeless in Gaza* in the
Criterion of October 1936, is a preparation for right choices.
Yet Eliot assimilated the Guru's wisdom, or something resem-
bling it, into "Little Gidding." Only, he did not use the vocabulary in the same way. In the common acceptance, with which
a poet must reckon, the word "indifference" suggests careless-
ness, tedium, insensibility. Where May Sinclair used "indifference," he used the word every book on mysticism, including her
Defence, offered him: "detachment." That left him free to
apply "indifference" in keeping with the common usage:

> There are three conditions which often look alike
> Yet differ completely, flourish in the same hedgerow:
> Attachment to self and to things and to persons, detachment
> From self and from things and from persons; and, growing
>   between them, indifference
> Which resembles the others as death resembles life.

Here "indifference" becomes the loss of love, the inability to
love (like Edward's and Lavinia's before they have learned to
see themselves). "Detachment" becomes freedom and serenity
(like the Guru's). But then the poem proceeds, and it is as
though detachment and its freedom are not an end but a beginning: they make possible the ascent to a love beyond the carnal.

Praising Lady Julian in the *Defence,* May Sinclair compared her with Kabir, from whom she quoted: "Few are the lovers who know the Beloved. The devout seeker is he who mingles in his heart the double currents of love and detachment." Perhaps by some such unexpressed connection, Eliot went from the slow movement of "Little Gidding," and its recommendation of the Buddhist detachment, to the lyric of Christian love and then to the phrases from Lady Julian.

Certain *Criterion* contributors — Mario Praz in his review of Bremond's *Prayer and Poetry,* and T. O. Beachcroft in his article on the Metaphysical poets — stressed a discrepancy, and a necessary discrepancy, they thought, between mysticism and poetry. As if spurred to a generous contention with them, Eliot wrote a work which, if it could not repair the discrepancy, brought the two elements closer together. And he answered, in the same sense of the word, May Sinclair. He wrote a poem free from the carnal imagery with which she had reproached the religious poets of the West: a poem that offered, and in its music betokened, a love beyond desire. She had complained that their work was not supremely devotional; he attempted a supremely devotional poem; and he succeeded in writing supremely devotional passages, or supremely devotional poems within the poem, though the more compelling passages are those that report the daily struggle, whether of fisherman or poet, rather than those which explicitly consecrate or pray.

The Form of the Quartets

Beethoven stands at the center of the European tradition. Greece, Rome, the Rhine and Vienna, if they unite anywhere, unite in him. Eliot deeply admires his last quartets; has long admired them; and we know from the New Haven lecture, which Matthiessen rescued, that in 1933 he cited them as exemplars of the poetry at which he aimed:

to write poetry which should be essentially poetry, with nothing poetic about it, poetry standing naked in its bare bones, or poetry so transparent that we should not see the poetry, but that which we are meant to see through the poetry, poetry so transparent that in reading it we are intent on what the poem *points at*, and not on the poetry, this seems to be the thing to try for. To get *beyond poetry*, as Beethoven, in his later works, strove to get *beyond music*.

Now it may not be every listener's interpretation, that the late quartets allow us to forget that they are music. They lift us to extraordinary and mysterious experiences, but the very act of going "beyond music," the unusual treatment of the form and the instruments, the departure from habits, remind us that we are listening to music. Possibly the music of Beethoven's middle life is the more truly "transparent." But interesting though it is to admirers of Beethoven to debate this question, and especially interesting as it would be to hear Eliot, if he felt inclined, deal with it in some essay or lecture, the fact sufficient for the immediate discussion is that he valued the last five quartets as masterpieces of the transparent style, and that in composing the Quartets he had them in mind.

"Burnt Norton," the first of the Quartets, was an attempt to write of the flowing and the permanent, of time and the stillness behind time, of the movement and the pattern. That subject made it especially fitting to adopt the form used by the greatest of the European composers at his moment of most intense insight. For music is the art that comes nearest to representing the simultaneous flow and permanence of which the philosophers have spoken and of which Eliot was to speak. When it is at its highest, and when we are listening at our best, we "are the music While the music lasts"; it raises us above our limitations and sets us at a serene point where riddles intersect and explain and justify each other.

Once a reader becomes aware of Eliot's love of Beethoven's last quartets and of his emulation of them, he inescapably finds himself drawing analogies, which perhaps only hold good for himself as reader, between Eliot's design, method, and effects, and Beethoven's. In particular, he is likely to find himself comparing the Quartets with Beethoven's Quartet in A Minor, Opus 132, for that is divided, like "Burnt Norton" and its successors, into five movements. Beethoven's movements are:

(1) allegro

(2) a scherzo and a contrasting trio

(3) a slow movement: which begins in somber depths; then

changes, "neue Kraft fühlend."

(4) a very short alla marcia

(5) allegro appassionato — in rondo form, with an extended coda.

"Burnt Norton" is divided into:

(1) a rapid first movement

(2) a scherzo in short, rhyming lines, excited, "trilling"; followed by a contrasting section in long, reflective lines

(3) a slow somber movement; if there can be said to be a contrasting section, it is yet slower and more somber

(4) a very short rhyming lyric

(5) a movement of statements or "answers": first passionate, even agitated; then more serene with sudden clearings and visions.

There are some indications in each movement that an effect comparable with Beethoven's is being sought; but there are also developments in which Eliot lets any attempt at a correspondence go and follows the different needs of his material. The pace of the opening is comparable with Beethoven's: more, the texture is comparable with that of a string quartet; it is as though he has said to himself that nothing better captures man's sense of fleeting time, of the world's dazzling impressions behind which he half senses a meaning or an all-comprehending image, than the elusive gusts of Beethoven's strings, and has attempted to find the poetic equivalent for these. At the end of the movement the repetition of phrases from the opening lines gives a token hint of sonata form. The beginning of the second section is a triumph of equivalence for Beethoven's scherzo: the rhythm and speed, the images, especially the "trilling wire," and the provocatively shifting syntax, convey the same excitement. Yet brilliant as the passage is, I have never found it wholly satisfying as poetry; never talked it to myself; indeed, it is the penalty of writing poetry that successfully represents the dazzle and elusiveness of the gleams of the real, that it will dazzle and elude. But the long lines of the contrasting trio, where Eliot uses the voice of introspection, stay more readily in the memory. There is no attempt in the trio to find a verbal equivalent for the curious bagpipe sound of Beethoven's trio; and after the eight lines of "trio" he makes no return to the scherzo, but continues his introspective probing of the enigma of experience. The third movement opens like the profound slow movement of Opus 132. Over that movement Beethoven wrote "Heiliger Dankgesang eines Genesenen an die Gottheit" and the opening seems to recall the darkness of his suffering. Eliot's movement tells of "a place of disaffection." Then again, as in the second section, the movement takes its own way: instead of quickening where Beethoven writes "Neue Kraft fühlend," it slows and deepens:

> Descend lower, descend only
> Into the world of perpetual solitude,
> World not world, but that which is not world.
> Internal darkness . . .

At the end of this passage Eliot recalls the beginning of the poem by repeating the phrase "time past and time future." This deliberate act of connection gives one the impression that he doubted whether a section or movement of a poem, at least a section using no traditional form, could be so *obviously* an organic unity as a movement in a musical composition, and that he felt it wise to bind section with section by the repetition of his leading motifs and so establish at any rate the unity of the whole quartet. The fourth movement, though not "alla marcia," imitates Beethoven's in its brevity. The questions lend it delicacy, and so do the shortening lines at its center; and very quick and delicate is the image of the kingfisher's wing. It is debatable whether Eliot gains or loses by the last line and a half, in which he says

> the light is still
> At the still point of the turning world.

One recognizes that he is again recalling a leading motif to keep the unity of his poem; it is not the power of that device that I am now questioning. I question the cloying rhetoric. In *Ash-Wednesday* he plays with the word "still" and the image of stillness within motion: "the unstilled world still whirled." The renewal of the figure here suggests his pleasure in it; yet does it not pall quickly? Has he done well to depend on it again? The fifth and last movement of the poem implies, like the first, something of the flights and quiver of string music. The first part of it, however, is more powerful, less elusive, in its images than the first movement. The second part corresponds to Beethoven's extended coda, at least in this respect: that it makes statements which are answers to the questions of the poem, exposes the discoveries made in all the preceding exploration.

Four years later Eliot wrote the second Quartet, "East Coker," and adopted the same five-movement pattern. The first movement again seeks a swift pace, and this time achieves it without that overelusiveness which is at once beautiful and frustrating in "Burnt Norton." In the second movement he again begins with the trilling scherzo form, and again changes to longer lines in his personal idiom of self-questioning. In the slow

movement he again describes the dark of illness and his acceptance of its necessary place in experience:

> I said to my soul, be still, and let the dark come upon you
> Which shall be the darkness of God.

Then, without quite making the distinct contrast that Beethoven makes in Opus 132, he lets his line stir and lift: in the very
moment of renunciation —

> I said to my soul, be still, and wait without hope
> For hope would be hope for the wrong thing; wait without love
> For love would be love of the wrong thing . . .

— there is the first trace of refreshment. It leads to glimpses of
ecstasy, "the wild thyme unseen and the wild strawberry."
And then follows a sudden thrust into a new passage, for which
nothing in the form of Opus 132 furnishes a model; in the manner of the great mystics, he makes a statement of the contraries
which are the key to health. With the fourth movement he
makes another thrust beyond Beethoven's form. In "Burnt
Norton" he has represented the brief alla marcia with a brief
lyric. Now, in the light of his statement of the contraries on
which health depends, he writes a compact lyric interpreting
the world in terms of sickness and surgery. Mallarmé had
said the world was a hospital; and in 1910, already susceptible
to the idea of the crucial illness, serious enough for the knife
which may kill or cure, Eliot had thought of the evening sky as
a patient on the operating table, and had exploited the analogy
to shock the languid contemporary taster of poetry and make
him read on. In maturity, thirty years later, he elaborates the
image in the conviction that it is a fitting notation of man's life.
The movement is a remarkable essay in neoclassicism. From its
first words, "The wounded surgeon," it is a contemporary study
in the oxymoron; and all the colors and turns are the work of a

man remembering, but reconstituting, the poetry of the English Petrarchans. The lyric illustrates, no less than the more obvious case of the sestina in "The Dry Salvages," Eliot's remark in *The Music of Poetry* that he has "seen signs of a return" to "forms such as the sonnet, the formal ode, the ballade, the villanelle, rondeau or sestina." This is of interest to the student of the poetic act; and perhaps of even greater interest is the way the poet, working at a poem comparable in pattern with its predecessor, suddenly sees an unexpected way forward: suddenly realizes how he may redispose the design. He has been concentrating on an equivalent for a pattern, and suddenly — his powers heightened, it may be, by the act of concentration — he finds himself turning from the equivalent to something entirely unforeseen, which, in the outcome, is a new masterpiece.

In the last movement of "East Coker" he keeps the two-part shape of the last movement of "Burnt Norton," and extends his subject matter. He has written in "Burnt Norton" of the difficulty of using words as compared with music. He now determines that the first part of his last movement shall be an examination and record of his lifelong struggle with words; and this decision leads him to poetry which moves his readers and seizes the memory as the poetry of "Burnt Norton" does not. Perhaps arising from that development, the second part or coda, which again identifies the discoveries of the poem, is more urgent than its counterpassage in the previous poem. All in all, Eliot controls the form of the Quartet much more powerfully in "East Coker" than in his first experiment.

Now that he has the command of his form, he writes two more Quartets, plying it and playing with it; and the variations he introduces into the pattern exhilarate a reader who cares for technique.

At the beginning of "The Dry Salvages" the theme of the river is set against the theme of the ocean, resulting in a semblance of the contrast provided by the two subjects of sonata form. For the scherzo he drops the trilling-wire meter, which has been decoying him into "worn-out" periphrasis, and replaces it by a modern study in an antique form: a quasi sestina, in which each line of the first stanza rhymes with the corresponding line in the following five stanzas; and the rhymes are an undertow, the deeper element in the sea rhythm the poem needs to sound its meaning. This leaves the previous scherzi and the example of music far behind; yet it has become possible because they were the steppingstones to it. The management of the trio through long probing lines, which proved satisfactory in both preceding quartets, is retained. In the slow movement the two-mood division is let go as Eliot finds himself writing a sermon on the symbol of the Voyage — writing the *poésie des départs* which has long attracted him, in a way in which it has never been written before: profound, noble, intense with the fullness of the reading and thinking of fifty years. The image of the sea voyage, together with the image of the fishermen in the second movement, suggests a new form for the short fourth movement: a prayer for toilers and travelers. In the fifth section, although no break is made, there is a shortening of the rhythm which gives the effect of a change to the second part or coda of the fifth sections in "Burnt Norton" and "East Coker."

The "Dry Salvages" cannot be called a greater poem than the preceding Quartets. But it gives, when read after them, an effect of increased power, increased comprehension. Though written as separate poems, published as separate poems, and capable of being read any one of them alone, the Quartets are also one poem, thematically bound together, and a progressive poem: the permanent for which they search beyond the flowing draws nearer; all that is swift and blurred at the start comes near, grows sharp and strong; they speak ever more strongly of what they see. One of the ways, perhaps the most important

way, by which Eliot instills "The Dry Salvages" with a sense of
higher power is his development of unexpected, powerful forms
for the three middle sections. Throughout the Quartets the
thought progresses as the poet concentrates on the form, and
the form bursts and reassembles in new modifications as the
poet struggles with the thought.

In "Little Gidding" there are further flowerings of the form.
In the second section Eliot allows himself to return to the
rhymed lyric for the scherzo, but it is not of the same texture as
his scherzo in "Burnt Norton" and "East Coker"; it is rather
closer to "The wounded surgeon" lyric, neoclassical, deliberately severe, dry with an extraordinary intensity. For the trio
he builds a new structure. He no longer is feeling for answers
with probing, questioning, tentative lines. In the empty streets
of bombed London he meets the ghost of those writer ancestors
who have gone before, and they foretell his future: the public
crowning for the wrong reasons, which has since occurred,
and which may be the source of the profoundest dissatisfaction
to him. For the drama of the meeting and the prophecy, and
for the passion of the experience, the probing line will no longer
do. A different form must be invented. Eliot invents an English equivalent for Dante's terza rima. In the *Criterion* of April
1934 Ezra Pound, who had long considered the problem of
translating Dante, pointed out a technical difficulty of keeping
the form of *The Divine Comedy:* "In the matter of rhyme,
nearly every one knows that Dante's rhymes are 'feminine' . . .
There are feminine rhymes in English, there are ENOUGH, possibly, to fill the needs of an almost literal version of the *Divina
Commedia,* but they are of the wrong quality: BLOWETH, KNOW-
ING, WAITETH." Eliot solves the problem by dispensing with
rhyme; he builds Dante's structure and holds it by interlocking
masculine and feminine endings; he does it so that the lines
appear to be as firmly held as by rhyme, and satisfy the ear as
if they rhymed. They have a higher austerity than one has ever

met in translations of Dante, perhaps, higher than one has ever met in terza rima in English. They have a dignity outstanding even amid Eliot's dignified poetry: an awful dignity; and at the end a bitter dignity — which is actually out of keeping with the reconciliation towards which the Quartets are at this stage closing, but the lines are supreme, erect with self-knowledge.

In the slow movement of "Little Gidding" the two-section pattern is resumed and the animation of *Neue Kraft fühlend* completely realized in the passage:

> Sin is Behovely, but
> All shall be well . . .

The fourth movement is again a short lyric as in "Burnt Norton," but not a mere bridge, not tentative. It combines Eliot's long-ingrained Arnaut Daniel image of the fire of purgation with the fire that consumed London and Europe and the fire that consumes musician and poet.

The "extended coda" of the last movement of "Little Gidding" is the culmination of the whole group. Accordingly Eliot designs it not so much in Beethoven's manner as in the manner of the musical generation of the first years of this century — in the manner of Sibelius, perhaps. All the themes are called in. He recapitulates the theme of exploration: recapitulates "In my beginning is my end"; recapitulates the river theme; recapitulates the stillness of "Burnt Norton"; recapitulates those elusive, time-swift gusts. He draws the material together.

Did J. W. N. Sullivan's book, *Beethoven — His Spiritual Evolution*, come to Eliot's hands and heighten his conception of the last quartets? In 1927 the centenary of Beethoven's death had been celebrated all over Europe. The composer was in the mind of the public — and in the mind of the *Criterion* contributors. Roger Hinks, Eliot's art chronicler, wrote about Blake, whose centennial celebrations also fell that year, and Beethoven came into his article for purposes of comparison:

"Just as Beethoven tried to say more than can be said in music, so Blake from time to time tries to compress into a phrase a whole tract of meaning which no mind can gauge . . ." In March 1928 the music chronicler J. B. Trend summed up on the Beethoven centennial books: how many of them were really useful? "Among the newer ones there was Mr. J. W. N. Sullivan's study; among the old ones Paul Bekker."

Sullivan was a Londoner with a gift for the clear exposition of mathematics and the sciences, which helped him to a living, and a love of music. He had been encouraged in his literary work by Middleton Murry, who had employed him with Eliot, Conrad Aiken, Aldous Huxley, for the *Athenaeum* pyrotechnics of 1919-21. Eliot was acquainted with him.

Stephen Spender knew Sullivan's book on Beethoven and quoted it in the essay on Eliot which he included in *The Destructive Element* in 1935. That essay attempts to correlate Beethoven's Opus 132 in A Minor with *Ash-Wednesday*. Is it possible that Eliot had spoken to Spender of his interest in Beethoven, perhaps, too, of his interest in Sullivan's book, and that Spender had thought that Eliot was telling him about a poem already undertaken in an attempt to follow Beethoven's example, and decided that *Ash-Wednesday* must be the poem? Whereas Eliot was describing a design still under consideration?

There are phrases in Sullivan's study which bear a likeness to key phrases of the Quartets. Writing of the *Grosse Fuge*, "in which the apparently opposing elements of life are seen as necessary and no longer in opposition," Sullivan translates it as Beethoven's realization that

his creative energy, which he at one time opposed to his destiny, in reality owed its very life to that destiny. It is not merely that he believed the price was worth paying; he came to see it as necessary that a price should be paid. To be willing to suffer in order to create is one thing; to realise that one's creation

necessitates one's suffering, that suffering is one of the greatest
of God's gifts, is almost to reach a mystical solution of the problem of evil.

"The wounded surgeon" lyric says, not in the language of an
epoch of storm and stress, but in neoclassical terms, that "suffering is the greatest of God's gifts." The phrase near the end
of the Quartets, "Costing not less than everything," is like a
splendid transformation of Sullivan's words, "necessary that a
price should be paid." Three times in the course of his book
Sullivan refers to "Beethoven the explorer." Eliot endorses:
"Old men ought to be explorers." "Submission, absolute submission to your fate," Beethoven wrote in his diary. Eliot
speaks of a creator's victory won by "strength and submission."
Beethoven had said of Gneixendorf, where the B♭ quartet,
Opus 135, was finished, "The name sounds like the breaking of
an axle-tree." The "East Coker" scherzo is perhaps tinged with
the memory of that: there is the suggestion of the danger to the
mind of an artist exploring a mental frontier. The first movement of the A minor quartet ends, says Sullivan, "as only Beethoven would end with what sounds like a startling and celes-
tial trumpet call." In "The Dry Salvages," where Eliot is in
complete command of the form, the first movement ends

>   Clangs
>   The bell

which is startling, admonitory of the eternal. A transposition of
Beethoven's effect, as Sullivan interpreted it, into the terms of
his own ocean-music?

Resemblances of detail apart, the Quartets are written with
the sense of age approaching, therefore with an urgent will to
understand Beethoven who had triumphed over age by exploring the utmost potentialities of his medium. Hofmannsthal, in
an article for the *Dial*, had written of Beethoven's last years in

Vienna when he was aging and ailing, changing lodgings twenty times, nursing his loneliness. Sullivan had told of Beethoven's illness, his disappointments, his last conversations with his physician. One of the themes, if a subtheme, of the Quartets, is the artist as the aging, ailing, and yet — and thereby — creative man.

The Quartets are a great work, but in one respect they fall short of Eliot's intention. They are not poetry beyond poetry. Some passages make statements so intently that they almost are. But then the voice alters, begins again with poetry that is surprising and beautiful, but for that reason is not what he had thought he was seeking. Instances of evident poetry are "the salt is on the briar rose," and the simile of the train halted in the subway tunnel, and the image which astonishingly blends St-John Perse and Tennyson:

> Out at sea the dawn wind
> Wrinkles and slides

These three moments would justify us in saying that evident poetry may also be transparent poetry, for the object is seen with clarity or sensed sharply even though we know that we are reading poetry. But if poetry is beyond poetry only when we forget that it is poetry, they are not what he desired. But though the Quartets did not produce the result he had purposed, they showed him, in the contest with the material, more about the difficulties and the possibilities than he had known before. They enabled him to proceed, after a characteristically lengthy pause for assimilation, to the poetry beyond poetry of *The Cocktail Party* and *The Confidential Clerk*.

Experiments: 1924-1925

Eliot's eventual success was to contribute to the English language a new dramatic poetry, dependent not on the language of the strong, nor the speech of men who would have appealed to Whitman, but on the twitter of men and women gathered for urban occasions. He evolved it in the same work in which he projected the contrasting figure of the ballad-howling Hercules and the myth of the dead restored. Yet twenty-five years before he completed *The Cocktail Party* some of the contributors to the *Criterion* were experimenting in a method very close to that which he slowly perfected.

Their experiments described suffering in a sophisticated gathering. Their method was to filter the suffering and its poignancy through a flimsy, elegant web of description and dialogue. Feiron Morris, in the *Criterion* of October 1924, told about the miseries of Felice and Sibylla at a *Thé Dansant,* and in April 1925, about Sibylla at a *Night Club* — this latter story shot with the Scott Fitzgerald sense of the emptiness of the bright twenties. Also in April 1925 a poem, signed F.M., asked *Necesse est Perstare?* — describing the breakup of a lunch party and catching the assault of its literary clamor and vacancy. A *Diary of the Rive Gauche* had been appearing over the signature Fanny Marlow. In July 1925 Fanny Marlow was reported ill and unable to continue the diary, and in place of the third installment Eliot printed her story "Fête Galante"; and this turns out to be another Sibylla tale, only the setting is some notable man's home where the dancers are drifting in to be entertained after their performance at the ballet. The F.M.s came to Eliot attempting a style which, though it was flirtatious, brittle, pleasure-grabbing, hollow-echoing, like the mood it represented, offered the possibilities of a manner.

He made at least one experiment like theirs and printed it in January 1925. He has never reprinted it. Yet its title is the index of a serious intention: "On the Eve," borrowed from Turgenev. Edward Garnett, in a study of Turgenev which Eliot reviewed for the *Egoist,* had devoted a chapter to *On the Eve* and to the "depths of meaning which at first sight lie veiled under the simple harmonious surface"; behind the lightly spun picture of a quiet household he saw the "wavering shadow" of a nation's hopes and ambitions and its coming changes. Eliot seems to have intended an equivalent double effect in his story: on the one level he would mimic, like his social-occasion contributors but better, the voices of the well-to-do, foppish, dunderheaded folk, and he would add the charlady commenting in Cockney (and he obviously enjoyed mimicking that); on the under level he would suggest the thud of emptiness, the bad dream of class collapse, bank failure, and national catastrophe. If you do not know that Eliot wrote it, and if you come on it unprepared as I did, it is an odd story to meet on a lonely night in a library while the snow gathers in the Montana spruce by the window; but on further acquaintance, and considered in the perspective of the years since 1925, its purpose is clear. Telling himself for some time that a modern poet must do as Dryden did, restore the diction and rhythm of conversation to poetry, Eliot had divined — with hints from the aspiring if vapid practice around him — that drawing-room gabble was the speech he must take and tool. He took it and reproduced, with his sharp ear, the foppish chatter, but only reproduced it. In a short story, in prose of any length, he could hardly do more. When he began to wrestle with the accommodation of chatter to metrics and to the requirements of stage dialogue, then he would find his art. The short story form did not suit his special problem, and it was a form for which he had no gifts.

One other story of the genre appeared in the *Criterion:* Aldous Huxley's "The Monocle," specifically a cocktail-party story, and adorned by a few words about a lion huntress which may have quivered in Eliot's memory when he designed the curtain-up conversation for Edward's drawing room years later. But the *Criterion* of 1926 was to be markedly different from that of 1924 and 1925. Viscountess Rothermere, to whom literature has a debt for founding the *Criterion,* had decided not to continue her support; there had been no autumn number. The January 1926 number was the first of a new series under the Faber imprint, and with it Eliot introduced a policy of greater austerity.

So ended his sponsorship of the vivacious stories in the "party" style. But there is one thing to be added: in the new *Criterion* of 1926 and 1927 Eliot published his Aristophanic Fragments, "Sweeney Agonistes." The scene between Dusty and Doris, and then between Dusty, Doris, and their visitors, shows Eliot already transforming the method of his storytellers into his own poetic method:

> What about that poker game? eh what Sam?
> What about that poker game in Bordeaux?
> Yes Miss Dorrance you get Sam
> To tell about that poker game in Bordeaux.

When he wrote that, Eliot was on the threshold of his late style. But to possess the technique perfectly, to make it capable of dealing with many situations, many moods, he evidently needed a withdrawal from it and a long interim, spent in the solemn scrutiny of the problems of man and society to which he conducted his readers.

Hofmannsthal's Death

On the obituary page of the London *Times* of July 17, 1929, a dispatch from the Vienna correspondent told how Hofmannsthal's eldest son, Franz, had committed suicide, how the poet had endured calmly till called to start for the funeral service, and then had collapsed and died; how he had been "more than once on the brink of entering a monastery" and now would be buried, "in obedience to his frequently expressed wish," in the garb of the Franciscan order. Eliot wrote a single sentence for the next issue of the *Criterion*, October 1929: "Of your charity pray for the soul of Hugo von Hofmannsthal." Nothing more. None of the material with which, writing obituary tributes, such as that to Virginia Woolf, he has sometimes both expressed his loyalty to the dead and attempted to avoid a judgment. The formal sentence bespeaks a community with the poet who had taken a way to which he felt himself called: to monasticism; but to the secret and taxing life of the tertiary, whose monastery is the heart while he follows the routine of the world.

As long as a man lives he conceals many things, and sometimes we know him better after his death, and can draw strength or sweetness from a new intimacy with him. In the four years following 1929, articles appeared in appreciation and interpretation of Hofmannsthal, which may have accentuated Eliot's sense of community. One was a study by Curtius for the *Neue Schweizer Rundschau*, describing Hofmannsthal as "a representative of the restoration, the 'conservative revolution,'" and comparing him in this respect with Eliot and Maurras. That article was not, of course, a *Criterion* contribution, but it was summarized by A. W. G. Randall in his survey of German-Swiss periodicals in the *Criterion* of January 1928. Six months later the *Criterion* published an essay by Max Rychner, a most attractive writer. Rychner centered his discussion on *Lord Chandos' Letter:* on the phase of development at which creative genius can no longer tolerate the inefficiency of words; abstains from speech rather than fall into falsity; can only revive if it can find a new language: "a tongue of which not a single word is known to me, a language in which dumb things have spoken to me." He applied the *Letter* to the heroes of the works Hofmannsthal had written before 1902:

So rich is their inner life that they feel themselves estranged in the outer world of sense, and almost come to doubt its reality. They dimly guess that the language they have heard and

learned from others can only supply an approximation to what
they feel to be the most living thing within them, and it is as the
logical outcome of such a state of mind that Lord Chandos condemns himself to silence.

and then he added:

The poet Hofmannsthal overcame this tragic stage, he passed
through this dark borderland of mystical world negation and
emerged as victor.

On the occasion of the Braille Centenary Eliot took part in a
meeting held at the National Book League's London headquar-
ters in the cause of the blind. A blind reader was to recite
from *The Rock;* and Eliot told, in some prefatory remarks, how
he had doubted during the two or three years before *The Rock*
was composed, whether he had any more poetry to write.
When the London churches had asked him to collaborate in
the pageant with E. Martin Browne he had agreed as an act
of conviction and obligation. In the result his numbed powers
were revived by the exercise, and he was able to proceed to
the second half of his creative life. There seems to me — one
can only speak for oneself in suggestions of this kind — to be
a parallel between that experience, in which he doubted his
power to write poetry again, and the experience which Hofmannsthal described in the *Letter;* and Rychner's interpretation of Hofmannsthal's success in passing beyond the borderland to a long, rich, second life as a writer may, at once or
soon, have spoken to Eliot of his own difficulty and encouraged him to endure it and persevere.

When he returned to London from his Harvard lectureship
in 1933, he found waiting on his desk, in Mary Hottinger's
animated translation, Marta Karlweiss' *Letter to a Doctor about
a Poet* — memories of Hofmannsthal which are also an analysis. It described Hofmannsthal's self-control, his masking of his

psychic energy behind lightness and buffoonery, the "dissimulation he practised in view of the vulnerability of mankind and from the instinct of self-preservation"; his conversation "without emphasis or insistence," his "dark equanimity" and "expectant resignation," his "incorruptibility by love" (for he wore, like William Greenleaf Eliot, the intimidating aura of the judge); his habit of ceremony, and his prescription, in cases of grief, of the discipline of manners:

> During a profound crisis in my life, he once said to me: "Surrender yourself utterly for a time to your surroundings. Don't neglect the least service, the smallest courtesy. Return every visit punctually, answer every letter carefully. Neglect nothing which good manners, in the broadest sense of the word, demands. In the seventeenth century, you would have gone into a convent for a time: this way is harder, but it is the only way."

He had surrounded himself with beautiful pictures, Chinese porcelain, fine furniture and had understood and absorbed their hidden life, but gradually said a farewell to beauty, "pushing the possession of things ever further from him." "His bedroom in the farmhouse which he occupied for years looked like a cell." "In youth," he said, "we find the so-called interesting remarkable: in later years, the good." And Marta Karlweiss displayed the paradox, not unlike that which young English contributors to the *Criterion* were, at much the same date, discovering in the English seventeenth-century religious poets: that Hofmannsthal was at once a moral being, deeply rooted in Christianity, occupied with "the poetic development of the Christian virtues and their constant contemplation," and the primitive seer:

> Saints and martyrs are never seers. If they possessed the gift, they would have to sacrifice it. The ultimate essence of poetry springs from the ultra-Christian stratum, and that it appeared pure in Hofmannsthal makes his uniqueness and at the same

time the strangeness of his soul among us. For there was a night
of strangeness in him before which he himself shuddered, which
did not reveal itself once or again — it never left him. And that
he *ganz vergessener Völker Müdigkeiten nicht abtun konnte von
seinen Liedern* was not the aimless and exquisite incantation
of romanticism and decadence, but the monstrosity of an ultra-
Christian pre-existence, thousands of years old, consciously
lived.

The essay, published in the *Criterion* in October 1933, makes
any reader brood, searching for understanding of the secrets
it is ever on the point of unfolding. How much more it may
have meant to a poet long in sympathy with Hofmannsthal
and who shared some aspects of his nature, some of his punc-
tilious, self-disciplined habits, his passion for austerity and experience of the poet's delight, his double watch on the transi-
tory and eternal. It is tempting to think that, as Eliot read his
contributors' interpretations of the dead poet, he thought of
him as a fraternal figure and was the better able to learn from
him and especially to perceive and use the lessons of his dramatic art.

The Bound Volumes

Most magazines stand or fall by their impact on their readers. Was the *Criterion* as important for its readers as it was for
its editor? A friendly French critic in 1927 was doubtful
whether it was quite so exacting as it should be, if its readers
were to be led anywhere. Shocked by the news that Middleton
Murry's *Adelphi* would be suspended after four years for lack of
subscribers, Charles du Bos wrote in his diary that Murry
posed ultimate problems and disturbed his readers, therefore
had lost them; Eliot treated every question with clarity, but
treated it in isolation, and avoided showing how one inter-
locked with another, with the result that he was not too dis-

turbing and his readers were free to enjoy the contributions without any intolerable degree of self-searching. But in 1927 the *Criterion* was not yet making all its demands, was only now about to be visible in all its austerity. Five years later the predominantly severe complexion was unmistakable. Eliot seemed to himself, as his "Last Words" of 1939 show, to be increasingly conscious of the interdependence of major questions and to be insisting on it. If lack of subscribers is a proof of virtue, he could claim to be not far behind Murry.

But he was reaching one class of reader more than any other. He was reaching younger writers. The magazine which nursed the creativity of its editor nursed the creativity of young writers; it nursed them, however different from him in outlook, hopes, style, and manners, both by what it published of other men and what it published of their own. Up to 1926 and 1927 his British contributors were, broadly, of two groups: old stagers, Saintsbury, Sturge Moore, Yeats, Whibley, May Sinclair; and new stagers, who are old stagers now, but who were coming up with Eliot himself, either just ahead, or a leg behind, or *pari passu:* Pound, Aldington, Flint, Wyndham Lewis, Herbert Read, D. H. Lawrence. In the second half of the twenties, he noticed and began to use, of the critics, J. B. Trend, I. A. Richards, John Hayward; of writers, Liam O'Flaherty. But the young, his juniors by twenty years and more, he began to discover on the first bell of the thirties. The significant date is January 1930 when he published Auden's charade, "Paid on Both Sides." From that moment the new university wits came in one by one: Empson in July 1930, Spender in October 1930, Ian Parsons in July 1931, Bronowski and James Reaves in January 1932, MacNeice in October 1932. Later came Charles Madge with poems and reviews of anthropology; Dylan Thomas; Ronald Duncan; Kenneth Allott; John Short; Roger Roughton; Lawrence Durrell, in whose *Black Book* Eliot discerned the later novels on the way. When he looked through the *Evocations* of Henri Massis, Eliot was struck by a story about Péguy. The Péguy of 1905-1911 was convinced that he was forming a party: the party of the next generation: "le parti des hommes de quarante ans." He promised Massis a place in it: "Un jour, vous serez mûr." Eliot reflected, in his Commentary of April 1934, "I wonder whether we should make that prediction, with equal assurance, to our juniors today." A depressed and doubting sentence! The gloom was unwarranted. He was engaged in forming the party through the *Criterion*.

In retrospect the *Criterion* is a monument. Not the only one in its England. For criticism *Scrutiny* challenges it. For poetry *New Verse* challenges it. But, though not impeccable as *Scrutiny* was, nor a fire as *New Verse* was, it attempted much more and accomplished much more. It represented the best critics and the best creative writers of three cultures — insular Britain, all Western Europe, America. Many of its articles are of lasting significance, many of its reviews, especially some in which Eliot asked a critic to survey a writer's whole work compendiously (C. Henry Warren's survey of T. F. Powys, for example). Major poets and major poems and some of the best minor poets of the two decades appeared there. The stories, for all that Eliot has sometimes been accused of lacking discrimination for creative prose, included A. E. Coppard's, Lawrence's, Dylan Thomas', together with others which history has not, or has not yet, celebrated, but which have beauty: Frances Gregg's "Locust Street," Maria Cristina Chambers' "John of God, the Water Carrier." Certainly there were mishits and imperfections. Unmatchable in diagnosis, Eliot was apt to fling into wild and wide prognosis. As an editor he would, rather than interfere with his contributors, let by their oddities, such as the announcement that *Mary Rose* was a masterpiece, or an appeal to Joyce to try his hand at a play — ten years after he had written *Exiles*. He occasionally passed curious misprints, and no doubt he suffered the agony every periodical editor suffers when he detected them a month or a year later. But these become, for the affectionate reader, part of the pleasure of the *Criterion,* part of the picture of Eliot's mind which it composes.

But the *Criterion* is also a picture of the critical-creative mind of the West between the two wars, as he had hoped it might be when he drafted the manifesto of January 1926. When the second war had come, come despite Europeanism, classicism, and theology, Eliot (like Faber in those three sonnets) spoke bitterly of "Twenty years largely wasted." But if we judge by the *Criterion* the time was not wasted. "It is after all a grrrreat litttttterary period," Pound had written to him after doctoring *The Waste Land* in 1921. So it was. Classical work was done; and the ground was laid for more work in the next half century.

9. Drama

IN "Prufrock" and the "Portrait of a Lady" Eliot was already a dramatist, and a dramatist employing his later theories of which he was yet unaware. "Let us go then, you and I . . ." That beguiling invitation involves the reader in the poem, as Eliot was to maintain that the audience must be involved in a drama. He has moved from the instinctive, vivacious dramatic poem to observation of the living theatre and the extrication of principles from the observation, then from the principles to experiments and eventually to successful experiments, and at last from the application of a theory to freedom from it.

At Harvard Eliot had resisted or ignored those conspicuous figures who advocated the "drama of democracy." His next step, in London, was to resist the "drama of aristocracy," advocated by the most imposing figure on the British scene: Yeats.

Yeats at fifty was in a state of excited hostility to the Irish crowd at the Abbey Theatre, which had treated him and his movement with malcomprehension and bickering ever since the first production of 1899. He now wanted no audience unless a comprehending one. He imagined a secluded, drawing-room theatre for a few dozen cultivated friends, and, turning with Pound's help to Japan, set himself to adapt the Noh play to his purpose. In 1918 *At the Hawk's Well* was expounded and danced to private gatherings in London (Eliot was among the guests at one). Touring America in 1919-20 Yeats sometimes spoke of his new conception; the issue of *Poetry* for April,

1920, reported his speech in Chicago describing "the aristocratic theatre in which from a dozen to fifty of the elect shall see plays worthy of spirits highly tuned and keyed, and shall pass them on authoritatively to the next age."

By 1920 Eliot was gradually turning towards the high Toryism, the desire for the paternal tyranny of the enlightened few, which Yeats was embracing; yet he was apparently not convinced by the doctrine of a theatre for the enlightened few, which might seem to be its counterpart. He refused to be content with a small audience and a dubious underground transmission to the future. If he could not reach the people in his own time, was there really any likelihood that the people would be better prepared to hear him a century later? — they might be the less well prepared precisely because of his failure. To despise the general audience and to shirk the hazard of malcomprehension was to abnegate the poet's work. As Hofmannsthal said: "It is absurd to use the dramatic form and yet to be unwilling to have anything to do with the theatre. If one concerns oneself with the theatre . . . one has made a decision; one acts because one intends to make an impression on the public." Hofmannsthal had grown to believe that the poet's vocation was a "mingling with the throng," a "speaking to the crowd, into the crowd." Eliot came to a similar view, reaching it by his own route, favored perhaps by the traditions of his preacher ancestors, favored too by the very energy and ferocious power of Yeats' experiments, which enabled a critically developed mind to appreciate alike the case for and against the theatre of the elite.

In his essay on the prospects for a new poetic drama, contributed to the *Dial* of November, 1920, and included in *The Sacred Wood*, Eliot suggested that:

Possibly the majority of attempts to confect a poetic drama have begun at the wrong end; they have aimed at the small public which wants "poetry" . . .

Shakespeare, he pointed out, had worked from the other end:
he and his contemporaries had aimed at a public which
"wanted *entertainment* of a crude sort, but would *stand* a good
deal of poetry."

What kind of entertainment was there that the public
wanted and that a poet might have the interest and the aptitude to provide? Now was the time to remember the sagacity of
the *Advocate* writers who told the tiro dramatists to learn from
the box office: from Gilbert and Sullivan, Gus Luders, and
Trixie Friganza. Eliot appears to have frequented the theatre
at this date, sampling productions of many kinds, and observing the plays and their audiences with a concentrated scientific curiosity. Occasional remarks in his criticism and his
Criterion commentaries bear witness to his forays and record
some of the opinions he brought back from them. He has
been to see Seymour Hicks in a fashionable success on the
West End stage: who can learn a new art from the spectacle of
Mr. Hicks telephoning for nights on end? He has been to the
ballet, and observed the difference "between the conventional
gesture of the ordinary stage, which is supposed to *express*
emotion, and the abstract gesture of Massine, which *symbolises*
emotion." He commends Miss Ethel Levey, "our best revue
comedienne . . . Hers is not broad farce, but a fascinating in-
human grotesquerie." In Paris he has been to see Mistinguett,
and writes to the *Dial* that the role she adopted — presumably
one that sparkled with "directness, frankness and ferocity" —
would have been better understood and liked in the English
music hall than in the Casino de Paris.

Arthur Symons, whose book on the Symbolists led Eliot to
Laforgue, had in 1890 led his London contemporaries to the
"music-hall," searching, like the French Impressionists of the
seventies, from whom he and George Moore derived their outlook, for a new beauty in dingy places. The habit spread
among English sophisticates during the next three decades.

Now when Symons took his friends to the Alhambra, he was principally interested in the dancers. A reader of our time, when he meets the word "music hall," thinks of vaudeville, the stage of the juggler, the popular comedian, the diseuse. Since 1911 music hall has undergone a process of bifurcation: to vaudeville in one direction, to ballet in the other. Eliot visited both kinds, and it is hard to say which taught him most, for both opened his eyes to what he wanted to do.

In the music hall where Marie Lloyd, Nellie Wallace, George Robey were performing, he recognized an active, creative rapport between artist and audience. Marie Lloyd died in 1922. Ford Madox Ford has told how England paused at her death, as it pauses when royalty dies, as France pauses when Proust or Eluard dies. The paperboys ran down the streets shouting "Ma-*rie* dies! Ma-*rie*'s dead!" The traffic stopped for half a minute. Eliot, already devoted to her art, was evidently profoundly moved to realize how much she was a national figure. He wrote, for the second issue of the *Criterion*, the obituary notice in which he said:

> The working-man who went to the music-hall and saw Marie Lloyd and joined in the chorus was himself performing part of the act; he was engaged in that collaboration of the audience with the artist which is necessary in all art and most obviously in dramatic art.

And thus presented, I think for the first time, his doctrine of the involvement and participation of the audience.

A very different American poet, Vachel Lindsay, had already had an inkling of the theory. Lindsay thought that poetry might gain a new group validity if the audience would participate with the poet in speaking it, and devised poems in which the poet is leader and the audience an answering voice. Touring American cities and universities he incorporated the antiphonals into his programs. On a visit to England in 1920 he offered them to an Oxford gathering at Worcester College. A. E. Coppard, who heard him that evening, tells how he led the dons in the chant "I've been to Palestine," then asked them for the interjections to his John Brown poem:

> Lindsay eulogized his hero in eloquent contrast with the vileness of sundry noxious miscreants and untried villains of the world, such as
> "Judas Iscariot!" he hissed.
> There was a momentary silence, this seemed a little brash, but then he let go his second torpedo:
> "Matthew Arnold!" he roared
> and the entire audience yelled ecstatic approbation.

Coppard says, "I had no least liking for Matthew Arnold myself, but that Oxford, of all places, should acclaim a respite from that august menace, was a pleasant surprise to me . . ." It was really very much in Oxford's style, and Lindsay was lucky there and got his response. His attempt to give his crowd a voice was courageous, and Eliot eventually made a gesture of acknowledgment by his echo of "Daniel" in *Murder in the Cathedral*. But it must have looked, to a trained theoretician, like surface tinkering, and, if promising in America where the poet was welcome in the universities and lecture societies and where the meeting was a genuine rival to the theatre as a living institution, scarcely applicable in England. Eliot saw that the hope of the poet in England lay in mastering the secrets of the stage. He made progress when he recognized the vitality of the workingman's theatre of song and joke.

At the same date Cummings in America was in love with vaudeville. In Paris Cocteau was calling the legitimate stage *un vieil album de photographie* and listing the circus, the music hall, and the cinema as aids for the youngsters in lifting it to life. Eliot quoted Cocteau's argument in the *Criterion* in 1923.

An important word in Eliot's tribute to Marie Lloyd is "dignity." He asked why the working people loved her and joined in the choruses with her, and answered that her performance was "the expression and dignity of their own lives." The same word occurs almost forty years later in his remarks on John Davidson's "Thirty Bob a Week": "Davidson had a great theme, and also found an idiom which elicited the greatness of the theme, which endowed this thirty-bob-a-week clerk with a dignity that would not have appeared if a more conventional poetic diction had been employed." A view of mankind and of the arts seems to be inherent in the two comments. It is as though Eliot points out that the value that each man has in the eye of God is often obscured to the human eye, and lost in the welter of the day's work and the common difficulties; but that the artist may sense it; and the artist may rescue it if he can find a new technique right to express it — may rescue it and enable us all to see it and esteem it as God sees and esteems it. (And if it be alleged that to say this is to echo Browning's attitude to man, that only reminds us how much Eliot and Pound and other men of their age are the legatees of Browning.) All Eliot's plays deserve rereading with the question in mind that the two analogous remarks, forty years apart, invite: to what extent do they elicit the dignity of their characters and of the class to which their characters belong? In *Murder in the Cathedral* the poetry of the choruses elicits the dignity of the poor women of Canterbury, betokening the toil and patience of their lives, the sorrow and privilege of their witness in the play. In *The Confidential Clerk* every character emerges with his essential dignity discovered. And the result in *The Confidential Clerk* is of particular interest when weighed against a point which Eliot had made as he pursued his thoughts on Marie Lloyd: he had congratulated the working folk of England on their vitality by which they nourished the music hall as their spokesman; and he had deplored, like George Moore a generation earlier, the pusillanimity of the middle class which nourished no powerful theatre. In plays of his maturity Eliot gave the middle class (the term is notoriously inexact and elastic; the dramatis personae of *The Confidential Clerk* display its range) an art by which it might know itself and acquire a stronger and more productive character.

The Ballet

Eliot's debt to the ballet is even greater than his considerable debt to the music hall. It led him towards the discovery of entirely new rhythms for the English poetic drama.

When he was first in Europe in 1910-1911, the Parisian intellectuals were swept by the Russian ballet; the *N.R.F.* was acclaiming it; Rilke was writing to his Princess about the *Spectre de la Rose* and Nijinsky's leap through the casement. By the time Eliot came back to Europe in 1914 London was as delighted as Paris, the sophisticated young of Mayfair and Bloomsbury had taken ballet fever, Karsavina was a magic name. To the dress rehearsal of the Strauss-Hofmannsthal *Legend of Joseph* at the Drury Lane Theatre in June 1914 the intelligence of London had crowded, and the beauty too — it was here that Lady Diana Manners made her climb from box to box above the admiring stalls. In the seasons after the war the ballet gradually grew into the public enthusiasm which it has remained, combatting and correcting the dour gray tweed which otherwise preponderates in British life.

Delighted by ballet, Eliot interpreted it — whether under the impact of Stravinsky's *Rite of Spring*, which he immensely admired, or whether his interpretation had begun to crystallize before he knew that work — in terms of "ritual." As a result of his employment of that word it has become a touchstone of literary and dramatic criticism in this age, now so often to be met that it is losing its force. But its force has been enormous.

The reader of Eliot's plays and of the criticism which led up to them is likely to be conscious of two meanings of the word "ritual." In an article contributed to the *Athenaeum* of October 6, 1923, Eliot defined "ritual" in a way which looks back to Royce, but which must have been somewhat unexpected to his readers, to whom he afforded a preliminary hint in the title, "The Beating of a Drum." Aristotle, he said there, had classified poetry, music, and dancing together, because they all three depended on rhythm. Rhythm was the significant common element in the arts of Shakespeare, Charlie Chaplin, Massine, and the juggling Rastelli. It was not to be found, however, in *The Doll's House.* Rhythm, which is best induced by poetry, though it is not confined to poetry, should be brought back into the theatre. The audience desired to participate in a "ritual," that is, in "a set of repeated movements . . . essentially a dance." That is one meaning he attached to the word; and indeed the dance is superbly present in his plays. But in the plays up to 1950 there is also a deliberate use of "ritual" in the sense in which the ordinary person would understand it: a religious ceremony. An example may be given from *The Cocktail Party:* the beautifully integrated example at the close of the second act, when prayers are spoken for the building of the marriage hearth and the protection of Celia on her journey. In great theatre the very plots, or episodes of them, approximate to acts of sacrifice or consecration or communion, and the audience is the tribe gathered to participate as if in a cathedral or at Stonehenge.

Did Eliot have a general theory to which both applications of the word "ritual" can be referred? If he had, he has not set it out, and it is hazardous for any other person to try. Yet there seems to be the shadow of such a theory behind a review of 1925. Discussing Cecil Sharpe's *The Dance* and A. P. Oppé's *Mudras: the Ritual Hand Poses of the Buddha Priests and*

Shiva Priests, he suggested that the neurologists might track the secrets of the dance in the play of our nerves; and he asked, "Is not the High Mass — as performed, for instance, at the Madeleine in Paris — one of the highest developments of dancing?" The rhythms of the dance, he appears to suggest, correspond with rhythms latent in the human system and are capable of evoking them. Poetry (he does not interpose, but we may) evokes them. Religious ceremonies (he implies) demand of the congregation the responsive, participant dance of the nerves. If we read the review of 1925 together with the 1926 preface to *Savonarola,* in which he recalls that, writing a graduate essay for Royce, he had once questioned the assumption that ritual was evolved by men for their purposes, and had speculated that it may have preceded purpose, we may think that in the dance Eliot discerned the divine pattern: rhythm is its shifting kaleidoscope. In his plays the ritual which is rhythm and the rituals which are ceremonies are essentially the same and are doing the same work: evoking their corresponding rhythms from our depths, and disclosing to us, as we respond with that inner movement, the sudden sight of the eternal verity.

Eliot claimed that the revival of the drama in English depended on inspiring the dialogue with the same excitement that music and dance give the ballet. The playwrights who had taken up the methods of *The Doll's House* — the Harvard prose dramatists, and perhaps some serious-minded but limited English dramatists like Galsworthy — had thought it enough to probe a social problem compassionately, unaware how much they needed, unaware how much they lacked, the drum which wakens the nerves and displays eternity (and unaware, as Eliot himself still was, that Ibsen had the drum). The poets, from Keats through Browning and Tennyson to Masefield, who had attempted poetic drama, why had they not succeeded? Because, though they spoke with their own voices and rhythms

when they made poems, they forgot them when they wrote
for the stage, and borrowed the voice and rhythms of 1600 or
1610, and these no longer wakened excitement; instead they
touched the stops of prejudice: in a few listeners the prejudice of snobbery and fake respect; in the majority the prejudice
of a dislike for "poetry." In both cases the prejudice deadened
the nerves. With the help of the ballet and of his reading in
anthropology, and possibly also with some help from the Noh
plays, which he had rejected for a poet's theatre but which he
knew, no one better, how to appreciate (and a *Criterion* review, contributed by B. G. Brooks, tells how a Noh program
at the Maddermarket Theatre, Norwich, was performed to the
monotonous beating of a drum, which accelerated as the climax approached), Eliot formed the conception of a poetic
speech to invite the nerves back to their dance. He would require new metrics, a new language, a new tone.

Before the twenties Pound had apparently been feeling for a
new language for the theatre among those "dialects" which pep-
per his correspondence. At least, that is the impression conveyed by a paragraph in the *Dial*, recalling that he had experimented with a modern *Agamemnon* (one of the few plays really
worth the endeavor, he thought at that time) and had "tried
every possible dodge, making the watchman a negro, and giving him a *fihn Géoogiah voyce;* making the chorus talk cockney, et cetera." But Pound added a criticism to his recollection: that dialect "is a usual form of evasion in modern drama.
Ibsen makes his people provincial, Chekhov also, the Irish theatre
talks dialect, to get a 'language.' " Eliot thought that the dialect which is attractive in proportion as it is remote from the
familiar language of the audience could not be a real solution
for the theatre. He had already criticized it in Synge — and
Synge and the Abbey writers had the excuse that they were
reaching backwards into their nation's history and character.
Nevertheless, in *Sweeney Agonistes* he made some exploitation

of it, as he had already exploited it in his poem, *The Waste Land;*
but since *Sweeney* he has called on it only rarely as an ancillary.
The dialect he has adopted, to "get a language," is that familiar to a West End audience, so familiar that it would not be
recognized as a "dialect": the dialect which the "best people"
talk in a Seymour Hicks or a Noël Coward comedy.

He has distilled from it: new metrics from its rhythms; from
its vocabulary and idioms a new diction, not obviously poetry,
but casting now a piquancy, now a pleasure, now nostalgia, although it shyly hurries from any of these. It has taken him two
lifetimes, if a lifetime be measured by Keats, to do it. The result is comparable with Hofmannsthal's in *Der Rosenkavalier:*
it is "gesprochene Sprache" which "ist in keinem Buch zu
finden . . . liegt aber in der Luft." He had English predecessors — W. S. Gilbert, for example — but they had limited
their exploitation of the spoken language to a poetry of light
satire, spoofing, and sentiment within the spoofing and satire;
and part of the charm of their result was the manipulation of
the spoken idiom as rhyming verse — and often, with that
virtuosity, like Byron's, which laughs with the audience when a
phrase that can't be juggled into rhyme is forcibly but neatly
juggled into it. Eliot succeeded in the much more difficult feat
of eliciting the dance from the dialect without recourse to
forms which would betray that he was writing "poetry."

The Period of Fragments

There is an experiment of Ford Madox Ford's which invites
comparison with Eliot's experimental *Sweeney Agonistes.* It
is a "Modern Morality Play," *A House,* printed in the *Chapbook* in 1921. Ford called into use, bringing down the pitch a
little, the rhyming speech of the three poems which Pound had
singled out for praise when he read *High Germany* nine years
earlier:

If Dixon could pay . . . But he never will . . .
He promised the money for yesterday . . .
But poor old Dicky's been through the mill . . .
And it's late . . . It's too late to sit here railing at Fate!
He'd pay, if he could, but he's got his fix on
Too, poor Doddering Dixon.

Faltering, imperfect; the looseness and slanginess of phrasing did not quite blend with the rhythm; and the rhyme, evidently meant to strut the ordinary speech and give it form, was a little overpowering. But the movement was in the right direction. It was true to speech and, as Ford said poetry should be, "like one's intimate conversation with someone one loved very much"; and it had the rhythm of poetry, the dance of the nerves. In *Sweeney Agonistes* Eliot moved in the same direction, but advanced further: advanced by subtilizing the rhythms, while bringing them nearer to speech; keeping the slanginess, but mating it with other qualities; using rhymes, but making them defter, quicker; catching the obstinate echo and repetition of conversation.

Ford's views on the proper subject for poetry in his time bear comparisons with Eliot's practice in *Sweeney*. The fertile *Chapbook* printed in 1922 remarks it had received from poets in answer to a questionnaire, the third item of which asked:

Do you think there is any chance of verse being eventually displaced by prose, as narrative poetry apparently is being by the novel, and ballads already have been by newspaper reports?

Ford answered with the suggestion that, since gossip and sensation are as necessary to humanity as oxygen, the poets should recapture them from the press:

If the conductor of this periodical could secure a good rattling account in rhymed verse of a late murder, with the names of ladies of title hinted at with asterisks and startling insight into

the psychology of the murdered unfortunate . . . those
rhymed verses would sell two million . . .

In the twenties and thirties the English ate crime-fiction for
breakfast and supper. A plot that activated their pleasure in
criminal fantasy might entertain them as Shakespeare's studies
in crime had entertained, and might privilege the incursion
of poetry — only, a fresh poetry free of the habits they regarded as oppressive. It was to Eliot's taste to attempt the
drama of "a late murder." He had brought himself up on *The
Leavenworth Case* ("the first detective story I ever read"),
Poe, Wilkie Collins, Conan Doyle; had been haunted by the
Crippen trial; and soon was to allow himself the luxury of reviewing thrillers for the *Criterion*. *Sweeney Agonistes* is the
drama of the man who has committed the crime every man
wants to commit once in his life. *Family Reunion* is the drama
of the same man, expiating the crime; or expiating the desire
for it, which is scarcely less blameworthy. *Murder in the Cathedral* is a title which appeals to the sense of crime; at the
drafting stage it is said to have been *Who Killed the Archbishop?* or *The Archbishop Murder Case*. The audience par-
ticipates in the dramatist's "startling insight into the psychology"
either of the murdered unfortunate or the unfortunate murderer.
In *The Cocktail Party* crime fiction is no longer the point
of reference; a war has changed the public taste; the play captures from the press and the national experience the intrigues
that accompany breaking marriages, the appeal for help to the
psychologist. It makes use, too, of stories that have often
caught the imagination of writers and their audience, and have
in the last hundred years recurred from time to time in the
press, of devoted missionaries dying in remote places. And the
missionary is, if not "a lady of title," the daughter of a distinguished old English family. Eliot taught himself how to entertain and amuse: how to hold his audience as he knew that

Shakespeare held it, and to apply the techniques which he saw applied by contemporaries who were truly in touch with the crowd. He remarked in the *Dial* in 1923: "Fine art is the *refinement,* not the antithesis, of popular art."

For him, 1923 appears to have been a year of self-communing on drama; and it is tempting to think that Hofmannsthal's theatre may have become interesting to him and enriched his reflections. The *Criterion* recently inaugurated, Eliot was aware of Hofmannsthal as a spokesman of the European tradition, and he was shortly to publish his *Greece.* He may well have been following the essays by him and about him which were appearing in England and America. The *Dial* in New York was publishing contributions from Hofmannsthal, some of them describing his drama. Kenneth Burke translated his *Lucidor* for the *Dial.* Edwin Muir provided an essay about him to the New York *Freeman.* His *Jedermann* was mounted in London by Sir John Martin Harvey, and on January 7, 1924, the *Salzburger Grosse Welttheater* was performed in St. Edward's Church, Holbeck.

In 1925 Hofmannsthal visited London and was the guest of honor at a dinner given by the P.E.N. That spring the English press resounded with the shots of a battle for and against the opera *Elektra,* then playing at Covent Garden. *Punch,* which in those days guffawed at Epstein and everyone with a new idea, led the opposition; it advised its austere readers to buy and study

a pamphlet called "A Guide to the Music," one of the best works of pure undesigned humour that I have ever sampled.

You will be shocked at its very un-Greek lack of reticence, shocked in fact by Herr Strauss's sacrilegious treatment of a great tradition; but you will be careful not to say so aloud.

W. J. Turner was almost equally savage in the *New Statesman:*

. . . *Elektra* has no more relation to Greek tragedy than has
Oscar Wilde's *Salomé* . . . Without Wilde there would have
been no Hofmannsthal and without *Salomé* no *Elektra*. Both
Salomé and *Elektra* are dramatic frauds . . .

It may be noticed in passing how easily W. J. Turner assumed
that Hofmannsthal could be destroyed by classifying him
with Wilde; we might reply that it is a justification of Wilde if
he endowed Hofmannsthal and other Continental writers with
resources from which they built. But the reply to the detractors
in 1925 was, simply, that even if *Elektra* had faults, for instance the rather "summary" characterization of Chrysos-
themus, it compelled its audience as only a tragedy does. Edward Sackville-West, a critic whom Eliot knew and respected,
wrote that Olczewska, who played the queen, "sent us out
of the opera house shaking with fear at the potentialities of
hate and misery in human beings."

I would like to connect that critical battle of 1925 with
Eliot's first sketches towards a drama, *Sweeney Agonistes*. Some
years earlier Pound had encouraged him to attempt a version
of the *Agamemnon*. But nothing had happened; and perhaps
Eliot allows us to overhear him still reflecting on the difficulties
of the task in 1920 when he remarks that of the poets of the
Poets' Translation Series, though they are more serious than
Gilbert Murray, none "has yet shown himself competent to attack the *Agamemnon*." Possibly the epigraph to *Sweeney
Among the Nightingales* and its allusion to the Agamemnon
story indicate the thought he gave to Pound's challenge —
though the nightingales come from *Oedipus at Colonus*. But
he was to advance in his work for the theatre when he grap-
pled not with Agamemnon's story but the story of Agamemnon's son: to advance first to the vivid sketches, *Sweeney
Agonistes*, then to *The Family Reunion*. The hypothesis in my
mind in this paragraph is, that the battles over *Elektra* ex-

cited him: that he had not forgotten *Punch*'s attack ten years earlier on "Mr. Ezekiel Ton, the Montana poet"; that the combative spirit, with which he had assisted in the defense of Joyce and of Wyndham Lewis, revived; and that there resulted both an inner mobility favorable to a sudden step forward with long-meditated plans, and a fresh, perhaps a piercing, view of the subject of the opera, the story of Elektra and Orestes. Up to that date one might have said that none of the twentieth-century writers understood the significance of the Furies better than Hofmannsthal, who had once proposed a symphonic ballet, the music to be written by Strauss, in which Nijinsky would dance Orestes, expressing "his prodigious deeds, his prodigious sufferings," and in which "the lurking, expectant Furies" would finally break out "into a horrible song of triumph." But Eliot gradually made it his own theme. A myth of expiation, it was close to the conception of purgation which underlies the ending of *The Waste Land* and its image of Arnaut Daniel leaping into the refining fire. It involved an additional element: that the deed which Orestes must expiate was, though a crime, a duty. This may have been of significance to Eliot. In the late thirties when war was impending, and the contentions of the pacifist that war could never be justified, and especially not for the practicing Christian, were much heard and debated, he wrote: "Aeschylus, at least, understood that it may be a man's duty to commit a crime, and to accomplish his expiation for it." Eliot brooded on the theme of Orestes and the Furies and became its great modern expositor.

To recapitulate: when he addressed himself to the *Sweeney* sketches, he held, acquired by diligence in observing and theorizing for half a dozen years, a list of requisites for a new poetic drama. He must entertain, and entertain with a crime story. He must involve the audience. His words must move the nerves like music and dance: pulse like a drum; use the repeated figures of the dance. They must be authentically speakable, as Ford had, long ago and more recently, insisted; but the speech must be managed with a deftness no contemporary poet had shown. He must convert to his purpose the song forms that captivate English audiences. He must write comedy, and the more rather than the less because he intended a tragic reading of the world. Aldington had prescribed an "Aristophanic levity" to render the crimes of 1919. Tailhade had caricatured the generation of 1900 in *Poèmes aristophanesques.* Though he aimed at tragedy, Eliot must work like Aristophanes. Therefore the descriptive subtitle to *Sweeney:* "an Aristophanic Melodrama."

For all this state of preparedness he could not advance beyond a pair of sketches. Perhaps he had foreseen, at the date of *The Sacred Wood,* that he would not easily complete a drama; he had quoted Aristotle: "Novices in the art attain to finish of diction and precision of portraiture before they can construct the plot." *Sweeney* was the diction, or an approach to it, without the plot. But it is remarkable how this novice essay paved the way for Eliot's later drama. When he developed its constituents in the context of a satisfactory plot, he would produce his own theatrical form, Aristophanic melodrama and tragic farce combined. Doing so, he would link up with the most distinctively British contribution to theatre. Benda and Maurras notwithstanding, he would cultivate the anticlassical hybrid that appeals to the British temperament.

The Cathedral and the Community

Before he could protract the *Sweeney* fragments into the full-length *Family Reunion* he was required to perform two tasks under special conditions. His church asked him for poetry for a pageant, then for a cathedral play. The obligation was his good fortune. It was fate knocking on the door, precisely the kind of challenge to stir him: was he as good as his predecessors, from the saga minstrels through Mutanabbi to Shakespeare, who could perform a job on request? And the job had to be completed; the fragments, to which self-questioning and doubts circumscribe the writer who has only to please himself, would not do any longer.

The plot or scenario of *The Rock* was provided for Eliot by E. Martin Browne. The main question for Eliot was to discover what might be done with the chorus. In discovering it he made an advance which was to help him when he came to *Murder in the Cathedral:* he mastered a musical form to which the English middle-class audience listened with ready assent. In the twenties and thirties verse-speaking had replaced the piano-playing and ballad-singing of the nineteenth century as an aspiring art of the English towns and villages. Every elocutionist had her group. While Eliot had been casting about for a current form to pour his own kind of poetry into, this was waiting for him, and E. Martin Browne pointed to it; and, using it, he, who had in 1920 wiped the floor with Gilbert Murray's chorics, wrote the first English equivalent of Greek chorics. I say this without sharing Eliot's early disparagement of Swinburne, whose best choruses I used when bicycling to chant as loud as Q, and still do when teaching. But Eliot's choruses are not surging English lyric. They are a new way of statement in English, a way of presenting an English *collective* voice.

Teaching himself the choric art in *The Rock*, Eliot used it to perfection in *Murder in the Cathedral*. The choruses of *The Rock* are far above that "hackwork" which some critics have labeled them, and are often beautiful, but those of *Murder in the Cathedral* are among Eliot's greatest poetry, conducting the listener through the most tense and solemn of all dances of the nerves, gripping the listener with sudden pictures of English life, sudden sounds and cries from English life. And the Eng-

lish middle-class audience, ready to receive a choric art, responded to the voices which spoke to them of themselves, and
accepted *Murder in the Cathedral* as their play. This process
was, indeed, part of a larger process with the same result.
The practice of choral speaking with which Eliot made contact
was an offshoot of the amateur theatre movement. This is
strong in England. In every town groups exist to give plays.
Often they are connected with a church or a chapel, and, even
if they have no affiliations with a place of worship, they may
still perform in a hall belonging to one. England's amateur
drama is a popular art which looks back to the annual festival
plays of the medieval communities and the performances of the
craftsmen. In the years after the Armistice when Hofmannsthal, already the poet of *Jedermann*, wrote his modern morality play, *Das Grosse Salzburger Welttheater*, for the Salzburg
Festival, he explained that he felt free to revive the morality
in Austria because there and in Bavaria and nowhere else the
medieval stage tradition survived like "the last protruding
point . . . of a sunken island-continent." Thomas Mann, commenting on the *Grosse Welttheater*, made a similar point: the
medley of elements which distinguished the play was "natural
only to that Catholic, Austrian, South-German sphere in which
this poet is rooted." But Eliot, sensitive to Britain's folkways,
a student of her social biology, saw that in Britain, where
morality and mystery play once flourished, the medieval
tradition was not extinct. A new morality play could be as
legitimate in England as in Austria. When the task for Canterbury faced him, he grafted his play onto the tradition.

In another respect, too, the Canterbury play was perfectly
designed to engage the British people. It dramatized a saint
whose story is told to British boys and girls early in their school
years. It sounded on a gut of living legend. So in subject matter, in form, and in method and tone *Murder in the Cathedral*
was right for the amateur-drama public of the British prov-

inces, those eager men and women who, following new work
as well as their distance from the capital allows, and the more
hungrily because of the handicap of distance, are potential
mediators between the artist and the nation. And, in the total
outcome of its rightness in these several particulars, the play
was "the expression and dignity" of the middle class.

Writing a religious drama for performance in a cathedral,
Eliot could not use exactly the recipe which he had been elaborating with the commercial stage in mind. But he would not
admit a total cleavage between a play for a cathedral and a
play for the stage: that would have been to abnegate his theories. With ingenuity and tact he retained "requisites" which
either less adventurous or less steady minds might have abandoned. Comedy? He admitted it: startlingly, in the apology of
the Knights; and yet even there with discretion, and with a
tragic note underlying the surface gusto. Ritual? That was
most easy: the story itself was a rite; the cathedral setting prepared the audience to follow a ritual and to participate in it.
But Eliot apparently felt that he should not simply count on
the cathedral to involve the audience in the action. He developed a trick, very simple, as good theatre tricks usually are,
to engage them. His protagonist directly addresses the specta-
tors and tells them of their part. At the end of the first act
Thomas, who has been speaking as the introspective man interpreting himself to himself, turns and speaks to the audience,
and tells them

> for every evil, every sacrilege,
> Crime, wrong, oppression, and the axe's edge,
> Indifference, exploitation, you, and you,
> And you, must all be punished. So must you.

Then the Interlude sermon is addressed to the audience, who
participate as the Christmas morning congregation. When the
Knights defend the assassination, they address the audience

as Canterbury, England, and their (nonimpartial) jury. The audience has something in common with the chorus. Like the Women of Canterbury it becomes the common people, no matter in what place, "who shut the door and sit by the fire" and whose burdens a martyr transfers to himself.

Murder in the Cathedral is exemplary in that it has spoken to Britain and won something like popularity without any surrender of elevation. It is austere. Its verses are demanding; they range from the long chorics, as exploratory and encyclopoedic as Claudel's, to the terse, muscled remolding of the alliterative measures of the Middle English morality play. It examines the agon of one man, and presents his struggle and its difficult choice without concession to the frailty of our understanding.

Eliot's treatment of the crucial phase of the martyr's problem involves a theatrical difficulty which Hofmannsthal before him had encountered in the *Grosse Welttheater,* and had described with candor and with a characteristically incisive self-criticism in the *Dial.* The Beggar raises his axe to shatter society. Wisdom raises her hands in prayer, not for her own salvation nor for society but for the Beggar. And

> what next takes place in him is outside the province and possibilities of the truly dramatic, and could not be said in a regular play, but only in a miracle.

That is: the Beggar abstains from the destructive, abstains from the Wotanic blow (for the *Grosse Welttheater* is the neo-classicist's answer to Wagner and the *Götterdämmerung*). There is nothing more difficult in the theatre than a negative decision. Abstention from action is not undramatic but it is untheatrical. Tewfiq el Hakim's *Shahrazad* is a case in point: a play of interest and charm, but theatrically lost at the end because its drama mounts to the King's abstention from killing.

When Shakespeare had to deal with Hamlet's negations he saved him for the theatre by supplying heaps of substitute action, by the interest of the oscillation between decision and indecision, by the final resolution of the struggle in action: the drama mounts to theatrical physical violence. A *Hamlet* in which, at the last, Hamlet did not kill the King might have eluded even Shakespeare. In Hofmannsthal's Morality the whole point was the abstention, and he had to make it theatre if he could. He found two means: the Beggar's bewildered uncertainty, as he lets the axe fall, whether he has committed the crime or abstained; and the singing of Wisdom and the angels, teaching him that he has not committed the enormity. These, he admits in the article, would have been too slender in any but the special conditions of the miracle play.

Becket's resistance to the first three of his Tempters is clear, his victory over them perfectly clear. But his resistance to the fourth Tempter involves a problem beyond the common experience, at any rate beyond the common awareness: in what state of mind will he receive the death on which he has resolved? In abstaining from the Tempter's offer, he wins a victory the nature of which must be, at the best, only very dimly intelligible to most of us in the audience. Eliot undertook a difficulty more subtle than Hofmannsthal. And perhaps he did not wholly solve it. To some extent we take Becket's decision on trust, leaning on the traditional medieval theatre of the tempting for the illusion and on the poetry of the whole play for our confidence. But the peculiar order of the events in the play is rather beautifully arranged to help us. Becket's inner agon is over by the end of the first act; he has combatted his tempters and made his mysterious choice. Now there follow the interlude, with its sermon, and the whole of the second act, to clarify his victory. It is not clarified by exposition; but it is *dramatized:* the scenes are written so that the actor may convey by his bearing, his tone, as much as by his words, what his decision entailed. Becket must *act* his right reason for dying; and Eliot's script makes it possible for him.

And there is some likeness between the leading motif of the *Grosse Welttheater* and that of *Murder in the Cathedral*. Poor and oppressed, the Beggar of Hofmannsthal's play is the type of the submerged and forgotten, and he is also, accordingly, Christ. During the Induction he protests against the part assigned to him: let the cup be taken from him: "My soul thirsts for action. What scope is there for action in this miserable part?" But he undertakes it, and when he lets the axe sink, the Angel tells him

> Nach Taten, Seele war dein Drang!
> Untat war nah in finstrem Wahn,
> Doch herrlich ist des Spieles Gang!
> Statt Untat ist jetzt Tat getan!

or, as Hofmannsthal transcribes it in the *Dial*, tells him that "this very abstaining from action was the one great decisive act of his life." The corresponding motif in *Murder in the Cathedral* is the recurring

> acting is suffering
> And suffering is action.

Murder in the Cathedral is not the story of the Beggar, but of the hero, the exceptional man. But the common man has a part in it; the Women of Canterbury speak for the poor, the forgotten and overlooked. Eliot's motif is their justification: suffering, they perform their part in God's play of the world, as Hofmannsthal's Beggar does. Again, watching, witnessing, praying, they fulfill an essential role in the drama of creation. Yet the motif speaks for Becket, too; it defines the condition of mind in which, having refused the fourth Temptation, he suffers his martyrdom, and by suffering consummates his life.

Transparency, and the Work Accomplished

By one test, *Murder in the Cathedral* was not yet a poetic drama of the order Eliot had conceived. Its poetry was new and splendid; but it was palpably poetry. No question that it commanded the fake reverence as well as the true reverence of those who are prejudiced in favor of poetry, and that it was vulnerable to the disregard of those who are sure that poetry must weary them. A year later he noted in the *Criterion* that "any form of poetry restricts one's liberty; and drama is a very peculiar form: there is a great deal that is high and full poetry that will not go into it." If he had already sacrificed something in *Murder in the Cathedral*, it was not yet enough. More was to be discarded. Something was to be developed in its place: the "transparent" style of which he had spoken in his New Haven lecture in 1933.

The Family Reunion shows a little, not a great, advance towards transparency. At least four levels of poetry can be identified in the play. There is a style which reports experiences in language authentic but rich; and at times it is admirable; but it tends to be palpable poetry and overheavy with trappings (the Java Sea, the nightingale's thicket). There is a deliberate and hierophantic poetry. There is a faint sketch of the "transparent" style in lower-level, expository, bridge scenes: for example, the conversation between the Doctor and Harry about Lady Monchensey's illness. There is the comic poetry. In this last the play is at its best, and connects with *Sweeney Agonistes* and "Prufrock" before it, and with *The Cocktail Party* ahead of it.

The comic poetry of *Sweeney* had been Eliot's most valuable experiment in a new medium for the stage. He could build on its effects. On its repeated phrases, for example, which at once capture the verisimilitude of conversation and the abstraction

of the dance. In *Murder* he adapted them for the threats of
the Knights:

> Yes, we'll pray for you!
>   Yes, we'll pray for you!
> Yes, we'll pray that God may help you!

Now in *The Family Reunion* he uses them:

> I have always told Amy she should go south in the winter.
> Were I in Amy's position, I would go south in the winter.
> I would follow the sun, not wait for the sun to come here.
> I would go south in the winter, if I could afford it.

He expands the range of *Sweeney:* in the speech just quoted he
converts the repeated phrase to the purposes of nostalgia, recalling the opening of *The Waste Land;* elsewhere he adds
the Betsy Trotwood voice:

> A minor trouble like a concussion
> Cannot make very much difference to John.
> A brief vacation from the kind of consciousness
> That John enjoys, can't make very much difference
> To him or to anyone else.

There is one feature of *Sweeney* which, while retaining, he
disciplines. He had worked, when he composed *Sweeney,* to
beat the drum. Perhaps too violently. He now tells himself
that a whole play to that exciting beat would have been intolerable to the ear, and that he must seek variety: sometimes
the strong beat may be admitted, if more often he uses a moderated beat, often a very subtle one. In *The Family Reunion*
he discovers the quieter rhythms.

The central conception of *The Family Reunion* is the flight
of a man from his Furies and his progress, with the help of
wise counsel, to knowledge and self-knowledge, by which he

realizes that he must not flee but face them, and self-control, by which he sets out to face his expiation. An archetypal experience; and even by this alone the spectator may feel himself caught up in a ritual; certainly he should feel this, with a thrill of awe, at the moment when the Furies reveal themselves. But Eliot still introduces, whether or not they are really necessary to the fulfillment of his theory of ritual, moments of sacred character, moments of ceremony, rites. He intermittently suspends the flow of outward life for a revelation of the inner life, the eternal drama, of the characters. His dramatis personae cease their "naturalistic" conduct and conversations and move and speak as if in a trance: it might almost be said that they act the dance and intone the song of the timeless pattern in which they are held. In these trance segments of the play the poetry is stiff, hierophantic; the actors become stiff, archaic, Grecian-vased. "Agatha goes to the window, in a somnambular fashion," says a stage direction. Eliot had for some time been thinking that, as he said in his essay on Marston in 1934, "what distinguishes poetic drama from prosaic drama is a kind of doubleness in the action, as if it took place on two planes at once." So here, in 1939, he boldly separates the two "planes" of reality; adopts two distinct styles of poetry by which to mark the separation, and his actors mark the separation by changes from the naturalistic to the trance manner. It is bold; but it defeats his hope of disguising the "poetic" status of his poetic play. The hinter-phenomenal style must strike the audiences as "poetic" drama, not entirely clear of turgidity nor guiltless of affectation. Even when we lend them all the sympathy of which we are capable, the trance passages are an embarrassment. The best poetry of the play is not theirs. Eliot really mastered the "doubleness" of poetic drama in that distinctive comic poetry of his which sounds gaiety and warning, delight and grief, contrapuntally.

I should be sorry to seem to range myself with those who be-

little *The Family Reunion.* Easy for us to disparage, who have
not had the labor of constructing. Eliot had been unable to answer Pound's invitation to renew the *Agamemnon* in his first
decade in London, but now, twenty years later, he made an
English *Choephoroi,* and discovered an English way of doing
what the French, led by Cocteau, were doing; retelling the classical tales so that they shed the crust of overfamiliarity. Cocteau claimed that he had restored "une incroyable jeunesse" to
Antigone. Eliot elicits from the commonplace contemporary
scene a sense of almost unimaginable antiquity: the everlast-
ingly aged face of natural and unregenerate man and the
aboriginal everlasting ritual. In *The Family Reunion* he first
realized his method. Without this play *The Cocktail Party* could
not have been written. But though it is high praise of the *Reunion* to say that it made the later plays possible, there remains
a further word due to it: that, if Eliot had died in 1940 and
The Cocktail Party had not followed, this would have stood as
a considerable play in its own right.

But *The Cocktail Party* is the supreme result of Eliot's long
battle with and for the drama. Instead of alternating between
tragedy and comedy, he interfuses them. He manages speech
and poetry, so that the poetry sounds like speech yet dances.
He masters the doubleness of comic poetry. He leads into the
rites without suspending the action. He elicits a doubleness of
plot: working from Euripides' *Alcestis* so freely that one spectator may ignore it and enjoy the play, another, sensitive to the
hinter-phenomenal, may discern it, as if it were the psyche,
the unconscious world, beneath the conscious action of the
stage.

In 1938 he had published in the *Criterion* McEachran's article on the pattern of rebirth in the drama from *Alcestis* to *Hamlet.* It is not surprising if, long a student of anthropology, Eliot
was drawn to *Alcestis* as a pattern for a modern play, and if, as
a Christian and a polemicist of his faith, he wanted to apply

McEachran's principle: that the Christian dramatist reproduces the ancient ritual of the sacrifice of the hero-victim at "a higher level." He has recently told how his plan for *The Cocktail Party* grew as he thought about the Greek story and asked himself, "What happened afterwards?" After Admetus received Alcestis back from the dead, how did husband and wife put up with each other? Playing with the question, he invented a series of felicitous transpositions of archetypal material into terms at once acceptable in the commercial theatre and yet not overfamiliar there. In *The Beating of a Drum* he had noticed the peculiar importance of the doctor in English medieval drama, and he knew Jessie Weston's remarks on the role of the doctor in the *Rig-Veda*. He recognized that the modern doctor of souls, the psychoanalyst, the clinician-priest, is also the modern Hercules: he goes down to the tomb and recovers the souls of the living dead. So he pivoted his play on Harcourt-Reilly. He was also concerned, as always, with that proper theme of the Christian dramatist: the saint. In *The Rock* he had written:

> And the Son of Man was not crucified once for all,
> The blood of martyrs not shed once for all,
> The lives of the Saints not given once for all:
> But the Son of Man is crucified always
> And there shall be Martyrs and Saints.

Murder in the Cathedral had been the play of England's most famous saint. He now conceived the play of one of the saints who shall be. By a combination at first sight the most unpromising, the combination of the story of the emergence of a new saint with the story of a marriage, Eliot found a way to raise the pattern of rebirth to the "higher level." *The Cocktail Party* tells of a soul brought back from the dead; and tells it twice. Two souls are recovered from the dark in two different senses.

Hercules restores a selfish wife to a selfish husband, so that they can learn to endure each other and to endure the reflection of themselves in each other. Even this is, in its degree, a higher level. But at a higher level still, Hercules brings back Celia's soul from the dead; from destitution, desiccation, evacuancy, and inoperancy he restores her to life. And there is a third recovery. In restoring her to a life which is the saint's death, he restores the world from sickness to life. Again, in letting Celia go, as she chooses, to perform the Roycean act of atonement, Eliot restores life and meaning to the religious act of atonement — restores the meaning of the act in the minds of his audience and readers.

The myth of fertility, which underlay *The Waste Land,* underlies *The Cocktail Party.* And though Eliot is not normally given to Joyce's neatly naturalized equivalences, he admits one into *The Cocktail Party.* ". . . You do need to rest now," says Edward to Lavinia as they prepare their party in the Union days of the last act. Evidently the marriage is to be fruitful. The fertilization lacking in love at *The Waste Land* era now belongs to it. To Celia the glory, whose choice of death has fertilized the earth. But Eliot adds that a simple glory also belongs to those who choose the household life and decently endure and propagate. In fact the saint would have no vocation if there were no common men to save; they save the saint, if she saves them.

The Cocktail Party was the conquest of the West End and Broadway to which the Harvard of 1910 had marshaled its talent. In one sense the play was received at the expense of its meaning. Very few of the audience recognized the meaning, few accepted it if they were aware of it, some were shocked; for as Eliot had warned his Rochester audience in 1937, the original Biblical events are, "if we regard them with fresh eyes, profoundly shocking" — and the Imitation of a savior must be shocking. Yet the play made its points, and the beliefs out of which it grew are circulating wherever it has gone, for they are integrated with the art and the entertainment, and to enjoy it is to absorb them. Very few people come away without enjoying it. But where do the art, entertainment, and success reside?

Partly in the skill and knowingness (but this does not weaken the seriousness) with which the 1949 interest of England and America in psychoanalysis and the transactions of the consulting room is exploited. More, in the comedy. In *The Cocktail Party* he perfected his comic art. His comedy is alive as a succession of diverting incidents, especially in the sequence in which Julia and Alex appear and reappear to interrupt and safeguard Edward and Celia. It is alive in the conversational and debating thrusts of the dialogue. It is alive in the metrics of the dialogue.

I have earlier compared the "dialect" of Eliot's mature dramatic poetry with that of *Der Rosenkavalier*. It is tempting to compare the tone and setting of *The Cocktail Party* with a later work of Hofmannsthal's, *Der Schwierige*, which is written in prose, but a prose that has the dance, the nervous delicacies, and the flavors of poetry. Only the very great poet, who has looked into the profound perils of existence and suffered his frozen silence, can come through to lightness and jest, Hofmannsthal had written in 1902 in *Lord Chandos' Letter;* and he had conquered his comedy by that route of intolerable experience. "Leicht muss man sein" —

> mit leichtem Herz und leichten Händen,
> halten und nehmen, halten und lassen . . .
> Die nicht so sind, die straft das Leben und Gott erbarmt
>   sich ihrer nicht.

So he counseled in 1911; and in the twenties it seemed to him that powerful knowledge and the lightness of comedy were always joined, and he pointed out that Plato died with the farces of Sophron under his pillow. *Der Schwierige* was his first retort (the *Grosse Welttheater* his more considered retort) to the collapse of his world in 1918 and 1919. He put himself to the writing of *Der Schwierige*, which, in a succession of seemingly trivial stage intrigues, catches Vienna's dream of herself: catches her dream of grandeur with the lightest speed of wit.

The setting of *Der Schwierige*, after the first act which is a prelude to prepare the situation, is not quite a cocktail party, but a Viennese soirée. A well-known anecdote alleges that when a guest at a large London party remarked to Eliot "Very interesting," he agreed "Yes. If one can see the full horror of it." Count Kari, the difficult man, prefers to stay away from parties because he sees the horror: "A soirée isn't very alluring, if one considers it, my dear . . . I understand people *giving* a party, but I don't understand people *going to it*." He doesn't dislike the old codgers there, they're charming; he doesn't even dislike the flappers and their escorts. "But the thing itself, you know. It's a complete horror. The whole thing — the *whole thing* is such a hopeless tangle of misunderstandings. Ah, the perpetual misunderstandings!" His sister has her way, he attends, and the secrets of the heart are elicited, a conflict of souls is fought, amid the movement of the reception.

In Hofmannsthal's comedy the audience is peculiarly conscious of the social texture which encloses, presses, ex-presses, challenges, sometimes justifies, sometimes enlarges, his men and women in their pretensions and struggles. *Der Rosenkavalier* and *Der Schwierige* both exemplify his elaboration of this quality, this "breath of the play," which is just as necessary to its full meaning as the characters and the plot. Eliot's comedies in some degree depend on a comparable social texture; certainly he develops it in *The Cocktail Party*. He and his contributors seem, to an observer nearly forty years later, to have been feeling for it in those *Criterion* stories of 1924 and 1925 when they tried to display the human drama with a new, sharp clarity by folding it in the specific texture of some social gathering. There is a touch of poignancy in the stories of that date, and the technique was capable of the results they intended, but neither the craftsmanship nor the experience of the contributors was quite sufficient. Eliot's own experience and craftsmanship were not yet sufficient in 1925. After 1945 he had both; he wrote English comedy the equal of Hofmannsthal's. And to do it he wrote a new English poetry of speech which, like Hofmannsthal's, expressed each individual character distinctively and expressed the social fabric of which the character is part. It is a polyphonic poetry, voice responding to voice, voice blending with voice.

The poetry of *The Cocktail Party* is the poetry of speech which Eliot had imagined a quarter of a century earlier: the new mode for English poetic drama: with metrics delicately pulsing, with phrases which effloresce though they are authentic spoken phrases. It is an astonishing linguistic phenomenon: the dialect of Mayfair reproduced, and yet bettered, by a poet whose native dialect is a combination of St. Louis and Boston. It is tinged with the influence of great predecessors: of Hofmannsthal exploiting his own Viennese dialect; of Pound's excursions among the dialects in search of energy; of Ford's and Pound's insistence on the use of genuine speech; and of Browning's sense of the poetry of the spoken language. Yet it is peculiar to Eliot, who reached it by his gift for separating, in the work of friends and forerunners, what he could use from what he could not, and his perseverance in rumination and exercise.

The poetry was the *transparent* poetry for which he had been working. Towards the end of the play Eliot draws attention to his success. Harcourt-Reilly asks, "Do you mind if I quote poetry?" Edward and Lavinia are polite enough, or cowed enough, to encourage him, and he quotes the Zoroaster lines from *Prometheus Unbound*. It is a crucial moment of the play, and Shelley in his seer mood is right for it, but the humorist and the technical critic as well as the seer in Eliot have their part in the choice and want us to note that traditional poetry sounds unmistakably different from the new poetry, the transparent medium, that he has invented after a lifetime of discipline.

The Plays of the Fifties

In 1937 new translations of two Greek plays had come to Eliot's notice at the same time: Dudley Fitts' and Robert Fitzgerald's *Alcestis* and H.D.'s *Ion*. *Alcestis* was the foundation of *The Cocktail Party*. For the foundation of his next play he adopted *Ion*. The drama of parents seeking a child, and of a child in a god's service, it enabled him to debate — in several moving passages between Colby and Sir Claude — the beauty of a family reunion against the beauty of the lonely service of God. The skill of the transposition from Euripides is that the play debates the great issue entirely as the comedy of everyday.

But if *Ion* lends the work its foundation and strength, we are also to think, when we judge it, of Terence, Plautus, the *Comedy of Errors* and *H.M.S. Pinafore*. Eliot holds his audience with the two-thousand-year-old ins and outs of mistaken identity. The tricks of this tradition never fail if they are well handled, and Eliot handles them charmingly.

Charmingly, and with deliberate quietude. A little earlier I suggested that, as compared with *Sweeney Agonistes*, *The Family Reunion* sought a more subdued excitement. *The Confidential Clerk* is remarkable for the lowering of the pitch. The dance of the nerves is sustained with a system of extremely subtle accentuation. The diction is quieted; the play is a study in quiet English. This is right for a drama which develops as a result of the sincere self-searching of his characters. Eliot has always been a self-examining poet, and his claim on us has always entailed some suggestion that "This is how men *must* examine themselves"; the early dramatic poems suggest this; all the plays suggest it occasionally; *The Confidential Clerk* suggests it throughout. Part of the interest of this play to the student of dramatic forms is Eliot's success in turning the old comedy of mistaken identity into a play of the search for the self — without sacrificing comedy or the comic music which is his invention.

In *The Elder Statesman* there is some change. Eliot returns from the domestic and introspective quiet of *The Confidential Clerk* to his earlier comedy behind which the shapes of shock and violence cloudily loom. He returns to the Furies of *Sweeney* and *The Family Reunion,* to the crime which is repeated through the generations till it is faced and expiated. This time he examines his theme in Sophocles' version. *Oedipus at Colonus* is his point of reference. Lord Claverton, a public figure invested with a public myth, behind which he suffers the common human experiences, faces his past and hollowness after a lifetime of evasion; cleans himself; and finds a refuge and transforming death in the ceremonial peace of a beech tree, his groves of Colonus.

Once Eliot has devised a central situation which corresponds with the central situation of the Greek play, he works very freely. His memories of other works are mobilized in the act of writing, and any appropriate development or intervention which they suggest he is prepared to use. Sophocles never forgets in *Oedipus at Colonus* that the devoted daughter, tending her father in his blindness and his pilgrimage for repose, will on a later day sacrifice herself by burying his son. Perhaps Eliot was reminded of *Antigone,* and of the chorus marveling and trembling at "Love unconquerable," which was much in the minds of writers between the two wars. He intro-

duces into his *Elder Statesman* a remarkable passage which
seems to look back to it: the passage which exalts

> . . . love within a family, love that's lived in
> But not looked at, love within the light of which
> All else is seen, the love within which
> All other love finds speech.
> This love is silent.

In vocabulary and syntax there is nothing here that cannot
be spoken, and the lines indeed conform with Ford's dictum
that poetry should be "like one's intimate conversation with
someone one loved very much"; and yet, does not the passage stand out conspicuously from Eliot's "transparent" poetry? To raise this question is not to carp or condemn, but to
suggest that a question which Eliot proposed to himself as he
worked on *The Elder Statesman* may possibly have been:
how much of the "fuller poetry," sacrificed for ten years, might
he reintroduce? From that utmost point of quietude reached
in *The Confidential Clerk* might he not move back a little? But
he retains the very light beat of *The Confidential Clerk* for the
staple of his dramatic metrics.

When Yeats paraphrased "Love unconquerable" in the last
lyric of *A Woman Young and Old,* he construed love as irresistible physical passion and glorified its triumphs and wreckage.
Eliot's paraphrase understands it as "love within a family."
His lines, in their compressed beauty, suggest the completion
of the family reunion which has been one of his persistent
themes. The dedication page of *The Elder Statesman* allows us
to see that Eliot wrote the work in the happiness of his second
marriage and his acceptance of the household life, the claims
of which he had declared in *The Cocktail Party.* To say this
may be to overemphasize the ingredient of emotionalism in the
writing. A hostile critic might complain that it is easy to overemphasize the emotionalism, unexpectedly profuse, in a writer

who once wrote of the coldness of the genuine artist. (But
that early writer was fighting a disease of the time.) In fact, in
The Elder Statesman the doubleness which we have described
as the attraction of Eliot's dramatic poetry is provided by the
counterpoint of nostalgia and comedy. The spectator who soft-
ens under the poetry of feeling is recruited by the darting
comedy.

Did some memory, conscious or unconscious, of an early
play of a master of English comedy come to Eliot's assistance
as he planned *The Elder Statesman?* The early Eliot, concerned, like so many successors of Arnold, to emancipate middlebrow England from the tyranny of her popular heroes, regarded Shaw, Wells, and Kipling as his obvious enemies, the
Goliaths he must topple. The *Criterion* several times promised
articles in demolition of their pretensions. Articles which never
appeared. Only, in their place, intermittent sniping. Intermittent and diminishing sniping. Far from hurling the enemies
to oblivion, Eliot gradually recognized, since he genuinely likes
whatever of worth another writer has to offer, merits in each
of them: possibly the authentic odor of the early, pre-preten-
tious stories of Wells; certainly, the skills and authentic odor
of Kipling, which he had known instinctively in boyhood,
deliberately forgot at Harvard and in Bloomsbury, then found
again (Bonamy Dobrée's good sense helping), and described
in the Preface to his Selections; and the dialogue of Shaw, which
he acknowledged, in a *New Republic* article of 1928 and reaf-
firmed in his lecture on "Poetry and Drama" in 1951, to be the
best in English drama since Congreve. However drab he
thought Shaw's beliefs, however pernicious he thought him as
the disseminator of those beliefs, he owed him debts: for the
pleasure of the dialogue and of the well-manipulated situations;
and for proving that comedy is the way to say serious things to
a British audience which fancies itself resistant to ideas. It
seemed to him in 1951, reflecting on *Murder in the Cathedral,*

that he might have been encouraged by Shaw's *Saint Joan* —
presumably by the method of modernizing the medieval characters — to the robust treatment of the Knights in his own
Apology scene. It is just possible that, designing *The Elder
Statesman,* he was helped by the play which was Shaw's favorite, *Mrs. Warren's Profession.* The lively scenes with Gomez
and Mrs. Carghill uncover Lord Claverton's past in the manner
of that rapid and cogent comedy. It would be pleasant to say
that the Eliot who in 1926 wrote an Aristophanic *Choephoroi*
wrote in 1959 a Shavian *Oedipus at Colonus.* But of course it
would be to say too much. If Shaw's influence touches the play,
it touches it only lightly. But this may be said: there is a mel-
lowness in the late play, and it accords with that long process
by which Eliot gradually gave up his crusading against the
middlebrow writers and found in that part of himself which
sympathized with them a source of creative energy to put at
the service of his own higher art.

Eliot and Auden

A work does not have to be complete and rounded to be important. The fragmentary *Sweeney Agonistes* was and remains
exhilarating, was invaluable to Eliot as an experiment in the
application of his theories, and for the poets twenty years his
junior was scarcely less seminal than *The Waste Land.* Rupert
Doone's Group Theatre, that quickest force in the London of
the thirties, was the result of the impact of *Sweeney* on Auden
and his friends. It filled them with Eliot's own passion for a new
poetic drama and told them how to re-energize the theatre.
They saw how to use speech, speech rhythms, speech echoes in
their poetry. They saw how to use song and dance. Where
Eliot had thought of the music hall and ballet as his models,
they thought of the rhythms of jazz and wrote studied adaptations of the "popular poetry" of the jazz lyric. *Under the bam*

Under the boo led to the early Auden sketch "The Dance of Death." The reiterated, monotony-laden, doom-laden *Birth, and copulation, and death* led to the style of ferocious indictment of the world-as-it-is which became the staple of half the poetry of the thirties. The cry of the year of reaction from the Great War, 1919, had been for a poetry of angry exposure. Aldington had promised it, several had attempted it, Eliot had performed it at the level of a stern predication in *The Waste Land*. With *Sweeney* he inaugurated a new stage: the poetry of comic animosity — the comedy augmenting and directing the animosity. Auden and Day Lewis pounced on the style and developed it. Grigson adopted it as editor and critic. Dylan Thomas integrated it into his poetry and scripts. It was the hard-hitting in Kenneth Allott. Orwell borrowed from it. Lawrence Durrell took it into his violent caricature. It persisted in the so-called Angry Young Men, who are no new emergence but the inheritors of *The Waste Land* and *Sweeney*. Eliot and Aldington, restoring to English the anger which they accused their Georgian seniors of abdicating, reconnected the twentieth century with the tradition of Skelton, Ben Jonson, Pope, and the Browning of the hate poem. *Sweeney,* and its exhilarated reception by the undergraduates of Auden's day, were decisive steps in the development.

But if it is the business of an older writer to influence younger writers, it is wisdom in him to learn something from them in return. Yeats had that peculiar genius, as his reactions to Joyce showed. Eliot had it too. He had influenced Auden; and now in 1930 and the immediately subsequent years he learned from him. When he commented on Pound's version of *The Seafarer* as early as 1917 he had recognized the potentialities of the Anglo-Saxon meters and the tones that go with them, but the observation had apparently slipped from his mind until in Auden's work, which he published in the *Criterion* and claimed for the Faber series of modern poets, he saw a modern alliterative English and the saga style realized. "Paid on both Sides" and such a poem as "Doom is dark" showed Eliot how powerfully the "consonantal rhymes" (so C. L. Wrenn, who tutored Auden, used to call them), and the terse phrases they encourage, speak to the English ear. In 1934, electing the story of Becket for his Canterbury play, he acted on Auden's example and went to English alliterative poetry for a medium. Of course his use of it is not Auden's: not the shock of a new-old Scandinavian voice. Instead he has chiseled and polished the verse with such skill that you are scarcely aware of his form. You are sharply aware of Becket, aware of his power of thought, power of command; aware of his Temptations, strong because reflections of his strength; only afterwards, on examination, aware that the results have been realized through the old alliterative line:

> Think, my Lord,
> Power obtained grows to glory,
> Life lasting, a permanent possession,
> A templed tomb, monument of marble.
> Rule over men reckon no madness.

Its fault: that occasionally it is too elliptical. Its beauty: that it is "flowing sculpture," as verse for a cathedral play should be. And, together with the early English alliterative medium, Eliot renews the aphoristic style of early English.

Another glimpse in *Murder* of the young master's lesson to the old: the Apology of the Knights, that switch of tone that delighted audiences in the thirties. With its buffoonery, its parody of the British speech-making styles, its cracks at British institutions in the favorite British mode of self-criticism, it looks back to the deliberate buffoonery of *The Orators*. The "Speech for a Prize Day" had appeared in the *Criterion* in October 1931, and Faber had published *The Orators* a year later. It is illuminating how Eliot, the conscious institutionalist, could enjoy and apply the iconoclasm of the new writers. Of course the Aristophanic voice that Aldington and Eliot wanted in 1919 and had to cultivate came from the throats of the generation of 1930 as if it were the natural register of adolescence.

Snatches of a new middle-class poetry of the English parish had appeared in Auden and Day Lewis: the poetry of boys who

> Bicycling against wind to see the vicar's daughter

were peculiarly conscious of their less conscious fathers and their homescape. Eliot read it. When he wrote *The Rock* he found himself, in certain of the choruses, projecting the same class and its life, and composing phrases in the same idiom:

> the land of the lobelias and tennis flannel.

Auden devoured *The Rock*, saw the beauty and opportunities of the new choric technique, and assimilated it and regurgitated it in his own style. Meanwhile Eliot, probably unaware of the sudden impact of his innovation on the younger man, was developing and heightening his chorics as he prepared his Canterbury play. The result: 1935 was the year of English choruses, the rich choruses of *Murder* in which Eliot thoroughly dramatized the art of *The Rock*, the astringent and wind-shouldering choruses of *The Dog beneath the Skin* in which Auden converted the art of *The Rock* to his own idiom. Then Eliot and Auden both began to turn away from the choric art: to turn away from it because they had mastered it; and Eliot to turn away from it because a chorus is evidently poetry — the more beautiful, the more evidently poetry — and he bent to the pursuit of his para-poetry to evade popular prejudice. In *The Ascent of F6* in 1937 and *The Family Reunion* in 1939 there are the last vestigial choruses — in which the process of interaction between the poets can still be detected. The *F6*

couple, everyman and everywoman, who listen to the radio by
their hearth and make their "collective" comment on the world's
affairs, are conceived in terms of the claim of the women of
Canterbury to be the type of the men and women who shut
the door and sit by the fire. That is Auden working from Eliot.
And Eliot working from Auden: his *Family Reunion* chorus,
the brothers and sisters merging to make collective statements,
tells how

> We know about the railway accident
> We know about the sudden thrombosis

echoing the *F6* couple who tell how they know the train disaster
in the dead of night, the father's tired heart stopping where
he sits.

Of course, even when the two men are working with each
other's material, the character of their writing is different. Auden seizes on an effect, renders it boldly. He exhilarates.
Eliot's results almost always give the impression of long, persistent effort, of long meditation; his materials have been subdued, as Thibaudet said the passions were subdued in classical drama, by "la juste nécessité" till they take their proper
place, no more and no less, in the organization of the work
in which they appear. That makes them quieter, but sometimes they are the stronger for it, sometimes the deeper in
luster.

Notes and Index

Notes

THERE is no attempt to supply a complete apparatus. My general intention has been to provide such references as I fancy someone interested in the field might really want to use. I have also let the pleasure of acknowledgment guide me.

Sources cited frequently are:

C. C. Eliot, *William Greenleaf Eliot* (Boston, 1904), cited as Mrs. Eliot, *WGE;*

T. S. Eliot, *The Complete Poems and Plays 1909–1950* (New York, Harcourt, Brace, 1952), cited as *Poems and Plays 1909–1950;*

E. J. H. Greene, *T. S. Eliot et la France* (Paris, 1951), cited as *Greene;*

F. O. Matthiessen, *The Achievement of T. S. Eliot* (New York, second edition, 1947), cited as Matthiessen, *Achievement;*

Ezra Pound, *Letters 1907–1941*, ed. D. D. Paige (New York, 1950), cited as *Letters;*

H. W. H. Powel Jr., "Notes on the Early Life of T. S. Eliot," an unpublished dissertation (Brown, 1954), cited as Powel, *NEL;*

Grover Smith Jr., *T. S. Eliot's Poetry and Plays* (Chicago, 1956), cited as Grover Smith;

and the following Harvard journals: the *Crimson;* the *Advocate;* and the *Monthly.*

Several other major sources are acknowledged, and short titles allocated to them, at the head of the chapters for which they have been particularly helpful.

Chapter 1
Family Figures (pages 1–35)

WORKS which have furnished much of the material of this chapter are: *The Family of William Greenleaf Eliot and Abby Adams Eliot* (privately printed in accordance with the will of Edward Cranch Eliot, third edition, 1943); Mrs. Eliot, *WGE;* W. G. Eliot, *The Story of Archer Alexander* (Boston, 1885), cited as *Archer Alexander;* Earl Morse Wilbur, *Thomas Lamb Eliot* (Portland, Oregon, 1937), cited as *Wilbur.*

Page
1 Lectured at Washington University . . . See *American Literature and the American Language* (Washington University, St. Louis, 1953).

Barret Wendell . . . In his *Literary History of America* (London, 1901), p. 288.

James Freeman Clarke . . . Quoted from Clarke's journal in the blackbound scrapbook, the cover stamped "Henry Ware Eliot Jr.," in the Library of Washington University, St. Louis.

2 stay in one place . . . Wilbur says (p. 68) that Dr. Eliot counseled Thomas Lamb Eliot: "Do not change, stick to your post, and let your influence become cumulative."

3 "The love of my profession" . . . See Mrs. Eliot, *WGE,* pp. 95–97.

6 "blood of the martyr" . . . See *Archer Alexander,* p. 114. After telling Alexander's story, Dr. Eliot appended two chapters: one recording facts, known personally to him, to illustrate the evils of slavery in Missouri; one in commemoration of Lovejoy.

"I have waited" . . . See Mrs. Eliot, *WGE,* pp. 130–31.

"the booming cannon" . . . See the text of his sermon to the "Old Guard," in the black-bound scrapbook in the Library of Washington University, St. Louis. He was speaking to the middle-aged republican volunteers at a moment, in September 1862, when Sterling Price was threatening the city; therefore the martial excitement of his appeal.

8 intersecting tangles . . . On p. 44 of *Archer Alexander* Dr. Eliot says: "Right-minded men could hardly tell where the lines of right and wrong crossed each other. Living in St. Louis the whole time and long before, and knowing many of those engaged in the strife on either side, I thought I saw both sides as they really were, but in truth I saw neither. The complications of action and motive, both right and wrong, were past finding out."

Phi Beta Kappa . . . See Mrs. Eliot, *WGE,* p. 69.

9 back within the law . . . Here we touch on one of the basic problems of the Civil War, which excited many people to argument and action, and which troubled Dr. Eliot. When, if ever, may an appeal be made

from the Law to the Higher Law? It is a central problem of the American experience.

In the years preceding the Civil War the battle was waged in terms of the Fugitive Slave Law — the law which Dr. Eliot was offending as long as he sheltered Alexander. Article IV of the Constitution of the United States upheld the rights of slaveowners over their slaves, and required that fugitives be handed back to their masters, even in states which had laws against slavery. Men whose consciences were outraged by slavery claimed that where the law of the land involved an offense against the Higher Law of God, they were justified in refusing to comply.

For all his feelings against slavery, Dr. Eliot saw infinite dangers in the Higher Law doctrine. Once you conceded its applicability in one instance, where else might not your friends, where else might not your enemies, claim it? Might not someone invoke it to justify secession if his sense of the Higher Law of freedom were hurt? It might become the sanction of fragmentation and anarchy.

Suppose a Unionist took the position that the law of man and the divine law were the same, or, what amounted to this, that the law of the country, once made, stood as the symbol of divine law and might not be challenged by the judgment of the individual. Then he was secure. He would have to repress his compassion for the runaway slaves, but there could be no splintering of the Union. A novelist of St. Louis, Gabriel Woerner, put the city's philosopher, Brokmeyer, into *The Rebel's Daughter* and assigned to him a crucial speech in which he maintains this position and flails the poetic consciences whose instincts give them private audience of God's intentions:

Out upon such hypocritical cant! Such nursery-room morality, such St. Crispian virtue! You will not solve the eternal conflict between conscience and law by imposing your conscience as law upon others. Liberate your slaves, if you have any, and appease *your* conscience; but let your neighbour liberate or keep his, as his conscience may demand. That, sir, is the law of the land. Let no one violate it, pleading a higher law of God. Be warned by the fate of Antigone: she obeyed what she felt to be the law written in her breast by the gods themselves in preference to the king's decree, and perished because institutions are valid, though individuals deem them cruel or absurd. So shall they perish who lay sacrilegious hands upon the constitution, come they from the North, or come they from the South!!

But despite this hard definition, Woerner's philosopher later remembered the inescapable paradox, that America, which proposed to herself the security of indivisibility, was historically devoted to the Higher

Law: New England was colonized because the Pilgrims asserted the doctrine, the colony became an independent nation by asserting it. In a sermon of 1861 Dr. Eliot took as his text:

Submit yourselves to every ordinance of man, for the Lord's sake: whether it be unto the king, as supreme; or unto governors, as unto them that are sent by him for the punishment of evil-doers, and for the praise of them that do well.

Nothing could more clearly prove his conservative temper, his aversion for the Higher Law and its dangers. Yet as an intensely patriotic American he could not forget his country's traditions, and he admitted that the Higher Law may, though rarely, "stand in direct conflict with the 'authorities that be,' and peremptorily set them aside at whatever cost." Only, it was a last resort; and if it included *violent* resistance to the State it was a sin against God (even for the martyr to offer violent resistance was a sin against God); and, having made his stand, the protester was under the moral obligation to compensate his disobedience to the State by paying the penalty, whether with his wealth, his property, his freedom, his life, as the laws of the State required, and only by suffering patiently could he justify what he had done. Thus a man who protected a runaway slave might buy the man's freedom (whether by paying for it or suffering for it).

Faced with the test of the time in his own affairs, when Alexander was brought to his house, Dr. Eliot invoked the Higher Law. But he was ready to perform the act of redress, whether with his wealth or worse. It was his good luck that the owner, by sending kidnapers, broke the law of the land more flagrantly than he had done; as a result, suffering was not required of him; and Alexander remained in safety, and at last, by the general decree of abolition, had his freedom.

This issue of the Higher Law pervades American literature. It imposed itself on Melville's imagination, and, phrased as Justice against Law, resulted in *Billy Budd,* that myth of the paramountcy of the Form of the Law, implacable — as if, though the cosmos weeps for the crushing of a good man, it would crack and tumble to the ruin of us all were the frame of the law weakened by one exception. It wracked Pound to a cry for the Higher Law. Sometimes he has written as if he were the South fighting for secession and its own way of life. Sometimes as if he were the northern conscience and Antigone obeying the gods. Brokmeyer denounced Antigone; Pound made her his heroine. There is a "Paris Letter" to the *Dial* in March 1923 in which Pound explains Jean Cocteau's *Antigone* in works that echo the Civil War debates: art, in its passion for τὸ καλόν, fights against authority, and authority protests "in the words of Cocteau's Creon 'Tu as inventé la justice': You have invented justice, or τὸ καλόν . . ."

Eliot's lectures on modern heresy might be understood as denouncing not the Higher Law doctrine but the constant resort to it by the poetic consciences who pride themselves on private audience . . . His Becket, however, is a martyr, and every martyr appeals to the Higher Law. Becket appeals rightly, in two senses: he has indeed heard and answered a higher claim than his King's; and he affirms his position in the obligatory way, refraining from violence and offering all he has and all his capacity for suffering to redress the disorder his act involves . . . And I rather think, subject (as throughout this note, and indeed throughout this book) to correction, that Eliot's view of the relationship of Church and State implies the possibility of frequently renewed appeals to the Higher Law. The law of the land strives to represent, as well as human frailty allows, the law of God. But since perfect legislation is not within human power, and since the application of our imperfect laws will tend to yet more devious imperfection, the Church will constantly watch the State and call it back when it deviates; and since the Church is also liable to human error, she too must sometimes be recalled to her strict endeavors. Whenever the recall is uttered, it will sound, to the administrators whose action is either stayed or urged by it, like a presumptuous appeal to the Higher Law. Yet it is necessary. Only it is to be made with prudence as earnest as Dr. Eliot's, and with his acceptance of its terms.

10 A business enterpriser . . . James K. Hosmer tells the story in his introduction to Mrs. Eliot, *WGE.*
"from his knowledge" . . . See Mrs. Eliot, *WGE,* pp. 300ff.
"a poem" . . . Mrs. Eliot gives the text.

11 Pass Christian . . . The guidebooks sponsored by the Federal Writers' Project give an attractive account of the Mississippi resorts. I am drawing on their pages and on the memory of a visit to Pass Christian, the wind blowing from the Gulf.
one reviewer complained . . . In the *Nation,* June 9, 1904.

12 "our Church vilified" . . . See W. G. Eliot, *Discourses on the Doctrines of Christianity* (Boston), p. 98. The edition I have used is dated 1880, but the introductory address is subscribed "St. Louis, April 10, 1852," and that may be a guide to the date of the first edition.
"all that was sacred" . . . see Mrs. Eliot, *WGE,* p. 328. Cf. p. 342.
would have preferred . . . Loc. cit., p. 314.

13 his family persuaded Dr. Eliot . . . By using the argument that he should perpetuate the record for his grandchildren. Compare the dedication to Mrs. Eliot's biography. There was a family agreement that his memory should live.
lest it prove too excitable . . . Asked to explain some criticisms of the theatre which he had introduced into a sermon, Dr. Eliot wrote that, while he could not describe the theatre as positively sinful, "It stimu-

lates the imagination too strongly; it awakens dormant passions; it
overtasks the sensibilities . . ." The letter is quoted in *Glimpses of
the Past* (Missouri Historical Society), Vol. V (1938), pp. 123–26.

14 to his children . . . Wilbur writes that the youngest child, Rose
Greenleaf Eliot, "published some fugitive but beautiful verses" (p. 7).
Of Thomas Lamb Eliot he says, "Though he wrote little in verse, he
was a poet in temperament . . . Though not an artist beyond making
delightful pencil sketches, he had a fine aesthetic taste . . . He delighted in the best music" (p. 114); and that he would occasionally
play Beethoven and Schubert on the piano (p. 112).
a father should consciously . . . See W. G. Eliot, *Early Religious
Education considered as the divinely appointed way to the regenerate
life* (Boston, 1855), pp. 122–26.

16 he went to Geneva . . . See his article, "The Martyrdom of Servetus," in the *Unitarian Review*, January 1883. William Greenleaf Eliot
in *Discourses on the Doctrines of Christianity* tells how Servetus was
burned and "thereby gave another proof that 'the blood of the martyr
is the seed of the Church,' for Geneva is now one of the strongholds of
the Unitarian faith" (p. 97).

17 a book of festivals . . . Henrietta R. Eliot, *Laura's Holidays* (Boston,
1898).

18 "her dear father's hand" . . . And, saying that, Henrietta Eliot tells
us something about herself and something about America; and raises
the question: how that act of rebellion of the child against the father,
as Sidney Musgrove called the American Revolution, resulted in the
intense, loving communication of the legend between father and child,
and how it paradoxically encouraged that nineteenth-century pattern
of the authoritarian father and the pious child which we have heard
Dr. Eliot describe. Thomas Lamb Eliot, in a sermon on "Authority,"
said that every man grows by three stages: first, implicit obedience;
then, the restless assertion of independence; then, intelligent and loyal
cooperation with "that which is rightly over us." He explained the individual in terms of his country's experience.
in which T. S. Eliot grew up . . . And consider, for example, his image in *The Rock* and its integration of childhood memories of July 4:

> We are children . . . who are up in the night and
> fall asleep as the rocket is fired . . .

See *Poems and Plays 1909–1950,* p. 113.

22 Charles Chauncy . . . In the *Crimson* of December 5, 1907, there is
a contribution by Professor E. K. Rand, reviewing the *Graduates Magazine* for that month. It contains the sentence: "A valuable article on
Charles Chauncy makes it clear that aristocracy as well as democracy
presided over the inception of the University, and will doubtless at-

tract more visitors than before to the portrait of Harvard's second President in Memorial Hall."

24 women of middle life . . . Not that the interests *arose* in middle life, but that they were cherished intact, through twenty years of rearing children, till they could be *pursued* in middle life. Mrs. Eliot once described herself as "an American citizen who from childhood has been interested in public affairs."

26 to uncover . . . remedy . . . Another example appears in a press cutting from the *St. Louis Globe-Democrat,* kept in the scrapbook now in the Missouri Historical Society's Library: a city employee, earning $75 a month, has tried to have his three children sent to the house of refuge, on the plea that (Mrs. Eliot quotes) they "gave a great deal of trouble." She urges a law making it impossible for a child to become a public charge until a court has investigated and proved the parents unfit or unable to provide. (The cutting does not show the year of this letter, only the date April 3.)

28 translation from Schiller . . . The scrapbooks indicate that Mrs. Eliot had an interest in German literature, which contrasts with her suspicions of French. Pochmann in his book on *German Culture in America* (Madison, 1957) says: ". . . we must correct a common impression, namely, that Unitarians consistently and implacably oppose German ideas. Nothing could be further from the truth . . ." (p. 148). Dr. Eliot and Charlotte Stearns support him. They were attracted by the serious German outlook.

30 as one of themselves . . . See, for example, W. G. Eliot, *Discourses on the Doctrines of Christianity,* p. 97. James Freeman Clarke said, "We admire Shakespeare and love Milton" (quoted from "Nineteenth Century Questions" by D. K. Colville in his Washington University thesis, "James Freeman Clarke," 1953). Thomas Lamb Eliot memorized *Paradise Lost* during a 129 days' voyage to San Francisco around the Horn.

once recalled . . . Reviewing J. Middleton Murry's *Son of Woman* in the *Criterion,* July 1931.

31 Giordano Bruno . . . The scrapbook cutting shows the year 1890 but not the name of the periodical in which the scenes were printed. One of the difficulties of work on the scrapbooks is that the cuttings have been snipped without regard for the name of the source or the date. Sometimes one appears, sometimes neither, seldom both.

33 the poem he wrote . . . John Hayward has included it in his compilation of T. S. Eliot's *Poems written in Early Youth* (privately printed for Georg Svennson and his colleagues in the publishing house of Bonniers, Stockholm, 1950). The stanza beginning "Great duties call . . ." is interesting. One would like to know whether Eliot had already encountered Daniel's *Musophilus.*

H. W. H. Powel Jr. . . . In his *NEL*.
35 Mrs. Eliot died . . . The report in the *New York Times*, September
11, 1929, described her as "author and philanthropist."

Chapter 2
"Well-Near the Centre of Our National Demesne" (pages 36–63)

IN THE section of this chapter dealing with the St. Louis Movement I have
drawn especially on: H. A. Pochmann, *German Culture in America 1600–
1900* (Madison, 1957), cited as Pochmann; *The St. Louis Movement in
Philosophy: some source material*, edited by Charles M. Perry (Norman,
1930), cited as Perry; Cleon Forbes, "The St. Louis School of Thought,"
Missouri Historical Review, October 1930, *et seq.*; and J. G. Woerner, *The
Rebel's Daughter* (Boston, 1899), cited as Woerner.

Page
36 A writer depends . . . See the *Egoist*, December 1917 — a review of
Edward Garnett's *Turgenev*.
Some historians . . . See, for example, W. H. Ryle, Missouri: *Union
or Secession* (Nashville, 1931).
37 in his drab pages . . . The editions I have seen are the first, dated
1970, and the sixth, dated 1873.
38 Walt Whitman walked . . . The narrative and quotations are from
his *Specimen Days*.
41 Newman's cable . . . See p. 279 of Houghton Mifflin's 1907 (Riverside) edition of *The American*.
"Faith in the approaching . . ." See Pochmann, pp. 259–60.
Dreiser stepped . . . The narrative and quotations are from his *Book
about Myself* (New York, 1922).
42 under indictment . . . See L. Steffens, *The Shame of the Cities* (New
York, 1904); L. Steffens, *Autobiography* (New York, 1931); and the
article on Folk in the *Dictionary of American Biography*.
43 scrapbook . . . Now in the Library of the Missouri Historical Association, St. Louis.
45 "To be a millionaire . . ." See Mrs. Eliot, *WGE*, p. 105. There is a
text of the inaugural address in a scrapbook in the Library of Washington University, St. Louis.
Edward Cranch Eliot . . . Whose *Address upon the Laying of the
Cornerstone* of the James E. Yeatman High School, June 6, 1903, was
printed as a pamphlet.
It may be possible . . . See C. C. Eliot, *Savonarola* (London, R.
Cobden-Sanderson, 1926).
47 Sara Teasdale . . . Lindsay . . . See Eleanor Ruggles, *The West-
Going Heart* (New York, 1959), p. 221.

Saint Louis, a Civic Masque . . . Published by Doubleday, Garden City and New York, 1914. MacKaye dedicated the volume "To the citizens of St. Louis whose organized foresight for art has created an inspiring precedent in the socialization of modern cities."

48 "Nike!" Why is Greek the language of evil, and English the language of good? A simple-minded version of Whitman's casting off from the Old World?

50 A line at the end . . . See *The Cantos of Ezra Pound* (London, 1954), p. 576.

the causes of war . . . See J. J. Espey, *Ezra Pound's Mauberley* (London, 1955), p. 82.

51 "And now I pass . . ." C. Day Lewis, *Transitional Poem* (London, 1929).

the Triumphal March . . . See "Coriolan," *Poems and Plays 1909–1950*, p. 86.

53 his lectures in 1932 . . . I.e. *The Use of Poetry and the Use of Criticism* (London, 1933).

54 his Page-Barbour lectures . . . I.e. *After Strange Gods* (New York, 1934).

at Charlottesville . . . Loc. cit. With Eliot's view of the Civil War we may contrast his mother's. In *WGE* (p. 152) she called it "a struggle whose moral grandeur has never been equalled."

55 fifteen years later . . . See *Notes towards the Definition of Culture* (London, 1948), pp. 45–46.

"I feel drawn . . ." See Mrs. Eliot, *WGE*, pp. 9-10.

56 William T. Harris . . . See Perry and the *Dictionary of American Biography*.

The Germans . . . See Pochmann, Woerner, and W. H. Ryle, *Missouri: Union or Secession* (Nashville, 1931), pp. 10–17.

57 Forster's Schlegel . . . In *Howard's End*.

Matthew Arnold . . . *Letters*, ed. G. W. E. Russell (London, 1895), Vol. II, p. 255. The date is February 1, 1884.

"a strong German element" . . . See Perry, pp. 25–26.

"to obtain a land" . . . Loc. cit., p. 49. And see the admirable portrait by E. S. Bates in the *Dictionary of American Biography*, from which "his choice of the fairest" and other points are quoted.

58 Rauhenfels . . . See Woerner, pp. 279–80 and 289.

59 *The Epigrammatic Voyage* . . . was published by Ticknor and Co. in Boston in 1886. I am afraid that it does not quite answer the expectation Woerner's phrases arouse. And yet, as always with Snider, just a faint personal sound is to be remotely heard and may touch us to regret:

> Could I but give to thee half the delight in reading these verses
> That I feel as I make all of them leap to my beat . . .

60 to a Mrs. Lockwood's . . . See the *St. Louis Globe*, January 4, 1950.
Hosmer's son wrote . . . Quoted by Perry.
61 or scattered . . . See Perry for much of the material in this paragraph.
62 Balfour's compliment . . . Loc. cit., p. 67.
63 Herbert Read . . . Eliot remarks of Read, in the *Criterion*, October
1926, that, among living critics, he has the best understanding of
American literature.
the *American Mercury* . . . The article was by Arthur Strawn in the
issue of April 1927.
Eliot himself told . . . See *American Literature and the American
Language* (Washington University, St. Louis, 1953), p. 6.

Chapter 3
Undergraduate Courses at Harvard (pages 64–94)

THE Registrar of Harvard College kindly supplied a list of the courses
which Eliot followed as an undergraduate. Among those of his freshman
year there was one which I have not found opportunity to mention in the
chapter: Government I (Constitutional Government). The Harvard Catalogues for the years 1906–1910 have been useful. For impressions of the
teachers I am much indebted to the correspondents who answered the inquiry in the *New York Times Book Review;* their names are recorded on
p. 60 above. In this chapter, as elsewhere, Harford Willing Hare Powel
Jr.'s thesis, *NEL*, has been invaluable.

Before entering Harvard, Eliot spent a year at Milton Academy (Mr.
Powel says that Mrs. Eliot did not wish her son to enter Harvard at too
early an age). The University's historian, Samuel Eliot Morison, remarks
in *Three Centuries of Harvard* that "about 1890 the Episcopal Church
schools, together with Milton Academy and one or two Boston private
schools," secured the leadership among the establishments preparing boys
for Harvard, and that it was "almost necessary" after that date for the fellow with social ambitions to enter from the "right" sort of school. For his
freshman year Eliot roomed at 52 Mt. Auburn Street. The class of 1910
was to be almost torn apart by tension between the socially fortunate and
the rest. The simplest distinction between the two groups was made by
Walter Lippmann: "There are two ways of living at Harvard — on Mt.
Auburn Street and off it" (see the *Monthly*, January 1910).

Page
64 "without the least prospect" . . . See the Commentary in the *Criterion*, April 1934.
65 of Rostand . . . For the *Athenaeum*, July 25, 1919. Reprinted in
The Sacred Wood.

or Apuleius . . . For the *Dial*, September 1928.

a flourish . . . In the famous *Hamlet* essay for the *Athenaeum*, September 26, 1919. Reprinted in *The Sacred Wood*.

Abel Lefranc . . . Gave the Hyde Lectures at Harvard in the spring of 1909. The subject of the cycle was "French Literature of the Renaissance."

"neglect of Greek . . ." See the Commentary in the *Criterion*, April 1925. The text says "a relapse into unconscious." A note introducing the *Commentary* indicates that Eliot was suffering an illness when this issue was in preparation.

defended it as a discipline . . . In his paper to the Classical Club at Harvard in 1933. See his *Essays Ancient and Modern* (London, 1936).

66 imposed . . . And indeed Eliot means "imposed," fully appreciating that no word could be less generally welcome in his age, and deliberately choosing it. Compare the Commentary, "On popular education," in the *Criterion*, January 1931: "it will not do merely to call for better individuals; the new asceticism must first, certainly, be practised by a few, and it must be definite enough to be explained to, and ultimately imposed upon, the many; imposed in the name of something in which they must be made to believe."

Latin at twelve . . . His Commentary in the *Criterion*, October 1933, says "When I was a boy we began Latin at twelve or thirteen, and Greek a year later." Trying to match this recollection with the Houghton Library notes on his Smith Academy work, I rather think he must have begun Latin at twelve; had it not been for this reminiscence, I would have suggested before twelve.

"much more exciting" . . . The quotations here are from his "Virgil and the Christian World," given as a B.B.C. broadcast in 1951, reprinted in *On Poetry and Poets* (London, 1957).

The editor lamented . . . In the *Crimson*, May 23, 1907.

ancient art . . . Strictly, this course came within the classification of Fine Arts, and the course on ancient philosophy within the classification of Philosophy. Nevertheless . . .

67 Robert H. Allen . . . In answer to the *New York Times Book Review* inquiry.

Chase . . . The quotations are from Professor John I. Sewall's letter in answer to the *New York Times Book Review* inquiry.

Norman Foerster . . . In answer to the *New York Times Book Review* inquiry.

68 At the age of thirty-six . . . See G. H. Palmer, *The Autobiography of a Philosopher* (Boston, 1930).

History of Greek Philosophy . . . Published New York, 1923.

the early Dante essay . . . In *The Sacred Wood*.

69 "Only by the form . . ." See *Poems and Plays 1909–1950*, p. 121.

the Fox Club . . . See William R. Castle, *Fifty Years* (privately printed for the Fox Club, 1949).

What is a Classic? . . . An address delivered to the Virgil Society in 1944 and published in London in 1945. Reprinted in *On Poetry and Poets* (London, 1957).

70 Mr. T. S. Stensland . . . In answer to the *New York Times Book Review* inquiry.

71 Rivière . . . Says it in *Le Roman d'Aventure*. See *Nouvelles Études*, p. 270, in the ninth edition (Paris, 1947).

"the kind of power" . . . *The Sacred Wood*, second edition (London, 1928), pp. 117–18. Eliot instances Volpone, Busy, Fitzdottrel, the literary ladies of *Epicoene*, "even Bobadil."

"humors" . . . On May 20, 1839, Cranch wrote to James Freeman Clarke: "When all trades fail, let us take to caricaturing. We have humors that way." Quoted by D. K. Colville in his unpublished thesis (Washington University, St. Louis, 1953) on "James Freeman Clarke."

Tailhade translated . . . Pétrone, *Le Satyricon* (Paris, 1902). Tailhade's *Avis Prémonitoire* is dated April 25, 1902, from the Prison de la Santé. His epigraph to the Avis: *Auctor purissimae impuritatis.* He attacks the moralists who object to Petronius; declines "mettre un vertugadin aux priapées"; will make his readers free of the only realist tales which have come down from antiquity: tales in which

> Priapus et Cotytto s'y délectent de leur vigueur nue. Un remugle de parfumerie et de cuisine, de sueur humaine et de benjoin, une odeur âcre de fards et de sexes en rut flottent sur ces pages lubriques ou charmantes.

He has tried to conserve "le scandale du texte dans toute sa pureté."

73 "that sense of the past" . . . See Eliot's essay "The Hawthorne Aspect [of Henry James]," written for the *Little Review*, August 1918, reprinted in *The Question of Henry James*, edited by F. W. Dupee (New York, 1945).

Wendell has written . . . In Stelligeri (New York, 1893), p. 205.

74 in Wendell's *Letters* . . . See M. A. DeWolfe Howe, *Barrett Wendell and his Letters* (Boston, 1924), p. 173.

Eliot read Dante . . . He gives some account of the process in the 1929 essay (see *Selected Essays*), and further details, from which these quotations are taken, in his lecture, "What Dante means to me," delivered at the Italian Institute, London, in 1950, printed in the Institute's journal, *Italian News*, July 1950, and reprinted in the *Adelphi,* First Quarter, 1951. As the *Adelphi* may be a little easier to consult I will use it for later references to the lecture. But, I would like to take the opportunity to recall with pleasure the lectures which the Italian Institute in London organized about that time.

75 His 1926 review . . . In the *Times Literary Supplement,* December 16, 1926.

"even in the thirteenth century" . . . See the *Criterion,* January 1926. Compare, three months later, in the April issue, Eliot's question whether, even in France and Britain, never mind elsewhere, "the culture of ideas has still as much liberty as, let us say, in the Sorbonne in the Thirteenth century."

76 Robert H. Allen . . . In answer to the *New York Times Book Review* inquiry.

78 "Donne in our Time" . . . In *A Garland for John Donne,* ed. Theodore Spencer (Cambridge, Mass., 1931).

A number of critics . . . Listed by E. P. Bollier in "T. S. Eliot and John Donne," *Tulane Studies in English,* IX, p. 103n.

79 Ford . . . in 1916 . . . In a preface to his 1916 collection of poems. It is reprinted at the end of his very different volume, *Collected Poems* (New York, 1936).

Charles Eliot Norton . . . See the *Crimson,* November 16, 1908.

Reedy . . . See, for example, the *Mirror* of February 11, 1904, which contained "Love's Infiniteness." Three more poems of Donne followed, one in each successive weekly issue.

80 "As we walk . . ." Bernard Blackstone, reviewing A. L. Maycock's *Nicholas Ferrar of Little Gidding,* in the *Criterion,* October 1938.

the Clark Lectures . . . See Barrett Wendell, *The Temper of the Seventeenth Century in English Literature* (New York, 1904), pp. 214 and 264. Wendell was delighted to be the first American to be invited to give the Clark Lectures. Eliot gave them in 1926.

a recent book . . . J. Donald Adams, *Copey of Harvard* (Boston, 1960). See especially pp. 158–64.

fight for his individuality . . . Compare the wonderful paragraph in *Notes towards the Definition of Culture* (London, 1948), p. 59, in which Eliot says: "Fortunate the man who, at the right moment, meets the right friend; fortunate also the man who at the right moment meets the right enemy." He allows us to guess that he has often learned by friction and contention.

82 execrated by Raleigh . . . Miss Elizabeth Booth pointed out to me Raleigh's comment in the *Letters,* ed. Lady Raleigh (London, 1926), Vol. II, p. 306.

Entering Harvard . . . See George Santayana, *Persons and Places* (New York, 1944), p. 186.

83 "My relations with . . ." See George Santayana, *The Middle Span* (New York, 1945), p. 159.

the *Monthly* . . . Of March, 1912.

84 "History of Modern Philosophy" . . . Santayana briefly describes the genesis and scope of this course in *The Middle Span,* p. 157: ". . . I had always had a great respect for Aristotle, especially for his *Ethics and Politics;* and, out of these, with the help of a glance at Bacon, Locke, Montesquieu, and Taine (authors that my pupils could be expected to read a little) I composed my lectures on the 'philosophy of history,' which for me meant no providential plan of creation or redemption, but merely retrospective politics; a study of what had formed the chief interests of mankind in various epochs. Religion — my strong point in history — naturally came in, and I treated it, I think, without giving offence in any quarter." He says that his work for these lectures prepared the ground for his *Life of Reason.*
"critically . . . compulsorily . . ." Op. cit., p. 155.

85 "the Christian epic . . ." See George Santayana, "A General Confession," in *The Philosophy of George Santayana,* ed. P. A. Schilp (New York, second edition, 1951), p. 7.
a new book . . . I.e. *Civilization in the United States: an Inquiry by Thirty Americans,* ed. Harold Stearns.

86 C. W. Eliot . . . In this section I am drawing on: C. W. Eliot, *Harvard Memories* (Cambridge, 1923); *Charles W. Eliot; The Man and his Beliefs,* edited with a biographical study by W. A. Neilson (New York, 1926); Henry James, *Charles W. Eliot* (Boston, 1930).

87 "I have privately . . ." Quoted by James, op. cit., II, p. 87.
John J. Chapman . . . For the story of this volcanic figure and for a number of glimpses of the Harvard of this period, see M. A. DeWolfe Howe, *John Jay Chapman and his Letters* (Boston, 1937).
indignantly repudiating . . . See the *Crimson,* October 21, 1909.
the "elective system" . . . See Powel, *NEL,* for information and comments on the elective system at Harvard in T. S. Eliot's time and on the poet's aversion for it.

88 "the happiest age" . . . See C. W. Eliot, *The Durable Satisfactions of Life* (New York, 1910). Some students of T. S. Eliot's generation agreed with the President. Edward Eyre Hunt, for example: see *Essays in Memory of Barrett Wendell* by his Assistants (Cambridge, Mass., 1926).
the "Religion of the Future" . . . Was published in *The Durable Satisfactions of Life.*
"American universities" . . . The quotations in this paragraph are from the paper which he gave to the Classical Club at Harvard in 1933.

89 Eliot has fought . . . See, for example, his Commentary in the *Criterion,* October, 1937.
Professor Merriman . . . See M. A. DeWolfe Howe, *Barrett Wendell and his Letters* (Boston, 1924), p. 185.

90 "The atmosphere . . ." See *Harvard Celebrities,* A Book of Caricatures and Decorative Drawings by Frederick Garrison Hall '03, Edward Revere Little '04, Verses by Henry Ware Eliot Jr. '02. Printed
for the Editors by the University Press, Cambridge U.S.A., 1901.

91 "We are living . . ." DeWolfe Howe, op. cit., p. 255.
a British General Election . . . See the *Criterion,* April and July
1929.

92 "But if human nature . . ." Barrett Wendell, *Stelligeri* (New York,
1893), p. 13.

94 the significance of "corruption" . . . See *Selected Essays* (London,
1951), pp. 427–29.
"Wendell's new book . . ." Quoted by James, op. cit., Vol. II, p. 134.

Chapter 4
The Young Writers of Harvard — and the Shore (pages 95–125)

Page

95 William Chase Creene . . . In a letter to me. My inquiry had been
particularly prompted by his poem "Vignette" in the *Advocate,* September 29, 1910.

96 votes . . . Reported in the *Crimson,* December 7, 1909.
"fourmillante Cité' . . . Eliot said in 1950: "It may be that I am indebted to Baudelaire chiefly for a half a dozen lines out of the whole
of *Fleurs du Mal;* and that his significance for me is summed up in
the lines:

Fourmillante Cité, cité plein de rêves,
Où le spectre en plein jour raccroche le passant . . .

I knew what that meant because I had lived it before I knew that I
wanted to turn it into verse on my own account" (*Adelphi,* First
Quarter, 1951).

97 *Troop of the Guard* . . . Published by Houghton Mifflin, Boston,
1909.
performed at Harvard . . . See the *Crimson,* May 18, 1909. The
other one-act plays on the bill were: an adaptation from Lever's *Con
Cregan;* a prairie comedy, *The Horse Thieves;* and an adaptation
from Chaucer, *Death and the Dicers.*
"I am moved" and "Wipe your hand" . . . See "Preludes" in *Poems
and Plays 1909–1950,* p. 13.

100 Davidson influenced *him* . . . See the preface which Eliot contrib-
uted to *John Davidson: A Selection of his Poems,* edited by Maurice
Lindsay (London, 1961). See also J. B. Townsend, *John Davidson:
Poet of Armageddon* (New Haven, 1961).
Some British painters . . . And George Moore, whose interest in the

new way of seeing and its application to literature showed in his first novel, *A Modern Lover* (London, 1883); and he never completely lost it.

The urban sensibility has remained active in literature. For its persistence in the late twenties a contribution to the *Criterion*, November 1927, G. B. Angioletti's "A Northerner" might be quoted: "I feel an almost instinctive love for the great coalmines of the Ruhr, for the serried furnaces of Essen, for the constellations of street lamps in the acrid London fog, for the squares of Paris, and for the bridges over the Meuse in Holland. I seem to understand the kindliness of the hour between twelve and one, when armies of workmen set round the factory walls eating their dinners; I love the weary gaiety of parks enclosed in great capitals, the nocturnal solitudes of vast city squares and morning departures from great stations . . ."

There has been a steady diffusion of urban poetry into popular literature. At one level it can be seen in Graham Greene's work; at another in the setting of Raymond Chandler's stories; at another in the imitative post-Chandler literature.

the Armory Exhibition . . . There is a thesis on the Exhibition by Chloe Hamilton (Oberlin, 1950).

101 Webster . . . reviewed it . . . In a later number of the *Crimson,* that of June 6, the poem was apparently reviewed again: a curiosity which I cannot explain, and which may point to something I have overlooked or misunderstood. The reviewer on the second occasion was G. F. Moore, who found that "Mr. Eliot's 'Song' says 'Carpe Diem' agreeably . . ."

102 Fuller reviewed it . . . In the *Crimson*, November 20, 1908.

103 told H. W. H. Powel Jr. . . . See *NEL*.

104 the birth of a poem . . . Arthur Symons, *The Symbolist Movement in Literature* (London, 1899), pp. 132–34. Eliot may have used the second edition of 1908, in which the pagination is slightly different.
    at the Italian Institute . . . See "What Dante means to me" in the *Adelphi* (First Quarter, 1951).

105 "He has invented . . ." Symons, op. cit., p. 112.
    the Harvard style . . . The Ivy Orator of 1910 said, in a flourish of more sociological interest than literary charm: "Africa has its uncouth lion. America has its dandelion."
    to Schoenhof's . . . See *NEL*.
    the first man . . . to possess . . . See Greene, p. 20n.

106 J. Donald Adams reports . . . In *Copey of Harvard* (Boston, 1960), p. 163.
    crise de conscience poétique . . . Greene, p. 23.
    "Humouresque" . . . Is based on a poem quoted by Symons. So is another poem of 1909, "Conversation Galante."

"sentiment is squeezed out" . . . Symons, op. cit., p. 112.

107 his word for it . . . See Green: "En 1907 ou 1908 il lit Baudelaire, qui le bouleverse" (p. 8, and see footnote 4).

108 the Board of Editors . . . To carry the story of Eliot's work for the *Advocate* a little further: in December 1909 a special election of *Advocate* officers was necessitated by the resignation of Tinckom-Fernandez. Hallowell Vaughan Morgan, later to become a Philadelphia stockbroker, was elected president, and Thomas Stearns Elliott — so spelled in the official announcement — moved up to the place of Secretary. It was a short run, for the normal turn over came again in March 1910, when Conrad Aiken took the presidency and James Merriam Moore of Detroit the secretaryship. But he had bagged a whole page for the printing of "Humouresque" on January 12.

To the *Crimson* of February 13, 1909, P. la Rose contributed an unusually reproving notice of the current *Advocate:* had they been submitted to Professor Hill's English class, the efforts of the senior Editors would, all but Powell's, have secured collectively "the grade of 'C,' the traditional gentleman's grade."

109 aware of Brooks . . . As he recalls in a letter of 1920, now in the Van Wyck Brooks collection at the University of Pennsylvania, Philadelphia.

111 "J'erre toujours" . . . See "Mélange Adultère de Tout," *Poems and Plays 1909–1950*, p. 29.

112 In the *Advocate* is the second . . . Published May 25, 1909.

Briggs, reviewing . . . In the *Crimson*, May 29, 1909.

113 William Greenleaf Eliot . . . See Mrs. Eliot, *WGE*, pp. 43–44.

"From the wide window" . . . See "Ash-Wednesday," VI: *Poems and Plays 1909–1950*, p. 66.

114 recalled . . . Tinckom-Fernandez . . . See *The Harvard Advocate Anthology*, edited by Donald Hall (New York, 1950), p. 326. His article is reprinted from the *Advocate*'s special T. S. Eliot issue of December 1938.

The Harvard Advocate Anthology also reprints "Gentlemen and Seamen."

115 Dr. Conland . . . See C. E. Carrington, *Life of Rudyard Kipling* (New York, 1955), pp. 180–81. *Captains Courageous* is dedicated to the doctor.

A study of Eliot's changing attitude to Kipling would take account of the following evidence: the immense popularity which Kipling enjoyed in the first decade of this century, the extent to which he was imitated at Harvard (see W. F. Harris in the *Crimson*, October 8, 1909, and various instances of imitation in the *Advocate* and parody in the *Lampoon*); the "harsh" essay which Eliot read to Copeland; Eliot's remarks in the *Athenaeum* of May 9 and May 16, 1919; his remarks in the *Criterion* of October 1926; the two discerning articles by Bonamy Dobrée in the *Criterion* of January and December 1927, which, I imagine encouraged Eliot to reconsider his position; the remarks in the unsigned review of Charles Williams' *Poetry at Present,* in the *Criterion,* July 1930; Eliot's obituary remarks in the *Criterion,* April 1936 — and so to the rehabilitation of 1941, the preface to *A Choice of Kipling's Verse.*

and mentions it . . . In his Commentary in the *Criterion,* October 1926.

"with all respect" . . . In his preface to J. B. Connolly, *Fishermen of the Banks* (London, 1928).

116 Connolly was himself . . . See S. J. Kunitz and H. Haycraft, *Twentieth Century Authors* (New York, 1942).

117 visited the Harvard Union . . . See the *Crimson,* October 16, 1907.

118 guidebook author . . . Henry C. Leonard, *Pigeon Cove and Vicinity* (Boston, 1873). See also James R. Pringle, *History of the Town and City of Gloucester* (Gloucester, 1892).

119 The Rev. J. G. Adams . . . Quoted by Leonard, op. cit., p. 68.
"the fishermen" and "forever boiling" . . . See "The Dry Salvages," *Poems and Plays 1909–1950,* p. 132.

120 Captain Mesquita . . . See K. Parsons, *The Church of Our Lady of Good Voyage* (North Montpelier, Vt., 1945).
"the evening hour" . . . See "The Waste Land," *Poems and Plays 1909–1950,* pp. 43–44.
"dory" . . . For a definition see J. B. Connolly's *Fishermen of the Banks,* p. 17: "The dory is a flat-bottomed boat with flaring sides, and of about fifteen feet in length." On p. 20 he says it is built and equipped for two men. *The Fishermen's Own Book,* published by Procter Bros. of Gloucester in 1882, says it is a little boat of ten or fifteen tons burthen, about twenty feet long, or less.

121 "The salt" . . . See "The Dry Salvages," *Poems and Plays 1909–1950,* p. 131.
When Arnold Bennett . . . See his series "Your United States" in *Harper's* in the summer and fall of 1912.
Ross . . . put into his stories . . . See, for example, the *Advocate* of November 12, 1909.

122 "Damyata . . ." See "The Waste Land," *Poems and Plays 1909–1950,* p. 49.

123 "expected to wear gloves" . . . See the *Advocate,* June 24, 1908.
the Hasty Pudding Club . . . For details of which, see Owen Wister's *Illustrated History of the Hasty Pudding Club* (Cambridge, Mass., 1933).

124 in the *Dial* . . . Of December 1923.

Chapter 5
A Year of Diligence (pages 126–149)

ABBREVIATIONS used in the citations for this chapter are: *LAC:* Irving Babbitt, *Literature and the American College* (Boston, 1908). Memorial Volume: F. Manchester, and O. Shepard, *Irving Babbitt, Man and Teacher* (New York, 1941).

Page

126 the Italian Institute . . . See "What Dante means to me" in the *Adelphi,* First Quarter, 1951. Fournier, discussing Laforgue in a letter to Rivière on April 21, 1906, had rather similarly said: ". . . comme dit Remy de Gourmont, 'ce serait aujourd'hui notre adoré frère aîné' " (*Correspondance,* Vol. 2, p. 72).

versatility . . . athleticism . . . In an address at the Milton Academy in 1933 Eliot said much the same thing in the language of self-mockery. He imagined his specter reproaching him: "You did a great deal of smattering and not enough concentrating . . ." See the text, someone's shorthand record, published without correction, entirely delightful, in the *Milton Graduates Bulletin,* November 1933.

127 In boyhood . . . The biographical points are taken, mainly, from the Memorial Volume.

128 an important look . . . See Eliot's obituary tribute to Babbitt in the *Criterion,* October 1933.

"We . . . seem certain" . . . *LAC,* p. 81.

this parable . . . Ibid., p. 64.

129 We have seen . . . Chapman . . . Please see p. 87.

"His outspoken contempt . . ." This is from Eliot's contribution to the Memorial Volume (pp. 101–4).

quoted Goethe . . . *LAC,* p. 194 and pp. 231–32.

130 "The classical spirit . . ." Ibid., p. 174.

131 praised Hawthorne . . . In his review of *A History of American Literature,* Vol. II, contributed to the *Athenaeum,* April 25, 1919.

Chateaubriand's . . . "ils ne savent . . ." Babbitt, *Masters of Modern French Criticism* (Boston, 1912), p. 65n.

Petrarch and Bacon . . . *LAC,* p. 38.

glorifying his own weaknesses . . . Compare Maurras, *L'Avenir de l'Intelligence:* ". . . un Gautier devenait de plus en plus Gautier et abondait fatalement dans son péché . . ."

"the balance it maintained" . . . *LAC,* p. 135.

132 "There is needed" . . . Ibid., pp. 178–89.

reviewed *Quia Pauper Amavi* . . . In the *Athenaeum,* October 24, 1919.

heard him meditating . . . Please see p. 38.

133 breaking down their subject . . . Cf. "All knowledge is simply classification" — Thomas Lamb Eliot, *The Radical Difference between
Liberal Christianity and Orthodoxy* (Boston, n.d.).

134 "would be more important" . . . *The Sacred Wood*, second edition
(London, 1928), p. 42.
When the Professorship . . . Eliot's letter is in the *Dial* of July 1922.

135 His Lowell lectures . . . W. A. Neilson, *The Essentials of Poetry*
(Boston, 1912).

136 "My little island girl" and "I'd be bored" . . . See "Sweeney Agonistes," *Poems and Plays 1909–1950*, p. 82 and p. 80.

137 In W. H. R. Rivers . . . Eliot quotes the passage in his article in the
Dial, December 1922. It was still in his mind in 1931 when he wrote
Thoughts after Lambeth (London), p. 13: "Without religion the
whole human race would die, as according to W. H. R. Rivers, some
Melanesian tribes have died, solely of boredom."

138 call the critical world back . . . And at least one younger critic responded. Ronald Bottrall contributed to the *Criterion* of January
1939 an essay on "Byron and the Colloquial Tradition in English
Poetry." Analyzing Byron, Bottrall found himself criticizing the tendencies of Eliot's later poetry:

> . . . although Eliot is confining himself nowadays to drama he
> seems rather to be moving away from colloquial rhythms than
> towards them. To me the method of *Murder in the Cathedral* is
> a sad watering down of the methods of *The Waste Land* and
> *Sweeney Agonistes*. Eliot is making the same mistake as Byron
> made in *Marino Falieri* and *Sardanapalus* . . . In these plays,
> in an attempt to be "as simple and severe as Alfieri," he broke
> down his poetic language to a condition where it was at a far
> lower tension than his prose.

In the later plays Eliot certainly returned to colloquial rhythms,
though some critics have expressed doubts (mistaken, I think) about
the degree of tension.
Grover Smith . . . has half hinted . . . Grover Smith, pp. 3–4.

139 To read his book . . . G. P. Baker, *The Development of Shakespeare
as a Dramatist* (New York, 1907).

140 the Promethean theme . . . On the half title of *The Fire-Bringer*
(Boston, 1904) Moody wrote that it "is intended as the first member
of a trilogy on the Promethean theme, of which *The Masque of Judgment*, already published, is the second member . . ." In dramatic
construction the play recalls Shelley's *Prometheus Unbound*, and the
poetry descends from him:

> wailing like a broken bird,
> I heard her dropping down from rock to rock.

> Then for an endless season sat she here,
> Her head between her knees, and all her hair
> Spread like a night-pool in the autumn woods.

It is the work of a poet, but a poet who has not found his own subject or language. We have seen (p. 85) that when Santayana lamented the early death and extinguished promise of the Harvard poets of Moody's generation, he blamed America and said it was impossible "to live in familiar friendship with the Greeks and Indians" (the *Dial*, June 1922). But in making that distinction Santayana fell into the very error that had really trapped and crushed the poets of his age: the supposition that to write at the level of the past they had to cultivate the themes and methods of the past. The new Greeks wrote of living themes with living methods — i.e. Eliot caricatured the Harvard dandy in *Portrait of a Lady*, Edgar Lee Masters wrote about Spoon River's inglorious Milton, Frost wrote about a wood at night but a Vermont wood as he saw and felt it.

   The Fire-Bringer was reviewed by P. A. Hutchinson in the *Crimson*, January 16, 1907: "the drama is of unusual interest as an indication of the poetic unrest and experimentation of the hour, which, one likes to believe, is prophetic of a period in America of genuine and high poetic achievement."

141 "play-mad" . . . The *Advocate*, May 11, 1910.

a quarter page . . . The *Advocate*, May 25, 1909.

142 One of the documents . . . Robert Herrick, *His Great Adventure* (New York, 1913). Herrick, of the Harvard class of 1890, had been an early pupil of Wendell's. He was on the Faculty of the University of Chicago when he wrote this novel.

his book on Baker . . . W. P. Kinne, *George Pierce Baker and the American Theatre* (Cambridge, Mass., 1954). I am much indebted to this study (which is not, however, responsible for the view of Baker which I have ventured to adopt).

143 congratulated the Club . . . The *Advocate*, March 26, 1909. Does the phraseology of the paragraph suggest that Eliot wrote it, as an editorial duty?

Henry Arthur Jones lectured . . . Reported in the *Crimson*, November, 1, 1906. The spelling is the *Crimson's*. Jones had a "very large audience" to hear his address, "The Corner Stones in Modern Drama." In the course of two hundred years, he said, English dramatists had produced three permanent pieces of literature: *The Rivals, She Stoops to Conquer*, and *The School for Scandal*. Whereas the French dramatists were still producing drama which was literature: "French audiences know that their drama is intended to depict life, and not to amuse them by clownery."

a sense of the sadness . . . Note his words of regret and public censure at the end (p. 292) of *The Development of Shakespeare as a
Dramatist:* "ten years ago," he says, "we were flooded with plays that
held up for our scrutiny the sadder and seamier sides of life. As a
public we forced these plays off the stage by our delight in the mere
romantic story-telling that came in among the novels and by our satisfaction with the adaptations promptly made from these novels."

144 reread Ibsen . . . See Eliot's prefatory note to his *Religious Drama:
Mediaeval and Modern* (New York, 1954), in which he recalls that
the lecture was originally written in 1937 for delivery to the Friends
of Rochester Cathedral, and goes on:

> . . . it was written before I had re-read Ibsen's plays. As a re-
> sult of studying Ibsen's plays, and criticising my own plays of
> contemporary life, I have a very much higher opinion of Ibsen
> than I appear to have held in 1937. In fact, I repudiate what I
> have here said about Ibsen . . .

and we may imagine that what he said in 1937 was considerate compared with the opinions he entertained in earlier years when fellow
undergraduates regarded Ibsen as their model for an American drama.
But note the ambivalence of such passages as that in *The Sacred
Wood* in which he at once attempts to decry *Peer Gynt* as mixed art
and to recognize that it is "remarkable" (p. 66 of the London, 1928,
edition). Sometimes in his earlier criticism he can be seen enjoying
the act of destruction yet checked in the act by a voice which warns
him of a value he may not destroy. In his later criticism he is increasingly careful to extricate and acknowledge the value.

a handful of listeners . . . See the *Advocate,* January 31, 1908.

rapturously reported . . . See the *Advocate,* February 14, 1908, and
the *Crimson* two days later.

commended by . . . Neilson . . . In the *Crimson,* February 14,
1908.

"The Drama of Democracy" . . . My quotations are from the lengthy
summary in the *Advocate* of February 14.

145 MacKaye's "Civic Masque" . . . Please see pp. 47–48.

Eliot . . . differentiated . . . *Selected Essays,* second edition (London, 1952), p. 262.

"naturally clever craftsmen" . . . *Religious Drama* . . . (New York,
1954).

146 lacked beauty . . . See the Commentary in the *Criterion,* June, 1926.

"the small public" . . . *The Sacred Wood* (London, 1928), p. 70.

147 pre-1914 years of . . . theorizing . . . It might be interesting to
compare, sometime, MacKaye's enthusiastic theorizing with the practical, pedestrian theorizing of Montrose J. Moses in his chapter on the

poetic drama in *The American Dramatist* (Boston, 1911). Moses had not much sympathy with MacKaye. He counted *Sappho and Phaon* as one of the "wrecks beautiful in their dramatic inertia," in which the writer stopped to listen to his own words instead of advancing the action. He equally hated the *Canterbury Pilgrims,* bracketing it with the Harvard Stadium performance of Schiller's *Joan of Arc* as merely "for visual effect." He wanted the poet to learn the craft of the theatre; to discover the poetry of ordinary existence; to avoid "sublime images"; to combine the lessons of Ibsen and Emerson.

join in the chorus . . . See "In Memoriam: Marie Lloyd" in the *Criterion,* January 1923.

148 reviewing *All God's Chillun* . . . In the *Criterion,* April 1926. Very recently Eliot has uttered a new and favorable verdict on O'Neill; see *O'Neill and His Plays,* edited by O. Cargill, N. B. Fagin, W. J. Fisher (New York, 1961), pp. 168–69.

A student journalist . . . The *Advocate,* May 11, 1910.

149 "À bas Sudermann" . . . The *Advocate,* June 3, 1907. And compare Paul Davis' *Advocate* article of June 1, 1908.

advised the competitors . . . The *Advocate,* October 18, 1912.

Chapter 6
Some Gifts of France (pages 150–198)

I HAVE relied considerably on the four volumes of Jacques Rivière and Alain-Fournier, *Correspondance 1905–1914,* using Gallimard's edition of 1928. It is cited as R. & F., *Correspondance,* though where the text makes it clear that this is my source and indicates the date I have refrained from citing. The *Nouvelle Revue Française* is cited in the familiar form, NRF. In the Hofmannsthal section, and in other chapters, I have debts to H. A. Hammelmann, *Hugo von Hofmannsthal* (London, 1957), cited as Hammelmann.

Page

150 When Conrad Aiken arrived . . . See his *Ushant* (New York and Boston, 1952), p. 157.

151 On April 21 . . . R. & F., *Correspondance,* IV, p. 274.

On May 10 . . . *Letters of R. M. Rilke,* translated J. B. Greene and M. D. Herter Norton (New York, 1947/48), Vol. II, pp. 23–24.

a book Eliot recommended . . . In his Commentary in the *Criterion,* April 1934.

152 for *La France Libre* . . . Of June 15, 1944. The passage is quoted by Greene, p. 10.

whole book should be written . . . And it might include a section on the Paris theatre in Eliot's year. I very much regret omitting any consideration of this. It would be attractive to examine, for instance, the dramatization of *The Brothers Karamazov* at the Théâtre des Arts, the more so as Fournier reveals a zealous concern for it in *Correspondance*. Or, at a very different level, Bouhélier's *Le Carnaval des enfants,* which gave the audience pleasant shudders. The long run of the season was *Le Bois Sacré!*

from Camille Vettard . . . In the *NRF*, November 1912. A comparable passage by André Lacaze occurs in the *NRF* of April 1925. Longer, more important, but essentially similar, is the chapter on Bergson in Raissa Maritain's *Les Grandes Amitiés* (New York, 1941). Alun R. Jones provides a brilliant short study of Bergson's significance for literature and the arts in *The Life and Opinions of T. E. Hulme* (London, 1960).

There are references to Bergson's London lectures of the autumn of 1911 in Cobden-Sanderson's *Journals*. A practitioner of feeling made visible, and therefore a little impatient with philosophers, and the more so because he was an old man, Cobden-Sanderson went to hear one of the lectures at University College, and came away not in the least exhilarated by "the discovery that my soul is an individual movement." Yet the lecture teased his mind, and he found himself discussing it with acquaintances. He set out for another lecture the next week, but was late and the door was shut; no standing room, even, and a woman was brought out fainting. He decided that he would not have been late unless his soul had already concluded that Bergson's soul-history was preposterous; and he did not try to chase the "fashionable French professor" to the next performance . . . "It is to poetry that we must ultimately look for an adequate description of the soul," he told his diary on November 1. But still he took the English edition of *Creative Evolution* to Grasmere with him in December.

154 Vincent Cronin . . . He suggested it in his essay on "T. S. Eliot as a Translator" in *T. S. Eliot: a Symposium for his Seventeenth Birthday,* ed. Neville Braybrooke (London, 1958).

155 pitiable "à cause de . . ." R. & F., *Correspondance,* II, p. 72.

156 a lecture at New Haven . . . Quoted in Matthiessen's *Achievement,* p. 96.

a passage of Joubert . . . Quoted by Babbitt in *Masters of Modern French Criticism* (Boston, 1912), pp. 44–45.

157 Gide . . . complained . . . See his *Journal,* entry of January 2, 1933.

158 an English translation of *Bubu* . . . By Laurence Vail, first published at Paris, 1932 (Crosby Continental Editions), republished at New York after the war. I am using the New York edition of 1951 (Shakespeare House).

In 1910, Eliot noticed . . . Loc. cit.

159 "La Dispute" . . . Included in *Miracles* (Paris, 1924).
"Il m'est si doux" . . . See Letter XXI (in the *NRF*, December 1910).

160 "La Seine est" . . . Letter XV, in the same issue of the *NRF*.
Grover Smith . . . p. 24.

161 "smells of chestnuts" . . . See "Rhapsody on a Windy Night," *Poems and Plays 1909–1950*, p. 15.

162 In a reply . . . Greene, pp. 136–37.
For the material in this and the following paragraph, see R. & F., *Correspondance:* I, 250, 305–9, 330–31; II, 30, 65, 361–62, 392; III, 337.

164 "Our brains . . ." and "I have lain . . ." and "What sign" . . . See "Murder in the Cathedral," *Poems and Plays 1909–1950*, pp. 181, 207, and 201.

166 "La tête du poisson" . . . In the *NRF* of June 1911. I wonder whether another Perse poem of this period suggested a turn of rhetoric which Eliot used brilliantly in his 1915 poems. Perse has a poem about the morning which unfolds to this climax:

> et la journée est entamée, le monde
> n'est pas se vieux que soudain il n'ait ri . . .

> C'est alors que l'odeur du café remonte l'escalier

The break into the common world at the end reminds me of

> And I say "Cousin Harriet, here is the *Boston Evening Transcript*."

Pound was attacking . . . The hit at "fake-bigotry" is in the *Egoist*, May 1918. For "ninth-rate" see *Letters*, p. 205.

167 Hamburger's edition . . . I.e., H. von Hofmannsthal, *Poems and Verse Plays* (New York, 1961). The last phrase in the 1947 communication to Greene (p. 137) may already indicate a strengthening of Eliot's respect for Claudel: "Depuis 1911, il a fort peu lu de Claudel, et jamais, a-t-il dit, avec l'attention que mérite son oeuvre."
Eliot recognized . . . In his obituary tribute to Rivière in the *NRF*, April 1925.
Copeland had been struck . . . J. Donald Adams, *Copey of Harvard*, (Boston, 1960), p. 162.

168 a *marchand de valeur* . . . Rivière, *Nouvelles Etudes*, p. 100.

170 Gide . . . claimed . . . In the *NRF*, October 1910.

172 Pound and Eliot . . . Pound's recollection appeared in his essay in the *Criterion*, July 1932.

173 Salmon's poems . . . The volume from which I am quoting is *Cré-*

ances 1905–1910 (Paris, 1926). It contains *Les Clés Ardentes* of 1905, *Féeries* of 1907, *Le Calumet* of 1910. For Eliot's recollection of reading "one of Salmon's first volumes" in 1910, see Greene, p. 76.

175 he had sometimes wondered . . . See his conversation with Donald Hall, recorded in the *Paris Review*, Spring-Summer 1959.

176 a moment precious . . . See the Commentary in the *Criterion*, October 1932.

he answered: "Upon me . . ." In the article "M. Maurras and Mr. Ward" in the *Criterion*, March 1928.

The *NRF* study of 1913 . . . The first installment printed in the January issue, the second in the March issue.

Thibaudet . . . Bergson commemorated him in a farewell essay in the *NRF*, July 1936.

177 the institution . . . Maurras makes it clear that not only the Church is an institution, not only the monarchy, but the Army. So Eliot included military pageants among the significant public rituals (see p. 145 of this volume), and so he remembers with pleasure how the strikers in Paris paradoxically cheered the cavalry (*Criterion*, April 1934). Nevertheless, I fancy that the most powerful impact was made on him by Maurras' remarks on the Church; for example, by this: ". . . nos libres penseurs n'ont pas encore compris que le dernier obstacle à l'impérialisme de l'Or, le dernier fort des pensées libres est justement representé par l'Église qu'ils accablent de vexations! Elle est bien le dernier organe autonome de l'esprit pur. Une intelligence sincère ne peut voir affaiblir le catholicisme sans concevoir qu'elle est affaiblie . . ." (from the introduction to *l'Avenir de l'intelligence*. I am using the edition, *Romantisme et Révolution*, Versailles, 1928, where this passage is on p. 32).

understand Confucius . . . See *After Strange Gods* (New York, 1934), p. 43.

179 "A good poem" . . . In his article on Benda in *The New Republic*, December 12, 1928.

180 "approaches or even suggests" . . . See "The Idea of a Literary Review" in the *Criterion*, January 1926.

"more attention" . . . See *The Use of Poetry and the Use of Criticism* (London, 1933), p. 25.

181 "si quelqu'un" . . . See the *NRF*, June 1919, and *Nouvelles Etudes*.

182 Julien Benda . . . In this section I have debts to Robert J. Niess, *Julien Benda* (Ann Arbor, 1956).

"hand to the sword-hilt" . . . *Belphégor* (London, 1929), p. 91. Classicism too, he says, may be seized as a "lyric theme." Eliot's criticism of the indiscipline of Babbitt (in *The Sacred Wood*) is an echo of Benda's criticism of the over enthusiasm of Maurras. Subsequently, in his *New Republic* review of the *Trahison des Clercs*, Eliot said, advancing from echo to conversation, "M. Benda attacks Maurras and the 'neo-classicists,' for instance, on the ground that their neo-classicism is itself a phase of romanticism. I think he is right, though the charge does not seem to me to be nearly as deadly as he seems to suppose."

183 gives Pound the credit . . . In this introduction to Pound's *Selected Poems* (London, 1928), p. xxiii.

Eliot remembered . . . In the *New Republic*, December 12, 1928.

"la haine de l'intelligence" . . . I am afraid that the way I have placed this quotation makes it appear to belong to *Belphégor*. But, if I remember rightly, it is from *Sur le Succès du Bergsonisme* (Paris, 1914).

184 "Et qu'il soit jusqu'au bout . . ." He is quoting Boileau.

A phrase . . . P. 44 in the second edition of *The Sacred Wood* (London, 1928).

lets it be seen . . . For example, although he inveighs against the concern of modern critics with the work "en train de se faire," he admits that he can never see the curtain fall on the studio scene of the *Meistersinger* "without thinking how it was falling on twenty years of the life and thought of the Master, and being moved thereby." But he promptly adds that this sympathy is not an aesthetic emotion, and should be strictly separated from the aesthetic and critical activity.

Like Babbitt he took immense pleasure in some of the passages of the romantics he condemned.

185 heresy . . . "the overemphasis" . . . See Eliot's review of Clive Bell's *Civilization* in the *Criterion*, September 1928. Compare "Heresy is often defined as an insistence upon one half of the truth . . ." in *The Idea of a Christian Society* (New York, 1940), p. 52. We must have these definitions in mind when he read his "primer of modern heresy," *After Strange Gods*.

Conrad Aiken . . . In *Ushant*, p. 232–33.

Bubu . . . with rebuke . . . P. 46 of the second edition of *The Sacred Wood* (London, 1928).

186 consent of the sufferer . . . See, for example, the miracle in Gide's *Les Caves du Vatican*.

Yeats . . . See, for example, his *Letters*, ed. Allan Wade (London, 1951), p. 626.

187 "multiply distinctions" . . . A phrase from Babbitt's preface to *The Masters of Modern French Criticism* (Boston, 1912): "Instead of reducing the intellect to a purely utilitarian role as M. Bergson does, we should employ it in multiplying sharp distinctions." The sentence might have been written by Benda or Maurras.

188 the Acropolis . . . For an instance of the dissemination of the example, see W. A. Neilson's paragraph on the Parthenon and symmetry in *The Essentials of Poetry* (Boston, 1912), pp. 106–7. The adoption

of the example by English and American scholars of Neilson's generation and type was almost certainly due to Arnold.

he translated the essay . . . And printed it in the *Criterion,* Part I in
January 1928, Part II in March 1928, under the title "Prologue to an
Essay on Criticism."

189 a man of ideas . . . Recalling the early and middle days of the *Criterion* and his concurrent interest in foreign periodicals of the same order, Eliot has written: "The ideas with which you did not agree, the
opinions which you could not accept, were as important to you as
those which you found immediately acceptable" (*Notes towards the
Definition of Culture,* London, 1948, p. 117).

"with the hand to the broom" . . . See "Murder in the Cathedral,"
Poems and Plays 1909–1950, p. 220.

190 Borchardt . . . In his "Brief" in *Eranos* (the volume presented to
Hofmannsthal on his fiftieth birthday in 1924).

". . . the valour . . ." Marta Karlweis, "A Letter to a Doctor about
a Poet," in the *Criterion,* October 1933.

Richter . . . Quoted by Charles du Bos, Approximations: 4 (Paris,
1930), pp. 290–91.

191 *Chandos' Letter* . . . There is a translation by Tania and James Stern
in Hugo von Hofmannsthal, *Selected Prose* (New York, Pantheon
Books, 1952).

". . . to dramatize" . . . In a letter to Schnitzler, quoted in Hammelmann, p. 26.

"jusqu'au paroxysme" . . . Robert Brussel in an article in *Figaro,*
January 24, 1910.

Arthur Symons . . . Here is a passage from Hofmannsthal's text:

> und wir schlachten dir
> die Rosse, die im Hause sind, wir treiben
> sie vor dem Grab zusammen, und sie ahnen
> den Tod und wiehern in die Todesluft
> und sterben, und wir schlachten dir die Hunde,
> weil sie der Wurf sind und der Wurf des Wurfes
> von denen, die mit dir gejagt . . .

and here is Symons' version, departing from the original in moving
the weighty words to different positions in the line, but doing so in an
attempt to gain the equivalent rhetorical effect in English, and otherwise holding strongly to Hofmannsthal:

> and we
> Will slaughter your horses for you and gather them
> About your grave, and they shall snuff up death
> And neigh in the wind of death, and die; and we
> Will slaughter the dogs for you, because the dogs

> Are litter of the litter of that pack
> That hunted with you . . .

The repetitive device is used by Eliot in *Ash-Wednesday*, II (*Poems and Plays 1909–1950*, p. 62):

> Prophesy to the wind, to the wind only for only
> The wind will listen . . .

I do not know whether Eliot ever saw Symons' translation of *Elektra;* what I rather suppose, lacking such knowledge, is that Hofmannsthal and Eliot independently invented a voice of desolate strength leaning on the suggestions of the rhetoric of the Old Testament. A historian considering the development of Old Testament usages in the rhetoric of contemporary poets might also wish to compare the psalmic passages in Henri Franck's *La Danse devant l'Arche* with the psalmic voice in Eliot.

Lugné-Poë . . . See his (rather disappointing) *Sous les Étoiles: souvenirs du théâtre 1902–1912*, p. 236n.

192 Bonnefon . . . In *Figaro*, November 26, 1910, under the rubric "Lettres d'Allemagne."

again presented . . . *Figaro*'s artist attended the revival and drew a cartoon of Elektra, her face sunken, hair falling to her waist, fists clenched, her shadow blotting a high wall: in *Figaro*, December 18, 1910.

194 "Die Sprache . . ." Hofmannsthal's article was written for the Vienna *Merker* in March 1911. I have been unable to see a copy of the *Merker*, and am quoting from the reprint in *Festspiele in Salzburg* (Vienna, 1938) where, side by side with it, is an equally important essay in which Hofmannsthal in 1927 rephrased, but mainly confirmed, his original estimate of the libretto.

In the 1927 paper Hofmannsthal quotes his critic's squib about an eighteenth-century Volapük.

misunderstood . . . See the letters for the late winter and spring of 1911 in *Correspondence between Strauss and Hofmannsthal 1907–1918* (New York, 1927).

195 the Kaiser's . . . See E. Krause, *Richard Strauss* (Leipzig, 1955) and O. Erhardt, *Richard Strauss* (Olten, 1953).

196 It is said . . . See Grover Smith, p. 9.

Edmund Wilson . . . *Axel's Castle* (New York, 1936), pp. 97–98.

challenged . . . See pp. 314 15.

197 "the heart . . ." Letter of January 8, 1911, in *Correspondence* . . .

"Prufrock" . . . Some astonishing interpretations of the light brown hair are being taught in college classrooms. I have heard colleagues analyze the phrase in parenthesis as an expression of disgust!

"Yet when we came back . . ." See "The Waste Land," *Poems and Plays 1909–1950*, p. 38.

198 memoirs . . . See George L. K. Morris in *Partisan Review*, March-April 1954, pp. 231–34.

Whether the thought was connected with the opening of "The Waste Land" or not, Eliot was thinking about the Baltenland aristocracy when he wrote his Marianne Moore review for the *Dial* of 1923. He reverted to the thought to provide a pleasantly resonant — and nostalgic? — piece of dialogue about "One of the *oldest* Baltic families," for the beginning of *The Cocktail Party*.

Chapter 7
Eleven Years: and a Poem for Europe (pages 199–249)

Page

199 *Tancred* . . . Book II, Chapter XI — p. 123 in Longman's reprint of 1924.

Wendell vindicated . . . see *Stelligeri*, p. 89.

200 "obnubilated" . . . Letters, p. 427.

201 *Sanskrit Reader* . . . The quotation is from the preface to the edition of 1884.

"especially timely" . . . So he says in the preface to Vol. IV of the Harvard Oriental Series.

Patanjali . . . Yeats, in a work of his old age, recorded Eliot's view of Woods' translation of *Patanjali*, and contrasted it with his own view: "Some years ago I bought *The Yoga-System of Patanjali*, translated and edited by James Horton Woods and published by the Harvard Press. It is the standard edition, final, impeccable in scholastic eyes, even in the eyes of a famous poet and student of Sanskrit, who used it as a dictionary. But then the poet was at his university, but lately out of school, had not learned to hate all scholar's cant and class-room slang, nor was he an old man in a hurry" — *Introduction to Aphorisms of Yoga by Bhagwan Shree Patanjali done into English . . . by Shree Purohit Swami* (London, 1938, reprinted 1952).

radio talks . . . Published as an appendix to Eliot's *Notes towards the Definition of Culture* (London, 1948).

202 said to be elaborate . . . A. A. MacDonell, *A History of Sanskrit Literature* (London, popular uniform edition 1915), p. 345.

"The Dry Salvages" . . . See *Poems and Plays 1909–1950*, p. 134. And the corresponding middle section of "Little Gidding" opens with a phrase, "There are three conditions," which recalls the formula in Henry Clarke Warren's *Buddhism in Translation*, pp. 215–63: "There are three conditions, O priests, under which deeds are produced . . ."

203 "Rock and no water" . . . See "The Waste Land," *Poems and Plays 1909–1950*, p. 47.
"Let them build the hearth" . . . See "The Cocktail Party," *Poems and Plays 1909–1950*, p. 369.

204 The preacher . . . The scriptures tell how a thousand priests heard the Blessed One deliver the Fire Sermon, and while they listened they were enlightened and relieved of the depravities of the world.

205 acceptance . . . Harold E. McCarthy, in his article on "T. S. Eliot and Buddhism" (*Philosophy East and West*, Vol. II, No. I, April 1952, pp. 31–55) suggests that such acceptance has always been implicit in Buddhism, together with the doctrine of renunciation, and that consequently it has always been implicit in Eliot. But I think that we can scarcely find it in Eliot before the Arjuna episode of "The Dry Salvages."
The household . . . "a good life" . . . See "The Cocktail Party," *Poems and Plays 1909–1950*, p. 364.

206 Babbitt's *Literature and the American College* . . . P. 53.
More's memoir . . . In Manchester and Shepard's *Irving Babbitt: Man and Teacher* (New York, 1941).
a perpetual source . . . But of the two men Babbitt moved the nearer to the Buddhist position. Philip S. Richards, reviewing Babbitt's late essay on *Buddha and the Occident*, pointed out how he distinguished the Buddhist meditation from the "neoplatonic or naturalistic types of mysticism" — "the difference being that Buddhist meditation is ethically strenuous, and associated with renunciation, while the others are emotionally expensive." (The *Criterion*, October 1936).
Virginia lectures . . . *After Strange Gods* (New York, 1934).
bought a copy . . . See Grover Smith, p. 299.
Ushant . . . Pp. 215–16.

207 Anne C. Bolgan . . . In her brilliant doctoral dissertation (Toronto 1960), "Mr. Eliot's Philosophical Writings, or 'What the Thunder said.'"
visiting professor . . . According to the Harvard Catalogue, 1912–13, he gave Philosophy 13, "Leading Ideas of the Present Time"; Philosophy 14, "The History of German Philosophy"; and Philosophy 20, a Seminar in the Philosophy of Religion.
an "independent" . . . See S. H. Mellone in the *International Journal of Ethics*, July 1915, pp. 547–51.

207-8 "This life" . . . See Meyrick Booth in his "Translator's Introductory Note" to Eucken's *Main Currents of Modern Thought* (London, 1912).

208 an opponent . . . Bosanquet, writing in the *Quarterly Review*, August 1914, quoted by Mellone, op. cit. See also *Bernard Bosanquet* *and his Friends,* ed. J. H. Muirhead (London, 1935), pp. 155–56.

209 "That extraordinary" . . . See Eliot's preface to Charlotte Eliot, *Savonarola* (London, 1926).

John Jay Chapman . . . In an article in *Outlook,* July 2, 1919.

210 "red-headed boy" . . . See C. R. Lanman's speech to the American Philosophical Society, April 24, 1937.

As a child . . . See Royce's autobiographical reminiscence at the end of *Papers in Honor of Josiah Royce on his Sixtieth Birthday* (n.d., but apparently published by the American Philosophical Society, which celebrated his sixtieth birthday with two sessions of papers at the annual meeting in 1915).

If error . . . I am borrowing Santayana's exposition in *Character and Opinion in the United States* (New York, 1920), p. 100.

"The darkness declares" and "Those who deny Thee" . . . See "Murder in the Cathedral," *Poems and Plays 1909–1950,* p. 220.

211 "depth and vitality" . . . Preface to *The Problem of Christianity* (New York, 1914), Vol. I, p. ix.

"Loyalty . . ." Ibid., Vol. I, pp. 68–69.

E. A. Singer . . In his contribution to *Papers in Honor of Josiah Royce* . . . "the mind of Europe" . . . *The Sacred Wood* (London, 1920), p. 46.

212 "purify the dialect" . . . "Little Gidding."

"The Problem of Christianity" . . . Royce delivered some of the lectures to the Lowell Institute, Boston, at the end of 1912, and all of them at Manchester College, Oxford, in the Hilary Term of 1913.

"Create me" . . . *The Problem of Christianity,* Vol. I, p. 54.

Man is free . . . There is an essay on this aspect of Royce by Mary Whiton Calkins in *Papers in Honor of Josiah Royce* . . .

"The modern man" . . . *The Problem of Christianity,* Vol. I, p. 236.

213 held up Baudelaire . . . In the Baudelaire essay of 1930, reprinted in *Selected Essays* (London, 1951); see pp. 428–29.

the proof of Celia's differences . . . See "The Cocktail Party," *Poems and Plays 1909–1950,* pp. 361–62.

"Any serial" . . . The brackets in this passage are Royce's. The writing is rapid and rough, and I am not sure of the word "chronology."

defined "ritual" . . . In his *Athenaeum* article, "The Beating of a Drum," October 6, 1923.

214 Woods wrote . . . See Anne C. Bolgan, op. cit., p. 18.

215 Of Babbitt . . . See Eliot's Commentary in the *Criterion,* October 1933.

Of Matthew Arnold . . . See *For Lancelot Andrewes,* p. 77.

possess us and stay . . . So Eliot quoted

> They will come no more
> The old men with beautiful manners

in his review of *Quia Pauper Amavi* in the *Athenaeum*, October 24, 1919, and found himself remembering it and quoting it again in his obituary on Algar Thorold seventeen years later (in the *Criterion*, October 1936).

216 to Harriet Monroe . . . *Letters*, p. 40.

to *Purpose* . . . Of April–June 1938.

In 1920 he wrote . . . in *Chapbook*, No. 9, March.

217 "the fewest possible" . . . F. M. Ford, *It was the Nightingale* (London, 1934), p. 223.

speed is beauty . . . Cf. *Letters*, p. 255. Pound is speaking of Binyon's contrasting view: "Slowness is beauty" — "Which struck me as very odd in 1908 (when I certainly did not believe it)." In 1934 Pound evidently sees complementary virtues in the two views.

218 "consider the excellent" . . . *Letters*, p. 92.

219 "And even the Abstract Entities" . . . See "Whispers of Immortality," *Poems and Plays 1909–1950*, p. 33.

"Accident . . ." See *The Family Reunion*, Part II, Scene II, *Poems and Plays 1909–1950*, p. 279.

220 "Internal darkness . . ." See "Burnt Norton," III, *Poems and Plays 1909–1950*, pp. 121–22.

Eliot noted . . . In *Ezra Pound: his Metric and Poetry* (New York, 1917), p. 19.

Jean de Bosschère . . . See the *Egoist*, October 1917.

221 to Hawthorne . . . In the *Athenaeum*, April 25, 1919.

"flawless cold words" . . . Ford's poem, which deserves to be better known, appeared in *Chapbook* No. 13, July 1920.

222 "Sherlock Holmes" . . . See the *Criterion*, April 1929.

before April 1921 . . . He speaks about Andrewes in his article of that month in *Chapbook* No. 22.

223 "as precious" . . . *For Lancelot Andrewes*, p. 5.

commentaries . . . For example, those of October 1926 and January 1928. *The Rock* was devised on behalf of the churches, and presumably Eliot cooperated in it, regardless of the difficulty of composition at that date, in pursuit of his long sympathy with the cause.

"To one who" . . . See his "London Letter" in the *Dial*, June 1921.

to decry . . . Against Mortimer's disparagement might be set a passage by Frank Harris in *Pearson's Magazine*, October 1919: "Life in London is by far the richest and most varied in the world," etc. But I don't know whether Harris is quite so interesting a witness.

224 "the British writer" . . . In *Tyro*, 2, 1922.

"there is in" . . . See the "London Letter" in the *Dial*.

224 the post-1918 years . . . See his foreword to J. M. Murry, *Katherine Mansfield and other Literary Studies* (London, 1959). See also his memoir of Bruce Richmond in the *T.L.S.*, January 13, 1961.

225 "in touch with" . . . *Letters,* p. 107.

Arnold Bennett . . . See his *Journal 1896–1928* (New York, 1932), p. 639.

Coterie . . . "A Cooking Egg" had appeared in the first issue of *Coterie,* May Day, 1919. Eliot was at one point on the editorial board; he is listed in issues Nos. 3 and 4, but no longer in No. 5.

227 Louis Untermeyer . . . In a review for the *Freeman* (New York), June 30, 1920.

A Writer's Diary . . . Edited by Leonard Woolf (London, 1954), p. 47.

228 the sixtieth birthday book . . . Edited by Richard March and Tambimuttu (London, 1948).

Garsington . . . In the foreword to J. M. Murry's *Katherine Mansfield and other Literary Studies,* cited above, Eliot paid tribute to the circle of Lady Ottoline Morrell as a point of communication between writers before 1919. There he heard of Murry for the first time, there Murry heard of "Prufrock."

"In my earlier" . . . See the first paragraph of *The Classics and the Man of Letters* (London, 1942). For an instance of his early reputation for learning see Douglas Goldring's article on younger critics in *Chapbook* No. 8, February 1920: "His learning is prodigious." In *Coterie* No. 4 Goldring published a skit in not very economical couplets, complaining, under the persona of "a safe young Georgian," that "all is chaos, all confusion" —

and T.S.E.
Uses great words that are as Greek to me.

229 "with decency" . . . *The Cantos of Ezra Pound* (London, 1954), p. 557.

230 Whibley . . . Eliot's well-known essay on Whibley is in *The Sacred Wood* under the heading "Imperfect Critics." He had another word to say about him in the *Dial,* July 1922: "I . . . prize Mr. Whibley because he has read so many things that I have not read, and because he is not a Whig." The second term of the *Dial* compliment is important. Whibley was the biographer of Lord John Manners, once one of Disraeli's Young England group, which looked back to Bolingbroke. Eliot goes on to remark of Whibley: "I do not know who else could write about Bolingbroke"; and he had him write about Bolingbroke in the *Criterion.* Points of relevance to the historian who will plot Eliot's place in the English Tory tradition.

"He was right" . . . *On Poetry and Poets* (London, 1957), p. 205.

231 Little Tich and Nellie Wallace . . . See the *Dial,* December 1922.

233 Richard Aldington . . . The poem appeared in *Coterie* No. 2, September 1919.

the next issue . . . *Chapbook* No. 34.

234 surrender . . . According to Raymond Mortimer, in the *Dial's* "London Letter" for March 1922, *Le Sacre du Printemps* was withdrawn after three London performances.

told the *Dial* . . . Of October 1921. The "Letter" is dated September.

235 another *Dial* letter . . . Printed in August 1921, and dated July.

Rivière . . . See his article in the *NRF*, September 1911, and the two essays, one dated August 1913, the other November 1913, in *Nouvelles Études*.

236 Caesarian operation . . . *Letters*, p. 170.

237 one or two pages . . . Grover Smith, p. 70.

238 "Chaucer retold" . . . *Ezra Pound: his Metric and Poetry* (New York, 1917), p. 9.

designer of the panels . . . This was Edwin Austin Abbey. He contracted for the frieze in 1890; five panels were ready by 1895; the remaining ten by 1901. See *A Description of Edwin Austin Abbey's Quest of the Holy Grail* (Boston, 1936).

239 the mood . . . against these remarks it is only proper to weigh the following passages from Eliot: "I dislike the word 'generation,' which has been a talisman for the last ten years; when I wrote a poem called *The Waste Land* some of the more approving critics said that I had expressed the 'disillusionment of a generation,' which is nonsense. I may have expressed for them their own illusion of being disillusioned, but that did not form part of my intention" (*Thoughts after Lambeth*, 1931).

W. H. R. Rivers . . . See Eliot's "London Letter" in the *Dial*, December 1922.

"What shall I do now?" . . . See "The Waste Land," *Poems and Plays 1909–1950*, p. 41.

240 absence of lubricity . . . See Wendell's *Literary History of America* (London, 1901), pp. 217, 276, 307.

certainly marked . . . Wendell's protégé, the novelist Robert Herrick, has the hero of *His Great Adventure* enlist the help of a Parisian lady in a tour of Paris, has him wine and dine her generously, but never lets him enter her room — though on the last night she sentimentally invites him in, and is puzzled at his courteous refusal. "These Americans!" she sighs to herself.

Geoffrey Tandy . . . In the "Broadcast Chronicle" in the *Criterion*, April 1938.

243 "superb" . . . See Patricia Hutchins, *James Joyce's World* (London, 1957), p. 128.

244 parodied . . . See *Letters of James Joyce*, edited by Stuart Gilbert (London, 1957), p. 231.

247 Faber sprang . . . See the preamble to his *Oxford Apostles* (London, 1933). The book is dedicated "To T. S. Eliot with affection and respect."
248 he appeared . . . When originally drafted, this passage was in the present tense. I learned of Sir Geoffrey Faber's death only after completion of the typescript. The editor of the Christ Church *Bulletin* for 1961 says, reporting his loss:

> "Literarum quaesivit gloriam
> Videt Dei.

Landor's tremendous lines on John Wellerby might have been written for him."
The Buried Stream . . . (London, 1951).
his second volume . . . Called *In the Valley of Vision*. Eliot's review appeared in the *Egoist*, August 1918.
sonnets . . . In *The Buried Stream*, pp. 245–47.

Chapter 8
The Editor and His Contributors (pages 250–299)

Page
250 Yeats . . . See *Poetry* (Chicago), April 1920.
Allan Tate . . . On "The Function of a Critical Quarterly," in the *Southern Review*, Winter 1936.
MacAlpine . . . In the *Criterion*, April 1925.
Metta . . . Ibid., November 1927.
in defense . . . Ibid., July 1930.
251 protest . . . Ibid., January 1930.
"stupidity" . . . Ibid., December 1928. It should be added in fairness that Eliot is reviewing not a clinical work but *The Future of an Illusion*.
Rivière . . . Ibid., July 1923.
Thomas Mann . . . Ibid., July 1933.
Mairet . . . Ibid., April 1937.
253 Pound addressed . . . See J. J. Espey, *Ezra Pound's Mauberley* (London, 1955), p. 82.
254 In 1925 . . . In the *Criterion*, January 1925 ("Commentary").
255 Bain's portrait . . . Ibid., February 1924.
"refuse to identify" . . . Ibid., October 1931 ("Commentary").
256 monastic . . . Thibaudet once compared the Pontigny meetings of the thirties with Cluny: "C'est en multipliant ces lieux de rencontre, comme les abbayes d'autrefois, qu'on aménage une Amitié des Nations, qui corresponde dans le spirituel à ce qui est au temporel la Société des Nations . . . Que se multiplient ces abbayes temporaires,

ces libres sociétés spirituelles, ces lieux de dialogue aux carrefours. Il pourrait en sortir des abbayes permanentes. Au delà de Vienne, au delà de Genève, songeons a Cluny . . ." (See "Lettre à Albert" in the *NRF*, July 1936).

257 George Every . . . In the *Criterion* of April 1938.
Orage . . . Ibid., January 1935.

258 "that balance . . ." Ibid., January 1937.
"the detached" . . . See a reference in the *Criterion*, April 1938, to Eliot's contribution to *Twentieth Century Verse*'s special Wyndham Lewis number.

259 manifesto . . . Reprinted in *Festspiele in Salzburg* (Vienna, 1938) under the title "Der Erste Aufruf zum Salzburger Festspielplan."

260 a common tradition . . . The Commentary in the *Criterion*, August 1927, bears on the question.
"was only one" . . . See Eliot's contribution to *Freundesgabe für Ernst Robert Curtius*, edited by Max Rychner (Bern, 1956).

261 Rychner tracing . . . In the *Criterion* of December 1927.
a "Latin" country . . . Ibid., October 1923 (in "Notes").

262 born Teuton . . . Ibid., December 1928. And compare ibid., September 1927 and April 1933.
Marichalar . . . Ibid., July 1938.

263 broadcast talks . . . Appendix to *Notes towards the Definition of Culture* (London, 1948).
Hamburg lecture . . . "Goethe as the Sage" in *On Poetry and Poets* (London, 1957).

264 "Alcestis and Savitri" . . . In the *Criterion*, July 1923.

265–66 discussed *Harriet Frean* . . . In the *Dial*, September 1922.

266 "And when I say" . . . See "The Cocktail Party," *Poems and Plays 1909–1950*, p. 368.

268 "For good or ill . . ." See "Murder in the Cathedral," *Poems and Plays 1909–1950*, p. 179.

270 "What there is to conquer" . . . See "East Coker," *Poems and Plays 1909–1950*, p. 128.
"Time past . . ." See "Burnt Norton," *Poems and Plays 1909–1950*, p. 118.

271 Charles Smyth . . . For the *Criterion* of January 1939 — the last number. There is an interesting reference to Smyth, and to the High Church spirit that prevailed among his friends at Corpus Christi College, Cambridge, in Paul Elmer More's letters: see A. H. Dakin, *Paul Elmer More* (Princeton, 1960), p. 265.

272 the *Advocate* . . . Of November 8, 1907.
Bel Esprit . . . See *Letters*, p. 175.
she left . . . I am indebted for the information to Alan Denson who consulted the will.

273 *Defence of Idealism* . . . Published London, 1917.
   "unclean" . . . *Defence*, p. 248.
   "that most exquisite" . . . Loc. cit., p. 253.
   "admirable psychoanalysts" . . . Loc. cit., p. 270.
274 "Jones's Karma" . . . In the *Criterion,* October 1923.
276 "The Grandmother" . . . Ibid., February 1924.
   "There are three conditions" . . . See "Little Gidding," *Poems and
   Plays 1909–1950,* p. 142.
277 "Few are . . ." *Defence of Idealism,* p. 274.
   Mario Praz . . . In the *Criterion,* July 1929.
   T. O. Beachcroft . . . Ibid., October 1932.
278 "to write poetry . . ." Matthiessen, *Achievement,* p. 90.
280 "Descend lower . . ." See "Burnt Norton," *Poems and Plays 1909–
   1950,* p. 120.
281 "the light is still . . ." See "Burnt Norton," *Poems and Plays 1909–
   1950,* p. 121.
   "I said to my soul . . ." See "East Coker," *Poems and Plays 1909–
   1950,* p. 126. The lines a little lower, which begin with the same
   phrase, are on the same page.
283 in *The Music* . . . See *On Poetry and Poets* (London, 1957), p. 36.
   Among the "signs" Eliot had certainly seen was Auden's sestina,
   "Hearing of harvests rotting in the valley," published in the *Criterion,*
   July 1933, and probably certain poems of Empson's which appeared
   in the lively *Contemporary Poetry and Prose.*
284 *poésie des départs* . . . See *Selected Essays* (London, 1952), p. 428.
   The essay, on Baudelaire, is dated 1930.
285 builds Dante's structure . . . Perhaps I should have given Eliot's
   own account of his conquest of the form. It is part of his "Talk on
   Dante" in the *Adelphi,* First Quarter, 1951.
286 "Sin is Behovely . . ." See "Little Gidding," *Poems and Plays 1909–
   1950,* p. 142.
   Sibelius . . . One of the concert programs preserved in the Houghton Library shows that Eliot heard Sibelius' Fourth Symphony in
   Sanders Theatre on November 13, 1913. It was the first Cambridge
   performance.
   Sullivan . . . As preface to Sullivan's *Isaac Newton* (London, 1938)
   there is a memoir of the author by Charles Singer.
   Roger Hinks . . . In the *Criterion,* November 1927.
287 That essay . . . One or two confusions in it have been pointed out
   by Stanley Edgar Hyman in *The Armed Vision.*
288 "Clangs . . ." See "The Dry Salvages," *Poems and Plays 1909–1950,*
   p. 131.
288–89 in Vienna . . . See Hofmannsthal's "Vienna Letter" in the *Dial,*
   October 1922.

289 "Out at sea . . ." See "East Coker," *Poems and Plays 1909–1950*, p. 124.

290 ballad-howling . . . In Eliot's undergraduate years at Harvard John Lomax began his pioneer collection of the songs of Texas and the plains, and Wendell and Kittredge appealed to the students to supply him with any material they knew. Eliot was then playing the dandy and searching for strength in city corner, and my supposition, perhaps quite wrong, is that he affected to disregard the undertaking; and yet, with his usual curiosity and good sense, took in what was happening; and that later his interest in the strong voice of the open spaces grew as his interest in anthropology grew, leading to the ballads of Mrs. Porter and the One-Eyed O'Reilly.

for the *Egoist* . . . Of December 1917.

292 "What about that poker game?" See "Sweeney Agonistes," *Poems and Plays 1909–1950*, p. 78.

296 Charles du Bos . . . See his *Journal, III, 1926–27* (Paris, 1949), p. 275.

299 those three . . . See pp. 248–49.

"It is after all" . . . See *Letters*, p. 170.

Chapter 9
Drama (pages 300–340)

IN HIS lecture on "Poetry and Drama," delivered at Harvard in 1951, Eliot candidly discussed his objectives and progress in poetic drama from *Murder in the Cathedral* to *The Cocktail Party*. I have abstained from quoting it in detail and from rehearsing its points, an instead have tried to review the importance and interest of his plays in the light, first, of the theoretical studies which preceded them, secondly, of the theories and practice of contemporaries whom he respected. But it is both an essential document for the study of his work and one of his most illuminating essays. It is to be found in his volume *On Poetry and Poets* (1957).

Page

300 "Let us go then . . ." "The Love Song of J. Alfred Prufrock," *Poems and Plays 1909–1950*, p. 3.

301 Toryism . . . Sometimes he actually used the old nomenclature. In his article on "The Function of Criticism" in the *Criterion*, October 1923, he said that men who live according to the inner voice are "Whigs."

"It is absurd" . . . Quoted in H. A. Hammelmann, *Hugo von Hofmannsthal* (London, 1957), p. 25.

"mingling . . . speaking" . . . Ibid., p. 20.

302 the box office . . . See p. 149.

Seymour Hicks . . . See "Dramatis Personae" in the *Criterion,* April
1923.
"between the conventional . . ." Loc. cit.
Miss Ethel Levey . . . See the *Dial,* June 1921.
Mistinguett . . . Ibid., May 1922.
Arthur Symons . . . In *Ave* (p. 40 of Heinemann's edition of 1947)
George Moore writes: "We fell to talking about Symons, who spent
his evenings at the Alhambra and the Empire, watching the ballet.
Having written *Symbolism in Literature,* he was now investigating the
problem of symbolism in gesture. Or was it symbolism in rhythm or
rhythmic symbolism?" Frank Harris, writing in *Pearson's Magazine*
(New York), February 1919, says that Symons, when they first met
around 1890, "professed himself an admirer of the music halls, then
just beginning to be popular in London."
   An interesting recollection of the status of ballet in England in 1911
is printed by A. R. Jones, *The Life and Opinions of Thomas Ernest
Hulme* (London, 1960), p. 92. His informant is D. L. Murray, whose
memories are all confirmed by the last section of Compton Mac-
Kenzie's *Sinister Street.*
303 England paused . . . See F. M. Ford, *It Was the Nightingale* (London, 1934), p. 178.
the obituary notice . . . In the *Criterion,* January 1923. Eliot also
wrote about Marie Lloyd in his "London Letter" for the *Dial* of December 1922.
304 A. E. Coppard . . . In *It's Me, O Lord!* (London, Methuen, 1957),
p. 154.
Cummings . . . See Charles Norman, *The Magic Maker* (New York,
1958), p. 39 (for early curiosity at Harvard), pp. 132–39 (for the
period following 1918).
Cocteau's argument . . . See "Dramatis Personae" in the *Criterion,*
April 1923.
305 "dignity" . . . In the "London Letter" in the *Dial,* December 1922.
"Davidson . . ." In Eliot's preface to *John Davidson: a Selection of
his Poems,* edited by M. Lindsay (London, Hutchinson, 1961).
306 the *N.R.F.* . . . acclaiming . . . See, for example, Henri Ghéon on
"Les Ballets Russes," August 1910 and August 1911. And in the issue
of November 1911, Ghéon wrote, foreshadowing Cocteau and Eliot,
on the question of the popular theatre. The elite audience had withdrawn from the genuinely popular vaudeville and from police-plays.
What conditions were required for a new popular tragedy? Two:
"l'ardeur du verbe qui fera fondre et soudera entre elles les âmes mul-
tiples, diverses, contraires de tout un peuple rassemblé"; and plot.
Rilke . . . R. M. Rilke und Marie von Thurn und Taxis, *Briefwechsel*
(Zurich, 1951), Vol. I, p. 47.

Karsavina . . . See, for example, Charles Ricketts, *Self-Portrait* (London, 1939), pp. 174, 177, 179.

the dress rehearsal . . . Ibid., p. 236.

Rite of Spring . . . In his Commentary in the *Criterion*, October 1924, Eliot says: "The writer of these lines recalls his efforts, several years ago, to restrain (with the point of an umbrella) the mirth of his neighbours in a 'family house' which seemed united to deride Sokalova at her best in the *Sacre du Printemps*."

307 Stonehenge . . . In his paper on "Baudelaire in our Time," written in 1927 and reprinted in *For Lancelot Andrewes* and *Essays Ancient and Modern*, Eliot points out that the men of the nineties, Lionel Johnson and Symons, had some awareness of ritual.

I would add that no one understood better than Wagner how drama includes the ritual of ceremony (and how it requires a compelling repetitive pattern, which, however, he did not call ritual). But by an almost Yeatsian misconception, Wagner desired to restrict and reserve his last work, which is conspicuously ritualistic. *Parsifal,* he said, must be played only in his own music temple at Bayreuth. He resisted proposals from the commercial stage: "The Sacred Festival Drama 'Parsifal' — with its action touching directly upon the Mysteries of the Christian Faith — cannot possibly be included in the operatic repertoires of our theatres." King Ludwig agreed. The public did not. The public claimed *Parsifal* and abetted the managers in practically tearing it from him. *Reedy's Mirror,* describing the New York winter season of 1904, tells of special trains carrying audiences to *Parsifal* from every city: audiences which patiently sat through the early episodes waiting to participate in the ritual of the Grail. Freya Stark, remembering her student days, says that in 1913 London flocked to *Parsifal* "as to a ritual."

Although Wagner contended otherwise, a dramatic action which touches directly on the Mysteries may for that very reason be proper for the regular theatre.

309 B. G. Brooks . . . The review appeared in the *Criterion* in April 1925, but Brooks says that he is recalling "one Thursday evening in the autumn of 1923."

Eliot's *Criterion* "Commentary" of June 1926 reveals that he is an admirer of the Maddermarket Theatre.

in the *Dial* . . . March 1923.

criticized . . . Synge . . . In the *Egoist*, August 1917. Eliot was reviewing Fenellosa and Pound, *Noh, or Accomplishment*. His strictures on the Kiltartan speech arose from a remark by a *Times* critic who had found in one of Pound's exchanges a "not unpleasant reminder of *The Well of the Saints*."

Questions of dialect apart, intuition instructed Synge in a technique

Eliot learned very slowly: the incorporation of a rite into a play. See the marriage rite in *Deirdre:* "By the sun and moon and the whole earth, I wed Deirdre to Naisi. May the air bless you, and water and the wind, the sea and all the hours of the sun and moon." This might be set beside the prayers at the end of Act II of *The Cocktail Party.*

310 the *Chapbook* . . . No. 21.
"intimate conversation" . . . Quoted (from *Portraits from Life*) by Richard A. Cassell, *Ford Madox Ford, a Study of His Novels* (Baltimore, 1961, p. 63.
fertile *Chapbook* . . . See No. 27.

312 "the first detective story" . . . So he says in the *Criterion*, April 1929. And see his notes on the tradition of the detective story in the *Criterion*, June 1927.

313 "Fine art . . . " See his "London Letter" in the *Dial*, December 1923.
Edwin Muir . . . In the *Freeman*, October 24, 1923.
Punch . . . Of June 10, 1925.
the *New Statesman* . . . Of June 6, 1925.

314 Edward Sackville-West . . . In the *Spectator*, June 6, 1925.
reflecting . . . See *The Sacred Wood*, p. 77.

315 "Mr. Ezekiel Ton" . . . For Eliot's angry quotation of this attack see *Ezra Pound: his Metric and Poetry* (New York, 1917), p. 18, where he says that *Punch* "is always a pretty reliable barometer of the English middle-class Grin."
symphonic ballet . . . See *Correspondence between Strauss and Hofmannsthal 1907–1918* (New York, 1927), pp. 166–69.
"Aeschylus . . ." See Eliot's Commentary in the *Criterion*, June 1936.

316 "Novices . . ." *The Sacred Wood*, p. 70.

318 "protruding point" . . . See Hofmannsthal's article in the *Dial*, March 1923.
Thomas Mann . . . In the *Dial*, June 1923.

319 not admit . . . cleavage . . . Compare Eliot's *Religious Drama: Mediaeval and Modern* (New York, 1954).
"for every evil . . ." See "Murder in the Cathedral," *Poems and Plays 1909–1950*, p. 197.

320 described . . . In the *Dial* article of March 1923.
"acting is suffering" . . . See "Murder in the Cathedral," *Poems and Plays 1909–1950*, p. 182.

323 "any form . . ." In the *Criterion*, June 1936. Eliot was reviewing J. M. Murry's *Shakespeare*. Murry had said that drama was "the highest and fullest kind of poetry." Eliot made his point in qualification of this statement.

New Haven . . . See p. 156. And compare the italicized word "transparent" in his 1951 lecture on "Poetry and Drama" — See *On Poetry and Poets* (London, 1957), p. 75.

324 "Yes, we'll pray for you!" . . . See "Murder in the Cathedral," *Poems and Plays 1909–1950*, p. 204.

"I have always told Amy" . . . See "The Family Reunion," *Poems and Plays 1909–1950*, p. 225.

"A minor trouble" . . . See "The Family Reunion," *Poems and Plays 1909–1950*, p. 265.

326 "jeunesse" . . . See Cocteau's "Scandales," printed in French in the *Criterion*, January 1926.

McEachran's article . . . In the *Criterion*, January 1938.

327 recently told . . . In his interview with Donald Hall for the *Paris Review*, Spring–Summer 1959.

Jessie Weston . . . In *From Ritual to Romance* (Cambridge, England, 1920), pp. 96–98.

"And the Son of Man" . . . See "The Rock," *Poems and Plays 1909–1950*, p. 106.

328 "if we regard" . . . See *Religious Drama: Mediaeval and Modern* (New York, 1954).

329 "Leicht muss man sein" . . . H. von Hofmannsthal, *Der Rosenkavalier* (Berlin, 1924), p. 59.

330 Sophron . . . See his "Vienna Letter" in the *Dial*, July 1922.

grandeur . . . Carl J. Burckhardt wrote: "in diesem Stück wollte er einer sozialen Schicht, dem imperialen spanisch-deutschen Hochadel Österreichs, auf dem Wege des Sichtbarmachens durch eine leichte Übertragung, ein Denkmal im Augenblick seines Aufhörens und Versinkens setzen." And this not because he belonged to the Austrian aristocracy, but "alles Soziale, so fern es wirklich und nicht nachgeahmt ist, hatte für ihn eine sinnbildliche Bedeutung." See *Hugo von Hofmannsthal: die Gestalt des Dichters im Spiegel der Freunde*, ed. H. A. Fiechtner (Vienna, 1949), p. 128.

332 translations . . . Eliot gave them both to Guy Manton for review. The review appeared in the *Criterion*, July 1937.

334 "Love within a family" . . . See *The Elder Statesman* (London, 1959), p. 72.

reintroduce . . . Compare *On Poetry and Poets* (London, 1957), pp. 85–86.

335 *New Republic* . . . Of December 12, 1928. For an early exhibition of violence against Shaw, see the *Egoist* of May 1918, where, over the pseudonym T. S. Apteryx, Eliot said: "Shaw's work has nothing to do with literature, either for good or evil."

337 *The Seafarer* . . . See *Ezra Pound: his Metric and Poetry* (New York, 1917), p. 17.

338 "Think, my Lord" . . . See "Murder in the Cathedral," *Poems and Plays 1909–1950*, p. 185.

339 "Bicycling . . ." C. Day Lewis, *From Feathers to Iron* (London, 1931).
"The land of the lobelias" . . . See "The Rock," *Poems and Plays 1909–1950*, p. 103.

340 "We know about the railway accident" . . . See "The Family Reunion," *Poems and Plays 1909–1950*, p. 243.

Index

said, too, that it was a way in which we tempt Fate to bring down upon us the thing that we dread could happen – the disclosure of our secret. Shout it out and control it that way. That's how he explained it.

"But I didn't really care about the explanation; what moved me was the fact that I had found something that I didn't think could exist. And that thing – the thing that I found – was very simple. Most people know all about it and have never really doubted it because their lives have been such as to give them a glimpse of this thing that they were not sure about, which is love, of course: the sheer fact of feeling love for another, of finding the one person – the only person, it seems – who makes the world make sense. It's like discovering the map that you've been looking for all your life and have never been able to find – the map that makes sense of the journey."

"George …"

"No, I don't expect you to love me back, because that doesn't always happen, does it? So I accept that this is the way it is to be."

"Can't we just somehow get over this? I wanted …"

He brushed this aside; it seemed that he was determined to finish what he wanted to say. "I shall continue to do what I'm doing, which is to be a doctor sorting out people's minor medical problems most of the time and every so often, I suppose, being able to do something more important for them. And I shall do this in a place that I don't really like – a place that I think has a tainted notion at its heart – that money should be able to be stashed away without doing anything for the people who actually do the work to produce it. I'm stuck with all that because even in places like this there are poor people and people who are treated badly and who need help with their varicose veins and digestive

how she would indicate by a casual, friendly demeanour that she bore no resentment or disappointment; that whatever had happened was a long time ago – three years was sufficient for people to get over most things, she felt, except, perhaps, sexual involvement: that was more difficult – the memory of intimacy was always there in the background, no matter how casually treated; the other had been admitted to the personal realm as others, acquaintances, friends, colleagues, had not.

But none of the scripts she had prepared came to her in this setting, before the tennis club noticeboard, where the opening remark had been about crime and a missing tennis racquet.

Banality came to her rescue. "Sometimes I wish somebody would steal my racquet," she said. "My game might improve with a new one."

He laughed. "I saw that you were having a lesson. I'm beyond all professional help, I'm afraid."

He looked at her, as if expecting her to comment on his tennis – she had never seen him play   but she said nothing. He waited, before continuing: "I thought you were never going to return."

She looked askance. "Why shouldn't I?"

"I just made the assumption."

"Well, you were wrong. Here I am."

He nodded. "You have the kids with you – so I assume it won't be for long."

She confirmed it would be for the duration of the school holidays and then she would return to Scotland, but only for a short while. "I'm coming back more permanently. Billy's going back to the Prep."

She saw that he seemed pleased to hear this news, and she became guarded. "I don't think that we should …"

He interrupted her. "Should what? Talk to one another?"

"I didn't say that. But I don't think it would be wise, after what happened, for us to be seen together too often."

Again he queried her. "What counts as too often in this place? Once a month? Once a year?"

She spelled it out. "Too often means ever. I suppose I'd say that we shouldn't really see one another at all."

He raised his voice in protest, causing her to glance anxiously down the veranda; they were still by themselves. There was a note of frustration in his voice now. "I don't see what harm there is in two friends occasionally seeing one another."

"George," she said, "there's such a thing as disingenuousness. We can't pretend that we didn't, well, fall for one another."

He looked away, as if it was painful to be reminded.

"We can't pretend," she went on, "that people don't know that our marriages suffered as a result: you know what this place is like for gossip. We happen to live in a village of married couples. There are the keepers, with all their money, and the kept – and I'm one of the kept – and there are lots of us; it's just the way it is."

He interrupted her. "I've never heard it described that way …"

She ignored the interruption. "My marriage more or less came to an end and now I'm rekindling it. I don't want to go through a separation again – or, worse still, a divorce."

"Don't sell yourself short. You've got a mind. You're not one of these women with nothing in their heads but thoughts of their next cocktail party or shopping trip to Miami. You're not that at all."

"Maybe not, but the reality of the situation is that I have no career. David and I can get on. We have children, and one of

them is still quite young."

He looked at her with a mixture of disappointment and pity. "So you've made your bed and you're going to lie in it."

"You could put it that way. I'm being realistic."

He stared at her mutely.

"I'm sorry," she said. "I was very anxious about meeting you again. And now I've upset you."

He looked away. "You're right, though. We can't, can we?"

"Not really."

"It would have been …"

"It would have been good for both of us, yes, but I don't think we can."

He took a step away, and lowered his voice. "Let me tell you something," he said. "For the last three years, there has not been a day – not a single day – in which I haven't thought about you. Not necessarily for long periods, but even just for a few seconds – a fleeting thought, you'd call it – in which you have been there, in my mind, and I have let you in, so to speak."

She wanted to say: *me too, me too*. But she remained silent. *Do not tell your love.*

"Sometimes," he went on, "when I've been driving to work in the car, doing something as mundane as that, I've thought of you and I've whispered your name, or called it out, even, as if in agony. Why should I do this? Why should you have got under my skin to such an extent that I behave in a way that my psychiatric colleagues would find interesting? In fact – and this may amuse you – I mentioned this – disguising details, of course – to a psychiatrist friend and he said to me, 'Oh, that's not all that unusual; that's how agony is released, by shouting out the name of the person or the thing that haunts the mind.' And he problems and their conjunctivitis and, yes, their deaths. And I'll do that because I'm the one who happens to be around to do it. I'm not being Albert Schweitzer or anything like that, I'm just doing a job that I happen to do. And I won't mind too much that I can't talk to anybody about this – other than you – because I can't find the words with which to open up to them. So, fine, I give you your freedom from this thing that happened to us and I promise you I'll respect what you have to do, which is what you've told me."

He stopped, and she reached out to him instinctively. "George …"

She withdrew her hand. A man and two women had appeared at the end of the veranda and had tossed their racquets down on a table. One of the women had looked in their direction and had seen her reach out to George. She was sure of that.

21

Ted had said to Clover: "Listen, if you feel awkward about going to the party, then why not come with me? Why not?"

He did not wait for her to reply. "We could walk," he said. "It's not far. I'll swing by and collect you."

She was at pains to say that she felt no awkwardness, although she was not sure that he believed her. Ted had a way of looking at you when you spoke as if he were weighing up the truthfulness or otherwise of what you said; Ted could tell. "I don't mind," she said, looking away to avoid his scrutiny. "It's just that I'm not sure that I want to go."

"But everybody …"

She chided him gently. "You don't have to do something just because everybody else is doing it."

He grinned at her. "You do, actually."

"I don't know what you mean."

He had written an essay on conformity, and he told her about it. "I got an A for it, as it happens."

"Clever you."

"Well, I got quite a lot of it from the web, although I put it in my own words. There's this fantastic site about personal psychology – it's called something like *The Authentic You*. It says that at some stages in your life you really want to conform – you really don't want to stand out. And you know when that is?"

She shrugged.

"Now. Right now. The stage we're at. Where we are."

"That is – if we're at the same stage."

He looked at her blankly. "We're both sixteen."

She pointed out, half-playfully, that boys and girls developed at different rates. "Sorry about that, Ted, but we're more mature."

"That's what you think."

"No, it's what psychologists think."

He was not convinced. "You wish."

"It's true."

He returned to the subject of the party. "Please come. James will be pleased."

She looked away. "You said something about a Canadian girl."

"Laura."

She had remembered the name, but had not wanted to utter it. "Her. You said that she and James are seeing one another."

"Yes, they are. But you know something?"

Her heart gave a leap; perhaps he had heard that it was over. "What?"

"I don't think it's going to last."

She asked him why he should think this, and he replied that he thought that James was bored. "He may like her, but ..."

"But what?"

"She looks at him all the time, you see. I think I told you. Imagine what it must be like to have somebody looking at you all the time. Just think of it."

Her voice was even. "He probably feels ... probably feels guilty, or something. You shouldn't look at people."

"Not at all."

She hesitated. "Well, maybe a bit. Now and then."

He thought that everybody looked at people. "You can't go around looking away all the time. How can you?"

"You have to be careful not to become obsessed."

He was staring at her. "Yes," he said, thoughtfully. "You have to." And then he continued, "Please say you'll come with me.

You can't have anything better to do round here. Come on."

"If you really want me to."

"I do, Clove. I do."

She wanted to go, of course, and did not want to go. She thought of her mother's advice – if it really had been advice, and if it had actually been given: it was not pressed upon her, as advice usually is – rather it was trailed before her, hinted at. You could make yourself unhappy so easily by wanting something that you might never get; that unhappiness could be avoided by the simple expedient of thinking of something – or somebody – else. Of course that was right. She had seen it a hundred times in the magazines that she and her friends read at school: the problem pages spelled it out with wearying familiarity: don't allow a boy to ruin your life; don't waste your time; move on. They were right, of course – she knew that – but it was easier said than done. She should ignore James's party, but Ted wanted her to go with him and she could at least oblige him. Ted liked James; he was perhaps a little bit infatuated by him; could boys be infatuated with other boys, and not be gay? She had talked about that with a friend at school who told her that her brother constantly talked about another boy. "He drives me mad," she said. "He thinks this boy is just great. The great Anthony: Anthony the Great. He tells me everything *Ant* says. It's all the usual stuff, but he still tells me. I think he wants to *be* him. That's what it is, I think. He wants to *be* him. Go and be *Ant*, I said to him, and he just stared at me. "

Their conversation had come back to her later. It was not so much the question of how boys felt about each other that interested her – she thought that for the most part boys were indifferent to other boys; they liked to impress each other, but there was not much more to it than that. What fired her imagination was the thought that people might want to be somebody else. Was that what happened when you fell for somebody? Did you really want to be him, or did you want to be yourself *beside* him? She tried to imagine what it would be like to be James. She closed her eyes and then opened them as if she were inside James, looking out at the world with his eyes. It did not work.

No, she yearned for something quite different from what she imagined James wanted. She wanted to be with him; she wanted to listen to him because everything he said was somehow ... What was it? Was it anything different from what Ted or any other boy said? Yes, it was. It was different, but she could not decide why this should be so. James was funny. James looked at you in a particular way when he spoke and that made the words seem different. James was beautiful. James made everything seem special, as if the sheer fact of his presence cast a light upon what was around him that was simply not there in his absence. Margaret used to say that about Jesus. She said: *The Lord makes everything shine, you know. He makes it so different that you scratch your head and ask: is this the same place? Is this Jamaica? Is this Cayman? Or is it the Lord's special place?* Margaret had religion, and people who had religion said things like that; sang them too. But leaving Jesus and the Lord to one side, she wondered how one person, a boy, could do this? How could one person transform the world about him?

She had not allowed herself to use the word – at least about herself and James. But now she did. Now she thought she was approaching the heart of what was happening; she had fallen in love with him. This was the mysterious thing that people talked about so much, that was in almost every line of every song, written into the digital code of every mp3. Love. This is what it was. It was like a wave. It was like being covered by a great wave coming in off the open ocean; a wave that rolled you over and over, making you tumble helplessly in its force, rendering you unable to do anything about it because it was so strong. That was what it was like, and it was happening to her. She could admit that now. She loved James.

And what can you do if you are in love? What are you *meant* to do? Do you throw yourself at the person you love? Do you tell him how you feel and place yourself at his mercy? Or do you wait until the moment comes when what you are experiencing within yourself is somehow reciprocated and the feelings of two people coincide? The problem with that was that if she did nothing, James would be lost to her, and then somebody else – some girl from Vancouver – would step in and take him away. Lure him away with sex. Give him what every boy wanted and thought about all the time, if you could believe what you read about that.

Ted had hinted – in a smutty, childish way – that this is what had already happened. She could not bear to think about that. How dare she even *touch* him: slut. Even if they only kissed, that was too much. Her lips all over him, parted like the lips of a … mollusc. Mollusc. Her saliva in a little trail on his chin. Her teeth. Her disgusting, greedy lips. Her busy hands. Now she felt a new emotion: hatred. She hated that Canadian girl. She wished that she would die. No, she did not; you could not think that. She was a girl, just like she was. She had parents who probably loved her and would be upset if she were dead. You could not think that. Or just a little bit dead – dead for a short time – and then discovered still to be alive. No. Injured somehow. Run over, perhaps; not too badly, but enough to put her legs in plaster. No, that was cruel; you should not think cruel things about real people, and I will not. I will not. Sent away then. Sent back to Vancouver for doing something illegal in Cayman. Marched out of the country and being seen at the airport handcuffed to a fat Caymanian policewoman who ate too much unhealthy food and who wanted to get home to eat more fried conch and rum cake. Parents crying and waving goodbye; their only daughter disgraced on the front page of every newspaper; *We had no idea she was such a slut*, they said to the press. The Cayman Airways plane with its piratical, one-legged turtle painted on it waiting for her; people staring out of the windows and pointing at her. *Goodbye. Goodbye.* The sound of the plane's engine and its blast blowing leaves and sand back across the runway like one of those high winds. Back to a school in Vancouver – a girls' school – where there would be no boys to ogle or seduce. A school run by nuns, perhaps – if there were any of those left; they had them in Quebec still and they would come and scold you in French. A school where the dormitories were actually small cells with barred windows out of which, if you stood on a chair and peered, you might just see boys in the distance, all of them unaware of you; far away, out of reach.

She stopped herself. It was not in her nature to be unkind; in fact, she was naturally quite the opposite. *I am an ordinary girl, with ordinary feelings; that's all.* She would not think such thoughts; she would make a real effort to like Laura, to see her better points ... her hair, for instance. She stopped herself again.

In a moment of honesty, she said to Ted as they walked together up the short tarmac drive of the Collins house: "I feel nervous,

Ted. Sorry, but I do."

Ted turned to look at her. He smiled. "Of course you do, Clove. We feel nervous about people we like a lot. We feel worried in case they won't like us as much as we like them." He paused. "I feel nervous too."

It occurred to her that it was not just for her sake that he had suggested she accompany him to the party. "Because …" she began.

He hesitated. "Same as you," he muttered.

She reached out to him, but said nothing.

"I spoke to somebody once. He said I'd grow out of it. That's what he actually said."

"Maybe you will."

He laughed. "Nobody says that any more. But at least with James I know it's no use. I can be his friend – that's all."

She felt a rush of sympathy for the boy beside her. "Isn't that enough?"

"It'll have to be." He paused. "But don't think I'm unhappy – or all that unhappy. I'm not."

"Good."

"So let's go in."

James answered the door. She looked up and saw him; then she glanced at Ted. He was smiling, as was James.

"Clove?"

"Yes."

"Ages …" He stepped forward, grinning, and put his arms about her. "Ages and ages."

She felt his cheek against hers. "It's been …"

"Ages," he said. "Ted told me he had been in touch with you. Sorry, I haven't myself. I've …"

His explanation died away, and she helped him. "It doesn't matter."

"Cool. You must give me your e-mail."

He held her away from him, looking at her. She felt his eyes upon her, and she blushed.

James turned to Ted. "She's just as pretty as she always was, isn't she, Ted?"

Ted nodded. "More, even."

James gestured towards the inside of the house. "My folks are out until midnight. We've got the house till then."

"Great," said Ted. "Who's coming?"

James shrugged. "Everyone," he said. "You'll know everybody, or just about everybody." He smiled. "About twelve people max."

They heard voices from further inside the house, which, like many houses of its vintage on the island, was a rambling warren of cool interiors. "That's them," James continued. "In the kitchen."

Twelve, thought Clover, and winced inwardly. At a large party she could have avoided Laura if she chose to; with twelve it would be impossible. She glanced at Ted, who understood. "Laura?" he said. "Is Laura here?"

James shook his head. "They've gone to Florida for Christmas. Clearwater, I think."

For Clover, it was a release from dread. "I wanted to meet her," she blurted out, and immediately regretted it; he might ask how she knew; he might ask what Laura was to her.

But he did not. He smiled at her. "You'll like her. I think she wanted to meet you too." He paused. "She heard we were old friends."

"Oh."

"Yes. Next time, maybe."

They moved through the house, to join the other guests in the kitchen. There was music playing, and a couple of girls were emptying packets of snacks into bowls. There was a large container of popcorn and a bowl of what looked like fruit punch. One of the boys, whom she recognised as having been in the year above her at the Prep School, smiled at her as he poured a bottle of vodka into the punch. He poured her a glass, which she took gingerly. She did not like alcohol and would make one drink suffice for the evening.

They drifted out onto the patio, lit by a line of white lights strung along the eaves of the house. There was a pool, as there was with most of the houses in the area, shabbier than their own and with a water slide that leaned drunkenly to one side. "If you swim," said James, "don't get on that. Nobody's used it for five years."

She sat with Ted and James by the side of the pool, their feet resting on the first step below the water. For a brief moment she felt James's right foot touch her own, and remain there briefly until he moved it away. She glanced at him, and he returned her glance in a way that she thought was encouraging. She wondered whether she should move her foot back, but did not.

"I can't tell you how good it is to see you," he said. "And you, too, Ted. The three of us again."

"Like old times," said Ted.

"Yeah, like old times."

There was a burst of laughter from somewhere behind them; the party was getting going, but James seemed content to be talking just to them. He asked Clover about Strathearn and whether she liked it and whether there was anybody there he would know. Then Ted volunteered some information about the boarding school he was at. "It calls itself progressive," he said. "But none of us knows what progressive is meant to mean. Nor do the teachers. Nor do people's parents. Nobody knows."

"But it sounds good," said James.

Ted laughed. "Yes, it always sounds good to be progressive. *I believe in progress.* Great, so you believe in progress. Who doesn't?"

James looked thoughtful. "Some people," he said. "Some people want things to go backwards – to go back to what they used to be."

She asked why.

"Because they're conservative," suggested Ted. "Because they hate other people."

James looked sideways at him. "Not all ..."

"Yes," said Ted. "All."

"I don't think conservatives hate people," said James. "They're just ..."

"Uncool?" said Clover,

James shook his head. "Not necessarily. In fact, it's quite cool to be conservative these days. Ride a bike and so on, but be conservative."

"I'm not interested in politics," said Ted. "It bores me. Yabber yabber yabber. Build a road. Don't build a road. Build an airport. More taxes, no less taxes. Yabber yabber."

James looked at him indulgently. "So what gets you, Ted?"

There was a moment in which it seemed to Clover that Ted was wrestling with a question he found awkward. Then he said, "The same as you, James. The same things as you."

The answer came quickly. "I don't know what I'm interested in. You tell me."

"Things," said Ted lamely.

James teased him. "Come on!"

"Okay, sex."

She drew in her breath. Ted had looked away after he had said this, but James had looked briefly in her direction. He was embarrassed – she could tell that, and she decided to defuse the tension that had suddenly risen.

"What all boys think about all the time," she said lightly. "Or so we're told. Actually, I don't think they do."

"How do you know what boys think about?" challenged Ted.

"Boys tell me." It was untrue, and she could see that neither Ted nor James believed her.

Ted scoffed at this. "No boy is going to tell you what's in his head. He couldn't!"

"Maybe not," said James. "But the same applies to girls. Girls don't tell us what they're thinking. We have to try to work it out."

"Clothes," muttered Ted.

She rounded on him. "What did you say? Clothes? Is that what you think?"

Ted looked to James for support, but James put up a hand. "No. Don't go there."

"We do not think of clothes all the time," said Clover sharply.

"Some of the time then," said Ted.

They smiled at that, and were silent for a moment as the topic expired. Clover shivered. She wanted Ted to go away now, to leave her with James, but he showed no sign of moving. James looked over his shoulder towards the others, who were now standing around a pool table at the edge of the patio. Somebody had turned up the music, but nobody seemed to be paying much attention to it. "I have to go and talk to them," he said. "I haven't spoken to them very much."

He rose, leaving her sitting at the edge of the pool with Ted. He reached out and put a hand on her shoulder as he stood up. "I love your shoulders," he said.

She looked up at him in surprise. "What?"

"Just your shoulders," he said quickly. "They're so convenient for leaning on." Then he added, "Sis."

He turned to Ted. "And you, bro."

"Lean on me any time," said Ted.

James shook his head. "No thanks. I can stand now."

After he had gone, the two of them sat in silence. Ted moved forward and dipped his hand into the pool. His fingers made shadows in the water.

"Still like him?" he asked.

She nodded. "Yes."

"He called you sis," said Ted. "Nice."

"Do you think so?"

"It means that he sees you as a sister."

"And you as a brother."

Ted shrugged. "Okay with me." He hesitated. "But not with you?"

She stared up at the sky beyond the fronds of the palm trees that ringed the Collins's garden. "I suppose I'll have to settle for that. I can, I think. Maybe."

"Why does he get under our skin?" asked Ted. "What's it about him? What is it?"

She mentioned the first thing that came into her mind. "He's kind."

Ted looked doubtful. "Is that all?"

"That and other things."

Ted dipped his hand back into the water. "You won't tell anybody, will you?"

"Tell them what?"

"About me."

"About what you told me?"

He nodded.

"Of course not. Being friends is about keeping the secrets you've shared."

"Thanks. And I won't tell anybody about you. You and him, that is."

She thought there was nothing to tell, other than that she loved James and in return he regarded her as a sister.

Then Ted said, "You okay, my sister?" He had launched into a Caymanian accent – it was redolent of their shared childhood; the accent of the Caymanian children, the ones from West Bay, from the wrong side of the tracks, with whom they had played sporting fixtures at school, across such wide divides of wealth; of the Jamaican pool-man who scooped the leaves out of the water and cut the grass. It was comforting.

He touched her lightly on the arm. His hand was wet from the swimming pool. She liked him. She had always taken Ted for granted; she had never really seen him, in the way in which we see people we value.

She nodded. "Sort of, my brother."

He became serious. "Don't give up," he whispered. "Just don't."

Part Two

22

For the next two years, she did not see him, not by design, but because they were never on the island at the same time. James had slightly different school holidays, and often filled these with projects that took him elsewhere. There was a cricket tour of Australia, and a working trip to Malawi, where his school was renovating an orphanage. She heard about these things from Ted, whom she did see, and who sent her regular messages. She tried not to appear too interested – but in secret she was like an addict deprived, poring over each scrap of news Ted gave her about James as if it were a sacred text, an utterance to be dwelt upon, weighed for meaning.

"He doesn't do e-mails," Ted assured her. "It's nothing personal."

She was not convinced; Ted was trying to comfort her. "But you hear from him. He must e-mail you."

Ted explained that he heard the news indirectly, from other friends. "It's true, Clove. I swear. There are some people who just don't e-mail. It seems odd, but they don't."

"How can they? Everything's done by e-mail now. How can they do anything if they don't use it?"

He shrugged. "They use it a little. Now and then."

She shook her head. "They can't. They have to."

He did not want her in his life; that was clear to her. He was not hostile; he had been friendly, even encouraging, at that party, but it seemed to her that she was just part of his background – nothing more than that. Sensing this, she decided to fall in love with somebody else – she willed that to happen – but it did not. Unconscious, irresistible comparisons with James meant that other boys were found wanting. Nobody was as good-looking;

nobody made her laugh in quite the same way; nobody listened, as James did, was as sympathetic. In short, James had changed the world for her, had set a bar that others simply could not surmount.

Her education taught her self-awareness. Strathearn was a school that encouraged intellectual seriousness – it was what the parents who sent their children there paid for – and there was an English teacher, Miss Hardy, who opened eyes. Clover's reading was guided by her and she expanded the horizons of everybody in that particular class. Clover thought a great deal – about people and their emotions, about how things were in the world. By the time she was due to leave school at eighteen, she had as mature an understanding of the world as many in their mid-twenties – perhaps even more mature.

"University is not a finishing school," said Miss Hardy. "It is not a place to mark time for three or four years until you find yourself a job."

The conversation arose in Miss Hardy's study. Clover had called to say goodbye, and to thank the teacher. The following day, Commemoration Day, would be her last day at the school.

Miss Hardy closed the book that had been open on her desk before her. Clover squinted to read the title upside down: *Edward Thomas: A Life in Poetry*. She remembered that he was an enthusiasm of the teacher, and they had spent the best part of an hour talking about one of his poems about a train stopping at a station in the country, and steam escaping, and birds singing. She had wanted to cry, and almost did, because she knew the poet would be killed in the trenches of France.

"Edward Thomas," said Miss Hardy.

"I remember. That poem about the train."

Miss Hardy touched the cover of the book almost reverentially. "If you forget everything else I ever taught you, I suspect you'll remember that poem."

She assured her that she would not forget. "No, you're wrong. I'll remember a lot."

"You're kind … But, back to the topic of university. It's your one chance, you know. Or for most people it's their one chance."

"Of what?"

"Of opening the mind."

"Yes."

"Education – *educere*, the Latin for *to lead out*. How many times has somebody explained that to you while you've been here?"

"One hundred."

"Well, there you are. So choose carefully. And don't throw it away."

"Yes."

Miss Hardy looked at her thoughtfully. "Your family lives overseas, don't they?"

"In the Cayman Islands. My father's an accountant." Clover's tone became apologetic. "He works there."

The teacher smiled. "You don't have to explain. You don't have to justify it. At any rate, not to me."

She felt she had to; people had their views on the Cayman Islands.

"I didn't raise it for that reason," said Miss Hardy. "I mention it because I suppose it affects your choices. You're probably in a position to do what you want to do. Your choice need not be too vocational."

"What you mean is that I can do something indulgent if I

want to. Shouldn't you say what you mean? Haven't you tried to teach us that?"

It was not impertinence, although it may have sounded like it. This sort of bantering exchange was allowed – even encouraged – with the students about to leave; the school believed in independence of thought and in the ability to hold one's corner in debate. "Don't be too ready to read things into what people say. But, broadly speaking, yes. You can study something that isn't necessarily going to lead to something else. You'll have plenty of opportunity to do that later."

"Whereas most people can't?"

"No, they can't. A lot of people have debt to consider. They can't afford to study expensive subjects that don't lead to a paying career."

She looked down at the floor. "Should I feel guilty? Should I feel bad about it?"

"No. Not at all."

"Why?"

"Because sometimes in this life we're given things that we don't deserve – that we haven't done anything to merit, so to speak. We don't have to give those up if they come our way. And remember this: plenty of people are better off than you. Inequality is written into the way the world works, no matter how hard we try to correct it." Miss Hardy paused. "You may be fortunate in one respect and less fortunate in another. Nobody's guaranteed happiness across the board. Fate has her own ideas of equality."

"Nemesis? Isn't she the person you told us about?"

"Yes, Nemesis. She stalks us, we're told. If we get above ourselves, she may take action to cut us down to size."

"I'll be careful."

The teacher affected mock seriousness. "So you should be. But I suspect that you'll do nothing much to risk corrective action by Nemesis or any of the other gods and goddesses."

She laughed. "They were so nasty, weren't they – the Greek gods?"

"Horrible. Full of mean tricks and petty jealousies. Worse than the girls in the third form, although not by much."

"And punishing people too. Making them bear all sorts of things … Sisyphus."

Miss Hardy was pleased that she had remembered. In class they had read Camus's essay *The Myth of Sisyphus*. "Yes, Sisyphus – condemned to push a rock up a hill eternally. They certainly knew how to impose burdens." She paused, but only briefly. "Of course, we're quite good at imposing burdens on ourselves – without any assistance from Parnassus."

"I suppose we are," said Clover. "Unreturned love, for instance. That's a burden, isn't it?"

Miss Hardy looked at her with interest. She had not been able to make this girl out – not entirely. Other seventeen- or eighteen-year-olds were transparent – at least to those who spent their lives teaching them. Clover was more complex; there was something there that she could not quite put her finger on; some sorrow, perhaps, that was more specific, more focused than typical teenage angst. Now she had revealed it as clearly as if she had spelled it out in capital letters.

She would be gentle. She wanted to say: *don't worry.* Unrequited love was painful to begin with, but the passage of time dulled the pain – it always did. "The Greek legends have a fair dose of that."

Clover's voice was even. "Unrequited love?"

"Yes. Greek mythology may be full of instances of the revenge and pettiness we were talking about, but it also involved profound insights into the human condition – of which unrequited love is just one feature. Echo and Narcissus – remember?"

"Vaguely. She fell in love with him and he ..."

"He was too preoccupied with himself to return her love. He gazed at his reflection constantly and eventually wasted away. As did she. All that was left of him was a flower by the water's edge, and of her a sound. That was it."

Clover was silent for a while. In their art class they had looked at a Pre-Raphaelite picture of Echo and Narcissus, with Echo watching Narcissus crouching by his pool, gazing at his reflection. It was a perfect depiction of what it was to be cut out of somebody's life.

Miss Hardy was smiling. "Would you mind if I said something critical of your generation?"

"Why should we mind criticism? We criticise people who are older than us. All the time ..." She grinned.

"Oh, we know that," said Miss Hardy. "Any teacher who isn't aware of what is said about us must have her ears closed."

Clover waited.

"This is nothing personal," said Miss Hardy. "I'm not talking about the boys in this school."

"Of course not."

"It's a difficult thing to explain, but there are those who say that young men these days have been encouraged into narcissism. They've been presented with images of themselves that are essentially narcissistic. All those brooding pictures of members of boy bands sucking in their cheeks to make themselves look more intense. What's the message there? Be cool. Don't express your feelings. Gaze at yourself and your image ... The problem is that this doesn't leave them much time – or emotional energy – for other people."

"Maybe ..."

"Of course I overstate it a bit, but then you have to overstate some things if you're to see them in the first place. But there's a rather odd consequence to all this, I think."

"Which is?"

"It can leave the girls out of it. You end up with a lot of self-obsessed young men, all trying to fulfil the cultural expectation of the detached, moody young hero, and lo and behold, these young men don't have much time for the girls."

"But they do!"

Miss Hardy conceded. "For some things, yes. Disengaged sex, maybe. But not for others." She hesitated before continuing. "I think that's probably enough of that. You can make too much of a theory."

"It's an interesting one."

"You think so?"

"Yes, I do."

The teacher considered this. Then she said, "I suppose we can speak pretty frankly. You're about to leave this place, to go out into the world, and I don't have to treat you as a child any more. May I ask you one further thing?"

She waited for Clover to nod before she continued. "I get the strong impression that you've already been in love with somebody and that it hasn't worked out. I don't want to pry, and you don't have to speak about it if you don't want to."

Clover looked past Miss Hardy, out through the window behind the teacher's desk. The hills – gentle in that part of Perthshire – rose off towards the north; an attenuated blue now in the warmth of summer. She felt, more sharply now, the pang of regret that had first touched her a few weeks ago when she realised that she was shortly to leave a place where she had been happy. "I don't mind speaking about it. It's all right now."

"You're getting over it?"

"Yes, I think so. I'm forgetting him. That's what you have to do, isn't it?"

Miss Hardy sighed. "That's the conventional wisdom. And I suppose there's some truth in the conventional wisdom – there usually is. But it's not always entirely true. I'm not sure that you should forget entirely, because what you're forgetting may be something really rather important to you. Something precious."

It occurred to Clover that the teacher was talking about herself. "You didn't get married, did you?"

"I did."

"But your name ... Miss ..."

The teacher shook her head. "Don't go by names. I was married for three years. Just for three years – my fault as much as his, but I didn't want it to end. When it came apart, I went back to my own name. I'd been Miss Hardy, and I went back to that. My *nom de guerre*, so to speak – not that the classroom is a battleground."

"I'm sorry."

"Divorce happens. I hope it doesn't happen to you, but it happens."

"You said that we shouldn't forget."

"No, I didn't say that. I think that we need to forget a certain amount – just to be able to keep going – but we shouldn't forget everything. I suppose it's a question of forgetting to the extent that you don't think about it too much. But keep some of the memory, because it's part of what … of what you've had."

Clover's gaze returned from the window. "But if you keep thinking about …"

Miss Hardy interrupted her. "You don't have to keep thinking about him. You change the way you think about him – that way he won't dominate your life. What do they call it now? Moving on. I've always thought that a resounding cliché, but I suppose it has its uses, like any resounding cliché. Move on."

"I have. Or at least I think I have."

Miss Hardy looked relieved. "It's not easy to forget something, is it? But let's talk about university now. Where are you going?"

"Edinburgh. History of Art."

"Good. Where I was." She paused, and then added, with contrived wistfulness, "That's where I met him."

They both smiled.

23

"Colours," she said to a friend, much later. "That's how I remember the stages of my life – by the colours."

She had to explain. "I began in the Cayman Islands. The colours there were Caribbean – very intense."

"Blue?"

"Yes, of course. That was the sea. Blue or turquoise, depending on the depth. Deep sea was deep blue, like that intense blue ink. You don't find it elsewhere, I think. Or if you do, I've never seen it. But it wasn't just that blue. There was another blue that people liked – a much lighter shade that they used to paint houses. That and pink. They loved pink too. They were pastel shades, I suppose."

"I can see them. Houses with blue window-frames and doors."

"Exactly. Those were the colours I grew up with. And then suddenly I was in Scotland and ..."

"The colours were very different."

"Yes. Everything was gentler. There were no bright colours – just those soft greens and purples and, yes, white. There are lots of whites in Scotland. White in the sky and in the rain. Sometimes even the water seems white, you know. You look at a loch and the surface of the water seems white. White or silver, like a mirror."

"And grey."

"Yes, there is plenty of grey in Scotland. The buildings are made of grey stone – granite and so on – and they're grey. Hard and grey, though some of them are made of a different sort of stone. It's the colour of honey, actually; sometimes even almost red."

Honey-coloured … She looked up at the building that was to be her home during the university terms. The stone used for the four-floored tenement building was of just that stone. It was far softer than granite and had weathered here and there, softened at the edges, where the action of rain and wind had made its impression. The flat was on the top floor, tucked under the slate roof, reached by a shared stone stairway with a curving, ornate ironwork banister. The overall impression was one of nineteenth-century confidence and solidity. Stone was the right medium for that; stone was the expression of the values that lay behind these buildings; solid; designed to last for hundreds of years; crafted so as to allow the living out of whole lives within thick walls.

The flat belonged to a friend from school, Ella, who was starting at Edinburgh at the same time as Clover was. Or rather, it belonged to Ella's parents, who had bought it a few years earlier for their son, who had studied engineering at Edinburgh. The son had graduated and left for a job in Bristol, but the flat had been kept on for his sister. Ella had offered Clover a room, and had then let another by placing an advertisement in the student paper.

"I have no idea what she's like," she said to Clover. "I tactfully asked for a photograph, but she ignored my request."

"Why would one want a flatmate's photograph?" asked Clover.

Ella had looked embarrassed. "You never know."

"You mean that you want to make sure that you're not taking on a serial killer?"

Ella nodded. "Something like that. Don't you think that you can tell what somebody's like from their photograph?"

Clover was not sure. "Maybe. Maybe not. Some people look unpleasant but aren't really – not when you meet them."

"It depends on what you mean by unpleasant. I think I'd pay attention to what her hair looked like. And her make-up."

"Really?"

"If she was caked in make-up – you know, bags of mascara, and so on, then you'd think: this one's not going to be easy to live with."

"Why would you think that?"

Ella hesitated. "She'd hog the bathroom. We wouldn't get near a mirror."

They had laughed. And when Karen, the other flatmate, arrived – after Clover had moved into her room – they had been relieved to see that she was, outwardly at least, quite normal.

"You didn't send a photograph," said Ella. "But I assume it's you."

Karen looked blank. "Photograph?"

"I suggested that you should send a photograph – when you got in touch first. Remember?"

"No. I don't. I can give you one now, if you like."

"No, now we can see you. We don't need a photograph."

Karen later said to Clover: "Why did she want a photograph? Did you send her one before you got the room?"

"I didn't need to. We've known one another for ages. I was at school with her, you see."

"But why did she want one of me?"

"To check up."

"Why? What can you tell from a photograph?"

"Lots of things – or that's what Ella thinks."

The photograph was forgotten about; they liked Karen, who came from Glasgow and brought an entirely different perspective with her. "Glasgow," said Ella, "could be on the moon, you know.

It's that different."

Karen had the room at the front – a room that looked out onto the street four floors below – while Ella and Clover each had a room overlooking the drying green behind the building. This was effectively a great courtyard serving the line of buildings on every side and divided, like a medieval field, into small sections, each allocated to a different flat. In places the boundaries between these postage stamps of garden were marked with low fences, barely knee-height; elsewhere the owners had long since abandoned any attempt to distinguish their property from that of their neighbours and grass – and weeds – ran riot across human divisions. Cats, too, observed their territorial arrangements across the face of the map of human ownership, moving around any contested space on top of such stone walls as could be found, or surveying the green from windowsills or doorways.

It was Clover's first room. She did not count her room at home – mothers or younger brothers can enter your room at home with impunity – nor did she count the single room that she had eventually been given at school; that had been meant to be private, but never really was. Now she had somewhere that was at her complete disposal. She was paying rent for this and it was hers.

She stood in front of her window and looked down onto the green below. A woman in blue slacks, presumably one of the neighbours, was tending a small bed of discouraged-looking flowers; a pigeon, alighted on a branch of the single tree in the corner, was puffing up its breast in a display of bravado; the sky, a patch of blue above the surrounding rooftops, was enjoying one of its rare cloud-free moments. Greys. Greens. Light, almost whitened blue.

She thought about her mother. She would take a photograph and send it to her; she had asked for that. She looked at her watch; her mother would be up by now and might be having her morning swim in the pool. Or she might already have started a game of tennis at the club. She would not change places with her. Cayman, for all its colours, was boring, she thought. Money, money, money. Tennis. Parties. Gossip. And after that there was nothing, but the same all over again.

She smiled to herself, savouring the sheer joy of freedom. For the first time in her life – the very first – there was nobody to tell her what to do. If she wished, she could stay in this room all day. She could lie on her bed and page through magazines. She could drink as many cups of coffee as she liked. The course was due to start the following day with both morning and afternoon being given over to orientation. It was an odd word to use, she thought, and she imagined for a moment a group of confused and uncertain students standing in a room and being gently turned by assistants so that they faced north or south or whatever direction the authorities thought best. She smiled again.

Then lectures were to start the day after that, after everybody had recovered from the orientation party that she had already seen advertised. *Half-price drinks*, announced a poster, and underneath, somebody, presumably with experience of student parties, had written *Full-price hangover*.

She had already investigated the departmental offices in a restored Georgian house on one side of a square of such houses and had found out where the first lecture would be held. That first lecture would be at ten, she had been told, and since a large crowd was expected she should get there early.

"Some people sit on the steps," said one of the secretaries disapprovingly. "We don't encourage it, but if there are no seats, then there really is no alternative."

She went to the orientation party, which was solely for those enrolled on the art history course – almost three hundred and twenty students. The secretary who had advised her about sitting on the steps was there, standing at the entrance, at the same time giving the impression of being both disapproving and hesitant, as if undecided as to whether to join the party. "There are far too many people for this room," she said to Clover as she arrived. "I tell them every year to get a bigger room, but they ignore me. They just ignore me."

Clover, feeling that she was being drawn into some internal issue, some obscure matter of the workplace, was uncertain as to what to say. "They shouldn't," she said at last.

"Well, it's nice to hear that you think that," said the secretary. "Because others don't."

Clover looked around the crowded room.

The secretary noticed her wandering gaze. "And that's another thing," she said, taking a sip of her drink. "I tell them every year that they should recruit a few more young men. Look at all these girls." She sighed. "We used to have some very nice young men. But these days …"

Clover looked. There were a few boys, but those who were there were heavily outnumbered by young women.

"A group of women is always different," said the secretary. She glanced at Clover, appraising her reaction. "The atmosphere is more difficult. I don't think that women have as much fun as men, do you?"

"Oh, I don't know," said Clover.

"Well, I do," said the secretary. "Look at them." She gestured towards the group of students.

Clover's eye was caught by a group of three young women standing near a window. She was sure that she recognised one of them, but was not sure why she did. She stared harder. The ears were right. She always used to wear one of those odd hair-bands that showed the ears rather too prominently. She had some sort of patterned hair-band on now, although it was hard to make out exactly what it was. And the brow, too. That was unusually high, as it had been all those years ago.

It was somebody from Cayman, she thought; there was no doubt about it. She had met her. And then, as she detached herself from the disgruntled secretary and began to make her way across the room, the girl in the hair-band unexpectedly turned round and looked straight at her, as if suddenly warned of her presence.

They had not seen each other for some years. For a brief period, now suddenly remembered, she and Judy had been in the same class at the Prep; there had been a running argument over something – Clover tried to remember it – and sides had been taken, with each of them in a different faction. The *casus belli* was soon forgotten and they had briefly shared the same friend; then she had gone – somewhere, as people did when you were a child – although she had returned to the island with her parents some years later and they had acknowledged each other distantly, and somewhat warily.

Judy's face broke into a broad smile of recognition. "I thought it was you," she said as she came up to Clover. "You know something? I haven't met a single person – not one – I know since I came to Edinburgh, and now you … Would you believe it?"

Clover shrugged. "Big world," she said. "Not small, as some people keep saying."

"Well, big and small," said Judy. "Here I am. Here you are. Small, maybe."

Clover noticed the bracelet – a thin band of tiny diamonds. Who would wear something like that to a student party?

"A present from my dad," said Judy. "My eighteenth birthday, last year. He said I should wear it."

Clover showed her embarrassment. "Why not? I like it." She glanced at Judy's clothes. They were expensive; expensive jeans could be frayed and distressed as much as you liked, but they remained costly-looking.

"So you're on the course too?"

Clover nodded absently. She wanted to know what had happened to Judy in the intervening years. "Where have you been?" she asked. "I mean, where have you been the last five years?"

"My dad moved to Singapore," Judy said. "He got remarried – remember my mum died?"

Clover nodded. It was coming back to her now; it had been an overdose, people said, and her mother had found it awkward explaining what that was. *Too many pills, probably by mistake. People get confused, you see.* What do you think, Clover asked herself at the time, if your mother takes too many pills – by mistake? How do you actually feel about that? She could not imagine it; she could not see her mother doing that; she counted things out; she never made a mistake. Other mothers took too many pills, not hers.

"So my dad married this Chinese lady – well, actually she's Singaporean. We moved to Singapore because her family had a company and my dad went and worked for them. They're quite important, actually – my Singaporean relatives."

"You went to school there?"

Judy shook her head. "No. I came to the UK. Boarding school. It wasn't too bad, I suppose."

"I went too."

Judy raised the glass she was holding. "Yeah, well, we're survivors, aren't we?" She paused. "I've got a flat in Singapore. I lived there for five months before I came here. I'll go back to it in the university vacations. Come and visit me."

"Your own place?"

"I told you – my stepmother's family is rich. Sorry, I'm not boasting – just explaining. There's a difference."

"Of course. I didn't think you were boasting."

Judy cast an eye back to where she had been standing earlier on. "That girl … The one in red. Dreary! Seriously dreary! She went on about that museum in St Petersburg – the whatever it's called …"

"The Hermitage."

"Yes, that place; she says that her aunt knows the head conservator there and they've offered her an internship for a month next year. She went on and on about it. I told her that Russia was a ghastly place and that I wouldn't ever spend a month there if I could avoid it. She became very defensive."

"Oh well …"

"But the boy she's talking to – see him? He's called Graham and he's seriously cute. I don't think he's gay either. You can tell, you know. They start talking about the High Renaissance or Michelangelo and you say to yourself *Here we go!* But he hasn't mentioned Michelangelo once – not once! That's almost like declaring yourself a rugby player round here."

Clover laughed.

"Did I say something amusing?" asked Judy disingenuously. "I should hate to miss my own jokes."

"Michelangelo …" began Clover.

"Oh not you too!"

"No, I was going to ask why Michelangelo was …"

"The litmus? Search me. It may be something to do with his statue of David. Who knows? But that guy, Graham, is seriously interesting." She paused. "And you know who else?"

"Who else what?"

"Who else is in Edinburgh. Not that I've seen him, but I gather he's here. He's doing economics or something like that." And then she added casually, without knowledge of the effect of what she said, "His dad was that doctor."

Clover caught her breath. "You mean Dr Collins?"

"Yes. He was my mother's doctor. She liked him a lot."

Clover battled to keep her voice even. "James?"

"Yes. That's him. I didn't know him very well – did you?"

"I did. Quite well. I'm a bit out of touch now."

Judy took another sip of her drink. "He was gorgeous, if I remember correctly. Or he looked as if he would be gorgeous … with time." She smiled. "I heard he was here because that other guy who was in our class – the one who went to Houston – he's kept in touch in an odd sort of way. We never see one another and I never really liked him very much, but he still sends me e-mails sometimes and tells me that so-and-so has done whatever. Some people like that sort of thing – gossip, I suppose. There's no real point to it, but they don't seem to get it. He told me that James was coming to university in Edinburgh. That's how I know."

Clover was silent. She had been trying not to think of him, and had succeeded – at least to some extent. But every day, almost without exception, some thought would come to her unbidden; his name, or the memory of him, like a tinge of pain from tissue that has not altogether recovered from a wound – and perhaps never would.

When she spoke, her voice was level. "I didn't know that."

"Well, you do now. If I see him, I'll tell him you're here. We could all meet up – like a bunch of stranded expatriates – and talk about old times. Or maybe we won't. I can't stand that sort of thing. You know how it is? Remember how we … that sort of garbage."

Clover nodded absently. She suddenly wanted to leave the party. She had come hoping to meet her future classmates – to make friends – but now she just felt empty. She did not want to talk to anybody; she wanted to get away, to go somewhere where she could just sit and think of James. It was precisely what she had been trying to avoid – she had sat and thought enough about him in the past – and now she was starting afresh. But tonight was different; this was a shock, and she could allow herself to think through the implications of what she had just been told. James was in Edinburgh. *In Edinburgh*. And he was at the same university as she was. That meant that he was one of – how many was it? – twenty-five thousand students, maybe a few more. Edinburgh was not a large city – not as cities went – and you were bound to bump into somebody else sooner or later. There would be parties – university life was full of parties – and that meant that they could find themselves in the same room together. She would see him.

The thought both appalled and excited her. It appalled

her because she had stopped thinking about him; it was over – whatever it was. No, it was love, she told herself. You can't dodge love by calling it *whatever it was*; it was love, and you might as well admit it. Use the word, Miss Hardy had said to them in English class; use the short, accurate, expressive word – not the circumlocution. And a boy at the back had muttered, "Circumlocution isn't a short, accurate expressive word." They had all laughed – Miss Hardy included.

"*Touché*," the teacher had said. "And here's another suggestion: if you can't find an English word, use a French one."

She extricated herself from the party as discreetly as she could. Just outside the doorway, though, she met one of the lecturers, a thin, rather worried-looking man. He had interviewed her the day before in his role as her director of studies, and now he frowned as he greeted her.

"Clover – it is Clover isn't it? You're not leaving, are you?"

"Well, I was …"

"The Professor was going to make a speech – just going to say a few words of welcome. Can't you stay for that?"

She looked down at the floor. "I'm sorry, I just don't feel in the mood for a party. It's nothing to do with the Professor."

He looked at her with concern. "Are you sure you're all right? It can be a bit of a strain, the start of a new academic year; and this is your first year, which is always more stressful."

She looked up at him. "Thanks. I'll be all right."

But she felt the tears welling in her eyes and after a moment or two she could not disguise them.

His concern grew. "But you're crying …"

She wiped at her cheeks. "I'm sorry. I'm all right. It's just that …" Her voice tailed off. What could she say? *I'm in love with somebody who doesn't love me. I thought I'd got over him, but I haven't, I haven't at all …*

He was looking at her expectantly. "Something's obviously wrong. It's not my job to pry, but I don't like to see you leaving in this state. I really don't."

She reassured him that she would get home safely and that she had just been a bit upset about a personal matter; she would feel much better in a few minutes. Really. Honestly. He did not have to worry.

She went outside into the street and began the fifteen-minute walk back to her flat. Yellow sodium street-lights glowed against the sky; a bus moved by with a shudder, one of the passengers looking out and briefly making eye contact with her as she walked past. She thought: *this is the last news I wanted to hear,* and for a moment she felt an irrational anger towards Judy for being the messenger who conveyed it. But after a brief struggle that stopped, and she felt calmer. I shall put him out of my mind, she said to herself. He is nothing to me any more; just a boy I once knew and to whom I can be indifferent when I see him again. I shall not be unkind; I shall not cut him nor ignore him; I shall simply be indifferent. Like this. She closed her eyes, expecting to see nothing, which is what she imagined a state of indifference should produce on the inner eye. But it did not. She saw James, and he was smiling at her.

24

It was easier the next morning. The anguish she had felt the previous night – and it had been anguish – a feeling of sheer sorrow, of loss – had dissipated itself in sleep; now she was back in the ordinary world in which she had breakfast to make and there were lectures to go to. The Edinburgh morning, which could be cold and windswept, was anything but – a brilliant display of the sunshine that could accompany an Indian summer. From her window the rooftops on the other side of the drying green were touched with gold, the rounded chimney pots like a row of amphoras against the sky. She found it hard to believe that she had gone to bed in such a state of misery; it was almost laughable, in fact, that a childish crush on a boy could make you feel as if there was nothing to live for; ridiculous thought. She was beginning a new life in one of the most romantic cities in the world. She had everything – everything – to live for; she had no reason to feel bad about anything.

Over the weeks that followed, she busied herself with her course and with the social activities that accompanied the start of the new semester. There were societies to join, and these involved new people and the almost immediate friendships that at eighteen – or on the cusp of nineteen – are so easily made. Karen and Ella both had a circle of friends already – people they had known for some years – and these friends welcomed Clover too. But she sensed the importance of having a life independent of her flatmates, and they understood that too. "I don't want to live in your pocket," said Ella, adding, "but of course that doesn't mean that you can't live in mine, if that's what you want."

But she did not. She made friends with several people studying her subject – Padraig, a young man from Dublin whose interest was in the Post-Impressionists and who had come to university slightly later than most of their classmates. He had worked in a bank in Ireland but had hated it, he said, because art was what he really wanted to do. He intended to write about it, he said, and he gave her criticisms that he had written of various art exhibitions. These he sent off to the *Irish Times* and other newspapers, although they had never been published. "You carry on," he said. "You send them your stuff and then eventually they publish something. Their regular art critic gets sick – or is arrested – and then they think, *There's this guy who's been sending us this stuff – let's ask him.* That's the way it works."

"Really? Is that the way it works?"

He shook his head ruefully. "No. But it gives me something to do."

In the second week, she went to a film at the Filmhouse, the arts cinema, with Padraig. He had invited her because he had a spare ticket and he thought she might like the film. "Iranian," he said. "They make pretty impressive films."

"I've not seen any."

"Nor me. But they do."

"About?"

He paused. "Oh, about the clash between modernity and the old ways. That's a good theme for an Iranian film. There are lots of clashes between …"

"Modernity and the old ways?"

"Exactly." He paused. "You go anywhere there and you see it."

"You sure?"

He grinned. "I have no idea."

"You could be talking nonsense, you know."

"Of course it's nonsense. Life is nonsense, don't you think? How much of it actually makes sense? It's just us filling time because we know that we're tiny specks in a great broth of galaxies and black holes and gas clouds. We're nothing, and so we try to make structures and meaning for ourselves, but it's all nonsense underneath."

She thought that a bleak view, and said as much. "But some things aren't nonsense at all. Some things are deadly serious. Pain. Hunger. Human suffering. These things actually hurt people and only ..." She struggled to find the right way of saying it. "They only seem meaningless to people who aren't actually suffering them."

At the end of the film he turned to her and said, "You were right."

They were leaving the Filmhouse, but she felt she was still in Tehran, in the cramped house with the young woman arguing with her indoctrinated brother.

"I was right about what?"

"About suffering. About how simple human concerns mean a lot. How they mean everything, really."

She thanked him. "I'd forgotten our discussion. But thank you anyway."

"Like loneliness."

They were out on the street now. He had suggested they go to a bar – and there were plenty about – but she was tired.

"I have to get up early tomorrow." Then she asked, "Loneliness?"

"Yes. Being ... I don't know – separate from people and being unable to do anything about it. It's a form of suffering, isn't it?"

"Yes, it is." She smiled at him. "You're lonely, Padraig?"

He looked embarrassed. "I'm so cheesy. I say cheesy things. It's just that …" He looked up at the night sky. "I like you. That's what I was trying to say."

"Good. That's nice to know."

"Can't we go for a drink?"

"I told you: I'm tired. Do you mind?"

He shook his head. "Of course not. I'm not much good at these things."

She said nothing.

"At dates," he said.

It had not occurred to her that they were on a date, and she was about to say, "But an Iranian film is not a date …" but stopped herself. He now turned to her and said, "Maybe I shouldn't have asked you."

She told him not to be silly. "I'm glad you asked me. But …"

He winced. "But …"

"But, well, there's somebody else."

It took him a few moments to digest the information. "I thought so. I didn't imagine that somebody like you … I mean, somebody who looked like you would be … Not that I judge by looks, of course. I may study aesthetics, but philosophy and well, the way your hair looks and your …"

She laughed. "Padraig …"

"And you're three years younger than I am."

"So?"

"That counts. You're not going to be interested in somebody who's twenty-two."

"Don't be ridiculous."

"But you told me yourself. You've just explained. I'm Irish – I can take these things. We can take anything. Come to Dublin and speak to people and they'll say to you: *we can take these things …*"

She took his hand. "Don't be silly."

They were standing at the pedestrian crossing opposite the Usher Hall. They had not crossed, although the light had changed several times in their favour. He said, "We can't stand here. There's a bar over there – look – the Shakespeare."

She did not resist.

"So tell me about him," he said as he brought the drinks to their table.

She had ordered a cider, and the glass was cold to the touch as she moved a finger down its side, tracing a pattern in the condensation. "He doesn't really exist," she said. "Or at least, I don't exist for him."

Padraig shook his head in puzzlement. "I'm not sure if I understand. You're not actually seeing him?"

"No. I never see him."

He frowned. "But you have actually *met* him? We're not talking about some film actor here, are we? You don't harbour a secret passion for …" He named an actor. She would never fancy *him*, she said.

"Good," he said. "I can't understand why anybody would."

"Money, glamour, looks …"

"Small things. Irrelevant." His eyes lit when he smiled; she noticed it. "So, you do know him, but you don't see him? I get it. He's in Africa or South America perhaps, doing something really important – selfless, too – and you promised him that even if it takes ten years you'll wait for him and …"

"No."

She took a sip of her drink. She regretted telling him now, and she wanted to talk about something different. "I don't know if we should talk about it."

"I didn't exactly raise the subject." He looked at her over his glass. "I think that you probably need to talk about this."

She hesitated before replying. He was right, she thought.

"It's going to sound corny to you because … well, because men don't think like this, I know, but I do. It's just the way I think – the way I am."

"Of course. We're all different."

"I've known this guy forever. Since we were kids. He was my best friend, I suppose, or that's the way I thought of him. Then I realised – a bit later – that he meant more to me than that. I wanted him to know that but I couldn't tell him, could I? I left it."

He interrupted. "But you should tell people." He shrugged. "Otherwise they don't know. How can they?"

"Yes, maybe. But I didn't, and all the time I thought of him. And so the years went by and nothing happened. That's all there is to it, I suppose."

He stared at her in silence. "You still love him?"

She avoided his gaze. "I suppose I do."

The admission – to Padraig – made her feel light-headed, and what was more, seemed to carry with it an unexpected sexual charge. In the past, on the few occasions when she had talked to anybody about her feelings for James, it had been to a girl friend or to Ted, and that was different. Now, talking to Padraig, she felt in a curious way that James himself was there – that she was talking to him about her feelings for him.

But then it occurred to her: the sexual charge had nothing to do with James, or talking about James; it had to do with Padraig.

He probed further. "And is he seeing somebody else?"

"I don't know. I never see him. I told myself I shouldn't, and

I haven't. I haven't spoken to him for … for months. A year maybe."

"He probably is. People don't stay by themselves unless there's a reason."

She felt a stab of pain. But she knew that what he said was true – and applied to her, too. James was the reason why she was alone.

He lowered his voice. "I think it's sad … I mean it's sad in the sense of being bad luck for you."

She nodded. "Yes, you're right."

"You need to forget him, I think."

"I know. But it's not easy."

He smiled at her. "Can't I help you? I'm not him, I know, but if you got to know somebody else, then that might help you to forget this other person … what's his name?"

"James."

"James. Predictable."

"Are you laughing at me?"

"I'm not. I'm being unkind, and I'm sorry. I'm called Padraig myself, for heaven's sake – how predictable is that, if you're Irish, which I happen to be? There's nothing wrong with being called James. But let's not mention his name." He made a slicing motion. "James is now an un-person. It's official. James has been *abolished*."

He made her laugh. She liked that, and they had another drink. He said, "Feeling better?"

She felt the effect of the alcohol. The cider had not been very strong, but it had been strong enough. "Yes, much better."

He reached for and pressed her hand. "Me too."

She let her hand linger in his; returned the pressure.

That was the beginning of something that lasted for four years, throughout their university years in Edinburgh, until they both graduated. It was a friendship and a romance, but the emphasis was on the former rather than the latter. Each provided for the other what the other needed: Padraig was looking for something, for the perfect love, the head-over-heels affair that would bring him his life partner, but he knew that this would not be Clover. She had already found, she felt, exactly what she was looking for, and it was not Padraig – but it seemed that it was forever closed to her. Both settled for something less than they thought they might find; neither wished to hurt the other, and neither did. Clover, though, began to lead a secret life – out of desperation, out of disappointment, as most secret lives are led.

25

It was not until she had been with Padraig for a month or so that Clover first saw James. The beginning of the affair with Padraig had distracted her, and the upset that the news of James's presence in Edinburgh had brought to her had largely abated. She had decided that she could live with the knowledge that he was in Edinburgh and had persuaded herself that it did not matter to her. Padraig had suggested that James be abolished; very well, he was. And it surprised her to find out that the act of consigning him to oblivion in this way seemed to help. She thought of him, but only occasionally, and without the desperate tug, the almost physical sensation of pain, that such thoughts had previously triggered. I cannot have James, she thought. He is not for me. It was a form of self-hypnosis – a mantra of the sort that smokers used to abandon cigarettes or alcoholics their alcohol: *I do not need these things. I do not need these things.*

But if weaning from a dependence succeeds, it often does so intermittently, and there will be periods of back-sliding, of weakness, when the temptation to do the thing that you know you should not do is just too strong. For Clover that came shortly before her first sighting of James – a sighting that was not accidental in any way but was engineered by her in just such a moment of weakness.

It happened one afternoon. She had just attended a tutorial and was making her way out into George Square when she passed a university noticeboard. For some reason she stopped and looked at the notices pinned on that particular board. They had nothing to do with her course but she read the largest of them and saw that it was a schedule of classes in economics, which was the subject that she had been told James was studying.

The notice set out the names of those students in various tutorial groups and their time of meeting. Now she knew what she was doing, as her eye ran down the list. *James Collins*. She stopped at the words – words that were invested with such potent effect, as the name of someone we love always is. She thought, inconsequentially, absurdly: *the person who typed them can't have known what sort of person he was*. There were five other names in the groups. Olivia somebody; Jenny somebody; Mark, Mustafa, Terry. They would know, of course; these were his *companions*. She looked at Olivia's name and tried to picture her. She might even sit next to him, and if she did then she would be bound to want him – of course she would.

She turned away. These were ridiculous, stupid thoughts. They were unhealthy. This way lay obsession.

She turned back to look at the notice again. It gave the name of the building and the room number. It gave the time of the tutorial. She looked at her watch. James's tutorial would have started ten minutes ago, and it would be taking place not more than a few hundred yards from where she was standing. She went to the doorway and looked out. There was the other building. Third floor – the notice had said it would be on the third floor. She looked at the windows along the third floor façade. Behind one of those, Olivia, Jenny, Mark, Mustafa, Terry and James would be discussing whatever it was they discussed in economics tutorials. Prices, perhaps. Markets. Commodities. Rational economic behaviour – an expression she had seen in a newspaper article. Rational economic behaviour was behaving sensibly in response to economic incentives or disincentives. Irrational economic behaviour, presumably, was doing the opposite. *I, for instance, am now behaving irrationally …*

Why? Because a rational person does not stand and stare at a window because she thinks a boy she cannot get out of her mind is sitting with others behind that window. There was nothing rational in that.

She lowered her gaze from the third floor to the ground floor. She imagined that there was more than one door into the building and more than one door out of it. The front door, though, seemed to be the main entrance and exit, as she noticed, even as she was staring at it, students walking in and out. So when you went to your economics tutorial on the third floor that must be where you went in and an hour, or maybe slightly less, later where you came out. She looked at her watch again. Forty-five minutes from then he would walk out of that door. Forty-five minutes from then she could happen to be passing – the building was on the way to the main university library and everybody walked that way. She could be walking past just as James was coming out of the building and she would say …

"James! What are you …"

And, when it happened, as she managed to ensure it did, just over fifty minutes later, he said: "I don't believe it! I heard you were here and I was going to …"

Then why had he not? She put the question out of her mind. "Me too."

His smile was unforced. Even if he had not been in touch, the chance encounter clearly pleased him.

He had come out of the building with a girl and she was now standing next to him, smiling at Clover.

"This is Olivia," said James.

She looked at the other girl. She was a recognisable type; one of those well-groomed, expensively educated girls who chose to go to university in Edinburgh because it was a good place to find a husband. It was a crude generalisation, and one that Clover would have previously mocked, but once she had arrived there she had realised that, like so many stereotypes, it was simply true.

Olivia glanced from Clover to James.

"An old friend," he said. "We were at school together in Cayman back in the day."

Olivia smiled at her, and then glanced at her watch. "I have to meet Sue. I promised."

James nodded. "See you later."

"Yes."

Clover wondered what later meant. Later that day? Tomorrow?

"Eight-ish," said Olivia.

James nodded absent-mindedly. He was still looking at Clover; he was still smiling.

"We could get a coffee," he said. "It would be nice to catch up."

She felt her heart hammering within her. "Yes, of course. Why not?"

"There's a place at the top of Middle Meadow Walk. You know it?"

She did, and they walked there together, slowly.

"I don't even need to ask you what you're doing," he said. "Let me guess. History of Art?"

"How did you know?"

"Ted told me, actually," he said. "But it suits you. I always thought you'd do something like that."

"Well, maybe that's what people do. The things they're interested in."

"Most of the time," he said. "But not always. There was somebody in my year at school who's just started medicine and has realised it's a terrible mistake. He's squeamish. He threw up in the anatomy lecture theatre."

"I couldn't do it," said Clover. "I don't like the sight of blood."

"Blood doesn't worry me," said James. "It's spit that I can't stand. Mucus. That sort of thing."

"Well, you're not studying medicine. There's no mucus in economics."

"No," he said, and laughed. "Just sweat."

"And tears."

"Something missing there. Blood, I thought."

She glanced at him discreetly as he spoke. He had not changed; some softness had gone, perhaps, but that was what you would expect. He had been a beautiful boy, she thought, and now he was a beautiful man.

They sat down for coffee. Somewhere in the distance a bell chimed. He looked at her over the table.

"I'm glad that we bumped into one another," he said.

"So am I." She took a sip of her coffee. It was too hot, and she could feel it burn her lips. She wiped it away.

"Olivia," she said.

"What about her?"

"She doing economics with you?"

He nodded. "She's doing other subjects too. She wants to get a degree in economics and French."

The next question was blurted out unplanned. "Are you seeing her?"

He toyed with his coffee cup. "Yes, I am." He looked up. "And you? Are you seeing anyone?"

Her voice sounded hollow. "Yes. There's somebody on my course. He's Irish."

He looked away. "So. Good. I wouldn't like to think that you were seeing just anybody …"

Her surprise at his remark made her laugh. "Why?"

He reacted as if her question were an odd one. "Because … because we've known one another forever, more or less. Because you're a sort of sister to me, I suppose."

It cost her an effort not to wince. He had meant it well, but it was not what she wanted to hear.

"You don't have to worry about me," she said.

"Good," he said. "Well, what about … what about everything?"

"Where do we start? Do you hear from Ted?"

"All the time," he said. "He sends me e-mails about all sorts of stuff. Music. Movies. The works. Ted has views on a lot of things."

"He always did."

They talked for fifteen minutes before he said that he had to get back to his flat.

"I'll phone you," he said. "If you give me your mobile number."

She gave him the number. She watched him write it down on a scrap of paper; she watched his hands. They were brown because of the sun that had been on them and that now was so weak, so distant, so unconvincing. It was strange seeing him here in Scotland, detached from the setting in which they had both grown up. She feared for him, somehow; she feared that something would happen to him in this cold, northern country; that the light that was within him, that was nurtured by the Caribbean, would somehow weaken, would flicker and be extinguished in Scotland.

She watched as he tucked the piece of paper with her number on it into his pocket. You lost pieces of paper like that. He would lose that, she was sure of it, and she would not hear from him. And she wanted, more than anything else, to feel that she was somehow part of his life – not of his past, but of the life he was leading now. But it was far more than that: she wanted to be able to see him, to be in his presence. It was a patently dangerous desire and she knew she had been foolish in courting it again, to allow it oxygen when she was only too aware that all that it would do would be to bring her unhappiness. It was what people did, though, she admitted to herself; they knew that something was wrong for them, and yet they did it. Women fell for the wrong men, time after time, and men did the same thing in falling for the wrong women. We repeated mistakes, and that was why our mistakes were often so recognisable to us – why we were able to admit to them, just as we self-deprecatingly admitted to weaknesses – an inability to resist chocolate, a streak of laziness, human failings like that; our mistakes were familiar because we made them again and again.

She waited for him to call her. She said nothing about it to Padraig, because she had not mentioned to him that she had met James. It was surprisingly easy to keep a secret – one just said nothing, which was hardly difficult – although he noticed that she was anxious not to leave her phone behind when he came to collect her to take her to a concert. "Why take it?" he said. "You have to switch it off during the performance."

She said nothing, and then he asked her whether she was expecting a call. She shook her head.

"Then why take it?"

"Habit," she said.

She did not like to lie, but she could not bear the thought that James might call and the phone would ring unanswered. But he did not, neither that evening, nor the next. She tried to remember his exact words. He said he would phone, but did he say when? She could not remember. And was it significant, she wondered, that he had asked for her number and not volunteered his? People did that, of course; and they did it not because they did not want you to phone them, but because they intended to be the ones to call.

After a week he called. It was in the early evening and she was alone in the flat. She thought it would be Padraig, who had taken to phoning her at that time, and almost said *Hello, Padraig,* but stopped herself in time.

James hesitated at the other end of the line. "Clover?"

"Yes. James?"

He laughed. "Oh, sorry: I wasn't expecting to get you."

She wondered whether it was a joke. "Well, it is my phone."

"Yes, of course. It's just that I've dialled the wrong number. I wrote down somebody else's number and I think I had yours on a piece of paper too. I've mixed the two up. I thought ..." He uttered a stage groan. "This is getting complicated, isn't it?"

She struggled to sound unconcerned. "A bit."

"I thought I was phoning somebody else, you see, but I was dialling your number. A silly mistake."

"I see."

"Not that it isn't nice to speak to you. How are things?"

They spoke for a few minutes. She hoped that he was going to suggest a meeting, but he did not. Eventually he said that he would have to go as he had to make the call he had intended to make in the first place. He did not give the name of the person he was calling, and she did not ask. It could be anyone, of course; she understood that; it could be somebody from his course, or a male friend – he played squash, she remembered, and he might just be phoning to arrange a game. Or it could be that girl she had seen, or any one of the other girls who would be flocking round him.

She sat down. She threw the phone onto her bed. It rolled off and landed on the floor, on the threadbare rug by her bedside, the rug she had bought, third-hand, for her room in the boarding house at Strathearn, loved in spite of its coffee stains, its bare patches, its tendency to crumple. She lowered her head into her hands. She would be seeing Padraig later. He had asked her to go with him to the pub. He would be witty – as he always was – he would make her laugh. He would whisper to her; he would share everything; he would invite her to be his co-conspirator in the word games he played with the world. He was honest and good – and she was keeping secrets from him. She should tell him that she could not love him entirely, that there would always be part of her that would be with James; she should say that that was the way it was no matter how hard she tried to make it otherwise. She should tell him the truth and then ask him to understand, to help her to get over this, as he had already tried, although in a jocular way, to help her to do. But she knew that she would not say any of this, because the whole point of the feeling that she had for James was that others, for all their sound advice, would be unable to understand how she felt.

And of course she should have said something to James. She could have let him know how she felt for him – there were ways of doing that short of the sort of declaration that could spoil everything; because that is what would happen, she knew it; James liked her, but he was not in love with her. James did not think about her as she thought about him; his day did not start, nor end, with thoughts of her. Kind and considerate though he was, he phoned her only by mistake. *I am the sort of girl who gets called only by mistake* ... It was the sort of thing that Padraig would say, with his occasional flashes of Oscar Wilde wit, that came from being Irish and from having a father who was a director at the Abbey Theatre. Or it could equally well have been that woman her mother sometimes quoted, the one from New York who made witty remarks.

She wondered where James would be. In his flat presumably, unless he had already gone out with ... her, whoever she was. She tried to envisage him in the shared flat which would be a mess, like all those flats that boys lived in; dirty socks all over the place and unwashed plates festering in the kitchen sink, and a smell. She could see it, but there were details missing because she had no idea where it was. Flats on the south side of the town looked different from flats on the north side. You could always tell. She thought James might live in the New Town, in one of those Georgian streets, with the Firth of Forth visible through the window and the coast of Fife beyond it. He would be sharing with boys called Henry and Charlie and names like that, and they would spend half their time in the pub and going to parties. And they would be surrounded at weekends by girls like Olivia, who would laugh at their jokes and cook for them on the dirty cooker and then do the week's washing-up without complaint. She tried to picture the place again, and failed. She should find out. There would be no harm in finding out where it was; there was no harm in just looking.

26

She sent an e-mail to Ted. "I saw James the other day. You're still in touch with him, aren't you? Have you got his address (not e-mail – I have that – but his snail-mail address)? I don't seem to have it. We're going to meet up some time soon."

She read and re-read the message. Was it a lie? No. She had seen James – that was quite true – and it was also the case that she did not have his address – she did not have to say that he had not given it to her. They were going to meet, too, as James had taken her number and you did not take a number unless you intended to do something about it. So there was no deception in this message, even if she had not disclosed why she wanted to know the address. But there was nothing to be ashamed of in that respect, she told herself. It was quite understandable, she thought, to want to know where your friends lived. That was normal curiosity. It was. *It was.*

Ted was usually good about answering his e-mails, but on this occasion it was three days before he responded. The delay made her wonder whether he somehow knew that she wanted to … to what? To *spy* on James. But it was not spying. All she wanted was to be able to imagine the place where he lived, and that was definitely not spying. Wasn't there a song about that; somewhere in one of the old musicals that her father liked? About being on the street where a lover lives?

Ted's eventual answer set her mind at rest, giving her the address, including the postcode. She transcribed it into the back of the Moleskine notebook she used as a cross between a diary and a place for lists. It was, as she had imagined, on the north side of town; in Dublin Street, a street that ran sharply down

the hill from the Scottish National Portrait Gallery. It was just
the sort of place that she could see him living in, and from that
moment it was invested in her mind with a sort of glow. Of
course he would live in Dublin Street because it was … well, it
was just right for him.

The address revealed on which floor of the five-storey tenement
building his flat would be: the figure and letters "2FR" meant
that James would be on the second floor, in the flat on the right
hand side of the landing. Armed with this information, anybody
could, in theory, walk up the shared stone stairway and ring the
bell – provided, of course, that the lower door onto the street was
left unlocked. If it were locked, then there would be a bell system
allowing for the remote opening of the door. All you would have
to do would be to tug at the appropriate bell-pull and the outer
door could be answered from above.

Ted had other things to say in his e-mail. He was now
studying Romance languages in Cambridge. "You should come
and see me," he wrote. "I have a room in St John's looking out
onto a quad – they call them courts here – and if I put on the
right music – Tallis or somebody like that – you would think
you were back in the sixteenth or seventeenth century. It's the
opposite of Cayman, and I am *seriously* happy. I mean, seriously,
seriously happy. I have a friend who's an organ scholar here and
we're going to go to Italy in the summer. He knows people in
Verona and Siena. They say that we can stay with them. Can you
imagine it? And you? What about you? You'll see that I've put
James's address in at the end of this e-mail. I hope that you get to
see him, but … all right, I may as well be honest and say what I
want to say, or what I think I need to say. Don't die of a broken
heart. I mean that seriously. It's very easy to break your heart and

it may be – it may just be – that our hearts have been broken ever so slightly by the same person. Just a thought. Remember that he doesn't mean to make us unhappy – he's far too kind for that. But you know something? James may be like the sun. It's nice to have the sun out there but you can't look at it directly or get too close to it, can you? End of lecture. Be happy. Come and see me in Cambridge and we'll go out on the river in a punt. If it's summer, that is; if it's winter we'll go to a pub I know where they serve fish and chips and disgusting warm beer. You can sleep on my floor, or rather I'll sleep on my floor and you can have the bed. It's only moderately uncomfortable. Tuo amico, Ted."

She thought about Ted's invitation – it would be good to see him again, and he had proved a loyal friend. Those friends, she thought, were the ones whom one almost did not notice; the ones who were just there in the background, the unglamorous ones, the ones you took for granted and then, quite unexpectedly, might prove their loyalty by coming to your rescue in a moment of crisis. In her mind, Ted had remained, rather curiously, the little boy that he had been when they had first known one another; that was another feature of loyal friends – they were slow to grow up, and often, in your mind at least, failed altogether to get much beyond the age at which you first met them – that was an absurd notion, of course, but it concealed a more prosaic truth about old friends: they did not change. And yet here he was giving her advice, as one contemporary to another – which he was, of course, as they had entered the Cayman Prep on the same day, all those years ago, excited and frightened at the same time by the change that was occurring in their lives: that first step through the school gate is for most of us the biggest step we ever take – the step out of Eden into the world beyond.

She would accept the invitation, she decided, but then she stopped thinking about it because Dublin Street came back into her mind and now she had the address. She would go down there one morning – the following day, perhaps – and just take a look; that was all – just take a look. The timetable of the first year economics course was available online, and she consulted it. The first lecture on a Tuesday was at ten: *Macroeconomic Modelling*. How dull that sounded, and yet it was what James did, and that somehow rescued it. If the lecture were at ten, then he would have to leave his flat by nine-thirty at the latest to give himself enough time to walk up to George Square. Of course it was uphill most of the way, and that meant that he would need to leave somewhat earlier – by nine-fifteen perhaps.

If she were to be in Dublin Street by nine-fifteen, she would see him. He would come out of the door and she would be on the opposite side of the street – not too close – and she would see him. She could then walk behind him – sufficiently far off not to be seen – she could follow ... She stopped herself. It was not *following*. She was not the sort of person to *follow* somebody. All she was doing, she told herself, was taking the opportunity to see somebody, and there was nothing sinister about that. It was entirely natural to want to see friends in that way when you felt too shy, too proud, perhaps, to make the first move. And pride did play a part here; she acknowledged that; pride mixed with an element of tactics. Now that she had his address it would have been simple for her to go to see him, but she did not want to do that because he would think her pushy and she knew that men did not like being pursued – a woman who chases a man puts him right off, everybody knew that. Bide your time; wait for him to come to you. If she were to seem indifferent to James then there was a chance that he would come round to seeing her in the light in which she saw him; it might occur to him that she might be right for him. But if she made the running, it could spoil it all. He would back off … not, she reflected with a smile, that he had ever backed on. The realisation made her sad – that was the only word she could find for her feelings; James did not love her, or, if he did, he loved her as a brother, or as one friend of childhood may love another, platonically, fondly, and in no other way.

Of course there was Padraig. This, though, had nothing to do with him. This was her private business, and it was not as if she were being unfaithful to him. She would never have a love affair with somebody while seeing another person; her conscience, in that respect, was clear. Padraig did not need to know about James – beyond what she had already told him – because this was a private domain within her life, like a private enthusiasm, a self-indulgence that one did not discuss with other people because it was simply that – a private passion. You did not have to tell others you liked to listen to a particular piece of music and would play it again and again, or that you liked Rembrandt or Hockney and that you could spend hours poring over their paintings, experiencing the thrill that something entirely beautiful can impart; you did not have to share these things. You did not have to tell others that you loved a boy who you understood would never love you back but who was your secret treat, like a concealed box of chocolates. Nobody was harmed by such things.

"Why so early?" asked Ella.

She had made herself a slice of toast and a cup of coffee and was having these in the kitchen by herself when Ella came in, eyes still filled with sleep – Ella never got out of bed until ten unless absolutely obliged to do so.

"Seven-thirty isn't early. Not for me."

"It's virtually last night as far as I'm concerned," said Ella, making her way to the coffee pot. "May I pinch some?"

"Yes."

"So why so early? Are you going somewhere?"

"I thought I'd get some work done. I'm behind with an essay."

She thought: *this is what it is like to lie about a small thing; and there are people whose whole lives are built around lies, whose every move must be something like this.* For a moment she felt appalled at herself, and could have abandoned her plan, could have gone back to bed; but it was more powerful than she was – whoever the *she* was.

Ella poured herself coffee, cupping the mug in her hands, as if to warm them. "But the library doesn't open till nine."

"There's a departmental library. The Fine Art Library. That's open much earlier. It's a great place to work." This was half-true. The departmental library was sometimes open at eight-thirty, but not always; and she had never worked there.

Ella shrugged. "I've got a hangover. I don't deserve it. I had two glasses of wine – max – I swear it."

"Go back to bed."

"I will."

Clover left the flat ten minutes later and began the walk across town to Dublin Street. The streets were quiet at that hour, and barely light. It was technically late autumn, but there was a hint of winter in the air – a sharpness that was a harbinger of what was to come. Yet the sky was clear and when the sun rose properly it would be one of those sunny, exhilarating days that a northern city like Edinburgh can sometimes pull out of the hat – a day in which the senses are rendered more acute by the cold in the air; a day in which distances are foreshortened by clarity. The sunlight would not be warm, but it would still be felt, like the breath of an unseen creature upon the skin, a soft, slight touch.

She arrived at the top of Dublin Street a good half hour early. Broughton Street was not far away, and she thought that she might find a coffee bar there that would be open. There was one, a small room decorated with out-of-date posters advertising plays from the Festival Fringe. Even at this hour it was busy with people dropping in on their way to work; the people who were too busy to eat breakfast at home, or found they had no coffee in the flat, or simply wanted a few minutes to themselves before work started. She sat at a table with her steaming cappuccino and looked at the people about her. They were part of a world that seemed parallel to hers; a working world that she knew nothing about. What did people *do* in Edinburgh? She looked at the woman sitting at the table nearest hers; she was wearing a woman's business suit – a dark skirt and top under a neatly cut jacket. At her feet was a briefcase and on the table in front of her an open organiser-type diary. She was studying the diary, annotating it here and there; her days mapped out, thought Clover – her expensive time sold in little packages. She must be a lawyer. Or a financial adviser perhaps; telling people how to parcel out their own lives, how to move things about, how to move their money from one place to another.

Sooner or later, she would have to join them: everybody did. She would find herself in an office somewhere, working with people, doing the things that she currently had no idea about, living with one eye fixed on some goal or other – some promotion, some opportunity to do better than the next person, some inducement dangled before her. But for the time being she was spared all that and could sit and listen to people talking about art because … She hesitated, and then admitted it: because somebody else, somewhere else – her father – was doing exactly what this woman was doing. He went off to his office in George Town and sifted through papers and wrote figures on documents and looked out through air-conditioned air into the glare of the unremitting light until he went home and cooled off in the pool and was too tired to read or think very much. And he did all that not so much for himself – because he never seemed that interested in acquiring anything – but because of her and Billy and her mother, to enable them to do the things they did.

The woman at the next-door table glanced at her watch. Then, snapping her diary closed, she took a last sip of coffee and stood up. As she did so, she looked across at Clover and smiled. Clover, embarrassed at being caught staring, returned the smile guiltily.

The woman picked up her briefcase. "So, have a good day."

It was said in a friendly tone.

"I will. And you."

There could have been a barb to the exchange: the woman could hardly have missed the fact, from dress, from pace, from a number of other clues, that Clover had no job to go to, that she was a student and that none of this business of getting to work affected her yet. That might have produced a wry resentment, but had not.

Clover looked at her watch. Something had happened to her, and she thought that it was probably to do with having a brush with normality. The woman with her business suit and her diary had something real to do, as did all the others in the coffee bar. Their daily lives were real in a way in which the world she was creating for herself – a world of dreams – was not. She shook her head, as if to rid herself of an unwelcome idea. She did not have to go through with this; she could go back to the flat and forget that she had ever entertained the thought of coming down to Dublin Street.

She made her decision; she would do that, and immediately felt a sense of relief. She looked up. She was no longer a ridiculous love-struck girl on a pointless mission, not much more than one of those air-headed young teenage girls – as she thought of them – who swooned outside the hotels where boy bands stay on tour, ready to squeal with excitement when their heroes ran the gauntlet of their fans.

She finished her remaining coffee, savouring it though it was now lukewarm. Her thoughts turned to the day ahead. She had a tutorial at eleven and she would now have the time to finish the prescribed reading for it. She would throw herself into her work. She would lead a normal life. She would have one boyfriend, whom she would appreciate, and she would stop thinking of James.

And then, suddenly, he was there. She had not seen him come in because she was facing away from the entrance, and now, he was at the end of her table, half-turned away from the counter where he had been about to place his order, distracted because he had seen her.

His surprise seemed as great as hers. For a moment he was silent, but then he laughed and said, "Well, of all the people ..."

She made an effort to recover her composure. She had half-risen to her feet but now sat down again. She thought it possible that if she tried to stand again her feet would buckle under her.

"James ..."

The assistant waited patiently behind the counter. James turned to him and placed his order. Then he turned back to address Clover. "You're not in a hurry, are you? You looked as if you were about to go." He gestured to the other chair at her table. "Do you mind?"

"Of course not. I was about to go but I ..."

He interrupted her. "But you could do with another cup of coffee? Come on. My treat."

She acceded, and he called out to the assistant, "One more, Anton."

He sat down, casually resting his elbows on the table. "I've never seen you here before."

"No," she said. She was searching for an explanation, for an excuse for her presence, but her mind, for the moment, was blank.

"Somebody told me you live over on the south side. You do, don't you?"

She nodded. "A friend ..." she began. She wondered who had talked to him about her. And why?

He cut her off. "Yes, of course." He looked away, and changed the subject. "They make great coffee. The best in this part of town, I think, and it's just round the corner from me. I live on Dublin Street."

She almost said, "Yes, I know," but did not, and simply nodded at the information.

"You're lucky," she said. "New Town flats are nicer, I think."

"It depends. There are some that aren't. The rent's higher too."

It then dawned on her what he was thinking, and why he had dropped his enquiry as to what she was doing first thing in the morning on the other side of the city.

She felt herself blushing. "I don't usually come over ..."

He cut her short. "It's not the other side of the world," he said, and grinned. 'I sometimes go to that pub in Marchmont. You know the one?"

She nodded. She wanted to correct his mistaken impression, but could not see how to do it. She could hardly say *I came over here to see you walk out of your front door.*

Their coffee was brought over to the table. "I need this," he said. "A lecture at ten."

She spoke impulsively. "Something boring? Like macro-economic modelling?"

He laughed. He did not think it odd that she should know. "Right. Actually, it's not all that bad. It sounds it, but it isn't." He paused. "But ... well, I'm on the wrong course. It hasn't taken me long to discover."

"You're going to change? I thought you liked economics."

"Universities."

She caught her breath. "You're going to leave Edinburgh?"

"Yes, next semester. I can transfer the credit on the courses I'm doing this semester. Glasgow has exactly the right course for me. It'll fit what I'm going to be – an accountant." He smiled. "Like your dad. I should have chosen it first time round, but I wanted to come to Edinburgh. And I've really enjoyed Edinburgh – it's just that the subjects I want to do are right there in the Glasgow course."

She was silent.

"Are you all right?"

She nodded.

He was staring at her intently. "You don't seem happy, Clover. Are you homesick, do you think?" He gestured towards the street

outside. "This place is very different from Cayman. Obviously."
He paused. "I miss it too, sometimes. And will even more in the
future, I think."

She wondered what he meant. "Why the future?"

"You haven't heard? Sorry, I thought you knew. My folks have
left Cayman. Two months ago."

She felt her world slip further away.

"Where to?" Her voice sounded strained.

"Australia. My mother's from there originally, you know.
She wanted to go back, and I think my dad was a bit fed up
with Cayman. He wanted something new. He's got a job in a
medical practice in a place called Ballarat. It's not all that far
from Melbourne. I'll be going to see them over Christmas."

Clover struggled to keep herself under control. This was the end.
It was what she had decided she wanted, but it was still an end.

James was still looking at her. "I don't think you're happy," he
said quietly. "Boyfriend trouble?"

She shook her head vigorously.

He reached over and placed his hand on hers. "Are you still
with the same guy? The Irishman ... what's his name?"

"Padraig."

He took his hand away. "I hope he makes you happy." And
then, after a brief pause, "That's what I want, you know."

She thought: I have to tell him now. If I don't, I'm going to
have the rest of my life to regret it. There's a chance – just a
chance. I have to tell him.

But instead it was he who spoke. "You see, I never had a sister
and I suppose you're the closest thing I have to a sister."

She struggled with the words. "But I don't want to be your
sister ..."

He drew back, in mock apology. "Sorry! I don't mean to burden you."

"It's not that …"

But he interrupted her. He had remembered something and looked down at his watch. "Oh God, I've forgotten."

"Forgotten what?"

"I have to get a book back to the library by nine. And it's still in the flat. I'm going to have to run."

She could not say anything.

He wiped the foam off his lips. "I'll see you sometime," he said, and added, "Are you going home for Christmas?"

She nodded.

"I envy you."

She stared at the surface of the table, at the crumbs of something – a croissant, perhaps – that had lodged in a crack in the wood. She did not want her misery to show, but the thought struck her then – the strange, unexpected thought – that misery was not just in ourselves – it was in the things about us in the world.

"Then you'll see Ted," he continued. "Tell him to come up to Scotland and see us both. Either Edinburgh or Glasgow."

"I will."

"Good."

He waved to the assistant behind the counter, who waved back. Then, as if it were an afterthought, he blew a kiss to Clover. She blew the kiss back.

27

She went home for the full three weeks of the university's Christmas vacation. Amanda met her at the airport, accompanied by Billy, who was himself at boarding school now but had come home earlier. He was full of news of his soccer team, and regaled her for the whole journey home with his accounts of their last match. His goal, in the final minutes, had saved the match, he said, and had been mentioned at school assembly – enough to turn any head.

Her room was just as she had left it, but, and she found this curious, it was no longer her room: the things it contained were hers, but seemed like relics – exhibits in a museum of what had once been but was no longer. And it seemed strange, too, that her parents were leading the lives that they were: everything seemed so small, so limited; even people's conversation seemed to be stuck in a groove from which there was no escape. Her father still talked about the office; her mother about the tennis club; Billy about soccer and the doings of his friends; and Margaret about the people she knew at church, who, like everybody else, were doing, as far as Clover could work out, much the same things that they had always been doing.

A Christmas party had been planned, to take place a week before Christmas itself, and Amanda suggested that Clover could invite her friends too, or such of them as were on the island. "Ted's here," she said. "You'll know that."

Clover had yet to see Ted, although she had spoken to him on the phone. She would invite him, she said; he did not always like parties, but she would invite him.

"I thought everybody of your age liked parties," said Amanda.

"I did."

"Ted's different. Not everybody's the same, you know.""

"Ted's a nice boy, though."

She nodded. They were sitting together on the patio, on the edge of the pool. The water was cool and inviting, although neither had swum that morning.

Her mother glanced at her, and then looked away. "It's a pity that James isn't here," she said.

Clover reached down for a leaf beside her chair and twisted it in her hand. "Yes, it is."

"Because he'd be company for you. I'm worried that you're going to be bored, with all your friends in the UK now and nobody left here. Except for Ted, of course. And that Edwards girl – the one whose name I always forget. Her mother, by the way, has put on an immense amount of weight. She's as large as a house now. As large as a hotel, actually."

"That's a bit unkind. And she's called Wendy."

Amanda smiled. "Maybe. But if you're too worried about being kind to people, you end up saying nothing about anything."

"Possibly. But still ..."

"People lose control of themselves," Amanda continued. "They see food and they eat it. They lose their capacity for self-control. Look at the cruise ships."

"What about them?"

Amanda took off her dark glasses and polished them with the hem of her blouse. "The cruise ships that call in here ... the ones that come over from Florida. Look at the people."

"What about them?"

"They eat too much. Those boats are vast floating kitchens."

Clover shrugged. "It's the food manufacturers. It's the people who put the corn syrup or whatever it is in the food. They've made people into addicts, haven't they? It's not the fault of people themselves."

"So nothing's our fault? Is that what you're saying?"

"No, I'm not saying that."

They lapsed into silence.

Then Amanda said, "You have to make your own life, darling. You don't just accept what you're given ..." She left the sentence unfinished.

Clover waited, but when her mother did not continue, she asked, "Given by whom?"

"By life, I suppose. The cards we're dealt. Call it what you will."

Clover dropped the leaf she had been fiddling with. Her fingertips were now stained green by the sap. "Some people may not find it all that easy to do that."

Amanda agreed. "Of course not. Of course it's not easy." She looked at her daughter. "I'd never say it was easy." She closed her eyes. "It can be very hard."

There was a silence between them now that lasted for several minutes. Clover was conscious of the sound of her mother's breathing – and the sound of the water lapping at the edge of the pool. There was a rustle, too, in the undergrowth at the edge of the flower beds – a lizard or a ground bird pursuing its prey. Then Amanda said: "My darling, I know that you live with a big disappointment in your life. I know that because a mother can tell these things. You don't have to tell me that it's there because I know exactly what you must feel. Parents can put two and two together.

"And this disappointment isn't necessarily going to go away. It may get to hurt a little bit less as the years go by, but it may never go away entirely. So what you have to do is to get on with life and try to fill the place that one person once occupied with another. That may not work entirely, but it'll help. It's the only way of getting through life. You stop thinking about the things that haven't happened and think about the things that *are* happening, or might happen."

Clover was staring fixedly at the pool as her mother spoke. But she heard every word. "That's what I'm trying to do," she whispered.

"Good. I'm glad." And then, "Me too."

Clover turned to her mother. "You too?"

There was a moment of hesitation, but it was brief; the admission may not have been intended, but now it was made, and it could not be left where it was. "You must have wondered why Daddy and I spent that time apart. I know you never asked, and we gave you a very vague explanation about people not always getting on – that sort of thing. But you must have wondered."

Clover gave no confirmation.

"There was fault on both sides," her mother went on. "Your father seemed to lose interest in our marriage because he worked so hard. Men do that. It's nothing unusual. And then I discovered that I was becoming fond of somebody else. People do that too. Men and women. Everybody. It's terribly easy to do – particularly in a place like this."

She studied the effect of her words on her daughter. Clover was paying attention; she was not looking at her mother, but she was listening intently.

"I don't know what to say about what happened," Amanda continued, "and I've often thought about it since then and I've tried to be rational about it." She laughed. "It's the one thing, though – the one thing – that you just can't be rational about. And I think that's because love is fundamentally irrational – so how can you be rational about something that doesn't make sense?"

She paused, as if expecting Clover to answer, but she remained silent.

"It was as if a whole lot of colour had suddenly been injected into my life," Amanda went on. "You know those films where black and white suddenly becomes colour? The mood changes – everything lifts. Well, that's what it was for me. I found somebody I wanted to talk to, somebody who made the world about me seem different. I thought at the time that it was something special – that feeling – but of course it's the commonest thing in the world. It's what everybody feels when they fall in love. They just do.

"But it wasn't to be. Sometimes love simply isn't to be. It's as straightforward as that."

Clover spoke quietly. "So you had an affair anyway? Even if it didn't work out?"

"I wouldn't call it that."

"But that's what it sounds like to me."

"Well it wasn't – at least it wasn't in the way in which most people would use the word affair."

Clover felt relieved – but puzzled too. Did her mother mean that she fell for somebody but failed to take it any further? That must be it. In which case …

Amanda provided the answer. "It was maybe a bit like what happened to you. I became fond of somebody from a distance. It never went further than that."

Clover made a face; she could not help herself. But suddenly aware of what she was doing, she stopped. Amanda, though, had noticed. "I suppose it disgusts you. And I can understand that. Parents aren't really flesh and blood, are they? They're never quite the same as we are ourselves."

She rushed to apologise. "I'm sorry, Mum. I didn't mean it like that."

"I shouldn't have talked to you about this. It's my fault."

"No," insisted Clover. "It's mine."

They exchanged glances, tentatively, but feeling, rather to the surprise of both of them, fonder now of one another than at any time before, now that the transition to an adult relationship had been made. It had not taken much: just the admission of defeat, of disappointment, of human failing.

"Are you going to be all right?" asked Clover.

Her mother reached over and touched her arm gently. "Of course."

"Though it must be sad for you."

Amanda looked thoughtful. "Yes. I suppose it is." She hesitated. "But don't you think that sadness like that has ... well, I suppose, a special quality to it."

"I'm not sure."

"Well, I think it does. You're studying art history. You look at paintings, don't you? Some of them must have that in them – the sadness that goes with something being just out of your reach. Something unattainable."

"Maybe. I hadn't thought about it."

"Well, think about it now."

She had a question to ask her mother, and she was debating with herself as to whether she should ask it.

"There's something on your mind," said Amanda.

"Yes, there is. This person …"

Amanda looked away. The easy intimacy of the previous few minutes was suddenly no longer there. "I don't think I should talk about him. I hope you don't mind."

"You know about … about me and James."

"Yes, I know that. But I'm your mother. It's not surprising I should know."

"And shouldn't a daughter know about her mother's …" She was on the point of saying lover, but Amanda said it for her.

"Her mother's lover? That depends. In this case, there wasn't one. I told you: he never became my lover." She started to get out of her chair. "I think we should have a swim. Then we can go over to the tennis club. I know you say your tennis is rusty, but I'll play with one hand behind my back."

"You'll still win."

Amanda laughed as she reached down to give Clover a hand up. "Mothers have to win something. They lose a lot as it is, you might as well allow them to win at tennis."

Their party, planned to be held at the poolside, was threatened by rain. Heavy thunderclouds, towering cumulonimbus stacked high into the sky, built up in the afternoon, and by early evening were discharging sheets of rain. The tables, already laid out with linen – the bar, wheeled out on a trolley – were all quickly moved under cover by Margaret and her helpers. But then, their burden discharged, the clouds disappeared, and everything was moved outside again in time for the guests to arrive at seven.

Clover knew just about everybody, although there was a sprinkling of new friends that her parents had made amongst the shifting expatriate community. The old friends she had known all her life – her father's colleagues from the office, the same as they always were but slightly more worn-down; the dentist and his wife with their flashing smiles, walking advertisements for the benefits of cosmetic dentistry; the American dermatologist from over the road and his Colombian wife, smothered in gold jewellery; the Jamaican accountant, with his air of sad acceptance, and his stories of the times they had in Port Antonio before – and this with a shake of the head –"it all went wrong".

Ted was her guest, and she sat with him by the pool after they had filled their plates at the buffet.

She said to him, "You're going to come and see me in Edinburgh – remember?"

He nodded. "After you come to see me in Cambridge. I asked you first."

"Maybe."

She looked at him. His hair seemed a bit different, but it could have been ten years ago, and they could have been sitting in the tree-house.

Ted looked over at the knot of guests around the buffet table. "Look at them," he said.

"What about them?"

"Don't you find it hard to believe that they're … that they're still here?"

She laughed. "Yes, I do. Just like when I arrived at the airport and saw that it was still there. And when I think of other airports where there are thousands of people and you walk through tunnels and so on and there's no sky, nothing, and here you can pick flowers when you get off the plane and walk over to the building."

"Yes," he said. "Yes."

"And then there's everybody doing the same thing – and saying the same thing."

He had noticed too, he said. "I don't think I could ever live here again. Not permanently. Visits, maybe, but that would be all." He looked at her enquiringly. "What about you?"

"Probably the same."

He looked thoughtful. "Do you think that it's odd that here we are at our stage in life – we aren't exactly ancient – and we're already thinking about our past with a sort of nostalgia? Do you find that odd?"

She did – to an extent. "It's probably because we spent the earlier part of our lives in this rather peculiar place. It's like being … well, it's like being born in a garden, I suppose. And then you get a bit older …"

"And you step out of the garden," he interjected. "Yes, that's absolutely right. That's what it is."

"But we find a life on the outside," she said. "And we like it. It's more exciting. There's more of everything, not just the same old, same old."

"Yes," he said. "That's exactly what I feel."

She smiled. "We always agreed – you and I."

"Yes, we did."

She thought: *we were made for one another – except for one thing. For that reason, and then because I can't get over James. James, James.*

She looked at Ted. "Are you happy?"

He nodded vigorously. "Seriously happy. I think I told you that."

"You did. You sent me a nice e-mail. Just reading it, I felt really happy for you."

"I love Cambridge," he said. "I love the buildings. I love the sense of history. I love the gentleness of it all."

"Gentleness?"

"Yes, it's very … very civilised. People treat one another in a way that's very different from here. It's money here, isn't it? That's what really counts. Money."

She happened to see her father as Ted said this. "My father counts money," she said. "So do most of the people at this party. Or they do things for people who count money."

Ted laughed. "Very funny."

"That's the way it is."

She raised the subject gently. "And you've met somebody?"

He was slow to answer, and she wondered whether she had intruded. But he had told her about it first and so he must be ready to talk about it.

"I have," he said. "And I'm pretty pleased about it."

"Just pleased? That doesn't sound very enthusiastic."

"No, I am enthusiastic. Very. Yes, I've found somebody whose company I really enjoy. And I think he likes me too."

"That's important."

"Yes, it is."

"He's a really good musician. In fact, he can do most things really well. He's a keen skier too. I've never learned, but he's good enough to be in the university team. But he doesn't have time to do it – he's an organ scholar and they have to spend all that time in chapel."

"It sounds great."

"It is. I know it is. I think I mentioned we were going to go to Italy. He knows these people. His dad is pretty grand, actually, and they have all these wealthy friends with villas in Italy and so on. He's been invited, and he says I can come too. We're going to go in the summer."

"You must be very happy."

"Of course I am. But I know it's not going to last."

She looked at him with concern. "You shouldn't say that. How do you know?"

"Because these things don't. I'm being realistic. They don't last all that well in the straight world, let alone if you're gay. It's more difficult, I think. It just is. People don't meet at university and stay together. They get bored with one another."

"I thought that was changing."

He sighed. "A bit, maybe. But not all that much."

"I hope that it will for you."

"Thank you." He paused. "And you? What about you?"

She looked beyond the guests. The two helpers Margaret had brought – a Jamaican couple from her church – were laying out more plates. They both wore white, as Margaret did when she went to church.

"Me?" she said. "I'm fine. I suppose I'm fine. Yes, I'm all right. Yes …"

He reached out to her.

"Because of …"

"Because of him. Yes."

"You can't."

"I know I can't. I know what I should do. People keep telling me. My mother. You. Everybody. Although you told me once not to give up – remember? Then, when you wrote to me, you said something different. You said what everybody else says." She made an effort now, and composed herself. "I'm going to be fine.

I'm going to live my life, and I'll try to get as much as I can out of it, but all the time I know I'm going to think of him. Sad, isn't it?"

"I don't think so. Not sad in the sense of being pathetic. Sad for you otherwise, I suppose."

"It's forever," she said quietly. "Whoever is up there in the sky looked down on me and said – 'It's forever for you.'"

The tension was defused. "You sound like Margaret."

"Maybe. But she believes it. I don't."

"You don't believe there's somebody up there … allocating things for us?"

She shook her head. "I believe there may be something – I don't know why, but I just think there is – but it's not a man with a white beard."

"Or a woman?"

"No. If it were a woman, she wouldn't make things so hard for women."

They laughed, but she thought: *would it be less embarrassing to talk about a goddess than a god?*

"When I was a boy," he said, "I thought I would get struck by lightning if I said things like that."

"I saw some lightning today," she said. "In that storm."

"I wonder who was struck."

"I didn't see. But I bet they deserved it."

They looked at each other and smiled. She wanted to kiss him at that moment, and she wondered whether he would object. A chaste kiss, to the cheek; a kiss that would say everything about everything; about the value of old friends; about how she wanted him to be happy forever, in spite of his belief that happiness, for him, in his own view of his situation, was likely to be temporary.

But surely all happiness was temporary, she thought – or most of it. That was what made us aware of it – the fact that it was a salience, something that stood out from our normal emotional state. She would not describe herself as unhappy, and yet she knew that she could be happier than she was at present. She would be happy if James were with her, which he was not; and, she thought, he never would be. She heard a snatch of song on the radio – a line from a folk tune – that resonated and somehow seemed right for her. The singer reflected on things that could never be, or at least would never come about "until apples should grow on an orange tree". Until then, she thought; until then. The song finished and was gone, and she had not heard its title or the name of the singer. The plaintive line, however, remained in her mind. *Until apples should grow on an orange tree.*

28

James went to Glasgow at the end of the semester. He sent her an e-mail a few months later, but it did not say very much. She read it and re-read it, and then, resolving that she would treat it as nothing special, deleted it. Ted gave her news of him from time to time, and when Ted eventually paid his visit to Edinburgh she invited James to join them for a meal. The distance between the cities was not great – forty-five minutes by train – but they were different worlds, it seemed, and he rarely made the journey. On that occasion he was away – he played rugby for a university team and they had a match that weekend in Inverness. Ted seemed relieved that James would not be there.

"It is nice to have you to myself," she said. "And besides …"

He looked at her quizzically.

"I'm over him," she muttered.

"Are you? Really?"

She shook her head.

"You see," he reproached her. "You should listen to me."

"I will. Eventually."

He looked doubtful. "Try harder." And then added, "I like Padraig. What's wrong with him? I don't see anything. Mind, you get a bit closer to him than I do …"

"Padraig's fine," she said. "He's considerate and witty and I like him a lot."

"Like?"

"Like."

Ted shrugged. "That's the problem, isn't it? Liking and loving really are different. But I'm not here to lecture you."

The visit was a success, and he came back to Edinburgh later that year. She went to Cambridge, and Ted put on a picnic for her by the river. He took her to Grantchester and recited Rupert Brooke's "The Old Vicarage" by heart, learned, he told her, specially for the occasion.

"You're very clever," she said teasingly. "How many boys can recite Rupert Brooke and understand about art and everything? And be good-looking at the same time. How many?"

"I'm not good-looking."

"Yes, you are. You're everything a girl could want."

He laughed. "Except for …"

"Who cares about that?"

He affected surprise. "Are you asking me to marry you? Really, Clover, you're rather *forward*, aren't you?"

She said that she would be happy to be married to him. "We could have a pact. If nobody else ever asked us, then we could settle down together."

"I'd love that," he said. "No, I really would. I could promise that I wouldn't ever look at men and you could promise to look the other way." He became serious. "Does Padraig mind? Does he mind your going off to see another man like this? Some men would be jealous."

He said this with a smile, and then winked at her.

"He's not the jealous type."

"Good." Then after a pause, he asked, "Are you going to stay with him forever?"

She did not reply immediately. She had not really thought about it, but now that she did, she realised that this was not what she intended. And the fact that she had not thought about the question itself provided the answer.

"No." The word slipped out.

"I thought you wouldn't."

"Things are all right at the moment. We enjoy being together. It's ..."

"Comfortable? Is that the word?"

"Maybe. But what's wrong with being comfortable?'

He thought that nothing was wrong with it. But he pointed out that one could go to sleep if one became too comfortable.

"And what's wrong with going to sleep?"

What was wrong with being asleep, he said, was that sleep amounted to nothing, and that the more you slept the shorter your life – your real life – became.

"Oh well," she said.

"Yes," he said. "Oh well. So how long are you going to keep Padraig? Until you finish at Edinburgh?"

"I'm not that calculating."

"But that's what's probably going to happen."

It was, she conceded, and he was proved right. Over the three years that followed, she stayed with Padraig. They did not live together, but they spent much of their spare time in each other's company. In those three years, she saw James four times – twice at parties in Edinburgh when they happened both to know the host, once in a pub in Edinburgh after a rugby match between Scotland and Wales, and once, by chance, in the street. Although brief, each of these meetings seemed to open a wound that she had thought closed. James was kind to her – as he always was – and treated her as an old friend whom she saw very occasionally but was always pleased to meet again. But that was all. She did not see him with a girl, and hesitated to ask, even if he asked after Padraig. Ted had hinted that James had met somebody in Glasgow but he had been tactful and had not said much. She had closed her ears to the information; she did not want to hear it.

The meeting in the pub was the most difficult one for her. She was there with Padraig who had gone to the game at Murrayfield Stadium and had arranged to meet her for a drink before going out to dinner. Padraig was at the bar, ordering the drinks, and she was standing in a crush of people, looking for somewhere to sit. James had appeared beside her, and had leaned over and kissed her on the cheek. He was with several male friends, whom he introduced to her, but she did not get the names.

"You're here with Padraig?" he asked.

She glanced towards the bar. It was taking time for Padraig to be served. "Yes, I am. And you ..."

"Pity."

The word was muttered, and she thought she had misheard him. But it had sounded like it; it had sounded like *pity*. She caught her breath. *Pity.* Did that mean that he hoped that Padraig was over – that she was free to go out with him? She closed her eyes momentarily, feeling dizzy.

The moment passed, and she thought: *he did not say it. It was what I wanted him to say – that's all.*

He spoke about the rugby. "I've been at the game," he said. "Scotland played okay – not brilliantly, but okay enough."

"They try," said one of his friends. "They try but in rugby it's not a question of trying, but scoring tries."

She looked at James. I'm standing next to him, she thought. I could easily say to him, James, I've wanted to say something to you for years now and here we are standing in this bar and I have the chance and ...

The moment passed. Padraig returned with drinks and James went off with his friends. She could not stay.

"I don't want to stay here," she said to Padraig. "I'm really sorry. I'm not feeling well."

He was solicitous – he always was – but she turned down his offer to accompany her home and left by herself. The street outside was filled with rugby supporters. Some of the Scottish fans, draped in tartan, were singing a song about ancient wrongs; she avoided them and went down a quieter side street. She stopped and looked in a shop window – the first shop window she came to. There was camping gear on display, and outdoor clothing too. There was a large picture of a young man and woman standing on top of a Scottish mountain, a cairn of stones by their side. She looked at them, and at their smiles. She turned away and began to walk down the street again. She felt the tears in her eyes, and within her a bleak emptiness – a feeling of utter, inconsolable sorrow over what she did not have. For all the time that had passed – for all her efforts – he could still do that to her. It was her sentence, she decided, and it seemed that it was for life.

When the time came for her to graduate, Padraig, who was about to embark on a master's course, was awarded a six-month travelling scholarship. He chose to spend his time in Florence and Paris, with three months in each city. He told her of the award and shyly, and rather hesitantly, invited her to come with him. She sensed, though, that the invitation was less than whole-hearted, an impression strengthened by the fact that he seemed relieved when she said that she had other plans. These plans were barely laid – her parents had offered her a gap year, which she had decided to take, but beyond that she was uncertain as to what to do. She had thought of going to Nepal with a friend who had taken a job as a teacher of English, but nothing definite had been arranged.

"I think we need to split up," she said. "I don't think you really want me to come to Italy and France with you."

"But I do," he protested. "I wouldn't have asked you if I didn't."

"I'll just get in your way."

He seemed hurt. "What do you mean by that?"

She spoke gently. "Things come to a natural end, Padraig. It's nothing to get upset about. We've had three years – more actually – and now …"

He looked resigned. "Your problem, Clover, is that all the time you've been with me, you've been in love with somebody else."

She was unable to answer him. Had it been that obvious?

They sat and stared at one another in silence. She felt empty, but she could not rekindle something that she knew now, just as he did, had run its course.

Eventually Padraig spoke. "I suppose you can't help it. I don't hold it against you for exactly that reason. It's your … how should I put it? It's your burden. But I must admit I feel sorry for you. You're in love with somebody who isn't there. He just isn't in your life. I'm sorry, Clover, but I think that's really … really pathetic. Sad."

His words struck home. *He just isn't in your life.* But he was. He had been a friend to her over all these years. She rarely saw him – that was true – but he was always so nice to her when she did see him. He smiled at her. He clearly liked her. He was kind and showed an interest in what she said to him. He was in her life. He was. And as for Padraig's pity – she did not want to be pitied, and told him so.

"All right, I'm sure you don't – and I'll try not to. But for

God's sake, don't let it completely ruin your life. You only have one life, you know. One. And you shouldn't try to live it around somebody who isn't living his life around yours. Do you see that? Do you get that?"

She wept, and he comforted her. They would always be friends, he said, and she nodded her assent.

"Don't wreck your gap year, Clovie," he whispered. He rarely called her that; only in moments of tenderness. "People fritter them away. Do something with it. Promise?"

She promised.

"And don't spend it thinking about him. Promise?"

She promised that too, and he kissed her, gently, and with fondness, in spite of what he had said – and what he had thought – setting in this way, with dignity, the seal on an ended relationship.

29

Nepal proved easy to arrange, being simply a question of money, which her father, having agreed to fund a gap year, provided without demur. The organisers of *Constructive Year Abroad*, though, were unable to fit her in to their programme until six months after her graduation. They had other suggestions to fill the time – a three-month engagement as an assistant (unpaid) in a Bulgarian orphanage? She would be working for part of the time in an orphanage in Nepal – the rest of her time would be on a school building programme – and she was not sure whether she wanted to spend too much time on that. They understood, of course, and suggested a conservation programme in Indonesia. That, though, was unduly costly and she decided to save her father the expense. To stay in Edinburgh until she left for Nepal would be cheaper, she felt, and she could get a casual job for a few months to cover her expenses.

She wrote to Ted, who had arranged to spend a year teaching English in Lyons: "I feel vaguely guilty about the whole thing. The Nepal thing costs serious money and surely it would be better if we were simply to give them the money to do whatever it is I'm meant to be doing there. I can't get it out of my mind that this is all about people whose families have got money – you and me, Ted, let's be honest – pretending to do something useful but really having an extended holiday. A year off, just *off*. That's what it is, isn't it?"

He wrote back: "Yes, of course. They don't really need you in Nepal. But, okay, you won't be doing any actual harm, will you? I suppose if they sent gap year people to build schools that actually *fell down* then there'd be a case for not doing it at all, but you're not going to do that, I take it. There'll be people – *real people* – out there who will make sure that whatever you build is going to be done properly, or at least not dangerously. So don't feel guilty. Sure, don't feel heroic, either, but not guilty. And as for having money, well, we don't really have it, do we? Our folks are admittedly not on the breadline, and they do happen to live in a tax haven, but they're not going to support us forever and we're going to have to earn our living. On which subject, any suggestions? You know what I'm thinking of being after I finish teaching English to the French? A marketing trainee. There's a firm near Cambridge that has actually offered me a job one year from now, unless the economy takes a nose-dive. How about that for glamour? Would you like to join me? We could do marketing together; just think of it."

The job she got in Edinburgh was at a delicatessen that also served coffee. She was to be in charge of the coffee, which she found that she enjoyed doing. The owners, a middle-aged couple who had taken on the business only a few months previously, were still learning and were good-natured. She was happy in her work and made a number of new friends. She had remained in Ella's flat, which was not far from the delicatessen, and it occurred to her that it would be simpler not to go to Nepal at all. But if she felt guilt about her expensive gap year, how much more guilty, she decided, would she feel if she did nothing with the year. She remembered Padraig's advice – his exhortation – that she should not fritter the year away. Padraig had approved of Nepal when she had told him about it.

"Good," he had said. "That's exactly the sort of thing you should be doing – something useful."

She had heard from James, who had called her unannounced

shortly before her graduation and told her that he might be coming to Edinburgh a few days later and suggesting that they should see one another. She had agreed, and they had met in the same pub where they had met after the rugby match. This time it was worse. She had gone into the pub, looked around, and seen him sitting at a table with a girl. She had stopped and had been on the point of retreating when he saw her and waved. It was too late then, and she had to join them.

The girl was from Glasgow, and had accompanied him to Edinburgh. Clover had been able to tell immediately that the meeting in the pub had not been the main aim of the trip, and James confirmed this.

"We've got some friends over here," he said. "They've bought a flat and are having a flat-warming party."

Her heart sank at the word *we*, the most devastating word for the lonely. "I see."

"Yes. I thought it would be good to take the chance to catch up with you. I realised that I hadn't seen you for ages."

He was being his usual friendly self, she thought. He has always been nice to me – always.

James turned to the girl beside him. "Clover and I go back a long time. One of my first friends, aren't you, Clove?"

The girl looked at her and smiled. But the smile, Clover could tell, was forced.

"There's nothing like old friends," James continued. "There was Clover, me, and a guy called Ted." He paused. "Ted says he's going to France."

She nodded. "Yes. To teach English."

"Everybody does that," said James. "Except me, I suppose. You know I'm going to Australia in two weeks' time. Did I tell you?"

Clover absorbed the news in silence. She felt quite empty within. There was nothing.

"My folks are in a place called Ballarat – I think I mentioned that to you."

She nodded.

"Anyway, I've decided that since I can get a work permit because my mother's Australian and I'm going to be eligible for an Australian passport, I might as well do my training out there. I was going to one of the large international accountancy firms anyway, and they said they had no objection to my transferring my training contract to Australia. They have a branch in Melbourne. That's where I'm going to do it."

Clover glanced at the girl. "What are you doing?"

The girl shifted in her seat. "I've got a job in Glasgow. I work for the Clydesdale Bank."

"Shelley's doing a banking traineeship," said James.

"So you're not going to Australia," said Clover.

The question seemed to annoy Shelley. "No," she said tersely. "I'll go to visit James, though, won't I, James?"

It sounded to Clover like a territorial claim. "That'll be nice," she said.

"Yes," said James. "And you should come and see me there sometime too, Clover."

Shelley looked at her, and then looked quickly away.

"Maybe I will," said Clover.

"I mean it," said James. "You've got my e-mail address. Just let me know."

Shelley glanced at her watch. Clover noticed; she herself did not want to stay now.

"I have to go soon," she said.

James seemed disappointed. "But you've just arrived."

"We have to keep an eye on the time too," interjected Shelley. "Maddy and Steve said ..."

"Of course," said James. He turned to Clover and smiled. "I wish we'd seen more of each other. I suppose that my being in Glasgow and you being here – well, somehow I hardly ever seemed to get that train."

She felt a wrench at her heart. It had been a mistake to see him, she felt. And now she was to say goodbye, which would be for the last time, she thought, as Australia was a long way away. She said to herself: I am about to say goodbye to the person I have loved all my life. I shall never see him again.

She stood up.

"Don't go," he said.

"I have to," she said. "Sorry."

She felt the tears well in her eyes; she did not want them to see – neither of them. She turned away. James stood up. "Clover ..."

She reached the door without turning back, and only gave a glance then, and a quick one. Shelley was saying something to James, and then she looked at her. Their eyes met across the floor of the pub, across the void.

Her job became busier as the city filled with festival visitors. The streets around the delicatessen were lined with Victorian tenements, many of which during university term-time were occupied by students. During the summer months the tenants covered their rent by sub-letting to the waves of hopeful performers who came to Edinburgh for the Fringe, the rambunctious add-on to the official festival, bringing with them shows that for the most part would be lost in the programme of several thousand events. Optimism sustained them; the hope of a review, of being spotted by somebody who counted, of being heard in the cacophony of a festival that opened its doors without audition and sent nobody away unheard – even if it was by audiences that sometimes numbered no more than one.

She noticed the groups of Fringe performers drifting into the delicatessen, and spoke to some of those who chose to stay for coffee. The cast of a student *Midsummer Night's Dream*, brought from a college in Indiana, came in each morning shortly before their ten o'clock rehearsals, to rub shoulders with a group of *a capella* singers from Iceland and a dance ensemble from Nicaragua. Their regular customers, those whose normal lives continued over the festival month, were accustomed to the annual invasion, and calmly purchased their cheese and cold meats against this polyglot backdrop. For Clover it meant long hours, but it was what she wanted. Ella was still in the flat, and so she had some company to go back to, but she now found herself slightly irritated by her flatmate's laziness and failure to do her fair share of cleaning. For the first time since she had moved into the flat, she found herself wanting to move out, to get on with the next stage of her life.

With most of her university friends away, she struggled with loneliness. She missed Padraig more than she imagined she would, and she wondered whether he would be feeling the same. Probably not, she decided. He had now taken up his scholarship and was in Florence. He sent her a photograph of himself standing beside the Arno – *Me by the Arno*, he wrote – and he sent her a copy of a piece he had written for the *Irish Times* on a minor Italian artist of the nineteen-twenties who had met James Joyce in Paris and disappeared the next day. "Some people get depressed by contact with greatness," he wrote to Clover. "Some people get disheartened."

She was not sure whether the reference to being disheartened was personal. She did not think that he would miss her; not, she thought, when one could go and stand by the Arno. She toyed with the idea of writing to him and confessing that she missed him and wondered whether they had done the right thing in splitting up, but she decided that she would not. That would be going backwards, trying to prolong something that had come to a natural and not-too-upsetting end. She would meet somebody else, she decided. It was time. There were plenty of young men in Edinburgh; the Fringe seemed to bring them in their hundreds and surely one of them would be looking for somebody like her.

"How do you get a new man?" she asked Ella one evening when she was cleaning up the breakfast plates that Ella had left unwashed.

Ella laughed. "You joking?"

"No, I'm not."

Ella shrugged. "How did you meet the last one?"

"He came up to me and told me his name," she said. "It was at a party."

"There you are. Parties."

"If you get invited to them. What if you don't?"

"Internet dating," said Ella. "Haven't you seen the figures? Apparently that's where everybody meets these days. You go on an internet dating site and you say something such as 'likes eating out' or 'into jazz' or whatever, and then you get your replies. You take it from there."

Clover frowned. "I couldn't. I just couldn't."

"Then you'll have to go to a pub or a coffee bar and sit around.

Somebody will come and talk to you if you're there long enough. It's easy. All you have to do is look as if you're looking for a man. Then they come to you. That's the way it works."

"I couldn't."

"Then you're not going to get a new man, Clover." She paused. "Do you really think you *need* one? Men can be overrated, you know. Okay, they may be useful for one or two things – sometimes – but not for the whole weekend."

They both laughed. Then Ella said, "But isn't there one in the background? I thought there was some guy somewhere you were keen on. Didn't you tell me once?"

"There was," said Clover. "Not any more."

"Is he with somebody else?"

"Probably. Yes, I think he is."

Ella looked up at the ceiling. "Frankly I don't think that's always an obstacle – know what I mean?"

"You mean: detach him?"

"Exactly. Prise him away. Steal him."

"I couldn't," said Clover.

"Then you're never going to get a man, Clover. We'll be old maids together. How about it? We can stay here until we're fifty, bickering. We can go to the cinema and pilates classes together. We can talk about the men we knew a long time ago and about what happened to them."

"No thanks."

"Then you're going to have to be more proactive. Steal him – the one you always liked." She grinned. "Trap him. Or …"

"Or what?"

"Or spend the rest of your life regretting what you didn't do. That's how life is for lots of people, you know – it's made up of things they failed to do because they were too …" And here she gave Clover a searching look. "They were too timid."

"Is that my problem?"

"Could be. I'm going to say it once more: steal him, this … what's his name?"

"James."

"Sounds sexy," said Ella. "Steal him."

She wrote to her father: "I know that you said I could use the money for anything – and I really appreciate that. But I thought I'd just check up with you, in case you thought that I was throwing your money around. Everything is sorted out for Nepal, but it's not going to happen for a while yet – not until February, which still seems like a long way away – I'm counting the days. I've been working, as you know, in a delicatessen. It's been quite busy recently but I'm enjoying it. They're paying me just above minimum wage, which is not meanness on their part but because they've just started the business and they don't have much money themselves. I don't mind. What I earn there more than covers the rent for my room in the flat.

"What I wanted to tell you is that I want to spend some of the money on a ticket to Australia. I want to go to Melbourne for a few weeks – maybe three, I think. I've met a girl here who's with a drama company doing something on the Fringe – it seems like the whole world is here at the moment. She's a member of a group called Two-Handed Theatre and they're putting on a couple of plays at the Fringe. She's invited me to come to see her in Melbourne when they go back there in a couple of weeks and I thought: I don't get many invitations to Australia. So I thought I'd go. I can get a ticket through Singapore for under a thousand,

and since you've been so generous I can afford it. But I didn't want you to think I was being … what's the word – profligate? Yes, profligate. Is that okay with you?"

It was. David wrote back: "The whole point of a gap year is that you can do things you can't do at any other stage in your life. Of course you should go to Australia. Going there has been on my list for years but I've never done it. And that's another point to a gap year – it gives you the chance to do things that your parents would have liked to do but have never had the time to fit in. Like visiting Australia. Or Nepal. Or anywhere, really."

The invitation from Frieda, the Australian actress, had been repeated more than once and so Clover knew that it was not one of those casual "you must come and see me" invitations that nobody really intends to be taken seriously. Frieda had been coming in for morning coffee since Two-Handed Theatre had first arrived for their run on the Fringe, and Clover had engaged her in conversation. Frieda was seven or eight years older than she was, but she liked the Australian's easy manner and enthusiasm; Edinburgh, said Frieda, was a box of chocolates that she intended to consume entirely before returning to Melbourne. Her attitude to her show also intrigued Clover; while most Fringe performers had about them an earnest intensity, founded, perhaps, on their conviction that their contribution to the Fringe was on the cusp of artistic greatness, Frieda was realistic. "We're enjoying ourselves," she said. "I'm not sure if the audience is, but we are." And on her own ability: "I can't really act, you know. I sort of play myself all the time but since the audience has never met me before they think I'm acting. It seems to work."

After the second invitation, Clover said, "I could come to Melbourne, you know."

"Great. Come."

"For a few weeks? If I came for a few weeks? Just to see the place."

This would have been the time for Frieda to claim to be too busy, to say that she was going to be elsewhere, but she did not. Instead, she suggested that Clover could stay in the converted fire station that she shared with five of her friends. "Contribute something to the rent, and you're in. You get one shelf in a fridge. Not to sleep in, you know; you get a sort of cupboard for that, but it's not bad. It's quite a big cupboard. You don't exactly get a bed – you get what used to be a bed and is now a sort of mattress on the floor of the cupboard. But as fire stations go, it's not all that uncomfortable."

"It sounds irresistible. I'll come."

Frieda seemed genuinely pleased. "I'll show you round Melbourne. We may have a show on – you can help with front of house if you like." She paused, looking around the delicatessen. "What about this job? Will they hold it for you?"

Clover explained that it was not an issue, as she thought that the owners could manage without her or could easily enough find somebody else. And that proved to be the case.

"It's a relief," the husband said.

"It's not that we don't appreciate what you do," the wife explained. "We do, but paying you is difficult. We just can't manage any more. We'll get somebody more part time."

She confirmed the ticket with the travel agent, arranging to arrive a couple of days after Frieda would have returned home.

"One thing interests me," said Frieda. "Why are you coming? Sorry to sound rude – and I'm really pleased that you're doing it – it's just that I wondered why." She gestured to the street outside. "This place is so exciting. It's like living on an opera set. Why Melbourne?"

Clover hesitated. She had not admitted it to herself yet, and now she was being asked directly. If she found it easy enough to deceive herself, it was not so easy to deceive this new friend of hers, with her trusting openness.

"There's somebody I'd like to see there. I suppose that's why."

Frieda smiled. "A boy?"

Clover nodded.

"I guessed as much," said Frieda. "I thought there was something."

"But people can want to go to Melbourne for plenty of reasons."

"Oh yes," said Frieda. "That's true enough. But it wasn't just the fact that you wanted to go to Melbourne. It's something about you. There was something in your manner that made me think ..."

Clover waited for her to complete her sentence. She found the observation rather unsettling.

"A certain – how shall I put it? Sadness. Yes, I think that's it. You know, when I saw you first – here in this place, operating that coffee thing over there with all that steam and hissing and so on, I thought: that girl's sad about something."

Clover looked away.

"I'm sorry if this embarrasses you," said Frieda. "I'll shut up, if you like. We don't like to hear about ourselves. Or at least most of us don't. It disturbs our self-image because how other people see us is often wildly different from how we see ourselves." She shuddered. "The truth can be a bit creepy, I think."

"I don't know ..."

"Oh yes, it can be. Most of us have a persona we project to the outside world – it's the part of us they see. And then there's the bit behind that, which is the bit that remains with us when we turn the lights out. You know what it is? It's what people used to call the soul. But now, we're not meant to have souls." She smiled. "It's *really* old-fashioned to have a soul, Clover. But there's this … this *thing* inside us that's the core of what we are – what we are individually, that is. And in your case …"

Clover waited. "In my case …"

"In your case, that bit is sad. It's sad because it's incomplete. It's seen something that it wants more than anything else in the world, and it can't get it." She paused. "Okay, I sound like a New Age freak going on about auras and so on. But it *is* there, you know. That sadness. I'm sorry, but it's there."

"Maybe."

"Good. You're admitting it. Plenty of people won't."

"I don't want to conceal anything from you."

"That's good to hear. But listen Clover – this boy, tell me about him."

The owners were looking at her. Conversations with the customers were not discouraged, but there was work to be done.

"I can't now," said Clover. "But there's this boy I loved, you see. I've loved him ever since I was six, I think – or thereabouts."

Frieda beamed. "That's really romantic. I just love that sort of story. Eternal love. Enduring love. It's great. We need more of that. Roll it on. Roll it on." Her smile faded. "But he …"

Clover nodded.

"He's in love with somebody else?" Frieda probed.

"I don't know."

This brought surprise. "You don't know? How come? Haven't

you asked him?"

"No. Not really."

Frieda looked incredulous. "What's wrong with you people? Are you so uptight? Is this something to do with being English?"

"I'm not English," said Clover. "My father's from here originally and my mother's American."

"Then you've no excuse for being so English," retorted Frieda. "Listen, so this guy's in Melbourne?"

"Yes. He moved there quite recently. His parents live in Australia now – his mother's Australian."

"But he's in Melbourne, right? This ... what do you call him?"

"James."

"This James is in Melbourne. Well ... well, that's where you need to be, Clover. Welcome to the Old Fire Station." She fixed Clover with an intent look. "Do you need some help with this? I think you might."

"Thanks, but I don't see how you could help me."

"You don't? Well, you'll see."

The following morning, Frieda showed her a picture of the Old Fire Station. "Friendly building, isn't it?"

Clover said that she liked the look of it.

"That's where the fire engines came out," said Frieda, pointing to a large window. "It used to be a door. And we've still got the pole inside, you know, that the firemen used to slide down to get to the engines, but nobody slides any more. Somebody did when he was drunk, though. He forgot to hold on. You have to grip the pole quite tightly as you go down, or you go down too fast. He broke his ankle." She paused. "I can't believe you're coming, Clover. It's going to be great."

'Thank you."

"And that little problem with that boy. We'll deal with that. We'll get it sorted."

She swallowed. I've made a mistake, she thought. She wanted to say: *You can't sort things out just like that*, but there was something about her new friend that made her feel almost helpless.

Frieda reached out and patted Clover's arm affectionately. "Still sad?"

Clover shook her head – an automatic response to an intrusive question.

"I think you are," said Frieda. "But we can sort that out."

She noticed Clover's expression. "You don't believe me?" she said, smiling. "You don't believe I can sort boys out?"

30

"Did you think it would be like this?" asked Frieda. "Is this how you saw the fire station? Of course, I showed you that picture, didn't I – when we were in Edinburgh. But reality's always a bit different, isn't it?" She made a face. "Thank God for that too. When I look at a photograph of myself I think: reality's different, so no worries."

Somebody had created a door as well as a window within the large double door at the front of the building. This led into the hall in which Clover now found herself standing.

"Is this where the fire engines …" she began.

Frieda lifted Clover's backpack from the concrete floor. "Yes. That wall over there blocks off the main garage – and it's all changed, of course. But this is where they parked them. Actual red fire engines – as advertised. Big hoses. Bells – the works." She was an actress, and it seemed she could not resist. "The calls came through. *Big blaze over at the Convent of the Good Shepherd.*" She imitated the nasal tones of a telephone voice. "Nuns on fire! Come quick! Girls escaping left right and centre!"

Clover stared at her.

"Only joking, Clover."

"Of course."

"We did a play about those nuns, you see. They took in girls thought to be in moral danger. That was the expression. Girls in moral danger, and I played one of them on stage. Most of them weren't in real moral danger – whatever that is. Having affairs with boys, perhaps – off to the convent with you. I'd love a bit more moral danger in my own life."

Frieda gestured to the stairway behind them. "This way." They began their ascent of the stairway, which was badly in need of a coat of paint. "This place was converted for fashionable people," she said. "But the fashionable people went away, as fashionable people are prone to do. It was allowed to go bush and they started to let it out to students. Then they went one worse and let it out to actors. That's us. Some of us are real pigs – purely in the domestic department, of course. And only the men. They're the ones who never wash up. Or clean. They spend a lot of time in the shower, though. No problem there. It's just the kitchen where they show themselves to be a bit flaky. Poor boys – they try, I suppose. Do you think men try, Clover?"

Clover felt dizzy from the lengthy flight. She shook her head. "I can't think very much at the moment."

Frieda was solicitous. "Of course. You're jet-lagged. I slept for twenty hours when I came back from Scotland, you know. I was knocked out. I'm still waking up at odd hours."

There was a dark corridor that somebody had tried to brighten by sticking colourful posters for long-dead concerts on the walls; at the end of it, an open door. "That won't stay shut," said Frieda. "You have to tie it with a bit of string. The string is your key, so to speak."

"I see."

They reached the door.

"I warned you it was a cupboard," said Frieda. "But you can actually lie down – I promise. I tested it myself. I lay down in your cupboard, and it felt perfectly roomy. This is officially a one-person cupboard."

She needed to sleep and Frieda left her with the promise that she would be somewhere in the house when she woke up. The cupboard was really a room, Clover thought, as it contained not only a bed but a small wardrobe and chest of drawers as well. There was a window looking out over a yard outside, and beyond that to the backs of neighbouring houses. She gazed out of this window for a moment, taking in the details – the red Victorian brick, the corrugated iron of the roofs, the shabby guttering with its blistered paint; and above it a cloudless sky, washed of colour as the sky can be in the brief transition between day and night. She was struck by the thought that this was Australia; that in spite of its distance from where she had started her trip, the things about her, the brick, the earth, the sky were of the same substance that she had left behind her in Scotland, but were at the same time so different.

The following morning Frieda said to her, "I am that great cliché – the resting actress. I'm resting today and tomorrow, and working the day after that. So let me show you Melbourne – or at least let me show you our local coffee bar and the supermarket at the end of the road. There are other things – arts centres, museums et cetera – but you know how it is."

In the coffee bar, Frieda looked at her with mild curiosity and asked her what she wanted to do in Melbourne. "I'm not sure you can find two weeks' worth of things to see," she said. "You could look at the river, I suppose. There's something called the Yarra. You could look at it for hours, I imagine, but I'm not sure what conclusions you'd reach. It's a great place just to be, though. There's a difference between seeing and being, I think. This is a great place to be – not to do anything in particular – just to be." She paused. "But you've got your friend to see, haven't you? Have you made any arrangements?"

Clover shook her head. "No. He doesn't know I'm here. Not yet."

Frieda sipped at her coffee thoughtfully and then put down her cup. "You should have told him," she said.

"I didn't want to. I wanted it to … to look natural, I suppose."

Frieda's eyes widened. "To look natural? Oh, hello, I just happen to have dropped in from the other side of the world! That sort of natural?"

Clover did not answer. Frieda was right, of course.

They sat in silence for a few moments, and then Frieda said, "Invite him round. Tell him you're here, visiting friends, and then invite him round. Simple." She paused. "I take it you've got his e-mail address?"

"Of course."

"Then invite him round for tomorrow. Dinner. Seven o'clock. There'll be five of us altogether. You, me, him. Two of the other inmates are in residence, I think. Three are out for good behaviour."

Clover agreed.

"Tell me a bit about him," said Frieda. "Good-looking?"

"Seriously."

"I see. That's good. But it's also bad, isn't it? Good-looking boys often know it. They take advantage of it."

"He doesn't know it. Or he doesn't act as if he does."

Frieda said this was perfect. But she needed to know more. "Funny? Does he make you laugh?"

"Yes."

"It gets better. Tall?"

"Yes."

"Oh my God, this is Adonis we're talking about. So what's the problem? Likes girls?"

"Yes. He's had girlfriends." It caused her pain to say it.

"But not you?" said Frieda. "You and James haven't been a number?"

She looked down at her hands. "He refers to me as a sister."

Frieda was silent for a moment as she absorbed the admission. "Oh, my God, that's terrible," she muttered, reaching out to Clover in instinctive sympathy. "What a terrible thing to say. His sister!"

Suddenly, and at the same time, they saw the humour in the situation.

"My sister," said Frieda, with exaggerated concern, "my poor sister, to be his … his sister!"

"I'm making a fool of myself," said Clover. "I know it."

Now Frieda became serious again. "Send him that e-mail," she said. " I can't wait to see him. And then I'll be able to advise you, as long as …"

She left the condition hanging in the air.

"As long as what?"

"As long as you don't behave like a sister when he comes round here. You see, that might be the problem. He's been treating you like a sister because that's how you've been behaving towards him."

"But …"

"But nothing. But nothing. Think sex, Clover. Act – don't think about reasons for not acting." She smiled. "That's the way some people go through life. They sit about and think about the consequences. Make the consequences happen. Embrace consequences." She drew back. "Do you know something? I've just said something really profound. I think I'm going to write it down before I forget it. *Make consequences happen.* How's that for a really … a really important aphorism? *Make consequences happen.*"

You're talking about my life, thought Clover. You're not on the stage.

"What?"

Clover shook her head. "I didn't say anything."

"Well, don't think it, then. Act. Do you want me to dictate the e-mail for you? No? Yes?"

"I can write my own e-mails."

"You sure?" But there was a quick retraction. "I'm sorry – of course you can. God, I'm pushy! But go ahead and do it – because you're never going to be happy, Clover, until you take control of your destiny. That's another aphorism, by the way. I'm so full of them today I'm going to make myself sick."

James replied almost immediately. He was surprised, he said, but "really, really pleased" to hear that she was in Melbourne and yes, he would love to come round the following evening. He was going to play squash but he had been looking for an excuse to get out of it because the particular squash partner with whom he was due to play was a bad sport. "He's a mathematician," he wrote. "Not that that has anything to do with it, but he seems to want everything to work out neatly in his favour. That's the way his mind works. I don't like playing with him any more, but it's hard to get rid of him. I find myself wanting to lose so that he doesn't get into one of his bad moods. And that's not the point of squash, I think. Anyway, that's my problem – not yours. I'll be there tomorrow. And is it really a disused fire station? I'll find out tomorrow, I suppose. And Clover … thanks for coming all this way to see me!"

She dwelt on his last sentence. When she first read it, she had been aghast at the thought that he must somehow have guessed that her purpose in coming to Australia had been to see him. She felt the nakedness of one whose secret motives are suddenly laid bare; the shock that one has been *seen through*. But then she realised that he was joking; nobody would travel to Australia just to see a friend with whom contact had more or less been lost – nobody in her right mind, that is.

But at least he had accepted the invitation, and the general tone of his message was welcoming. Of course he had always been like that – apart from one or two moments when they had been much younger and for a short time he had seemed to lose interest in her company. For the rest, he had been friendly and interested in what she had to say. And that brought her back, as it inevitably did, to the thought of his kindness. It was like love, really – a kindness that grew from love; it must have, because things cannot come from nowhere – but it was not actual love, not love of the sort that she wanted him to feel and that he had given to others, but never to her. Could you make do with kindness rather than love? What if you were to lead a life in which you were never given the love that you craved, but found friendship and the kindness and consideration that went with that? She could not imagine that this would be enough, although she knew that there were people who had to make do with just that.

She offered to make the meal the following day and Frieda was quick to accept. "I was hoping you'd offer," she said. "We *love* our guests to do the cooking. It's why we have them. No, I'm not serious about that. We have them to defray the rent. No, I'm not serious about that either. We have them because we like them."

She went to the Victorian market and wandered about the stalls, returning with fish, fennel and wild rice. She realised that she did not know whether James had a favourite dish, and this led her to reflect that although she had known him for years, she still did not know all that much about him – the details of his life, the likes and dislikes, the music he liked to listen to, the books he read, what he liked to drink. Those things she thought, were the context against which a life was led, not the life itself. The person himself was something quite different from the surroundings of his life: he was a disposition, an attitude, a way of looking at other people, and as far as all that was concerned, she felt that she must know James better than any of his more recent acquaintances. It did not matter that she did not even know whether he liked fish.

She spent the afternoon worrying. It now occurred to her that although she wanted to see him, she did not want to hear about his life in Melbourne. She had only been in Australia for a couple of days but already she understood the attractions: the warmth, the spaciousness – even in a city; the high, empty sky; the sense of being on the edge of something that was just beginning. Surely this would be just as seductive for James as she suspected it would be for her, and he would be creating for himself a whole new life in which she would have no part. I am his past, she thought; I am not even his present, let alone his future.

Frieda was auditioning that afternoon and was not back until six. She thought she had not been successful. "They hate you if you look a day over eighteen," she said. "Let me warn you about casting directors."

Clover said, "But I'm not an actress. I don't know any."

"Look out anyway," said Frieda. She picked at an olive from the bowl that Clover had just prepared. "Nice. Olives are so ... I don't know. How would you describe an olive?"

"Small and round."

"Exactly. Small and round." She popped the olive into her mouth and looked at Clover thoughtfully. "A small round man is probably the answer, you know. He'd never stray. He'd be so appreciative of everything you did for him because small and round people usually are." She paused. "Small, round and maybe a bit rich."

Clover laughed.

"It's no laughing matter," said Frieda, reaching for another olive. "I can't even find a small and round man. Not in the theatre." She looked at her watch. "This man ..."

"James."

"Yes, James. Leave it to me."

Clover felt a surge of alarm. "Listen, Frieda, it's not that I'm ungrateful, but I thought ..."

Frieda affected hurt. "You think I'm going to be tactless? Do you really think I'd say something unhelpful?"

"I didn't say that."

"You *looked* it. There are some things you don't need to say; you just *look* them."

Clover made a soothing gesture. "I'm sure you understand how I feel."

"Nervous?"

"Yes."

Frieda put an arm about her shoulder. "No need. We're pretty relaxed round here. It'll be a really easy evening. And you know what? I've had an idea. I'll suggest we go out to this bar round the corner – have you seen it? The Atrium. Then I'll suddenly remember that I have to be somewhere else so that the two of you can go together. It'll be very natural."

"Very."

Frieda made a face. "Don't be so pessimistic. That's the trouble with you people – you just give up."

Clover was unsure what people Frieda was talking about: the British? Everybody who happened not to be Australian? People who weren't actors? People like her, who could be said to have given up because they allowed boys to think of them as sisters?

They were both in the kitchen when the doorbell rang.

"That's him," said Frieda. "Go and let him in. And Clover ..."

"Yes?"

"When you see him there on the step, kiss him. Okay? Kiss him."

She looked away, resentful of the advice. She felt her heart thumping within her; a shortness of breath. Her palms would be moist, she decided, and she wiped them against the side of her jeans. Frieda saw her and smiled.

"I know what it's like. I sometimes feel like that when I go on stage. Some people use talc, so that when the romantic lead takes their hand he doesn't think *Oh my God: dripping with sweat!*"

She left the kitchen and made her way towards the front door. This was the reason she had made this journey, and now those thousands of miles were culminating in a few short steps.

He stood there, smiling at her, and then stepped forward to embrace her. She closed her eyes, and felt the dryness of his cheek against hers. She was suddenly afraid that she might cry; afraid that the pent-up emotion within her would break its bounds. But those bounds had been long in place, and well founded, as are the defences behind which any concealed love must shelter. Lifetimes might be spent in tending such ramparts; and have been.

Later, she could not recall what he had said to her and she to him in those first few minutes. There had been an enquiry about her journey, and remarks about Melbourne. He had just seen something in the street outside, but she paid no attention to what he told her about it: a poster that amused him, or triggered some memory that he thought she might share. All that she was aware of was that she was in his presence; that he was real, he was there in the flesh, and that she had not been mistaken in her feelings about him.

She introduced him to Frieda, who looked at him from under her eyelids, her head slightly lowered, in that rather unusual and disconcerting manner that she had noticed before. But if he was taken aback by this scrutiny, he did not show it, and the two of them moved immediately into the relaxed, good-natured banter that the Australians excel at; an assumption of good will, a default position based on the understanding that there was enough for everybody – enough of whatever it was that people needed: space, food, the chance to make something of life.

She could tell that James liked Frieda, and for a moment she felt a twinge of jealousy as he quizzed her about her acting. He had seen her, he said, on television a few weeks ago in an episode of a serial to which his flatmate was addicted, and the recognition pleased her. It had been a small part, she said, but had paid well, as banal roles could do.

"If you're going to be boring," she said, "you might as well be well paid for it."

James turned to Clover and asked her about her plans.

"You should stay longer out here," he said. "You'd like it."

"Yes," said Frieda. "Stay longer." '

Automatically – and foolishly, she later decided – Clover

explained that it was a brief trip and that she had to get to the next stage in her journey. She said this as part of the pretence that she had not come to see James.

"Where?" he asked.

Again she spoke without thinking; her return journey would be through Singapore, but it was only for a change of plane.

"Singapore," she said.

James looked puzzled. "Why there?"

"There's a friend," she said. "I knew her in Cayman, ages ago; and in Edinburgh too. Judy. She has an apartment in Singapore and I thought I'd spend a bit of time with her. She said that she might be able to get me a job doing something or other. Just for a few months."

"Difficult," said James. "You can't just pick up a work permit there."

Clover was vague. "She didn't say ..."

They were joined by Frieda's two flatmates who had been invited to the dinner. Like Frieda, they were both actors, although one, Chris, was about to give up in despair after his last television role, his first for three months, had been as a parking attendant with one thing to say, which was *thank you*.

"I did it so expressively," he said. "I put my soul into it."

Frieda shrugged. "The theatre – what can one say?"

Chris said, "Thank you – which is what I said."

The two flatmates did not stay beyond the end of the meal. Frieda cleared up. "So James," she said as she took his empty plate. "You're pleased to see your friend?"

If he was surprised by the question, he did not reveal it. "Of course."

Clover squirmed.

Frieda seemed impervious. "And you, Clover?"

Her response was muttered. "Yes."

Frieda continued breezily. "You two go back a long way, don't you?"

Clover winced.

"Well you do, don't you?" persisted Frieda.

"To six, or thereabouts," said James. "Don't we, Clove?"

"Yes."

Frieda smiled. "Destiny," she muttered. "Childhood sweethearts."

James laughed. "Not really. More like friends."

Frieda waved a hand in the air. "Friends make the best sweethearts."

Clover glared at her, but Frieda was looking at James. He seemed to hesitate, and then, looking at his watch, said that since he had to be at work early the next morning, he would have to think of getting home. "I'm going down to Adelaide for the next four weeks," he said. "An audit. It's really dull." He looked at Clover apologetically. "It's bad timing, I'm afraid. Next time, I hope I'll be able to show you the town. And why not bring Padraig?"

She felt empty.

"Padraig's in Italy," she said. "And we ..."

She would have gone on to say that she was no longer seeing Padraig, but James had risen to his feet and had begun to thank Frieda for the meal. Then he bent and kissed Clover on the cheek.

"Write to me," he said. "I like getting e-mails from you."

Frieda saw him to the door and when she returned to the kitchen she found Clover in tears.

"I did my best, Clover. But what more can I do? I gave you every chance in the book."

Clover looked away. "I don't care. Just leave me alone please." Frieda sought to defend herself. "You can hardly blame me. You should have told him about Padraig, and what did you say? Just something about Italy. How pathetic!" She shook her head. "I despair of you, you know. I completely despair. You say that you want him, but you know what I think? You don't. Not really."

31

She left the Old Fire Station two days later, in spite of Frieda's apologies, that came the next day: *I always, always, always put my feet in things; I'm really sorry, Clover; you have every right to be cross with me, my God, I know that.* She made light of these, and told Frieda how grateful she was for giving her somewhere to stay, but she felt restless, and her restlessness was not helped by the irritation she felt over her older friend's ways – her over-statements and her extravagant way of speaking. The cupboard itself seemed less attractive now, and following up an advertisement in a give-away newspaper she found a room in a flat that the other tenants were happy to let her take for a few weeks. With James away, she had no real reason to be in Melbourne, but she somehow lacked the will to do the obvious thing and leave for a backpacking trip. She found herself brooding over her evening with James and how, before it had begun to go wrong, it seemed to be going so well. He had looked at her with fondness in his eyes – she was sure of that – and her recollection of what he had said – in so far as it went – was encouraging. If only she had been by herself, without Frieda, and her obvious, ham-fisted hints, she might have been able to convey to him what she had so long wanted to tell him but had found impossible.

There were moments of complete clarity when her situation presented itself to her realistically, just as she knew it to be. At such times – moments that came without warning when she was sitting in a coffee bar, browsing in a bookshop, or simply lying in bed looking at the ceiling – she understood exactly what she was: a young woman of twenty-two, who had been given every advantage, who had everything she needed in a material sense, who had parents who loved and supported her, who had never been obliged to struggle for anything or work against the odds. All of that she knew – and did not take for granted – but she was more than that young woman; she was also somebody who did not have the one thing she wanted in life and now, in such moments, understood and accepted that she might never get it.

At such moments, along with this self-understanding, there came an awareness – and acceptance – of what she had to do next. She had to wait out her remaining few days in Melbourne and then return to Scotland. She had to try to get her old job back – or something like it – and then in due course go off for the rest of her gap year. There was Nepal, and that school somewhere that she would help to build. Then she had to find a proper job, support herself, meet somebody else, and start leading the life that everybody else seemed to be prepared to lead without constantly hankering after something that was not to be. That was the plan, and as she marked time in Melbourne, it even began to have an aura of desirability about it. The rest of my life, she thought. The rest of my life.

But then James came to her in her dreams – not once or even occasionally, but every night, or so it seemed. He was just there – entering a room in which she found herself – a room that was somewhere geographically vague: not quite in Scotland, nor in Cayman, but somewhere in between. One night, in that dream that precedes wakefulness – the one that remains, if only for a few seconds, in memory – she was in Australia, because that was how it felt, and she was with James outside a house with a silver tin roof, and there were swaying eucalyptus trees behind the house, and he gestured to her that they should go in. She took his hand, and he let her place it against her cheek, and she kissed it, and he said: *Of course, Clover; of course*, and then was suddenly not there any more and she felt a great sense of having seen something that she had never seen before, of having been vouchsafed a vision of sorts, as a religious person might see an angel in the garden, or a child an imaginary friend. The house with its silver roof, of course, was love; she had read enough pop psychology to understand that.

She woke up and stared at the still darkened ceiling, and it seemed to her that James had really been in the room with her and had somehow sanctified it by his presence. Which is what he does, she thought. James makes everything whole for me. She thought that, and allowed the words to echo in her head, luxuriating in them; then she turned and closed her eyes for sleep again, if it would come, so that she might return to the dream in which he had been present. She hugged herself, imagining that her hands were his, but then let go, almost guiltily, struck by sheer embarrassment at the thought that she was one of those people who must rely on the embrace of an imaginary lover. She thought of Padraig, again with guilt, and asked herself whether he had meant anything to her. Had she treated him badly by allowing him to think that she loved him when all along she had only ever loved one person, and it was not him? Or had they both been a temporary solution for each other – an equal bargain between adults, a perfectly adequate way of filling an absence; in her case for the boy she remembered and in his case for the girl he hoped might one day come into his life. She had always known that he had such an idea; she had seen him glance on occasion at some girl and had said to herself, with the satisfaction of one who detects a clue to some mystery or conundrum, *So that's his type*; so different from her – self-possessed types, with hair swept back, and the confident poise that went with their education at south of England boarding schools. Their cool Englishness was the polar opposite of Irishness, and yet he obviously liked them. Yes, for all his advice to her not to live in thrall to an impossible love, Padraig had been doing exactly the same thing himself.

The thought occurred to her that perhaps most of us were like that; perhaps it was common to live with an image in our minds of what might be, of what we truly deserved if only the world were differently organised – in a way that gave proper recognition to our claims. So the lowest paid imagined the sumptuous life of the banker, the lame envisaged what it must be like to be athletic, the lonely closed their eyes and saw themselves surrounded by friends. We might all cope with a dissonance between real and unreal simply by making do, simply by admitting to ourselves that dreams are just that – dreams. Perhaps the real danger was to think that the thing you felt you deserved could really be achieved. And yet it was also possible that you could get what you really wanted, if you simply took it when it presented itself. She had come across a poem by Robert Graves that put it rather well; a poem called "A Pinch of Salt" about the bird of love, who came sudden and unbidden, who had to be clutched by the hand in which he landed, clutched and held tight lest he fly away. That had struck her as being true, and yet she had not done what the poet said you should do, and so the warning implicit in the poem, the warning of loss, applied to her.

She got on well with her temporary flatmates whose uncomplicated ambition, as far as she could ascertain, was to have fun. They were two young women and one young man. One of the women was an architectural student, and the other was marking time before going off on a working holiday to

London. The young man, Greg, who was loosely connected with one of the women in a way which Clover could not quite understand – he was an ex-boyfriend, she thought – worked as a copywriter in an advertising agency and had ambitions to be a novelist. The social life of these three consisted in endless outings to bars and restaurants, and they were happy for Clover to tag along with them. She did so, and met their friends, who were doing much the same thing as them, and accepted her with the same readiness that they seemed to accept everybody else. "Success," pronounced one of these friends, "is being able to eat out every night. Every night. 7/7." She thought he might believe it, even if he said it with a smile.

Greg flirted with her – mildly and with a certain wry humour – and she responded. But when he came to her room one evening after they had been in a bar together and said pointedly how lonely he found Melbourne and the worst thing was loneliness at night, she could not bring herself to an involvement that she knew would be short-lived and mechanical.

"I'm in love with somebody else, Greg," she said. "It's not that I don't like you. I do. It's just that I've loved somebody else for a long time and I can't ..."

"It's just sex," he said. "That's all."

She laughed at this, partly to defuse a potentially awkward situation, but also partly because what he had said struck her as being so completely wrong – not wrong in any moral sense, but in the sense of being psychologically reductive. Sex was not *just sex*; it was everything. It was ... She faltered. It was James.

"I'm sorry, Greg."

"No need to apologise. Should we watch a DVD instead?"

"It's just a movie," she said. "That's all."

He nodded his agreement. "DVDs are better than sex. Everybody knows that. Or at least everybody who's not getting any sex."

They watched together, and at the end she took his hand in a friendly, unthreatening way, and patted it. He grinned at her. "I'm glad you said no," he said. "I'm glad you're faithful."

She smiled at his tribute. *More faithful than you can imagine*, she thought.

"I'm going to miss you when you go next week," he said. "I've enjoyed having you around."

"Would you mind if I stayed a bit longer?"

She had not thought it through, but suddenly she did not want to go. James was in Melbourne – or would be – and she did not want to leave the place where he was; it was as simple as that.

"No, of course we wouldn't mind. Aly and Joy will be fine. They like having you here too."

Now the rest of her inchoate idea came to her. She would change her ticket for a later departure – her particular fare would allow for one change – and she would stay in Australia without telling James. She did not want him to know. She would allow herself a final ... she struggled with the period, and decided it would be a month. She would have a final month and then she would begin to do what she knew she should have done all along: she would begin to forget. And in that final month she would allow herself just a few glimpses of him. That was all. She had his address now, and could see him on the street. She could watch him coming out of his flat. It would be saying goodbye from a distance, slowly, as goodbye used to be said when you could actually see people leaving; when they left by trains that moved slowly out of stations, or by ships that were nudged gently away from piers still linked by paper streamers; or when people simply walked away and you could see them going down paths until they were a dot in the distance before being swallowed up by a world that was then so much larger. It was only watching; that was all. It was definitely *not* stalking. Stalking was something quite different; that was watching somebody else with hostile intent or with an ulterior motive. She had no such thing; she loved James, and that was what made it different; she was not going to make any demands of him. How could she?

James, of course, would think that she had gone on to Singapore to stay with Judy, and it would complicate matters to have him think differently; more than that, it would be impossible to explain what she was doing. She would write to him as if from Singapore, and in this way she could keep some contact; again, there was no harm done in *writing* to somebody. There was e-mail. You can't tell where e-mails come from, she thought; in a sense they conferred a limitless freedom, for they came from somewhere that could just as easily be Singapore as it could be Melbourne.

She told Greg. She had not planned to, but at the time it seemed right, and it helped her too. They were in the kitchen together and had shared half a bottle of wine. She felt mellow, and in a mood for confession. The disclosure made her feel less anxious, less burdened.

Once she had stopped speaking he looked at her in astonishment, and she wondered whether she would regret what she had just said. Her story, she knew, must sound absurd to others, and it *was* absurd. But then *we* are absurd when you come to think of it, she thought; we are absurd, every one of us, with our hopes and struggles and our tiny human lives that we thought mattered so much but were of such little real consequence. *Think of yourself in space, as a tiny dot of consciousness in the Milky Way*, one of the teachers at Strathearn had said. *It puts you in perspective, doesn't it?*

Greg's look of astonishment changed to one of puzzlement. "You actually told him that you had gone to Singapore?"

"Yes. I know it sounds stupid, but I did. I suppose ..."

He waited.

"I suppose I wanted him to think that I had a life of my own... I suppose I hoped it would somehow make me more interesting." She looked ashamed. "Does that sound odd to you?"

He looked as if he was making an effort to understand. "What do you expect me to say? No, it's quite normal to tell somebody you're in Singapore when you aren't? Is that what you expect?"

She did not answer.

"I suppose," Greg continued, "that people try to impress others in strange ways. Maybe being in Singapore would impress him – I don't know. But what bothers me is the point of it all. Why? I mean, most people would just tell him the truth, don't you think? They'd go up to him and say something like *I've always had the hots for you.*"

"Would they?"

He grinned. "I would, if I were a woman and there was this guy I wanted."

"That's what Frieda said. That's what everybody's said all along."

He shrugged. "Well, there you are. I think that's about it."

She wanted to explain – as much to herself as to him. "But the problem is this: I know how he feels about me. He doesn't think of me in that way. I'm just a friend to him – somebody he's known since he was six or whatever. That's all." She paused before the hardest admission. "And there's somebody else. He's seeing this girl."

Greg sighed. "Another girl? Oh well, that's not so good, is it? If somebody has somebody else, there's not much you can do."

"He'll never love me," Clover said. "I know that. And I know that if I were to go up to him and tell him how I felt that would probably end our friendship. He'd feel sorry for me and ... and that's the last thing I want. I'm a little bit of his life right now, but I'd be less if he decided that he had to keep me ... keep me at arm's length because I had gone and fallen in love with him and spoiled everything." She stared at Greg, hoping he would understand. "Do you see what I mean? If somebody falls in love with you and you don't fall in love with them, then they're just a nuisance. You're embarrassed. You want them to go away." She willed him to react. "Do you get what I'm trying to say?"

He tried. "Maybe. A bit." Now he looked intrigued. "So let me get this straight: you've told him that you've gone on to Singapore?"

"Yes. I know that sounds ..."

"Weird."

She said nothing, and he continued: "So now he's back from Adelaide and he thinks you're in Singapore staying with this girl ..."

"Judy."

He looked at her dubiously. "Who exists?"

"Of course she exists."

"I just wanted to make sure how big the fantasy is. That's all." He looked thoughtful. "It's peculiar, but you know what? I suppose it's harmless – and fun too. You're inventing a life for yourself there?"

She nodded. "It sort of grew. I sent him an e-mail telling him I'd gone and he sent one back. He asked me about Singapore and what it was like and I was so pleased that he had actually answered me that I wrote back."

"Telling him about it?"

She looked down at the floor. "It was an excuse to be in touch with him. I bought a book – a guide book. And one of those coffee table books with pictures."

He suddenly gave a whoop of delight. "Oh, Clover, you crack me up! You're serious fun – in a vaguely worrying sort of way."

"He wrote back ... again."

"And you continued with the story?"

"Yes."

"All of it invented? Made up?"

"I told you: Judy exists. And I was going to stay with her for a few days on the way back. So it's true – in a way. All I've done is to bring it forward by a few weeks."

They had been talking in the kitchen of the flat, and now he got up from his chair and walked over to the window. "You know what? Let's make one up. Could I try? Get your computer and write it down."

"Do you ..."

"Yes, come on. *Clover's day in Singapore.* You go shopping. That's what people do in Singapore. Big shopping place. And you buy ..." He broke off to consider. "You buy a T-shirt. Big deal. But that sounds just right because people do that sort of thing, don't they? They go out shopping and they come back with a tee-shirt. Yours says ... You know what it says? It says *Foreign Girl*, but you can't resist it because you think it says it all. You *are* a foreign girl, and here's this T-shirt that admits it. It's a very honest T-shirt."

He warmed to his theme. "And on the way back to the flat somebody steals your purse. You don't know how it happened, but it goes. Maybe there was this guy – yes, there was, I remember now – this guy brushes past you and he says how sorry he is but he's actually taken your purse and he goes off in the crowd."

"There's no crime in Singapore. My book said that. Or they have a very low rate of crime."

He laughed. "That's what they say. And maybe it's true. But even if it is, there's bound to be some crime. So you go to the police station and … and it's really clean. Clean policemen, clean desks, clean criminals – not very many of them, of course – and this sergeant … It was a sergeant, wasn't it?"

She entered into the spirit of it. "Yes. He was Sergeant Foo. He had one of those name badges on and it said *Sergeant Foo.*"

He said, "Oh, I like that guy. I wouldn't cross him, but I like him. Sergeant Foo takes your statement and then he says, *This is very regrettable. Rest assured, lady, that we will catch this … this malefactor. He will be severely punished.* And then you went home. And Judy had invited these people over for dinner and she didn't have any …"

"Arborio rice. She was going to do Italian and she needed some Arborio rice."

"So you went out to this shop round the corner," he said. "And there was this whole stack of Arborio rice because there were some Italians living nearby and they were always wanting Arborio rice. All the time."

They laughed together. "Silly girl," said Greg, gazing at her fondly.

She avoided his gaze. She did not feel silly. Nothing about her feelings for James was silly.

She had imagined that there would be one or two e-mails from Singapore, but she was to be proved wrong. James replied to each, often almost immediately, and began to include, in his responses, news of his own. There was a different tone to his e-mails now – something that she had not noticed in his earlier messages. He had been almost business-like before and had said little about himself and what he was doing; now he seemed more open, more inclined to chat. He told her about Adelaide and the hotel that he was staying in. "It's one of those old Australian hotels that were always built on street corners," he wrote. "There's a pub in it called the Happy Wallaby – I'm not inventing this; it really is – and this fills with rather rowdy locals each evening and it depresses me, I'm sorry to say, and I wish I were back in Melbourne. I like this country, and I know that I'm half Australian – just like you're half American, aren't you? – but there are little corners of it that seem ... I don't know the word. Is it *lost*? Is that what I'm trying to say? There are places where somehow everything is *lost* in the vastness of it all. The buildings stand there against a backdrop of emptiness, or mountains, or whatever it is and they seem adrift. It's like being on the sea. And if there's a wind, you find yourself thinking, *Where's this wind come from?*"

She wrote back to him: "I know what you mean about Australia. I liked it too – not that I saw very much of it. And I liked the people – I liked them a lot, but you could very easily feel lonely there, couldn't you?"

'Yes," he replied. "You could feel lonely."

She stopped saying very much about Singapore. This was not because she had no ideas as to what she was doing in her

Singaporean life – she and Greg spent hours imagining it, and his suggestions, although occasionally preposterous, would have made up a quite credible daily life – but she felt increasingly guilty about the fact that what she was saying amounted to lies. She was deceiving James, and she did not like doing it. And yet she had started it; the whole conception had been hers.

In due course she would tell him, she decided. She would make light of it – as if it were a long-drawn-out joke, and as harmless as a joke might be. He might be surprised, but surely he would not be hurt by what she would portray as innocent imaginative play.

"I'm going back early," he wrote. "The audit took less time than they thought we'd need and so it's back to Melbourne for all three of us. But not for long. Listen to this: Singapore. The firm has a big client there – it's an Australian engineering firm that does a lot of South-East Asian work and they're looked after by our office in Singapore. But one of their staff is in London for a month and another has been poached by an American firm. So … Singapore for two of us from the Melbourne office – for five weeks – quite a big deal for a first year trainee but that's par for the course with this firm, apparently. Right, then … dinner next week? I love Chinese food and somebody told me you can get it cooked on wood fires in Singapore. And there are these big food markets where you can eat – have you been? I leave here on Wednesday, which gives me three days to get ready after I get back to Melbourne. Tuesday or Wednesday suit you?"

She read the message twice, and then sat still, appalled by what she had done. She had known that there was a risk that her deception would be exposed, but she had not imagined that it would happen so soon. She went to Greg, who read the e-mail and then raised an eyebrow. "Exposure, Clove. It happens. So what are you going to do? Come clean?"

She shook her head. "I can't."

"I don't blame you."

"I'm going to tell him eventually. But I can't do it now. I can't face it."

He was silent.

She reached her decision. "I'm going there. As soon as I can."

"Singapore?"

"Yes. I was going to see Judy anyway."

He made a face. "Money?"

She explained about her father's gift. "I can afford it. I'll have to pay to change the ticket again, but I can do that."

He shook his head in disbelief. "I can't believe this, you know. You'll do anything it seems for this guy – anything. Except tell him the truth about how you feel."

"How can I?"

"Open your mouth and speak. It's that simple. Give him a call. Ask him. Say: *Are you still going out with that other girl?* And if he says yes, then end of story. If he says no, then you could say what everybody's been telling you to say. Get it sorted out one way or another."

"No."

"That's all you can say? No?

"Yes. I mean, no."

"I give up," he said harshly, and then, almost immediately, relented. "Sorry. I wish I could be positive, but how can you be positive about something that has disaster written all over it?" He repeated the word to underline his warning. "Disaster."

32

Judy gave her an enthusiastic welcome.

"I can't tell you how pleased I am that you're here," she said. "I've asked *tons* of people to visit me and not one has taken me up on the invitation. Not a single one – apart from you."

They were standing at the window of the spare room in her flat. This flat was in a building that was not high by Singaporean standards – four storeys, arranged around a courtyard dominated by an inviting blue swimming pool. Two young children, brother and sister, frolicked in the water at the shallow end of the pool, watched by a uniformed nurse. The nurse spoke constantly on her phone, occasionally getting up, mid-conversation, to admonish the boy for splashing his sister too enthusiastically.

"Those children," said Judy, "belong to some people on the floor below. You never see the parents with them – just one of the Filipina nurses. There are two of them – the Filipinas – and I've got to know one of them quite well, but not this one. They spend their lives working for other people, although they have children of their own back home. The other woman's sister works in the Middle East. She looks after the children of some ruling family over there. She says the children never even learn to tie their own shoe-laces because they have a Filipina to do it for them. Can you imagine that?"

Clover watched the children. She had grown up with that sort of thing in the Caymans, where the Jamaicans did the work of the Filipinas.

Judy looked at her and smiled. "The truth is – I'm bored stiff. I don't know what to do. I'm only here because my parents want me to be. I'm going to have to talk to them about leading my own life."

"Do another degree," said Clover.

"That's what I'm planning to do. That's what master's degrees are for, aren't they? To keep graduates out of the unemployment statistics." She paused. "How long do you want to stay?"

Clover suggested two weeks and Judy gave a cry of delight. "Oh my God, that's fantastic. I thought you were going to say two days. That's what most people do – they come here on their way to Australia or Bali or somewhere sexy like that and then they go. Or, in my case, they don't come in the first place."

Clover took a deep breath. She knew that she would have no alternative but to tell Judy about her deception, and now she did so. Hearing her own account of what happened only served to deepen her disquiet. "I know it sounds stupid," she said at the end. "But that's what I did."

Judy's reaction took her by surprise. "Totally reasonable," she said.

"So you don't disapprove?"

"Why should I disapprove? Nobody's died."

Clover said that she felt that she had involved Judy in her dishonesty.

"No," said Judy. "You didn't. It's entirely up to me as to whether I play along with this – and I'm cool with it. Absolutely. Men mislead women all the time – they're such liars – this is just a return match."

"You'll back me up? You'll go along with what I said happened?"

"Of course. Just give me the details."

She gave her the broad details of the imaginary life that she had created for herself. Judy listened with growing amusement. "We had a terrific time together," she said. "Our virtual life was much more interesting than real life."

"We're going out for dinner on Tuesday," Clover said.

"Tuesday? Good. I'm free."

Clover was silent for a few moments. She had invited herself to Singapore and she could hardly tell her friend that she was not welcome at dinner. Judy, though, picked up her hesitation.

"Sorry, it was going to be just the two of you. I shouldn't have …"

"No, I'd like you to come. You'll have the chance to catch up with him."

Judy did not protest. "All right. Thank you. I haven't seen him for ages. Not since Cayman, really – we didn't connect in Edinburgh."

"I'm sure he'll be keen to see you."

Judy smiled. "I know this really great place where everybody wants to go these days. My father knows the owner – we'll get in no matter what time we arrive."

She made a list of the places that she had mentioned to James in her e-mails to him, and asked Judy about these, reading out what she had written – the fiction of her created life.

Judy seemed bemused. "You wrote that about me?" she said. "You told him that we went out for a meal and saw that movie and so on? All of that?"

Clover nodded ruefully. What had started with so little thought, what had seemed so innocent and inoffensive at the time, had now taken on the appearance of a monstrous deception. "I don't know why I did it," she said. "Well, I do, I suppose … I suppose I wanted to be involved with him. I wanted him to pay attention to me and what I was doing. Does that make sense to you?"

"It does. In a way – as a form of attention seeking."

"I feel such a fraud," said Clover.

Judy laughed. "But you are," although she rapidly added, "No offence, of course."

And soon, rather sooner than she might have wished, James arrived in Singapore and telephoned from his hotel. She took the call with trepidation, signalling to Judy across the room. "Him?" mouthed Judy.

She nodded, and Judy gave the thumbs up signal.

After the call, Clover said, "He never phoned me before, you know. Or hardly ever. It was always me."

Judy was encouraging. "I've got a good feeling about this," she said. "I think that something's changed. I think it's over between him and …"

"Shelley."

"Yes. He wants to see you, I think."

"You really think so?"

Judy grinned. "Well, why else would he bother?"

"Maybe he just wants somebody to show him round Singapore."

Judy shook her head. "People don't need to be shown round Singapore," she said. "You get a map and places are where they're meant to be. It's very well organised. No, I think at long last he's come round."

"I feel as if I know this place," he said.

Judy had poured him a beer and was sitting opposite James in the flat. Clover was on the sofa next to him.

"You've been to Singapore?" Judy said.

"No. Not Singapore. This flat. Clover wrote to me and told me what she was doing. What *you* were doing."

Judy caught Clover's eye, and smiled. "Chick lit," she said.

"*Two Single Girls in Singapore*. How about that for a title? Fiction section, of course."

James seemed amused. "It wasn't very steamy," he said.

"The whole place is steamy," retorted Judy. "You've probably been in air conditioning since you arrived. Open the window. Let in the steam."

Clover felt uncomfortable about this exchange and tried to change the subject. "Judy knows this place for dinner," she said. "What's it called, Judy?"

The answer was addressed to James, and not to her. "Billy Lee's. It's mostly seafood, but you can get other things. He has this incredibly ancient chef – he's ninety or something like that, and he comes out and speaks to everybody and asks them whether they'd like to come and help in the kitchen. And when they say yes, as they tend to do, he says that it's the washing-up he was thinking of, and everybody laughs."

"That's where we're going?" asked James.

Again the conversation was between James and Judy. "We thought you'd like it," Clover interjected.

James turned to her. "But of course I will."

"I didn't know whether you liked Chinese food."

He smiled. "But don't you remember? We went for that Chinese meal in Cayman – a hundred years ago. Remember? It was Ted's birthday party – we were about twelve or something, and Ted's mother took us all to that Chinese restaurant near the airport and they had made a massive cake for Ted. Don't you remember?"

It came back to her. She remembered wanting to sit next to him, but he had been with other friends and she had watched him over the table. He had been her hero, the object of her admiration, her longing. It was well before she had an inkling of what love was like, but it was there, already planted, its first tender shoots about to take root; which would take over her life, she now thought.

For a moment she was back there. "I wanted to sit next to you," she said. The remark came unbidden.

James looked surprised. "To me? At Ted's party?"

Judy was watchful.

"Yes," said Clover. "I wanted to sit next to you, but you always seemed too busy for me. You wanted to be with other people." She stopped herself. She had not intended to say any of this.

James was abashed. "I'm sorry. I didn't mean to … to ignore you, or whatever it was I was doing."

Judy now entered the conversation. "Boys don't like girls at that age. They want to be with other boys. Look at groups of kids. The boys all talk together and so do the girls."

"Oh, I know," said Clover. "But they can still be friends, can't they? And lots of people are. Lots of people have best friends of the opposite sex when they're young."

Judy looked doubtful. "I don't think so. What do you think, James? Did you have a best friend?"

He picked up his glass. Clover noticed the pattern in the condensation where he had held it. His hand. James's hand. "I had a friend called Ted," he said. "I don't know whether you'd remember him from Cayman."

Judy shook her head. "No, I don't. We left so long ago."

"He's a friend of Clover's too. I suppose that Ted was my best friend for a long time. We went to different places, though, when we were sent off to boarding school."

"Ted's gay," said Clover. She felt a moment of doubt, and

wondered whether she had unwittingly betrayed a confidence: had Ted talked to James about that? She thought that he made no secret of it, but was not sure now that he had mentioned it.

James did not react. "Yes," he said. "Of course he is."

Clover thought she knew what Judy was thinking. Judy would be imagining that this was the thing that she – Clover – had failed to spot all along. James was not interested in her because of a very simple reason, and you, Clover, didn't pick up on it because you were too obsessed by him to see the glaringly obvious truth. Talk about naïveté!

But it was not true – it simply was not true. Ted and James had never been boyfriends because ... She hesitated. Ted had confessed to her that he saw James in that way but had never hinted that his feelings were reciprocated. And James had had various girlfriends, which pointed the other way, except, of course, if he were repressing something.

"Women," said Judy, "like to have a best gay friend. He's no threat. You can talk to him."

"Of course," said James. "Whereas you can't talk to straight men, can you?"

There was a sardonic note to his remark, and Clover watched its effect on Judy. The other woman had to think quickly. "You can," she said, adding, "If they allow you. Straight men have barriers."

"Oh?" said James. "Do we?"

Do we, thought Clover. And she wanted to say to Judy, "That settles that." But then it occurred to her that it did not. It depended on the sincerity of the *we*. Or the possible irony.

Judy looked at her watch. "I reserved for about twenty minutes from now and we need to go." She turned to Clover.

"How should we get there, Clover? What do you think?"

She was taken aback by the question, and it occurred to her that in entrusting Judy with the story of her subterfuge she had created a hostage. She did not think that Judy was about to reveal her secret to James; rather, she thought that she was playing with her here – taunting her with the possibility of exposure.

"It's up to you," she said evenly. "I forget how we did it last time. Taxi?"

Judy grinned, acknowledging that Clover had batted back the verbal grenade.

"Taxi, then," she said.

They made their way to the restaurant. James was clearly excited to be in Singapore and asked Judy a series of questions as they made the taxi journey. Judy seemed to enjoy the attention; she knew the city well and he listened attentively to what she had to say about it. Clover sat back and stared out of the window. Everything was going wrong, and it was all Judy's fault. Somebody on their course in Edinburgh had once described Judy as selfish, and Clover had defended her; but the criticism must have been justified, as she was selfish here; an unselfish friend would never have suggested accompanying her as Judy had done.

In the restaurant, Judy paraded her knowledge of the menu and her few, mispronounced words of Chinese, patiently received by the staff.

"I'm trying to remember what we ate when we came here," said Judy, picking up the menu. "Do you remember, Clover?"

Clover looked at the selection. "You had far too much," she said dryly. "You felt sick. Remember?"

This brought a sharp glance, and Clover bit her lip. She would have to tolerate Judy, because a word from her could spoil everything. She did not trust her.

After the dinner, they picked up a taxi directly outside the restaurant. Judy asked James the name of his hotel and then said, "It'll make sense to drop you first. It's on our way."

James accepted. And then to Clover, "I'll call you. Are you free on Friday evening?" That was three days away.

Clover noticed Judy staring at her, and wondered whether she assumed she would be included in the invitation. "Fine," she said quickly. "I'm free." She stressed the *I*.

"I …" began Judy, but James cut her off.

"Maybe you should come round to the hotel," he said. "We could go out somewhere from there."

She noticed that the remark was very clearly addressed to her and that it excluded Judy.

James turned to Judy, and said, apologetically, "School reunion time."

Judy made a carefree gesture. "Of course. Clover will know where to take you, won't you, Clover?"

"Yes," said Clover. "No problem there."

They dropped James off at his hotel and continued their taxi journey home. The tension in the atmosphere was palpable, although the niceties were observed.

"A good evening," said Clover. "Thanks for the recommendation of the restaurant."

"You're very welcome," said Judy icily.

"What did you think of him?" asked Clover.

"He's okay," said Judy. "Average. I can't see why you're so keen, frankly, but *chacun à son goût*, as they say."

Clover chose her words carefully. "I thought you took quite a shine to him."

"Did you?"

"Yes, I did."

"Well you were wrong," said Judy. "I like them a little bit more mature. But I suppose one has to take what one gets."

They reverted to silence.

Their dinner together had been on a Tuesday. That Wednesday, Judy had to attend a family lunch party with Singaporean relatives on her stepmother's side. It was the birthday of an aged uncle, and she explained that although she would have liked to invite Clover she would not inflict the extended family on her. "They'd give you no peace," she said. "They love asking questions. And you'd have to eat and eat in order not to appear rude."

Clover did not mind. She wanted to visit the Asian Civilisations Museum.

"Sure," said Judy. "You can go there."

"And I could take us for dinner tonight. Somewhere … Maybe you could choose."

Judy looked doubtful. "Our lunch will merge into dinner," she said. "Sorry."

"Oh well …"

"We could do something tomorrow," said Judy. "I have to meet some people, but we could go and have tea in Raffles. Everyone's ancient, but it's the thing to do in this place."

The suggestions were made without enthusiasm, and Clover decided that there might be a good reason for Judy's having received so few visitors. Judy was bored, she decided, and any visitor, she felt, would be sucked into her vortex of boredom. It was a state that Clover recognised from people she had known in Cayman: the boredom that comes with having money.

They both spent Thursday afternoon in the flat. The weather seemed particularly sultry, and they cooled down with a swim after lunch. There was a group of Russians staying in one of the flats, and they were in the pool too, shouting exuberantly. One of the men made a remark in Russian that was clearly directed against Judy, and was censured by one of the Russian women, who wagged a disapproving finger at him.

"These people are ghastly," said Judy in a loud voice. "Don't worry: their English isn't good enough to know what ghastly means. They're disgusting."

They went inside to escape the Russians and the heat. The air in the flat was chilled and Clover felt her skin tingling to its touch. Judy said that she was going to go to her room to read. "We can meet some people for a drink tonight," she said, "since your friend seems to be too busy."

"He said he has to work in the evenings," said Clover. "He won't be free until tomorrow."

"Of course," said Judy. "I forgot. Work." She sounded as if she didn't believe it.

"He does," said Clover. "They work all hours. They just do."

"Yes," said Judy. "Okay. They work."

Clover went to her own room and lay down on the bed. She picked up the magazine she had been reading and began to page through it. She dozed off.

She awoke twenty minutes later. She was thirsty – the effect of the dehumidified air. She sat up on the bed. There was a telephone in the kitchen and it was ringing insistently. She heard Judy open the kitchen door to answer the phone. The door closed behind her. She heard her talking, but could not make out what she was saying. There was laughter.

The conversation seemed to last about ten minutes. Then she heard Judy come out again.

"I'm going out to get some stuff for the kitchen," Judy called out. "I'll be about an hour or so. If you want to go down to the pool again, remember to take your key."

Clover replied that she would remember. The front door was opened and then clicked shut again.

Clover left her room and went into the kitchen. There was a large bottle of Badoit water in the fridge, and she poured herself a glass. She finished the glass and poured herself another half glass.

The telephone rang again. She hesitated. She could let it ring because it would be for Judy and not for her, but she was a guest, and guests had certain responsibilities.

She picked up the receiver.

"I'm sorry to call back," said a voice. "I forgot to give you the address to pass on."

It was James.

"James?"

There was a silence at the other end of the line. "Is that you, Clover?"

"Yes."

He sounded surprised. "But Judy said you were out. I called a couple of minutes ago and she said you would be out all day."

Clover said nothing.

"You still there, Clove?"

"Yes, I'm here. I'm surprised she said that. I was here all the time. In my room."

"Oh well, I called – the first time – to tell you about a change of plan. I've found a fantastic place for tomorrow. I gave her the name of the place but not the address. That's what I phoned back about."

"I see."

"It's just that I thought it would be easiest for us to meet there because I'm going to be near the restaurant. We have a meeting a couple of blocks away and it would save me going back to the hotel." He paused. "Would that be all right with you?"

"Of course."

"I suppose she thought you were out."

"I suppose so."

She wrote down the details and he rang off. She returned to her room and waited for Judy to come back.

"Did James call?" she asked.

Judy did not flinch. "I don't think so," she said. She had several shopping bags with her and she placed these on the kitchen table. "Were you expecting him? I thought he was working."

Clover shook her head. "No," she said. "I just wondered."

She decided to go for a swim in the pool by herself. She slipped into the water and swam slowly across to the other side.

They went out that evening with Judy's friends – two young men of about their age – both Australian – and a slightly older woman from Hong Kong, a barrister who had just started her practice. Clover enjoyed their company, but could not get out of her mind her distrust of Judy. One of the Australians whispered to her during the evening that he found Judy difficult. "How well do you know your friend?" he said.

"Not all that well."

He grinned. "Careful," he said.

"Oh yes?"

He winked. "Yes. Very careful."

"What do you mean?" she asked.

"Men," he said. "She likes men."

Clover smiled. "So?"

"Other women's," he whispered.

That night, Clover dreamed of her mother. It was a very clear dream, in which she was sitting with Amanda in the garden in the Caymans. Her mother was wearing her tennis outfit and a blue headband.

"Darling," said her mother, and then stopped.

Clover said, "I know what happened. I know who you loved and how hard it's been for you."

Her mother stared at her. "Do you really?"

And then she woke up. She thought of her mother, and the insight that she had had in the dream came to her, as knowledge now. *Her mother loved her father.* Suddenly she wanted to speak to her; to give her the forgiveness that a child may feel he or she must give to a parent – a forgiveness that usually comes only much later, when we come to understand that our lives have at heart been much the same life led by our parents, even if led differently in their externals.

She closed her eyes. The air conditioning was humming and a clock beside her bed ticked loudly. It was clear to her now. Her mother had survived it, and she would too. You can love and not be loved in return. You can live without the thing that you want above all else; you can be free of it. We all have to do that; we all have to make a compromise. She would let James go, as people everywhere gave up on the unattainable. And in giving up, there was a certain freedom, for herself as much as for him.

The pursuer abandons the pursuit and the quarry gets away; both are free, for the moment. Let some other girl – anybody ... but maybe not Judy – have him. He did not want her, and it was foolish, and ultimately self-defeating to carry on thinking that things could be otherwise.

She steeled herself to say goodbye. She would not say it in so many words, of course, but she would say it nonetheless, in any of the other ways in which goodbye could be said.

The restaurant was busy, and they were asked to spend some time waiting for their table in the small bar. It was an intimate place, and they had to sit close to one another on an upholstered bench.

"Your friend, Judy," said James.

"Yes," said Clover.

He shook his head in amusement. "At that restaurant – you know when you went out to the Ladies?"

"Yes?"

"She turned up the flirting. Full blast."

Clover said that she was not surprised. "But you didn't respond?" she said.

"Of course not," said James.

"She's not your type?" asked Clover.

James shook his head. "It's not that. It's because ..."

She waited.

"It's because I've always loved you," he said.

33

Amanda had suggested it.

"Picnics should be spontaneous," she said.

Clover thought about this. "Everything should be spontaneous – sometimes. Kissing people. Eating chocolate. Dancing."

That reminded Amanda of a newspaper headline that she had read about: *Dancing breaks out*. Dancing, like peace, could break out – could overturn what was there before – when people decided that they had had enough. "Yes," she said. "Yes."

They went to the place they always went to. Amanda parked the car in the shade of a tree, as it was mid-day, and if she did not, the car would be a furnace on their return. The heat pressed down like an invisible hand, seeming to hold down even the surface of the sea, dark blue and sluggish. There was the shriek of insects in the air, an ever-present tinnitus, that Clover now realised she had missed. In Australia it had been birdsong; in Scotland it had been the sound of the wind; here it was the chorus of insects that had always been there, a background sound to her childhood.

They did not bring much with them – a plastic sheet that they had always used for picnics and had never replaced in spite of the scars it bore; a thermos flask of iced water; a couple of bread rolls into which Amanda had tucked a slice of ham and the mayonnaise that she knew her daughter liked. It was too hot to eat, but she thought a picnic required at least a nod in the direction of food.

They looked at the sea.

"I'll swim a bit later," said Amanda. "I have to summon up the energy."

"The sea's going nowhere."

Amanda smiled. "That's very profound, darling."

Clover lay back and closed her eyes. She had never thought about it before, but the only time that she would close her eyes in the open, outside, was when she was with her mother. She thought about this. Trust. Protection. It was something to do with that.

"Where do you think you and James are going to live?"

"We'll see. He has another year in Australia."

Amanda nodded. "I suppose we're always going to live apart. The family, I mean. Us."

Clover opened her eyes and looked at her mother. "It's because of this place, isn't it? It's because everybody here is from somewhere else."

"Yes, it is. But that's what the world is like. That's what it's becoming. Everybody comes from somewhere else. Living apart from the people you grew up with is nothing unusual."

"I'm not complaining," said Clover suddenly.

"I didn't think you were. But thank you for saying that."

"I mean it."

Amanda looked at her. It was a whole separate life that she had created; that was the miracle of parenthood, and it never seemed to be anything less of a miracle; you made a whole world; several worlds – one for each child. And then you let go of those worlds, as a creator might do of a world he has created; you let go and watched. "Why did he never say anything to you?" she asked.

Seeing her daughter's hesitation, Amanda was on the point of changing the subject, anxious not to intrude. "Sorry, I shouldn't pry."

"I don't mind. I don't mind at all."

Amanda waited. A small child had appeared out of nowhere,

it seemed, and was making her way on unsteady feet to the edge of the water. The mother followed, wrapped in a towel. They exchanged brief glances – acknowledgements of sharing the tiny beach – and then a hand raised in passing greeting.

"He thought I wasn't interested in him."

"Really?"

"Yes."

Amanda smiled. "Well, he was wrong."

Clover shook her head. "Maybe it was my fault. Maybe I should have told him, rather than letting him think that. And he said that he thought I was with somebody else."

"And you were."

"Yes, but only because I couldn't be with him."

Amanda pointed out that James was not to know that. "We all make that mistake, don't we? All the time. We imagine that people know what we're thinking, and they don't. We misunderstand one another."

They were silent as they watched the mother lift her child and dangle her toes in the water. The sea could not be bothered to respond. The child gave a squeal of delight and struggled to escape her mother's grip.

"We used to do that with you," said Amanda. "We used to swing you over the edge of the water. You loved it. I suppose you thought that we would let you go and you might end up in the sea."

"But you never did."

"No."

Clover looked away. "Thanks for all of that. All of it."

"For what?"

"For making the sacrifices you did. In your life …"

Amanda weighed each word carefully. "I didn't make any sacrifices. I found out that I didn't need to."

"I thought that," said Clover. "Or rather, I found it out. It came to me – sort of."

"That your father and I ..."

"Loved each other. After all."

"Yes, after all."

Amanda brushed sand off the edge of the plastic sheet, but stopped herself. You could not keep sand off you on a beach picnic. You had to give in. "People believe that love lasts forever. Or theirs will. That's what they believe." She glanced at her daughter. "I think that you've been ... well, just amazingly lucky. The two of you. Sometimes you find that. People meet one another when they're very young and they stay together for their whole lives, which is as close as we get to forever."

"Yes, maybe we've been lucky. I love him so much, Ma ..."

"Of course you do. Of course you do."

"I love him so much I could cry."

"Well, you mustn't. Not on a picnic ..."

They were distracted at that moment. The child had slipped from her mother's arms and fallen into the water. But she did not seem to mind. She was buoyant.